A Guide to Examining
BUILDING ENGLISH SKILLS Gold Level—Grade 6

This book is one of a series of composition/grammar books for grades 6–12.* The Gold Level is recommended for use in Grade 6. This Teacher's Edition contains:

- The entire student text, not reduced in size
- Answers to all exercises, printed in blue
- Marginal notations giving lesson objectives, preparatory lessons, additional exercises for enrichment
- Seventy-nine pages of reproducible copy masters at the end of the book (see pages 404–484) providing additional exercises, diagnostic tests, and mastery tests.

As you examine this text, note the following features:

1. Readability. This text is written at a 5th-grade reading level. It is printed in large type, in an attractive, open format. Illustrations are used functionally to enhance the content and to motivate students, not as mere ornamentation.

2. Organization. The text contains chapters on writing skills, grammar, usage, and other language skills. Each topic or skill is developed completely in one chapter, rather than on pages scattered throughout the text.

3. Emphasis on writing. The series contains far more material on fundamental writing skills than other leading series. It contains more writing models and many more writing exercises . . . both important tools by which students learn to write clearly and effectively. Chapters on vocabulary development and using the library and reference materials enhance this emphasis on written English.

4. Developmental approach to grammar. The text features an exceptionally clear, developmental approach to basic grammar, usage, and the support skills of capitalization, punctuation, and spelling.

5. Numerous exercises and opportunities for review and testing. A wealth of exercises are included at regular intervals to insure mastery of basic language concepts. In addition to the exercises in the student texts, the series provides hundreds more exercises in the accompanying workbooks, in duplicating masters, and in the concluding pages of this Teacher's Edition.

*Books for grades K–5 are in preparation.

Building English Skills

Purple Level

Yellow Level

Blue Level

Orange Level

Green Level

Red Level

GOLD LEVEL

Silver Level

Aqua Level

Brown Level

Plum Level

Pink Level

Building English Skills

Gold Level

McDougal, Littell & Company

Evanston, Illinois

Authors

Kathleen L. Bell, Arizona State University. Formerly, Chairperson, English Department, Lincoln Junior High School, Mount Prospect, Illinois

Donna Rae Blackall, Chairperson, Language Arts Department, Thomas Junior High School, Arlington Heights, Illinois

Kraft and Kraft, Developers of Educational Materials, Stow, Massachusetts

Susan Duffy Schaffrath, Specialist in Educational Materials for the Elementary and Middle Grades

Consultant: Barbara Wirth Sirotin, Language Arts Coordinator, Arlington Heights Public Schools, Arlington Heights, Illinois

Editorial Direction: Joy Littell

Assistant Editor: Patricia Opaskar

Design: William A. Seabright

Acknowledgments: See page 404.

ISBN: 0-88343-564-0

Contents

Handbook: The Mechanics of Writing

Chapter 1

How Our Language Grows

The English language is always changing and growing. New words come into our language all the time. There are many ways in which new words are added to our language. Here are seven ways.

1. Words are borrowed from other languages.
2. Words are made from initials.
3. The name of a famous person or place becomes a word.
4. Sounds are imitated and eventually become words.
5. Old words are shortened.
6. Two words are put together.
7. Technical terms from jobs and science become common words.

In this chapter we will talk about these seven ways in which new words come into our language.

Chapter Objectives

1. To recognize seven ways that new words are added to our language

Borrowed from other languages
Words made from initials
Names of persons or places
Imitations of sounds
Old words shortened
Two words combined
Technical words

Preparing the Students

Write the following paragraph on the board. Ask students to read it carefully. Do they notice anything unusual about it? A number of words are not part of the modern vocabulary of students. Have the class use dictionaries to "translate" the paragraph.

> Walking through the portiere to great-grandma's garret was like walking into a time machine. There, under a layer of dust, was the old davenport from her parlor. There was the icebox that used to stand next to her pantry. In the drawer of the elegant highboy was a tintype of my great-grandpa standing proudly next to his tin lizzy. My, how times have changed!

Additional Resources

Mastery Test—pages 435 and 436 in this T.E. Recommended for use after teaching the chapter.

Additional Mastery Test—Recommended for use after any necessary reteaching. (In separate booklet, *Diagnostic and Mastery Tests, Gold Level,* pages 11 and 12.)

Skills Practice Book—pages 1–4

Duplicating Masters—pages 1–4

Part 1

Objective

To become aware of words borrowed from other languages

Presenting the Lesson

1. Read and discuss page 1. Make it clear that these seven ways of adding words to the language do not explain all of our words.

Part 1 Words Borrowed from Other Languages

Throughout its history, the English language has taken many words from other languages. Even today English is still borrowing words. Some of the languages that English has borrowed from are American Indian, French, Spanish, Dutch, and German. The following lists give some examples for each.

American Indian

squash
raccoon
pecan
squaw
chipmunk

French

pumpkin
chowder
rapids
bureau
cent

Spanish

alfalfa
ranch
taco
plaza
bonanza

Dutch

cookie
waffle
cole slaw
sleigh
boss

German

pretzel
noodle
hamburger
loafer
seminar

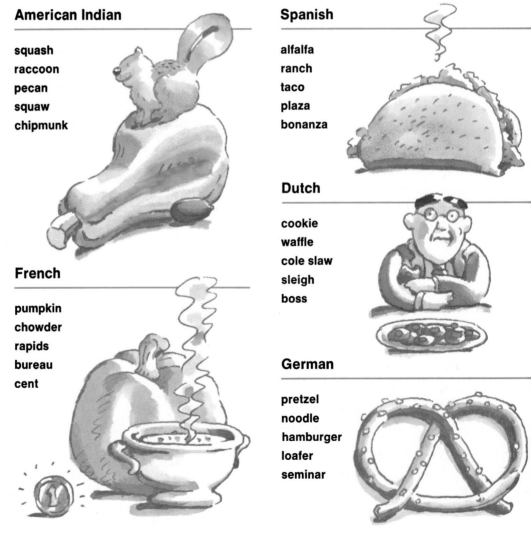

Exercise Borrowed Words

From what language was each word in the box borrowed? Number from 1 to 10. Write the correct abbreviation after each number.

Algon. = Algonquian (American Indian)
Fr. = French
Sp. = Spanish
Du. = Dutch
G. = German

A dictionary will give you the answers. Practice pronouncing each word you look up.

1. kindergarten G.	6. moccasin Algon.
2. chaise longue Fr.	7. ersatz G.
3. wigwam Algon.	8. snoop Du.
4. sombrero Sp.	9. patio Sp.
5. margarine Fr.	10. snorkel G.

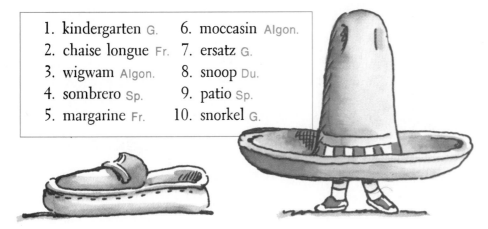

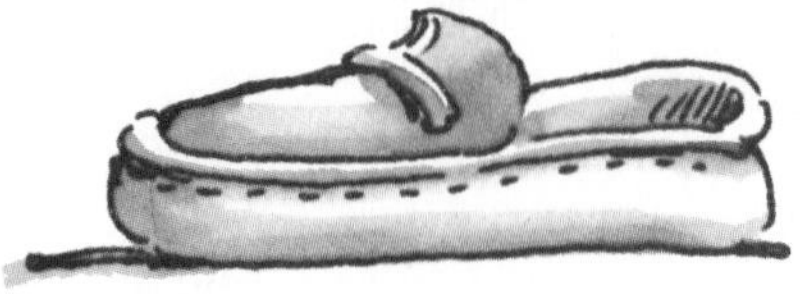

Part 2 Words Made from Initials

Sometimes the initials of a group of words are put together to make a new word. These words are called **acronyms.** They give us shorter ways to say and write things. For example, it is easier to say VISTA than to say Volunteers in Service to America. Acronyms are pronounced as words. However, some groups of initials used to make new words are pronounced as separate letters. For example, UN is a shortened way to write or say United Nations. There are over 12,000 acronyms in our language. More come into use every year.

2. Read and discuss page 2. Identify the geographic location of each language discussed.

German—Germany
Dutch—Netherlands
Spanish—Spain, Mexico, South America
French—France
American Indian—North American continent

3. Point out that most words have a history of sources. Perhaps a word we borrowed from Spanish was borrowed by the Spanish from the early Latins.

4. Explain that American Indian is not one language, but a general category for many different languages: Sioux, Algonquin, Crow, Navaho, etc.

5. Assign and discuss the Exercise on page 3. The authority for the definitions and word sources used in this chapter and exercises is *Webster's New World Dictionary of the American Language,* Students Edition.

6. See Exercise A on page 10 for additional practice.

Part 2

Objective

To understand the creation and use of acronyms

Presenting the Lesson

1. Read page 3 and discuss it. Emphasize that an acronym is initials that form a word. Point out that often the small words in a phrase are left out in the formation of an acronym. For example, the acronym for the Organization of Petroleum Exporting Countries, OPEC, does not include a second *O* for *of*.

2. Assign the Exercise on page 4. Discuss the answers with the class. Be sure to pronounce each acronym as a word.

3. See Exercise B on page 10 for additional practice.

Extending the Lesson

Have students explain each of these acronyms:

SCUBA *Self contained underwater breathing apparatus*
UNICEF *United Nations International Children's Emergency Fund*
WAF *Women's Air Force*

Part 3

Objective

To be conscious of words relating to specific people and places

Presenting the Lesson

1. Read and discuss page 4 with the class.

2. Assign and discuss the Exercise on page 5.

3. See Exercise C on page 10 for additional practice.

Optional Practice

Have students trace the source of these words:

pasteurized diesel
sideburns saxophone

Exercise Acronyms

Tell what acronym is used as a short form for each of the following names.

1. Strategic Arms Limitations Talks SALT
2. Job Opportunities for Better Skills JOBS
3. Fabbrica Italiana Automobili Torino FIAT
4. Congress of Racial Equality CORE
5. North Atlantic Treaty Organization NATO
6. Cooperative for American Relief Everywhere CARE
7. Women's Army Corps WAC
8. United Nations Educational, Scientific, and Cultural Organization UNESCO
9. People United to Save Humanity PUSH
10. National Aeronautics and Space Administration NASA

Part 3 Words Made from Names of People and Places

In 490 B.C. the Greeks won a war against the Persians at the battle of Marathon. One of the victorious Greek soldiers ran twenty-six miles to bring the news of the victory to Athens. Today the word *marathon* usually means a twenty-six mile race. Sometimes it means another type of endurance contest.

The Earl of Sandwich, who lived about 200 years ago, loved to gamble. He did not even want to leave the gambling room for meals. Therefore, he asked for a more portable kind of meal, something he could eat as he played. Eventually, his snack was known as a *sandwich*.

Exercise Words from Names of People and Places

Look up each of the following words in the dictionary. Find out what name or place each came from. Write the name on your paper.

Amelia Bloomer bloomers	Earl of Cardigan cardigan	Hamburg hamburger
John L. McAdam macadam	Tuxedo Park tuxedo	Pierre Magnol magnolia
Calicut calico	Earl of Chesterfield chesterfield	John Philip Sousa sousaphone
Samuel Maverick maverick	Marquise de Pompadour pompadour	John Macadam macadamia nut

Part 4 Words Made from Sounds

One way in which language might have begun was by imitating the sound that something made. English has a number of words that imitate actual sounds. These are called **echoic words.** They echo real sounds. Some of them are *pop, buzz,* and *clop.*

Exercise Echoic Words

Think of an echoic word that describes or names each of the following sounds. Number your paper from 1 to 12. After each number, write the echoic word. These are suggested answers.

1. The sound of water when someone jumps in splash
2. The sound of a person telling secrets buzz
3. The sound of brakes squeal
4. The sound of cloth tearing rip
5. The sound of a dog bark
6. The sound of heavy boots clump
7. The sound of a ringmaster's whip in an animal cage crack
8. The sound a pencil makes when you break it snap
9. The sound of scissors snip
10. The sound of a leaky faucet drip
11. The sound of a person with a cold wheeze
12. The sound of thunder rumble

Part 4

Objective

To understand the concept of echoic words

Presenting the Lesson

1. Read and discuss page 5. What additional echoic words can students think of?

2. Assign and discuss the Exercises on page 5. There will be more than one acceptable answer for most items. Encourage creativity.

3. See Exercise D on page 11 for additional practice.

Extending the Lesson

Have students bring copies of comic books to class. Examine them for examples of echoic words. Ask students to note how the words are illustrated. Create a bulletin board of student-made echoic word signs.

Part 5 Shortened Words

People who speak the English language like to shorten long words. They use only a small part of a word. For example, they say *fan* for *fanatic, auto* for *automobile,* and *burger* for *hamburger*. Each short form of such words eventually becomes a new word itself. Using only part of a long word is called **clipping.**

Exercise Clipping

Here are the long forms of some English words. Can you give the clipped form for each?

omnibus	gymnasium	mathematics
laboratory	influenza	examination
taximeter cabriolet	telephone	submarine
advertisement	airplane	dormitory

Part 5

Objective

To understand how clipping can create a short word from a longer one

Presenting the Lesson

1. Read and discuss page 6. Note that some word clipping is a part of regional slang: *burger* for *hamburger, frig* for *refrigerator, shake* for *milkshake, rec* for *recreation.*

2. Do the Exercise on page 6 aloud with the class.

3. See Exercise E on page 11 for additional practice.

Part 6 Words Put Together

Sometimes two words are put together to make a new word. The new word is called a **compound word.** English has many compound words. New ones are being made all the time. Some compound words are *bookkeeper, football, outdoors, downtown,* and *input.*

Sometimes when two words are put together to make a new word, some of the letters are dropped. The new word is then called a **blend.** The word *smog* is a blend of *smoke* and *fog. Paratroops* is a blend of *parachute* and *troops.*

Exercise Compounds and Blends

Each of these words is a compound or a blend. Tell what each word means. Tell what two words it is made from.

bedtime	doorknob	bedspread
motel (motor hotel)	skyscraper	chortle (chuckle, snort)
cloudburst	telethon (television marathon)	motorcade (motor cavalcade)
drugstore	bellhop	brunch (breakfast, lunch)

Part 7 Technical Words

People who work at a job have a special vocabulary for that job. The special language of a job is called shoptalk. It is made up of technical words. These words have specific meanings that are related to the job. For example, the space agency NASA has such terms as *countdown* and *blastoff*. Athletes have such terms as *tackle* and *hurdle*. Sometimes these words are useful for talking about other things besides the job. Then the words become part of everybody's vocabulary. In other words, a person "tackles" a problem or overcomes a "hurdle." The technical word changes slightly in meaning when it comes out of its original setting. It becomes a common word,

Part 6

Objective

To recognize the formation of compounds and blends

Presenting the Lesson

1. Read page 7. Be sure to distinguish between a compound and a blend.
2. Assign and discuss the Exercise on page 7.
3. See Exercise F on page 11 for additional practice.

Extending the Lesson

Have students create some new blends for these ideas:

1. What would you call a cross between a pig and a squirrel?
2. What would you call a new flower made from combining a daisy and a rose?

Part 7

Objective

To become aware of the absorption of technical words into daily language

Presenting the Lesson

1. Read and discuss pages 7 and 8. Pay special attention to the chart on page 8.
2. Assign the Exercise on page 9. Have students share their lists. Here is a chart of possible answers:

bottom line, from business: originally the bottom line of the earnings report of a company; now the most important factor, the final decision

ballpark, from baseball: originally a stadium for playing baseball; now designating an estimate or figure thought to be reasonably accurate

strike out, from baseball: originally, to be put out as the result of three strikes; now, to fail, to be a failure

knockout, from boxing: originally a victory won when the opponent is knocked out; now a very attractive person or thing

acid test, from chemistry: originally a test of gold by acid; now a crucial, final test that proves the value or quality of something

stalking horse, from hunting: originally a horse, or figure of a horse, used as cover by a hunter stalking game; now anything used to disguise or conceal intentions, schemes, activities

spark plug, from mechanics or engineering: originally a part of an internal-combustion engine that ignites the fuel mixture; now a person or thing that inspires, activates, or advances something

Extending the Lesson

Have students discuss the meaning of these terms:

jargon slang
dialect colloquialism

a new word in our language. The following chart gives some examples of shoptalk, the job from which it came, its job meaning, and its general meaning.

Word	Job	Job Meaning	General Meaning
southpaw	baseball	left-handed baseball pitcher	a person who is left-handed
grandstand	baseball	seating for spectators	to show off before people
shill	carnival	a helper in the audience permitted to win money so that others will take a chance	a person who works with a gambler, auctioneer, etc., by pretending to bet, bid, or buy so as to lure others
sucker	circus	circusgoer	a person easily cheated
fade-out	movie	picture slowly disappearing	slowly disappearing
third degree	police	harsh questioning of criminals	any harsh questioning
feedback	computers	return of data	reactions between people, answers to questions

Exercise Technical Words

Can you think of examples of technical words that have become common words? Try to think of five such words. Explain their sources and original meanings. Then tell their common, new meanings. Answers will vary.

Review Exercise How Our Language Grows

Here are the seven ways that words are added to the English language:

1. By borrowing
2. By making a word from initials
3. By using the name of a person or place
4. By imitating a sound
5. By using part of another word
6. By putting two words together
7. By using technical terms as common words

Decide how each of the following words came into our language. Write each word on your paper. After each word, write the number of the way that applies. Use your dictionary for help.

sunrise 6	jersey 3	fizz 4	camouflage 1 or 7
mike 5	HUD 2	roommate 6	pasteurize 3
honk 4	boycott 3	memo 5	basketball 6
raglan 3	gas 5	UNICEF 2	garage 1
chassis 1	bookcase 6	deb 5	mackintosh 3

Review Exercise

Assign and discuss the Review Exercise on page 9.

Additional Exercises

If these Exercises were not used with each lesson, they may now be assigned for chapter review.

Additional Exercises

How Our Language Grows

A. Borrowed Words (Use after page 2.)

Look up each word below in a dictionary. Number your paper from 1 to 10. Write the abbreviation of the language it was borrowed from.

Algon.	= Algonquian	It.	= Italian
Fr.	= French	Du.	= Dutch
Sp.	= Spanish	G.	= German

1. barbecue Sp.
2. piano It.
3. totem Algon.
4. frankfurter G.
5. chocolate Fr.
6. woodchuck Algon.
7. levee Fr.
8. delicatessen G.
9. balcony It.
10. alfalfa Sp.

B. Acronyms (Use after page 3.)

Tell what acronym is used as a short form for each of the following names.

1. Internal Revenue Service IRS
2. National Organization for Women NOW
3. Very Important Person VIP
4. Extra Sensory Perception ESP
5. Distant Early Warning line DEW line

C. Words from Names of People and Places (Use after page 4.)

Look up each of the following words in a dictionary. Find out what name or place each came from. Write the name on your paper.

James Watt watt — bayonet Bayonne, France

Vulcan volcano — bobby Sir Robert Peel

Elbridge Gerry gerrymander — atlas Atlas

D. Words Made From Sounds (Use after page 5.)

Use each of the echoic words below in sentences of your own.

clash	plop	whoosh	Answers will vary.
crunch	rap	crash	

E. Shortened Words (Use after page 6.)

Here are the long forms of some English words. Can you give the clipped form for each?

caravan	penitentiary	memorandum
periwig	champion	promenade
curiosity	askutasquash	graduate
turnpike	drapery	convict

F. Compounds and Blends (Use after page 7.)

Each of the words below is a compound or a blend. Tell what each word means. Tell what two words it is made from.

twinight (twilight, night)	earth|worm	news|magazine
bath|robe	back|bone	dish|pan
candle|holder	smog (smoke, fog)	copy|reader
foot|bridge	hand|bag	head|ache

B102

Chapter 2

Developing a Vocabulary of Specific Words

There are two kinds of words: **general** and **specific.** A general word is one that covers a whole range of ideas or feelings. A specific word has a more limited meaning. For instance, *go* is a general word. It means "move along." *Sail* is a more specific word. It means "to be moved forward by means of a sail or sails." He *sailed* across *the river* describes more exactly what he did than *He went across the river*.

Specific words pack a lot of information into a small space. They make writing lively and interesting. They say exactly what you mean.

Six general words are *go, make, big, small, good,* and *bad*. This chapter will show you how to choose specific words for each of these general words. The specific words will express your meaning exactly.

Chapter Objectives

1. To appreciate how specific words can convey a more exact meaning than general words

2. To use specific words to communicate exact meaning

3. To develop a vocabulary of specific words for each of these general words: *go, make, big, small, good,* and *bad*

Preparing the Students

The writing and speaking of sixth graders abounds with general words. Bring this to the attention of students by writing this phrase on the board: *kids with boats.*

Ask students to analyze how exactly this phrase describes the picture on the opposite page. Can this phrase be improved? What is wrong with the word *Kids*? Does it mean boys? girls? goats? What about *boats*? Are they toys? real? what kind? What specific phrase can be created to describe the picture?

Additional Resources

Mastery Test—pages 437 and 438 in this T.E. Recommended for use after teaching the chapter.

Additional Mastery Test—Recommended for use after any necessary reteaching. (In separate booklet, *Diagnostic and Mastery Tests, Gold Level,* pages 13 and 14.)

Skills Practice Books—pages 5–8

Duplicating Masters—pages 5–8

Part 1

Objective

To develop a vocabulary of specific words for the general word *go*

Presenting the Lesson

1. Read pages 13 and 14. Discuss the difference in meaning of *dash, trudge, stampede,* and *flutter.*

2. Explain the different forms of *go: go, went, gone, going.* Be sure students understand that each of these forms is still a general word.

3. Ask students to begin a master vocabulary list to be continued throughout this chapter. All specific words for *go* in Part 1 should be on this list. At the end of the lesson, review these words.

4. Assign and discuss Exercises A and C on pages 14 and 15. It is suggested that only more advanced students be assigned Exercise B.

5. See Exercise A on page 26 for additional practice.

Optional Practice

1. Have students write new sentences using the second word choice for the sentences in Exercise A on pages 14 and 15.

2. Ask students to explain the difference between these words. They should be able to use each in a sentence:

crawled	galloped	bounced
jogged	inched	bounded

Part 1 Specific Words for *Go*

Think about the general word *go*. It does not give much information. It tells only that something moved. If you say, "Tony went home with his report card," you have told where Tony went. What if the report card was wonderful? Would *went* accurately describe how Tony got home? Maybe *dashed* would be a better word, since it shows that Tony was happy. However, if the report card was bad, *dashed* would be the wrong word. In that case, saying "Tony *trudged* home with his report card" would be better.

Many specific words may be used instead of *go*. Each word will have a slightly different meaning. For example, the word *stampede* has a different meaning from the word *flutter*. You could use *stampede* to describe the "go" of a herd of buffalo. But you could not use *stampede* to describe the "go" of a butterfly. Instead, you would use *flutter*.

Specific Words for *Go*

sail	ride	roll	tumble
run	walk	plunge	trot
skip	trudge	dash	glide
charge	drift	jump	fly
wander	hurry	flutter	race
stampede	rush	streak	plod
hike	march	climb	drive

Exercises Specific Words for *Go*

A. Choose the better word for each sentence.

1. Donna (trudged, dashed) into the room shouting "Fire!"

2. During the fire drill the students (charged, walked) out of the school building in single file.

3. Andy was daydreaming. He just seemed to (wander, trudge) around with his head in the clouds.

4. The old horse (plodded, skipped) along the path.

5. The swimmer was so enthusiastic that he (tumbled, plunged) right into the cold water.

6. The butterfly was not hurt. It (fluttered, rushed) away.

7. She (walked, ran) to get to the store before it closed.

8. I watched the sailboat (skip, glide) over the water.

9. You will have to (jump, fly) over the puddle.

10. The family dog proudly (trotted, trudged) along beside the new baby carriage.

B. Choose five precise words for *go*. List them in order of increasing speed. Start with words that mean "go slowly." For example, *plod* would come before *race*. Answers will vary.

C. Replace the italicized word in each sentence. Use a more specific word that fits the idea in the sentence. These are suggested answers.

1. When the last day of school ended, the students *went* out the door. dashed, streaked, raced

2. The wind made the lifeboat *go* off course. drift

3. After I had delivered the last paper, I *went* home and collapsed into a chair. trudged

4. The car *went* down the race track at nearly 300 kilometers per hour. charged, streaked

5. The dancers *went* lightly across the stage. glided

6. John and Jim *went* to the shelter on their overnight camping trip. hiked

7. My family is thinking of *going* across the country next summer. traveling, driving

8. Wait till you see the lions *go* through a burning hoop. jump

9. Diane's homerun blast *went* over the center field fence. sailed, flew

10. If you *go* right in, the water won't feel cold. plunge

Part 2

Objective

To develop a vocabulary of specific words for the general word *make*

Presenting the Lesson

1. Read and discuss page 16. Students should become familiar with the meanings of the specific words listed.

2. Present the different forms of *make: make, made, making.*

3. Have students continue their master vocabulary list. All specific words suggested in Part 2 should be included.

4. Assign and discuss Exercises A and B on pages 16 and 17.

5. See Exercise B on page 26 for additional practice.

Optional Practice

Have students write new sentences for the unused words of Exercise B on page 17.

Extending the Lesson

Have students use each of the words in the green box on page 16 in an original sentence. They should compare sentences with those of other students in the class. Discuss other specific words for *make.* Ask students to use them in sentences.

Part 2 Specific Words for *Make*

Some words are so general that they can be confusing. The word *make* is a good example of a word that is not clear. Suppose you said that someone "*made* a house." Did someone design the house? Was someone hired to build it? Did someone actually take hammer and nails and put the boards together?

The word *made* does not say exactly what the person did. If you said instead that a person *designed* a house, or *built* a house, your meaning would be clear.

Specific Words for *Make*

create	compose	design
invent	manufacture	concoct
build	construct	fashion
forge	devise	prepare
produce	cause	form

There are many other specific words for *make*. They are words for the work that is needed to make specific things. Do you *make* cloth or *weave* cloth? Do you *make* a picture or *draw* a picture?

Exercises Specific Words for *Make*

Replace the italicized word in each sentence. Use a more specific word that fits the idea in the sentence. You may use words that are not on the list. These are suggested answers.

1. Hurricanes and tornadoes can *make* destruction. create

2. Thomas Edison *made* the electric light bulb. invented

3. The only tools you'll need to *make* this birdhouse are a hammer and saw. construct

4. This jacket was *made* to allow easy movement. designed

5. My aunt spends her evenings trying to *make* a hit tune. compose

6. Use a spade to *make* a trench around the tent. form

7. If I had known you were coming, I would have *made* a cake. baked

8. Even if you can't thread a needle, I can teach you to *make* your own clothes. fashion

9. In this plant we *make* television antennas. manufacture

10. *Make* the dough into a ball. shape

11. I've *made* a new kind of bubble gum! produced

12. Donna *made* a watercolor picture of the forest. painted

13. Can you *make* a meal for two hundred hungry hikers? prepare

14. Juan is always able to *make* some excuse for being late. concoct

15. We watched the spider *make* a web. spin

B. Choose the better word for each sentence.

1. We (built, fashioned) a fishhook from a safety pin.

2. The Wright brothers (built, formed) the first successful airplane.

3. Directions that are not clear may (manufacture, cause) confusion.

4. Most bicycles are (created, designed) to carry only one person.

5. The United States is (composed, built) of fifty states.

6. With a sharp knife, Dan (carved, concocted) a grinning face in the pumpkin.

7. I (manufactured, concocted) a stew from some leftovers.

8. As a hobby, I (build, invent) model boats.

9. Carol hopes to become a writer; she's good at (creating, preparing) stories.

10. We have to (build, devise) a plan for getting across the river.

Part 3

Objective

To develop a vocabulary of specific words for the general word *big*

Presenting the Lesson

1. Read page 18. Discuss the meanings of the specific words listed.

2. Choose a more specific word for *big* in each of the following sentences. Rewrite the sentences with the new words.

1. They live in a *big* house.
2. He received a *big* raise last week.
3. The student showed a *big* improvement on his latest report card.
4. How *big* is your dog?
5. Washing the windows is a *big* job.

3. Students should continue their master vocabulary list, adding specific words for *big* from Part 3.

4. It is recommended that you do exercises A and C on page 19 with the class. Assign and discuss Exercise B.

5. See Exercise C on pages 26 and 27 for additional practice.

Optional Practice

1. Have students write new sentences for the words not selected in Exercise B on page 19.

2. Ask students to select the word from list B that most closely matches each word in list A.

Part 3 Specific Words for *Big*

Action words are not the only words that you should choose carefully. Descriptive words are just as important.

Big is a general word. *Tall* is more specific; so is *fat*. Each of these words tells in what way something is big. A word like *monstrous* tells even more. Something *monstrous* is frightening as well as big.

Think of different words you might use to describe a house. *Spacious* might fit, or *substantial*, or *huge*. What about *imposing*? That could be used, too. But a word like *fat* would not work.

However, if you were describing a person, *fat* might be a better word than *huge*. The correct word will depend on the particular thing you are writing about.

Specific Words for *Big*

great	**hulking**	**substantial**
fat	**vast**	**bulky**
imposing	**gigantic**	**massive**
spacious	**monstrous**	**heavy**
huge	**tremendous**	**strapping**

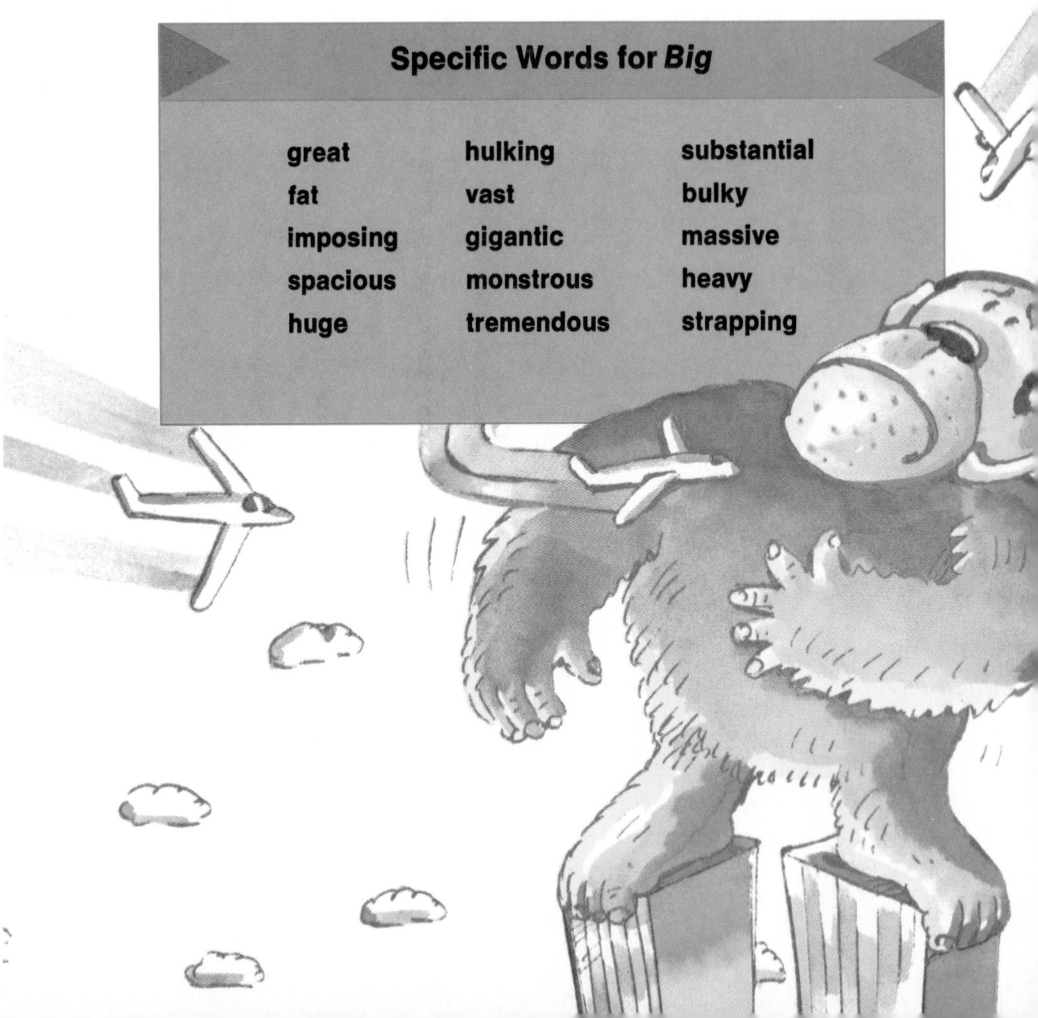

Exercises Specific Words for *Big*

A. Look at the word list. Find the word that matches each definition. For some definitions, more than one word will fit. Discuss your choices with the class. These are suggested answers.

1. big and solid and strong substantial, imposing
2. big and healthy strapping, great
3. big and scary hulking, monstrous
4. too big fat, bulky
5. big and hard to move bulky, heavy
6. big and full of room vast

B. Choose the better word.

1. The doorway to the cathedral certainly was (fat, imposing).
2. We wandered through the airy, (spacious, hulking) rooms.
3. Everyone hoped to get a (huge, heavy) piece of cake.
4. The elephant had (massive, tall) feet.
5. The furniture was much too (spacious, bulky) to move.
6. The circus was held in a (tremendous, strapping) canvas tent.
7. We looked out over a (monstrous, vast) field of wheat.
8. My aunt and uncle have a (strapping, substantial) house in the suburbs.
9. We went to the store during its (gigantic, imposing) clearance sale.
10. The airplane searched over a (vast, heavy) area.

C. Choose at least three specific words for *big* that you might use to describe each of the following things. Answers will vary.

1. a big place
2. a big shipping crate
3. a big dragon
4. a big baby
5. a big rock

A	**B**
enormous	large
sizable	unselfish
roomy	gigantic
generous	spacious

Discuss the reasons for the choices of the students.

Extending the Lesson

Introduce the terms *connotation*, general meaning, and *denotation*, specific meaning. Discuss how words of the same connotation can denote widely different meanings: *Big* can mean "fat" or "important."

Part 4

Objective

To develop a vocabulary of specific words for the general word *small*

Presenting the Lesson

1. Read and discuss page 20. Point out how words of similar meaning can convey very different feelings.

2. If students are curious about the microscopic animals pictured on page 20, identify the organisms as an amoeba, a euglena, and a radiolarian.

3. Which word in the box on page 20 best fits each of these descriptions?

1. A small room with a glowing fireplace
2. An apple core left in the sun for several days
3. A one-room apartment with ten roommates
4. A shoe that is a little tight
5. Germs on the lid of the garbage can

4. Students should update their master vocabulary list with words for *small.*

5. Do Exercise A and B on page 21 aloud with the class. Assign Exercises C and D. Have students compare their paragraphs for Exercise D.

6. See Exercise D on page 27 for additional practice.

Part 4 Specific Words for *Small*

Many words that describe an object also show how the speaker feels about the object. Take, for instance, the word *small. Small* is a general word that means "not large."

If you said that a cat was *small,* you would merely be describing the size of the cat. If you said the cat was *scrawny,* you would also be telling how you felt about the cat. A listener would imagine a stray cat that looked underfed and unhealthy. A *scrawny* cat does not sound very attractive.

A *delicate* cat describes a prettier cat. *Delicate* still means small. It would be a better word to use if the animal were slender instead of unhealthy.

People have different feelings about what size is the "right" size. If large rooms make you feel lost, you might call a small one *snug.* If large rooms are what you like, you might think a small one was *cramped.*

Some specific words are complimentary. Some are insulting. Your feelings will help determine which you use.

Specific Words for *Small*

tiny	microscopic	modest
petite	dainty	shrunken
miniature	cozy	puny
little	snug	scrawny
cramped	delicate	shriveled

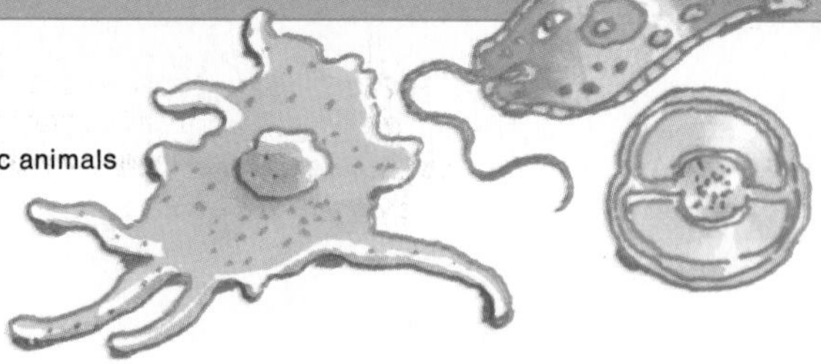

microscopic animals

Exercises Specific Words for *Small*

Look at the list of specific words for *small.* Use them to fill the blanks in the following sentences. Choose a word that fits each sentence. More than one word might be correct. Use only one.

These are suggested answers.

1. The ___dainty___ golden slippers were beautiful.
2. We felt at home in the ___modest, snug___ living room.
3. It was hot and sticky in the ___cramped___ bus.
4. My hobby is collecting ___miniature___ car models.
5. The ring was covered with ___tiny___ diamonds.
6. The ___puny, scrawny___ puppy was the last to be bought.
7. The spider wove a ___delicate___ web in the corner of the doorway.
8. We won the game by a ___modest___ number of points.

Some words are used mostly to describe things that are alive, like people or animals. From the word list for *small,* choose the words that you think might be used to describe a person or animal. Try to list at least five words. Answers will vary.

List six specific words for *small.* Use words from the list or make up your own. Put a + by each word that makes smallness seem good. Put a — by each word that makes smallness seem bad. Put a 0 by words that do not make smallness seem good or bad.

Answers will vary.

Write two short paragraphs describing a small person. In the first paragraph, imagine the person is someone you like. In the second, imagine he or she is someone you dislike. Answers will vary.

Part 5 Specific Words for *Good*

Good is a general word we use frequently. It can describe how something looks, how much it is worth, or how well it works. Most often it tells how the writer feels about a person or thing.

Part 5

Objective

To develop a vocabulary of specific words for the general word *good*

Presenting the Lesson

1. Read pages 21 and 22. Discuss the various shades of meaning for the word *good.*

2. Students should continue their master vocabulary list with specific words for *good.*

3. Present the comparative and superlative forms of *good: good, better, best.* Explain that these words are also words with general meanings.

4. Assign and discuss Exercises A, B, and C on pages 22 and 23.

5. See Exercise E on page 27 for additional practice.

Extending the Lesson

Encourage students to create an advertising campaign for Bubbo Soap. They might design posters and write radio and TV commercials. Have them presented to the class for discussion.

Specific words for *good* cover a wide range of feelings. If you said that a party was *passable,* no one who missed it would feel sorry. If you said the party was *perfect,* anyone who missed it would be full of envy. If you said that the party was *proper,* people would have still different feelings about it.

People often use certain words in spoken English to mean "nice" or "fine" or "excellent." Some of these are *okay, terrific, wonderful, great, neat,* and *super.* These words are not specific words for *good.* They are merely other general words that mean the same as *good.* They may be used in speaking. However, they should be avoided in writing.

Specific Words for *Good*

nice	**suitable**	**pleasing**
fine	**perfect**	**useful**
passable	**adequate**	**satisfactory**
excellent	**rare**	**proper**
superb	**valuable**	**moral**
delicious	**sound**	**enjoyable**

Exercises Specific Words for *Good*

A. Read the word list. Make sure you understand all the words. Then choose a more specific word for *good* in each sentence. You may use a word more than once. You may also use a specific word for *good* that is not on the list. These are suggested answers.

1. My parents thought the sweater looked good on me. nice
2. The plump cream puffs dripping with chocolate sauce looked good. delicious
3. That movie was so good that I'm going to see it again. enjoyable
4. The winner of the race was a good horse. valuable
5. Joe! I haven't seen you since last year! It's good to see you again. nice
6. Diane is good, honest, and trustworthy. moral
7. It rained every day, but my vacation was still good. enjoyable
8. The car isn't in the best shape, but it has four good tires. excellent
9. Here's a coat that's good for rainy weather. useful
10. My job is to separate the good apples from the bruised ones. passable

B. Imagine that you are a salesperson. You are trying to persuade a customer to buy Bubbo Soap. What words for *good* would you use to describe Bubbo? List them in a column labeled *Bubbo.* What words for *good* might you use to describe Flubbo, a competitor's soap? List those words in a column labeled *Flubbo.* Answers will vary.

C. Choose the better word in each sentence.

1. I'm going to practice this trick until it is (perfect, adequate).
2. Unfortunately, the food at camp is only (proper, passable).
3. Claude's father congratulated us for the (excellent, passable) weeding job we had done.
4. This is the only (superb, suitable) coat I have for winter.
5. My teacher told me that my work is barely (satisfactory, fine).
6. Let's go to see that comedy movie that got such (proper, excellent) reviews.
7. It's not a fancy ring, but I think it's (superb, nice).
8. The museum had a display of (adequate, rare) antique pottery.

Part 6

Objective

To develop a vocabulary of specific words for the general word *bad*

Presenting the Lesson

1. Read and discuss the words listed on page 24.
2. Students should complete their master vocabulary list with words for *bad*.
3. Assign and discuss Exercises A and B on pages 24 and 25.
4. See Exercise F on page 27 for additional practice.

Extending the Lesson

Ask students to choose a specific word for each italicized word in the following sentences.

1. I have a *bad* headache.
2. Don't do that. It's *bad* for you.
3. The babysitter scolded the *bad* child.
4. We had a *bad* winter this year.
5. The rock star told the reporter, "My new song is really *bad*."

Part 6 Specific Words for *Bad*

The word *bad* has as many different meanings as *good* has. It is important to think about exactly what you mean when you use a general word like *bad*. Do you mean *evil?* Or do you just mean *wrong?* Or *defective?* Or *illegal?* Or *dangerous?* Or *harmful?*

Specific words for *bad* range from mild words like *mischievous* all the way to *repulsive* and *disgusting*.

If you were talking about an alarm clock that did not work, would you call it *defective* or *evil?* What about a poisonous gas? Would you call that *unfortunate* or *terrible?* It makes more sense to save strong words like *evil* and *terrible* for serious things. Do not waste strong words on small matters.

Specific Words for *Bad*

poor	worthless	evil
terrible	horrible	harmful
defective	wrong	vicious
shoddy	wicked	inferior
immoral	naughty	dishonest
illegal	vile	devastating

Exercises Specific Words for *Bad*

A. Read the word list. Choose specific words from it to fill the blanks in the following sentences. Some answers may vary.

1. I took a ___wrong___ turn somewhere, and got lost.

2. The handle on the door was ___defective___ and had to be fixed.

3. We thought the movie was a cheap and ___shoddy___ job.

4. It is not only dangerous to speed, but also ___illegal___.

5. The room has a ___vile___ odor of spoiled meat.

6. People used to think that witches were charmed by ___evil___ spirits.

7. My little brother isn't really nasty, but he can be ___naughty___.

8. The tornado left a ___horrible___ path of destruction behind it.

9. A balloon is ___worthless___ after it bursts.

10. Cigarette smoking is ___harmful___ to health.

B. List a specific word for *bad* to match each definition.

1. Not as good as something else inferior
2. Not worth anything worthless
3. Not made correctly defective
4. Not made well shoddy
5. Causing terror terrible
6. Not correct wrong
7. Causing harm harmful
8. Causing horror horrible
9. Showing slightly bad behavior naughty
10. Not honest dishonest

Additional Exercises

Use pages 26 and 27 for review of the chapter if they have not been previously assigned.

Developing a Vocabulary of Specific Words

A. Specific Words for *Go* (Use after page 14.)

Number your paper from 1 to 5. Choose the better word for each sentence. Write the word on your paper.

1. The icebreaker (plowed, streaked) through the frozen harbor.
2. The frightened chipmunk (trotted, scurried) into its hole.
3. A hot air balloon (rushed, drifted) over the countryside.
4. John and Linda (skipped, plodded) through the deep snow.
5. A bee (charged, flitted) from flower to flower.

B. Specific Words for *Make* (Use after page 16.)

Number your paper from 1 to 5. Choose the better word for each sentence. Write the word on your paper.

1. Handel (manufactured, composed) the music for *The Messiah.*
2. The colonists learned to (build, manufacture) the goods they couldn't buy.
3. Cuba (produces, constructs) much of the world's sugar.
4. The usher asked the crowd to (devise, form) a line.
5. Lures are (designed, concocted) to look like the food fish eat.

C. Specific Words for *Big* (Use after page 18.)

Number your paper from 1 to 5. Choose the better word for each sentence. Write the word on your paper.

1. This coat is too (bulky, tremendous) to wear skating.
2. The moon landing was a (great, monstrous) accomplishment.
3. A (strapping, vast) area of Russia is still unpopulated.

4. A (gigantic, fat) wave crashed over the sea wall.
5. The truck was too (heavy, vast) to cross the old bridge.

D. Specific Words for *Small* (Use after page 20.)

Number your paper from 1 to 5. Choose the better word for each sentence. Write the word on your paper.

1. Jim has a collection of (shrunken, miniature) trains.
2. My (cramped, scrawny) seat on the plane was uncomfortable.
3. The (tiny, microscopic) bird struggled in the storm.
4. The acrobat lifted his (puny, petite) partner easily.
5. Though the Rands were wealthy, they lived in a (shriveled, modest) home.

E. Specific Words for *Good* (Use after page 22.)

Number your paper from 1 to 5. Choose the better word for each sentence. Write the word on your paper.

1. Greg's touchdown pass was (suitable, perfect)!
2. Bird-watchers enjoy sighting (pleasing, rare) birds.
3. This bread is (delicious, nice). Please give me the recipe.
4. Doris said I did a (fine, rare) job fixing her hem.
5. The (moral, proper) thing to do would be to invite the whole class.

F. Specific Words for *Bad* (Use after page 24.)

Number your paper from 1 to 5. Choose the better word for each sentence. Write the word on your paper.

1. Money is (defective, worthless) on a deserted island.
2. The lumber was (inferior, harmful), so it warped easily.
3. I apologized for dialing a (poor, wrong) number.
4. Some laws protect customers from (dishonest, naughty) salespeople.
5. A warning light shows if the brakes are (wrong, defective).

Chapter 3

Learning About Sentences

When you learned to talk, you began slowly. You probably started out with the names of people around you, like *Mama* or *Dada*. Then you added some action words to let others know what you wanted—words like *come* and *give*. Still later you learned words to describe things you saw, like *pretty flowers* or *funny clown*.

Now you know thousands of words, and how to put many of them together to express your needs and ideas. But you may have found that now and then you still have trouble making others understand you. You can still grow in your ability to use your language.

This chapter will describe the rules for arranging words to make good sentences. Learning these rules will help you understand more of the sentences you hear or read. It will also help you to express yourself to others, in speaking or in writing.

Chapter Objectives

1. To distinguish between fragments and complete sentences
2. To identify the four kinds of sentences:

declarative	imperative
interrogative	exclamatory

3. To use the correct end punctuation for each kind of sentence
4. To identify and form the two basic sentence parts: subject and predicate
5. To understand the function of the verb (simple predicate) and to identify verbs in sentences
6. To understand the term *simple subject* and to identify simple subjects in sentences with regular word order
7. To identify subjects in unusual positions
8. To identify and form compound subjects
9. To identify and form compound predicates

Preparing the Students

Remind students that a sentence is a group of words that expresses a complete thought. Explain that this chapter will help them to understand and write good sentences. Read aloud and discuss the introduction on page 29.

Additional Resources

Diagnostic Test—pages 425 and 426 in this T.E. Recommended for use before teaching the chapter.
Mastery Test—pages 439–442 in this T.E. Recommended for use after teaching the chapter.
Additional Mastery Test—Recommended for use after any necessary reteaching. (In separate booklet, *Diagnostic and Mastery Tests, Gold Level,* pages 15–18.)
Skills Practice Book—pages 9–19
Duplicating Masters—pages 9–19

Part 1

Objective

To distinguish between fragments and complete sentences

Presenting the Lesson

1. Read pages 29 to 31. Discuss the concept of sentence fragments and what is needed to make complete sentences.

2. Ask students to match the following sentence parts to form complete sentences. Do not discourage humorous combinations. They will help to reinforce the need for careful sentence composition in serious writing.

that white rabbit
the TV repairman
cheered for the winning team
many excited fans
ran past the matador
munched on a carrot
bloomed in the garden
a charging bull
some yellow daisies
fixed our broken television

3. Assign and discuss Exercises A and B on page 31.

4. See Exercise A on page 58 for additional practice.

Part 1 Complete Sentences

A **sentence** is a group of words that expresses a complete thought.

If people hearing you talk do not understand you, they can ask you questions. If they are reading a story, or a report, or a letter you wrote, they cannot ask your paper any questions. Your story, report, or letter by itself must make your thoughts clear.

When you are writing, make sure your sentences answer such basic questions as these: *Who did it? What happened?* If a group of words does not answer these questions, that group is not a complete sentence.

Example 1. His stack of newspapers.

What happened? Did someone do something to the stack of newspapers? Did the stack do something? The example does not give you enough information to answer the questions. It is only part of a sentence, or a **fragment.**

By adding words to a fragment, you can change it into a complete sentence. Here are two sentences that give complete thoughts about the fragment "His stack of newspapers."

Richard delivered *his stack of newspapers.*
His stack of newspapers fell to the ground.

Example 2. Played in the water.

Who or what played in the water? Again, the group of words does not give a complete thought. Here are two ways you might complete this fragment:

The seals *played in the water.*
Kristen and Gene *played in the water.*

Can you add words to the two fragments below to make them complete thoughts?

Threw out the first ball of the season
The TV special yesterday

Exercises Recognizing Complete Sentences

A. Number your paper from 1 to 10. Study the groups of words below and decide which of them are sentences. For each word group write "Sentence" or "Fragment."

1. A pocket of my jeans Fragment
2. Sold ten tickets Fragment
3. Two trucks blocked the intersection Sentence
4. The day before the school races Fragment
5. We visited Mount Rushmore Sentence
6. Between the laundromat and the corner Fragment
7. Carefully climbed out on the roof Fragment
8. Louis was asleep Sentence
9. A fountain in Lincoln Park Fragment
10. Three pounds of hamburger Fragment

B. All but one of the groups of words below are sentence fragments. Add words of your own to make complete sentences. Write the sentences. Copy the one complete sentence just as it is.

Answers will vary for all but item 3.

1. On Friday
2. All the bus drivers
3. Jill came at six o'clock Sentence
4. Half the night
5. The automatic door at the supermarket
6. Across the bridge
7. Exploded in mid-air
8. Cautiously tried the ice on the pond
9. Too much water
10. A block from school

Part 2

Objectives

1. To identify the four kinds of sentences:

declarative — imperative
interrogative — exclamatory

2. To use the correct end punctuation for each kind of sentence

Presenting the Lesson

1. Read and discuss pages 32 and 33. Point out that students are probably familiar with other names for the four kinds of sentences.

declarative = statement
interrogative = question
imperative = command or request
exclamatory = exclamation

Ask students to identify the kinds of sentences used in the illustration on page 32.

2. Do Exercise A on page 33 aloud with the class. Assign and discuss Exercise B.

3. Read and discuss page 34. Stress the importance of careful end punctuation for sentences.

4. Assign and discuss Exercises A and B on page 34. Assign Exercise C and D to those students who demonstrate good understanding of the work in this lesson.

5. See Exercise B on page 58 for additional practice.

Part 2 Four Kinds of Sentences

SON OF STAR WAR
I like space movies.
Have you seen 2001?
Go home.
How slow this line is!

The girls and boys in the picture above have used four different kinds of sentences. Each kind expresses a complete thought.

1. A **declarative sentence** tells something. It ends with a period (.) .

The movie begins at two o'clock.

2. An **interrogative sentence** asks something. It ends with a question mark (?) .

Do you like popcorn?

3. An **imperative sentence** requests, instructs, or orders. It usually ends with a period.

Sit near the front of the theater.

4. An **exclamatory sentence** expresses joy, surprise, anger, excitement, or other strong feeling. It ends with an exclamation point (!).

What a huge crowd came to this show!

Begin every sentence with a capital letter.

Exercises Identifying the Kinds of Sentences

A. The following sentences do not have punctuation marks at the end. Number your paper from 1 to 10. Write *Declarative, Interrogative, Imperative,* or *Exclamatory* to show what kind each sentence is.

1. Measure the length of the table Imperative
2. May we watch Channel 11 Interrogative
3. Birds' bones have air pockets Declarative
4. Take a break Imperative
5. What a scary feeling I got Exclamatory
6. Do you have an eraser Interrogative
7. Is the pressure in the tires too high Interrogative
8. Ms. Minden's cat had a rabies shot Declarative
9. Does a chipmunk have a white stripe down its back Interrogative
10. Tell me all about your problem Imperative

B. Follow the directions for Exercise A.

1. John Singleton Copley painted portraits of great Americans Declarative
2. Turn off the hose, please Imperative
3. The melon rolled down the steps Declarative
4. Can you lift the 100-pound weight Interrogative
5. May I come, too Interrogative
6. What a fast runner Vincent is Exclamatory
7. The ballerina wore toe shoes Declarative
8. Wait for the next elevator, please Imperative
9. Are you rooting for Peggy Interrogative
10. Guava is a tropical fruit Declarative

Extending the Lesson

Demonstrate the differences in the four kinds of sentences by reading them aloud with expression.

Declarative:
I want an apple.

Interrogative:
Do you want an apple?

Imperative:
Please give me an apple.

Exclamatory:
What a delicious apple!

Have students read the sentences in the Exercises on page 33 and 34 aloud and with expression.

Punctuating Sentences

The kind of punctuation mark you put at the end of your sentence helps the reader figure out your meaning. Remember these rules:

1. Use a period after a declarative sentence.
2. Use a question mark after an interrogative sentence.
3. Use a period after an imperative sentence.
4. Use an exclamation point after an exclamatory sentence.

Exercises Using Correct Punctuation

A. Copy and punctuate these sentences.

1. Which seats are ours?
2. Remember to bring a sweater tonight.
3. Call Debbie to the phone, please.
4. Oil floats on the top of water.
5. Have you ever visited the Everglades?
6. Place your stamp in the upper right-hand corner.
7. How far can you swim under water?
8. The Swiss flag is red with a white cross.
9. Oil slicks kill hundreds of birds.
10. What a lot of questions you ask!

B. Follow the directions for Exercise A.

1. Proceed to gate G-7.
2. What a great time we had at Disney World!
3. Follow the rules of the game.
4. Now, which tooth is loose?
5. Elvis Presley Boulevard is a street in Memphis.
6. Do twenty push-ups.
7. Lauri practices the tuba down in the rec room.
8. Does Michael wear his hair in an Afro style?
9. Whales are guided by tiny pilot fish.
10. What is the Continental Divide?

C. Write two declarative sentences, two interrogative sentences, two imperative sentences, and two exclamatory sentences. Begin and end each sentence correctly.

D. Write a paragraph or a story about something exciting, funny, or different that has happened to you. Use the four kinds of sentences.

Part 3 Every Sentence Has Two Parts

Every sentence has a **subject** and a **predicate.**

1.	**The old car**	**lost its tailpipe.**
	This part is the subject. It tells what the sentence is about.	This is the predicate. It tells what happened.
2.	**Our team**	**won the pennant.**
	This is the subject. It tells whom the sentence is about.	This is the predicate. It tells what happened.
3.	**My friend Sue**	**hit a home run.**
	Subject	Predicate

Finding the Subject and the Predicate

Every sentence states a complete thought. A complete thought has two parts: the subject and the predicate.

> The **subject** of a sentence tells what or whom the sentence is about.
>
> The **predicate** of a sentence tells what the subject did or what happened.

Part 3

Objective

To identify and form the two basic sentence parts: subject and predicate

Presenting the Lesson

1. Read and discuss pages 35 and 36.

2. Stress that the usual sentence pattern is subject followed by predicate. Examples:

Subject	Predicate
The large dog	scared my baby sister.
Thunderstorms	occur often in spring.
Two different answers	confused us.

3. Assign and discuss Exercises A and B on pages 36 and 37. It is suggested that Exercises C and D be done orally.

4. See Exercise C on page 59 for additional practice.

Optional Practice

Use Exercises C and D on page 37 for a small group oral activity. Each member of the group is to complete each sentence with an appropriate predicate or subject, different from those already stated. The group should complete one sentence at a time.

Extending the Lesson

Have students create a set of subject and predicate flash cards. They can be used for individual practice or for a classroom activity.

An easy way to understand the parts of a sentence is to think of the sentence as telling who did something or what happened. The subject tells *who* or *what*. The predicate tells *did* or *happened*. You can divide sentences in this way:

Who or What (Subject)	Did or Happened (Predicate)
All my friends	came to my party.
The old elm	was blown down by the storm.

Exercises Finding Subjects and Predicates

Copy these sentences. Draw one line under the subject of each sentence. Draw two lines under the predicate.

Example: The yellow car was going too fast.

1. Dad locked the house.
2. Thanksgiving will fall on November 28 this year.
3. The first batter struck out.
4. My socks have shrunk.
5. A robin's nest was in the pear tree.
6. Jay's cat eats beetles.
7. The second-string players watched from the bench.
8. We could not see through the water.
9. Lisa took her bathing suit with her.
10. The team can count on Mandy.

Follow the directions for Exercise A.

1. Maria found an old gold watch.
2. My little brother swallowed a dime.
3. A pound weighs less than a kilo.
4. My sister's Chevy uses unleaded gas.
5. The sunlight sparkled on the water.

6. Terence's cookies taste best.
7. The final whistle blew.
8. A butterfly struggled in the spider's web.
9. The inventor experimented with the wooden gears.
10. The air conditioner in the family room works.

Write an interesting predicate for each of these subjects. Begin each sentence with the words given. Answers will vary.

1. The pizza
2. The black hearse
3. My terrier
4. Our front door
5. Stacy's science project
6. The drive-in
7. Charlie Brown
8. The sly old cat
9. The best game
10. The quarterback

Write a good subject for each of these predicates. Answers will vary.

1. knows all the latest dances
2. is jumping next
3. are going rock climbing
4. has twin engines
5. is allergic to peanuts
6. squeaks a lot
7. saw the movie on Saturday
8. went fishing every day
9. stopped
10. wants to be an engineer

Part 4 The Verb

The subjects and predicates you have been studying so far are called **complete subjects** and **complete predicates.** The complete subject includes all of the words that tell *who* or *what.* The complete predicate includes all of the words that tell *what happened.*

There is one part of every complete predicate that is more important than the rest. This part is the **verb.** It is sometimes called the **simple predicate.** In the rest of this book, we will speak of it as the *verb.*

Part 4

Objective

To understand the function of the verb (simple predicate) and to identify verbs in sentences

Presenting the Lesson

1. Read and discuss pages 37 and 38. Stress the fact that *verb* and *simple predicate* are both names for the same thing. Point out that the verb is only a part of the complete predicate in most sentences.

2. If a student raises the question, explain that the verb may be more than one word long. However, in this lesson, all verbs are one word long. (Verbs consisting of more than one word will be presented in Part 5.)

3. Assign and discuss Exercises A and B on pages 38 and 39.

4. See Exercise D on page 59 for additional practice.

Extending the Lesson

This activity is suggested only for those students who understand the role of the verb in the sentence.

Each sentence pair below uses a particular word two ways. In one of the sentences, the underlined word is a verb. In the other it is not. Choose the sentence in each pair whose underlined word is a verb.

1. The charge for the meal was low.
   The cavalry charged up the hill.
2. Run home and get your baseball mitt.
   He scored a run in the first inning of the game.
3. That light is too bright.
   Light a match.
4. Please set the alarm clock.
   I bought a paint set.
5. They drive to Florida every year.
   The drive home seemed long.

Finding the Verb

The words in italics in these sentences are the verbs.

We *went* to the beach.
Three girls *brought* their goggles.

Some verbs tell of an action:

Charlene *hit* the ball.
The boys *ran* home.

Other verbs state that something is:

The doctor *is* here.
You *are* first.

A **verb** is a word that tells of an action or a state of being.

Exercises Finding the Verb

A. Copy these sentences. Draw two lines under the verb.

Example: The tornado carried Dorothy to Oz.

1. A pack of dogs runs loose on my street.
2. Reggie does unusual stunts on his skateboard.
3. Diana Ross went from singer to movie star.
4. In spring, northern farmers boil maple sap into syrup.
5. The bike marathon lasts all day.
6. The guide told our group about the state capitol.
7. One of my cousins writes for *Newsweek*.
8. A worm was in that apple.
9. Sacajawea guided Lewis and Clark in their exploration of the Northwest Territory.
10. Nobody believed Esther's story.

B. Follow the directions for Exercise A.

1. Queen Elizabeth I ruled England for forty-five years.
2. Water freezes at 0°C or 32°F.
3. All the students went home half an hour ago.
4. The mail arrived early today.
5. Barry rode his bike to school.
6. The baby eats nothing but cereal.
7. Medicine Hat is the name of a town in Canada.
8. My mother once met Pearl Bailey backstage.
9. Alex found a dollar bill in the mall parking lot.
10. The lightning storm caused static on the radio.

Part 5 Main Verbs and Helping Verbs

The verb is often only a single word. Read each sentence below and notice the verb, in italics.

Eddie *laughed* at the joke.
Georgia *whistled* a tune.
The students *cheered*.

Other verbs are made up of more than one word. Notice how you can build a one-word verb into a verb with several words:

Beth and David *collect* shells.

The verb, *collect*, tells what Beth and David do.

Beth and David *will collect* shells.

The verb we began with, *collect*, now has another verb, *will*, before it. We call *collect* the **main verb**, and *will* the **helping verb**. The helping verb changes the meaning of the sentence slightly.

Beth and David *were collecting* shells.

Part 5

Objective

To differentiate between main verbs and helping verbs

Presenting the Lesson

1. Read and discuss pages 39 to 41.

2. Students should become familiar with all the listed helping verbs. Special attention should be paid to those verbs at the top of the page that can be used either as main verbs or as helping verbs.

Some students may challenge the rule that certain verbs can be used only as helping verbs. They may point out that the following is an acceptable sentence: *I can.* However, that sentence is not complete in itself. Its meaning depends on its context.

Examples: Can you ski?
I can (ski).
Can you knit?
I can (knit).
Can you type?
I can (type).

When *can* is used alone, it is still a helping verb. Its main verb is known from the sentences preceding it, and simply understood.

3. Assign Exercises A and B on pages 41 and 42. It is suggested that Exercises C and D be assigned only to those who demonstrate mastery of the basic concepts.

4. See Exercise E on pages 59 and 60 for additional practice.

Optional Practice

Students who are having difficulty should identify the complete predicate for each sentence in Exercises A and B before looking for the helping verbs and main verbs.

Extending the Lesson

1. Have students follow the directions for Exercise C on page 42, using each of the verbs at the top of page 41. Note that when some of these verbs are used as helping verbs with *go, go* changes its form to *going* or *gone.*

2. How many different sentences can be created from this base sentence by adding helping verbs, changing the verb form where necessary?

The dog barked.

The verb *collect* has changed its form now to *collecting*, but it is still the main verb. The new helping verb is *were*. This helping verb changes the meaning of the sentence, too.

Beth and David *have collected* shells.

Here, the main verb is *collected*, another form of the verb *collect*. The helping verb is *have*.

As you have seen in these examples, the main verb may change forms when helping verbs are added to a one-word verb. The endings *-ing*, *-ed*, and *-en* are frequently used on main verbs. Adding helping verbs and changing the ending do not change the basic action of the main verb. However, these changes do modify the meaning slightly.

In the following examples, decide which word is the main verb and which word or words are helping verbs. Then look at the chart to see if you were right.

Grace *was skating*.
The vase *was broken* by accident.
Randy *has combed* his hair.
The old Ford *has been making* strange noises.
The back door *should have been locked*.

Verb	Helping Verbs	Main Verb
was skating	was	skating
was broken	was	broken
has combed	has	combed
has been making	has been	making
should have been locked	should have been	locked

Some words can be used either as verbs by themselves or as helping verbs:

is	was	have	do
are	were	has	does
am		had	did

Examples:

Tomorrow *is* a holiday. (verb)
The pump *is broken.* (helping verb with *broken*)

Ardis *has* a cold. (verb)
She *has stayed* home. (helping verb with *stayed*)

Some words can be used only as helping verbs:

can	may	should
shall	must	would
will	could	might

Examples:

We *may go* with you.
Dad *will finish* the pie.
Jackie's project *might win* an award.

Some verbs are made up of a main verb and helping verbs.

Some words can be used either as verbs by themselves or as helping verbs.

Some words can be used only as helping verbs.

Exercises Finding the Main Verb and Helping Verbs

A. Label two columns *Helping Verbs* and *Main Verb.* Find all the parts of the verb in each sentence. Write them in the proper column.

Examples:	Helping Verbs	Main Verb
a. I have enough potato chips for the party.		have
b. Eighteen customers have demanded refunds.	have	demanded

1. I have (HV) seen (MV) the dinosaur bones in the museum.
2. The blizzard stopped (MV) all traffic in the city.
3. The Cubs might (HV) beat (MV) the Braves.
4. Pennsylvania is (MV) the Keystone State.
5. Chris has (HV) completed (MV) four passes in this quarter.
6. Rick should (HV) be (HV) waiting (MV) for you.
7. Terri can (HV) somersault (MV) in the air.
8. The chemical had (HV) poisoned (MV) the fish.
9. McDonald's invented (MV) the Egg McMuffin.
10. The fireworks in Candlestick Park will (HV) begin (MV) at eight.

B. Follow the directions for Exercise A.

1. You should (HV) have (HV) seen (MV) the game last Tuesday.
2. Those peppers may (HV) burn (MV) your tongue.
3. The water was (MV) 26°C in the pool.
4. On Saturday the rides will (HV) cost (MV) a quarter.
5. Seattle was (HV) named (MV) for an Indian chief, Seathl.
6. The whole house would (HV) shake (MV) with each new tremor.
7. The Grand Canyon is (MV) more than a mile deep.
8. My sister has (HV) driven (MV) six hundred miles a day.
9. I might show (MV) Lion at the pet show tomorrow.
10. You must (HV) have (HV) taped (MV) that noise at the basketball game.

C. Write sentences in which you use the words *do, does, did* as verbs by themselves. Then write sentences using these words as helping verbs with the main verb *go.* Answers will vary.

D. Use the helping verbs given on page 41 with the main verb *call.* See how many different verbs you can make. Answers will vary.

Part 6 Separated Parts of the Verb

never not often
The baby **has** **cried.**
always just usually

The words that make up a verb are not always together in a sentence, like *could have been,* and *might have been.* Sometimes the helping verbs and the main verb are separated by other words that are not verbs:

can hardly **wait**	**could** not **have come**
has always **been**	**did**n't **understand**
is usually **found**	**must have** already **gone**

The parts of the verb are in red. Notice that *not* and the ending *n't* in contractions are not parts of the verb.

Exercises Finding Separated Parts of the Verb

A. Label two columns *Helping Verbs* and *Main Verb.* Find all the parts of the verb in each sentence. Write them in the proper column.

Example: The kitten didn't scratch me.

Helping Verb	Main Verb
did	scratch

1. Jenny has[HV] always been[MV] my friend.
2. Bruce would[HV] often take[MV] the bus.
3. Slacks are[HV] usually found[MV] in the sportswear department.
4. The logs are[HV] normally floated[MV] down the river.
5. We will[HV] probably see[MV] the movie this weekend.
6. Judy had[HV] just cut[MV] the lawn.
7. Lynn is[HV] always whistling[MV] that song.
8. The carpet is[HV] usually vacuumed[MV] once a week.

Part 6

Objective

To identify and use verbs with separated parts

Presenting the Lesson

1. Read and discuss page 43. Pay particular attention to the verb contractions. Stress that the *n't* is not considered part of the verb.

2. Students will often incorrectly identify adverbs as helping verbs, especially those in positions between helping verbs and main verbs. Suggest that students review the lists of helping verbs on page 41. Most helping verbs are included there.

3. It is recommended that students who experience difficulty with Part 5 not be assigned Part 6. They should use the time for additional practice on identifying helping verbs and main verbs not separated by adverbs.

4. Assign and discuss Exercises A, B, and C on pages 43 and 44.

5. See Exercise F on page 60 for additional practice.

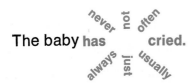

9. My brother didn't [HV] understand [MV] the instructions in the cookbook.

10. Maurie must [HV] have [HV] already finished [MV] his lunch.

B. **B.** Follow the directions for Exercise A.

1. My mother was [HV] actually looking [MV] for a new car.
2. The hot days of July and August are [HV] sometimes called [MV] dog days.
3. That catbird is [HV] always mimicking [MV] all the other birds.
4. Ms. Washington doesn't [HV] often assign [MV] homework.
5. Valerie can [HV] really walk [MV] a tightrope.
6. Mr. Lang must [HV] not have [HV] called [MV] very loudly.
7. A Venus fly trap can [HV] really catch [MV] flies.
8. Greg would [HV] rather have [MV] a corn roast.
9. In Australia, badgers are [HV] sometimes called [MV] bandicoots.
10. New York was [HV] originally named [MV] New Amsterdam.

C. The following sentences have main verbs but no helping verbs. On a sheet of paper numbered from 1 to 10, write helping verbs that will fit the blanks. Some answers may vary.

1. My parents _____have_____ often watched "60 Minutes."
2. Marsha _____has_____ already performed.
3. Jason _____is_____ n't going to the art fair today.
4. Dottie _____has_____ never visited a factory before.
5. Robin _____will_____ surely come tomorrow.
6. Last month the sewing class _____would_____ usually end at three o'clock.
7. The skyscraper _____is_____ probably equipped with eight elevator shafts.
8. The sound equipment _____is_____ n't working.
9. Larry _____should_____ not _____have_____ put his ticket on the windowsill.
10. You _____have_____ hardly looked at the geology display.

Part 7 The Simple Subject

In a complete sentence, every verb has a subject.

	Subject	Verb
1.	**Ginny**	ran.
2.	Your **popsicle**	will melt.
3.	The old **man**	laughed.

The subject of the verb is sometimes called the **simple subject** of the sentence. The simple subjects in the sentences above are *Ginny*, *popsicle*, and *man*. From here on in this book, the simple subject will be called the **subject of the verb.**

To find the subject of the verb, first find the verb. Then ask *who?* or *what?* before the verb.

Examples:

The crowd at the rock concert cheered loudly.

Verb: *cheered*
Who or what *cheered?* the *crowd*
Crowd is the subject of *cheered.*

After dinner my whole family watched television.

Verb: *watched*
Who or what *watched?* my *family*
Family is the subject of *watched.*

Exercises Finding the Verb and Its Subject

A. Copy each sentence. Draw two lines under the verb. Then draw one line under the subject of the verb.

1. Carol coached our team.
2. The space shuttle was first tested in 1978.
3. Joel is our next-door neighbor.

Part 7

Objective

To understand the term *simple subject* and to identify simple subjects in sentences with regular word order

Presenting the Lesson

1. Read and discuss page 45.
2. Ask students to suggest other sentences. Have the class identify the simple subjects.
3. Assign and discuss Exercises A and B on pages 45 and 46.
4. See Exercises G on pages 60 and 61 for additional practice.

Extending the Lesson

Use this activity only with those students who understand the difference between the subject and the verb.

Have students write two sentences for each of the following words, first using the word as a simple subject and then using the word as a verb.

Example: ring
The golden ring was beautiful.
Terry will ring the bell.

box plant light play trap

4. The hornets under the window buzzed angrily.
5. The cows didn't even look at the train.
6. The grandfather clock struck twelve.
7. The treasures of King Tutankhamen were found in Egypt.
8. We were flying over the airport for an hour.
9. All three boys could play the guitar well.
10. The cat's eyes shone in the dark.

B. Follow the directions for Exercise A.

1. Aretha worked the problem easily.
2. In July and August, the Dog Star rises with the sun.
3. Heavy traffic frequently jams the Holland Tunnel.
4. Trespassers will be prosecuted.
5. The steer in that pen was branded at Lazy T Ranch.
6. The fragrance of popcorn filled the theater.
7. Now Carl can dry the dishes.
8. The hedge behind the tennis court was loaded with balls.
9. My older sister must have dropped the vase.
10. The lettuce in that salad was grown in my garden.

Part 8 The Subject in Unusual Positions

In nearly all the sentences you have studied so far, the subject comes before the verb. There are many sentences, however, in which the subject comes after the verb. Notice these sentences:

1. The *shark* lingered off the shore.
   (Subject before the verb)
2. Off the shore lingered the *shark*.
   (Subject after the verb)

Sometimes you can find the subject more easily if you turn the sentence around.

Part 8

Objective

To identify subjects in unusual positions

Presenting the Lesson

1. Do not assign this section to students who are still experiencing difficulty identifying the subject in usual positions. Provide additional practice with subject identification in regular sentence patterns.

2. Read and discuss pages 46 and 47.

Sentence: Through the cloud shot the missile.
Rewritten: The missile shot through the cloud.

Always find the verb first. Then ask *who?* or *what?* before the verb.

The subject always follows the verb in sentences that begin in these ways:

Here is	Where is	There is
Here are	Where are	There are

1. Where are the *keys?* (*Keys* is subject of *are.*)
2. Here is your *guitar.* (*Guitar* is subject of *is.*)
3. There is our *boat.* (*Boat* is subject of *is.*)

3. In working with subjects in unusual positions, emphasize that students first locate the verb in the sentence.

4. Assign and discuss Exercises A, B, and C on pages 47 and 48. It may help to invert some of the sentences before analyzing them. Be sure that students understand Part 8 before proceeding with Part 9.

5. See Exercise H on page 61 for additional practice.

Exercises Finding the Subject in Unusual Positions

A. Copy each sentence. Draw two lines under the verb. Then draw one line under the subject of the verb.

1. There is a funnel cloud in the distance.
2. Into the pool the diver plunged.
3. The girls zipped the tent windows.
4. Where is the key to your locker?
5. Over the haunted house floated strange shapes.
6. There are many irritating commercials on that program.
7. Across the street darted Mr. Walter's cat.
8. Slowly Sandy understood.
9. Up the bank scrambled Patti.
10. Two hours after lights out, Kevin crept from his tent.

B. Follow the directions for Exercise A.

1. Here is my idea.
2. Overhead were all our helium balloons.
3. Up the river glided the barge.
4. Suddenly the rocket backfired.
5. In the tropical waters are many unusual creatures.

6. There is room for Miki.
7. In last year's competition, Al's team won easily.
8. Over the plains thundered the herd.
9. Her bracelet is made of a souvenir spoon from Niagara Falls.
10. Where is a public telephone?

C. Follow the directions for Exercise A.

1. The sand glittered with gold dust.
2. There are already five teams in our bowling league.
3. Into his burrow whisked the fox.
4. Here is the electrician now.
5. Out of the canyon roared the river.
6. Heather collected the carwash money.
7. Down the tower stairs the knight clattered.
8. Time waits for no man.
9. Where is the latest newspaper?
10. In the shed was an old Victrola.

Part 9

Objective

To identify subjects in interrogative and exclamatory sentences

Presenting the Lesson

1. Review interrogative and exclamatory sentences as explained in Part 2 on pages 32 and 33.

2. Read and discuss page 48. Point out that a given sentence may be rewritten into several patterns, to suit the style of the writer.

3. It is recommended that you do Exercise A on page 49 with the class. Assign Exercise B only to the more advanced students.

4. See Exercise I on pages 61 and 62 for additional practice.

Part 9 Subjects in Interrogative and Exclamatory Sentences

You may have to rewrite or rethink some interrogative and exclamatory sentences to find the subject. Here are examples.

Interrogative Sentence:	Did you see that touchdown?
Rewritten:	You did see that touchdown.
Exclamatory Sentence:	Was that movie boring!
Rewritten:	That movie was boring!

Sometimes you need to drop some words to make a rewritten sentence sound normal.

Exclamatory Sentence:	What terrible weather we're having!
Rewritten (Awkward):	We're having what terrible weather!
Rewritten (Smooth):	We're having terrible weather!

Exercises Finding the Subjects and Verbs in Interrogative and Exclamatory Sentences

A. Change the word order in each sentence below. You may need to drop some words to make your sentence smooth. Then write the new sentence. Underline each subject.

Example: Will we never get home!
We will never get home.

1. Were you the winner? You were the winner.
2. What a long time you took! (Drop *What.*) You took a long time.
3. Has the dog been fed? The dog has been fed.
4. How orange the moon looks! (Drop *How.*) The moon looks orange.
5. Have they painted the library? They have painted the library.
6. Did your friend win the calculator? Your friend did win the calculator.
7. What a dark cave we saw! (Drop *What.*) We saw a dark cave.
8. May I help you? I may help you.
9. How fast the baby has grown! (Drop *How.*) The baby has grown fast.
10. Won't this snow ever melt! This snow won't ever melt.

B. Copy the sentences below. Draw two lines under the verb in each sentence. Draw one line under the subject of the verb. (If you need to, change the word order mentally to find the subject and verb.)

1. Does that hamburger have onions on it?
2. How did you find the right answer? (Drop *How* mentally.)
3. What a noisy bird that crow is! (Drop *What* mentally.)
4. Does Marianne Moore write poetry?
5. Have the Indians played in the World Series since 1970?
6. How ugly you look in your witch's costume! (Drop *How* mentally.)
7. Did Angel Cordero ever ride Affirmed? (Drop *ever* mentally.)
8. What a feast we had at Thanksgiving! (Drop *What* mentally.)
9. Has Marcia read today's newspaper already?
10. Am I hungry!

Part 10 When the Subject Is Not Given

Look at the two sentences on the signs in the picture. *You* is the subject of each of these sentences. In imperative sentences the subject is understood to be the word *you*.

Examples: (You) Keep off the grass.
(You) Do not feed the animals.

Exercises Telling the Subject

A. Copy the following sentences. Draw two lines under the verb in each sentence. Draw one line under the subject of the verb. If the subject is not given in the sentence, write it in parentheses in the place where it is understood.

Example: Memorize your new phone number.
(You) memorize your new phone number.

1. Play ball. (You) play
2. Marianne almost forgot her umbrella.
3. Take another turn. (You) take
4. Finish your game before supper. (You) finish

Part 10

Objective

To be aware of the understood subject of imperative sentences

Presenting the Lesson

1. Before the lesson, write the following sentence on the board:

Please open your book to page 50.

Ask students to identify the verb in the sentence (*open*). Ask them *who* or *what* is supposed to do the opening. They should easily see that they themselves are being indicated. The subject, the person being asked to do something, is always understood to be the word *you*.

2. Read and discuss page 50.

3. It is suggested that the class do Exercise A on pages 50 and 51 together. Have the students identify each sentence by kind: declarative,

5. Did Joe bring the net?
6. Give me your autograph, please. (You) give
7. How bumpy this road is!
8. Is the story true?
9. Proceed with caution. (You) proceed
10. Do you know Steve Fowler?

B. Follow the directions for Exercise A.

1. Wait a minute. (You) wait
2. Does Rosalie speak Spanish?
3. The violin players had not arrived.
4. Did the explorers come from Portugal or Spain?
5. Listen to that rain. (You) listen
6. Can everyone hear me?
7. How many legs do insects have?
8. Shop at Safeway. (You) shop
9. Turn left at the first stop light. (You) turn
10. Some of my friends play handball every afternoon.

Part 11 Compound Subjects

Look at these two sentences:

	Subject	Predicate
1.	Tom	saw a traffic accident.
2.	I	saw a traffic accident.

Since the predicates are the same, we can join the two sentences together. Here is the new sentence:

	Subject	Predicate
3.	Tom and I	saw a traffic accident.

interrogative, imperative, or exclamatory. Assign and discuss Exercise B on page 51.

4. See Exercise J on page 62 for additional practice.

Part 11

Objective

To identify and form compound subjects

Presenting the Lesson

1. Read and discuss pages 51 and 52. Stress that *compound* means "more than one."

2. Point out that the conjunctions *and* and *or* can both be used to form compound subjects, but that they have different meanings.

3. Assign Exercises A, B, and C on pages 52 to 54. Discuss the various possible answers. Note that other words may come between the words of the compound.

4. See Exercise K on pages 62 and 63 for additional practice.

Extending the Lesson

Have the students rewrite each of the following sentence pairs as a single sentence with a compound subject.

1. Tom earned an A in math.
   Amy earned an A in math.
2. My aunt visited the Grand Canyon.
   My cousin visited the Grand Canyon.
3. The rabbit ate the lettuce.
   The gerbil ate the lettuce.
4. Many rainstorms occur in April.
   Many windstorms occur in April.
5. Sandwiches are served for lunch.
   Salads are served for lunch.

Now the subject has two parts. When two or more subjects are used with the same predicate, they are called a **compound subject.** The word *compound* means having more than one part.

In sentence 3 the word *and* joins the two parts of the subject. The word *or* is also used to join parts of a subject.

A word that is used to join words or groups of words is called a **conjunction.**

Simple subject: **Darren** may win.
Simple subject: **Alicia** may win.
Compound subject: **Darren** or **Alicia** may win.

When three or more subjects are combined in a compound subject, use commas to separate them. The conjunction is placed before the last subject.

Example: The *trees*, the *bushes*, and the *flowers* need rain.

Exercises Writing Compound Subjects

Copy the following sentences. Draw two lines under the verb in every sentence. Then draw one line under each part of the compound subject. (Reminder: Be careful to copy every comma.)

Examples: a. The wind and the sudden rain ruined the picnic.

b. John Lennon, Paul McCartney, George Harrison, and Ringo Starr became famous as the Beatles.

1. Emily, Charlotte, and Ann Brontë wrote novels.
2. The Knicks or the Celtics may win the playoffs.
3. Shirley, Della, and Pat are best friends.
4. In *Star Wars*, C3PO and R2D2 aid in the fight against the evil Darth Vader.
5. Radishes, carrots, and potatoes grow underground.

6. That stuffed dog or the rubber duck would be a good gift for the baby.

7. George Burns and Gracie Allen performed in vaudeville, on radio, and on TV.

8. Marisa and Juan tied for first place in the essay contest.

9. Cereal, milk, and toast make a nutritious breakfast.

10. The Mohawks and four other Indian tribes joined forces as the powerful Five Nations.

B. Think of a compound subject for each sentence below. Copy the sentences, filling in the blanks with a compound subject.

Example: ________ and ________ rent canoes at Bow Lake.
Mr. Walker and his daughter rent canoes at Bow Lake.

1. Answers will vary. and ________ are the busiest streets near us.

2. ________ or ________ whistled.

3. Gooey ________ or ________ tastes good on ice cream.

4. ________ and ________ are my favorite sports.

5. ________, ________, and ________ were coming down Cherry Street.

6. Many ________ and ________ grew in the greenhouse.

7. ________, ________, and ________ have thirty days.

8. ________ and ________ clung to the overturned boat.

9. My ________ or my ________ is my oldest relative.

10. Over-ripe ________ and day-old ________ were on sale.

C. Think of a compound subject for each predicate listed below. Then write the complete sentence. In some sentences, try to use a compound subject with three parts. Use correct punctuation.
Answers will vary.

1. suddenly rounded the corner
2. are waiting outside
3. were my best subjects
4. have never been afraid of spiders
5. covered the ground
6. were not ready yet
7. ran for the last bus
8. are in the tool kit
9. were blocking the supermarket driveway
10. tied down the trunk of the car

Part 12

Objective

To identify and form compound predicates

Presenting the Lesson

1. Read and discuss page 54.
2. Discuss the different meanings of the conjunctions *and, but,* and *or.*
3. It is suggested that you do Exercise A on page 55 aloud with the class. Assign and discuss Exercises B and C. Point out that Exercise B asks for verbs to complete the compound predicates.
4. See Exercise L on page 63 for additional practice.

Part 12 Compound Predicates

When two or more predicates are used with the same subject, they are called a **compound predicate.**

By using a compound predicate and a conjunction you are often able to combine two or more sentences.

Subject	Predicate
1. The dog	growled.
2. The dog	bit the paperboy.

Subject	Predicate
3. The dog	growled and bit the paperboy.

When three or more predicates are combined in a compound predicate, commas are used to separate them. The conjunction is placed before the last predicate.

Example: Katherine saw the bear, dropped the camera, and ran off.

Exercises Writing Compound Predicates

A. Copy the following sentences. Draw one line under the subject of each sentence. Then draw two lines under each part of the compound predicate. (Reminder: Be careful to copy every comma.)

Examples: a. Chris Evert practiced long hours and became a top tennis player.

b. My father jacked up the car, took off the flat tire, and put on the spare.

1. I left the cake in the oven too long and burned it.
2. Ice covered the streets and caused numerous accidents.
3. Lydia's family went to the Grand Canyon, rode burros down the trail, and spent the night at the bottom of the Canyon.
4. The Angels scored four runs in the first inning and stayed ahead during the rest of the game.
5. Frederick Douglass escaped from slavery and became a speaker for anti-slavery groups.
6. Our class rented a bus and visited the Natural History Museum.
7. King Kong broke loose in New York City, climbed the World Trade Center, and fought off fighter planes.
8. On the field trip, you bring your lunch or buy a hot dog at the cafeteria.
9. Mary Pickford starred in silent movies and was called "America's Sweetheart."
10. Ector came to bat, ignored three wide pitches, and smashed the fourth pitch into the stands.

B. Think of a compound predicate for each subject listed below. Copy the sentences, filling in the blanks with verbs to complete the compound predicates.

Extending the Lesson

Have the students rewrite each of the following pairs of sentences as a single sentence with a compound predicate.

1. The poodle ran around the yard. The poodle jumped over the fence.
2. Marla cut out the dress pattern. Marla sewed the dress.
3. My pen rolled across the desk. My pen spilled all its ink.
4. Eric called the restaurant. Eric ordered a pizza.
5. The science club held a contest. The science club awarded a prize.

Example: The lean gray cat ________ on the shed, ________ itself, and ________ the sparrows.

The lean gray cat sat on the shed, sunned itself, and watched the sparrows.

1. The photographer __Answers will vary.__ for buffalo and finally ________ a herd.
2. The lion cub ________ and ________ his food.
3. The gymnast ________ on the balance beam and ________ a prize.
4. Noisy crows ________ over the field and ________ the corn.
5. A 747 ________ very big and ________ many passengers.
6. My little sister ________ her food, ________ her shoes, and ________ with her toys.
7. A foghorn ________ a loud noise and ________ ships about rocks and other dangers.
8. Benjamin Franklin ________ electricity, ________ bifocal glasses, and ________ *Poor Richard's Almanac.*
9. Satellites ________ the earth below and ________ information about the weather.
10. A huge Christmas tree ________ in the shopping mall and ________ many shiny ornaments.

C. Think of a compound predicate for each subject listed below. Then write the complete sentence. In some of your sentences, try to use a compound predicate with three parts. Answers will vary.

1. The catcher
2. A shrewd detective
3. The Statue of Liberty
4. The big band
5. Stars and planets
6. The ice cream
7. Rotten floor boards
8. Forest fires
9. An octopus
10. The snowstorm

Sentence Patterns **Word Order and Meaning**

Sentences are made up of words. To make sense, the words must be put together in a special order. Look at the groups of words below. Which group makes sense?

Ralph jumped up.

Jumped Ralph up.

The first group makes sense. The words are in the right order for an English sentence. The second group does not make sense. Our experience tells us that the words are not in the right order for an English sentence.

Sometimes there is more than one right order for a group of words. Each order makes sense and expresses a message, but the messages are not always the same. Read the following pair of sentences.

Elaine saw Hugh.

Hugh saw Elaine.

The words are the same in each sentence. Only the order of the words makes the sentences different. But the difference in order makes an important difference in meaning.

Exercise Word Order and Meaning

Read each sentence. Then change the order of the words to change the meaning. Write each new sentence on your paper.

Phyllis spotted Tom.
1. Tom spotted Phyllis.

The dish covered cake crumbs.
2. Cake crumbs covered the dish.

The Lions beat the Tigers.
3. The Tigers beat the Lions.

My best friend knows Carol.
4. Carol knows my best friend.

Some plants eat insects.
5. Some insects eat plants.

Some nurses are men.
6. Some men are nurses.

The cat heard Donna.
7. Donna heard the cat.

That dancer is a boy.
8. That boy is a dancer.

Sentence Patterns

Objective

To recognize the usual word order of sentences

Presenting the Lesson

1. Ask the class to listen carefully and follow the instructions below. Read them no more than twice, and wait for the students to figure them out.

1. Books your open.
2. Find 57 page.

Explain that their difficulty in understanding was caused by the unusual word order in the directions.

2. Read and discuss page 57.

3. Assign and discuss the Exercise on page 57.

Additional Exercises

If these Exercises were not used with each lesson, they may now be assigned for chapter review.

Additional Exercises

Learning About Sentences

A. Recognizing Complete Sentences (Use after page 31.)

Number from 1 to 10 on your paper. Study the groups of words below and decide which of them are sentences. For each word group write "Sentence" or "Fragment." Then add words to the fragments to make complete sentences. Complete sentences will vary.

1. Just bought a new ten-speed bike Fragment
2. Peanut butter and jelly Fragment
3. United Airlines flies to Los Angeles Sentence
4. Quickly chose players for their teams Fragment
5. The lights of New York Fragment
6. Won a prize in the broad jump Fragment
7. We have already mailed the boxtops Sentence
8. The satellite monitored the weather Sentence
9. Cars for rent Fragment
10. The Colorado River flows through the Grand Canyon Sentence

B. Using Correct Punctuation (Use after page 34.)

Copy and punctuate these sentences.

1. What a good mood you're in !
2. Cotton is cooler than polyester .
3. From the airplane the thunderheads looked huge .
4. Can you repair this cuckoo clock ?
5. Call me at five .
6. Does Kim's jackknife have a can opener ?
7. Give the baby her bottle at two o'clock .
8. Rustler is my cousin's horse .
9. How tan you're getting !
10. Do a cartwheel on the mat .

C. Finding Subjects and Predicates (Use after page 36.)

Copy these sentences. Draw one line under the subject of each sentence. Draw two lines under the predicate.

1. Our class hung the posters in the gym.
2. The seaplane revved up its motors.
3. A six-foot drift covers our driveway.
4. The final score for the game was tied.
5. Mr. Lewis will take our class picture next week.
6. A huge brown eagle glided over the mountain top.
7. The book from Japan shows pearl divers.
8. The old apple trees by the barn are loaded with green fruit.
9. The woolly mammoth became extinct in prehistoric times.
10. A heavy fog hid the old lighthouse.

D. Finding the Verb (Use after page 38.)

Copy these sentences. Draw two lines under the verb only.

1. Sequoia invented the first Indian alphabet.
2. All the guests brought birthday presents.
3. Jennifer pitched three scoreless innings.
4. Clothing styles change every few months.
5. Mrs. Figueroa runs a grocery store on West Fourteenth Street.
6. The rug had a lump in it.
7. My pencils are in my desk.
8. Roger Bannister ran the first four-minute mile.
9. The empty car rolled down the hill.
10. Many cats act very independent.

E. Finding the Main Verb and Helping Verbs (Use after page 41.)

Label two columns *Helping Verbs* and *Main Verb.* Find all the parts of the verb in each sentence. Write them in the proper column.

1. Veronica can (HV) speak (MV) German.

2. The camera had(HV) slid(MV) under the seat.
3. Gayle has(HV) been(HV) shoveling(MV) snow for half an hour.
4. The maple sap is(HV) boiling(MV).
5. My cousins are(MV) in Mexico.
6. The White Sox were(HV) winning(MV).
7. Janice could(HV) read(MV) the sign in the moonlight.
8. My brother will(HV) be(MV) in boot camp for three months.
9. You should(HV) taste(MV) this mild cheese.
10. Spencer might(HV) have(HV) taken(MV) the short cut.

F. Finding Separated Parts of the Verb (Use after page 43.)

Label two columns *Helping Verbs* and *Main Verb*. Find all the parts of the verb in each sentence. Write them in the proper column.

1. Kirk could(HV) hardly avoid(MV) the chuckholes.
2. My aunt had(HV) just finished(MV) that sketch.
3. The arctic bush pilot has(HV) already flown(MV) a thousand miles today.
4. The weather will(HV) very likely be(MV) worse in February.
5. My family has(HV) always gone(MV) to the Octoberfest.
6. Grass will(HV) never grow(MV) under your feet.
7. Montreal was(HV) originally settled(MV) by the French.
8. The girls will(HV) certainly like(MV) these blueberry muffins.
9. I don't(HV) often watch(MV) the Saturday morning cartoon shows.
10. Corky might(HV) have(HV) been(HV) seriously hurt(MV) in that accident.

G. Finding the Verb and Its Subject (Use after page 45.)

Copy each sentence. Draw two lines under the verb. Then draw one line under the subject of the verb.

60

1. The tallest girl in the class was Nicole.
2. Eric usually takes his flippers with him.
3. The first official flag had only thirteen stars.
4. The joggers circled the field again and again.

5. The water is dripping onto the bookshelves.
6. The bus on Euclid Avenue doesn't run after seven o'clock.
7. The high iron gate swung soundlessly on its hinges.
8. Rob can water-ski on one foot.
9. Out of breath, Sara just grunted.
10. A light on the instrument panel flashed on and off.

H. Finding the Subject in Unusual Positions (Use after page 47.)

Find the verb in each sentence. Write it on your paper. Then find the subject of the verb and write it in front of the verb.

1. Here comes Mark. Mark comes
2. Under the eaves several long icicles formed. icicles formed
3. Where is the other plate? plate is
4. Here are the statistics for the Yankees. statistics are
5. Out of nowhere came a sonic boom. boom came
6. After the argument Holly left. Holly left
7. On the Mississippi are many dangerous sandbars. sandbars are
8. During our vacation we went to Disneyland. we went
9. In today's newspaper there is an article about our school. article is
10. Over the city was a double rainbow. rainbow was

I. Finding the Subjects and Verbs in Interrogative and Exclamatory Sentences (Use after page 48.)

Change the word order of each sentence below. You may need to drop some words to make your sentence smooth. Then write the new sentence. Draw one line under the subject and two lines under the verb.

1. How awfully strong you are! (Drop *How*.) You are awfully strong.
2. Has Robert found the answer? Robert has found the answer.
3. How delicious that big cake looks! (Drop *How*.) That big cake looks delicious.
4. What exciting stories Nancy tells! (Drop *What*.) Nancy tells exciting stories.
5. Did the rabbit get into the garden again? The rabbit did get into the garden again.

The Floorwalker is a Charlie Chaplin comedy.

6. Is *The Floorwalker* a Charlie Chaplin comedy?
7. What beautiful flowers you have in your garden! (Drop *What.*) You have beautiful flowers in your garden.
8. How can I thank you? (Drop *How.*) I can thank you.
9. Doesn't this rain ever stop! This rain doesn't ever stop.
10. Are all the songs from the movie on the record?
All the songs from the movie are on the record.

J. Telling the Subject (Use after page 50.)

Copy the following sentences. Draw two lines under the verb in each sentence. Draw one line under the subject of the verb. If the subject is not given in the sentence, write it in parentheses in the place where it is understood.

1. Untie the boat. (You) untie
2. Return these empty bottles for the deposit. (You) return
3. There are only five minutes before liftoff.
4. Did Tandra have the ace?
5. Spin the game dial for your turn. (You) spin
6. Is Leonard collecting the money?
7. Look at that flash of lightning. (You) look
8. What did Luis find inside the box?
9. Come in an hour. (You) come
10. Ask the ranger for information. (You) ask

K. Writing Compound Subjects (Use after page 52.)

Think of a compound subject for each predicate listed below. Then write the complete sentence. In some of your sentences, try to use a compound subject with three parts. Answers will vary.

1. hibernate in winter
2. are loaded with calories
3. stopped playing their trumpets
4. were piled on the table
5. have the biggest appetites

6. headed out to sea
7. fluttered around the streetlight
8. graze in the fields
9. are countries in South America
10. should be oiled

L. Writing Compound Predicates (Use after page 54.)

Think of a compound predicate for each subject listed below. Then write the complete sentence. In some of your sentences, try to use a compound predicate with three parts. Answers will vary.

1. The garage attendant
2. Abraham Lincoln
3. Rain
4. The Ping Pong ball
5. Three players
6. Early American Indians
7. The elm tree
8. A delivery truck
9. The *Tyrannosaurus Rex*
10. A plumber

Chapter 4

Writing Good Paragraphs

Think about the last thing you read. Maybe it was a story or a magazine article. Maybe it was directions for how to make something. You were probably so interested in *what* you were reading that you didn't even notice *how* it was written. How something is written can make a big difference, however. It can help you understand what you are reading.

One of the most important things a writer does is to arrange ideas into paragraphs. In this chapter you will learn about things that make a good paragraph. Later, you will use what you learn. You will write good paragraphs of your own.

Chapter Objectives

1. To understand the function of the paragraph and to recognize good paragraphs

2. To identify a topic sentence in a paragraph by its function

3. To write good topic sentences

Preparing the Students

Introduce the idea that the paragraph is a basic unit of writing by asking the students to open several textbooks at random. Help them to see that the texts are divided into paragraphs. Point out that *Building English Skills* is also organized into paragraphs.

Additional Resources

Mastery Test—pages 443 and 444 in this T.E. Recommended for use after teaching the chapter.

Additional Mastery Test—Recommended for use after any necessary reteaching. (In separate booklet, *Diagnostic and Mastery Tests, Gold Level,* pages 19 and 20.)

Skills Practice Book—pages 20–24

Duplicating Masters—pages 20–24

Part 1

Objective

To understand the function of the paragraph and to recognize good paragraphs

Presenting the Lesson

1. The composition chapters in this book present a highly structured type of paragraph, a basic model that consists of a topic sentence developed by several additional sentences. This model is useful in getting students to discipline their thinking and their writing. However, it should not be presented as the only way to organize a paragraph. Therefore, you may want to mention occasionally that the sample paragraphs represent one way to write a paragraph.

2. Read the introduction on page 65. Emphasize that a paragraph is a way of organizing ideas.

3. Read the examples and the explanations of the examples on pages 66 to 68. Emphasize that a main idea is what a paragraph is about, that each paragraph must have one main idea, and that each sentence in a paragraph must tell something about the main idea.

4. Discuss the answers to Exercise A. In paragraph 2, the fourth sentence is the extra sentence because it does not explain how to make a pizza. In paragraph 3, the last sentence is the extra sentence because it does not discuss Flapjack's habits. In paragraph 5, the fourth sentence is not a general suggestion for getting ideas, so it does not belong.

5. In Exercise B, paragraphs 2, 3, and 4 are good paragraphs because all of their sentences stick to

Part 1 What Is a Paragraph?

A **paragraph** is a group of sentences that work together to explain one idea. Here's an example of a paragraph. As you read it, ask yourself: What is this paragraph about?

> Ramo's eyes were unusual. They were black like a lizard's and very large and, like the eyes of a lizard, could sometimes look sleepy. This was the time when they saw the most. This was the way they looked now. They were half-closed, like those of a lizard lying on a rock about to flick out its tongue to catch a fly.—SCOTT O'DELL

The first sentence tells you that Ramo's eyes were unusual. This is the main idea. Each sentence after the first tells you something about Ramo's eyes. The second sentence, for example, tells you that they were black and large and could look sleepy. The third sentence tells you that this is when they saw the most. The last sentence tells you that now they were half-closed, like a lizard's eyes.

Sticking to the Main Idea

Here is another paragraph. The first sentence tells you the main idea of the paragraph. The rest of the paragraph contains one sentence that does not help to explain the main idea. See if you can pick out that sentence.

> Baseball is truly an international sport. The major U.S. leagues include two teams in Canada. The sport is popular in Latin American countries, such as Venezuela and Panama. Our Little League team won the division championship last year. Baseball is also a major sport in Japan, where games sometimes attract over 30,000 fans.

The paragraph explains that baseball is played in many countries. This is the main idea. However, the sentence "Our Little League team won the division championship last year" does not tell about baseball in different countries. It tells about the writer's Little League team. Now go back and reread the paragraph. This time omit the sentence that does not fit. See how much better the paragraph sounds.

You may have noticed that the first line of a paragraph is indented. It is moved a few spaces to the right. This is the way to signal the beginning of a paragraph. It is the way that is used in this book.

Writing About One Main Idea

The next group of sentences looks like a paragraph. However, it is not really a paragraph at all. See if you can figure out why.

> Pigeons are good at living in the city. Some pigeons are brown, some are gray, and some are black. Once my brother caught a pigeon and tried to train it. Carrier pigeons have flown thousands of miles.

This group of sentences does not have one main idea. It has four. One idea is that pigeons are good at living in the city. Another is that pigeons come in different colors. A third is that the writer's brother tried to train a pigeon. A fourth is that carrier pigeons have flown thousands of miles. Each one of these sentences could be the main idea of a separate paragraph.

Look at the following paragraph. The first sentence tells the main idea. All the rest of the sentences tell something about that main idea. The whole paragraph sticks to one idea.

> Pigeons are good at living in the city. They can live in just about any sheltered place—under railroad tracks, tucked under the edges of roofs, in gutters, in garages. Loud city noises don't scare pigeons a bit. People don't frighten them, either. In fact, they like living near people because people often feed them.

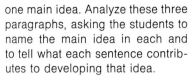

one main idea. Analyze these three paragraphs, asking the students to name the main idea in each and to tell what each sentence contributes to developing that idea.

6. The astronaut pictured on page 69 is Dr. Anne L. Fisher, of Rancho Palos Verdes, California, a physician.

7. See Exercise A on page 81 for additional practice.

Extending the Lesson

From a source outside the classroom, have each student provide an example of writing that is divided into paragraphs. These sources might include an encyclopedia, a favorite book, a magazine, or a newspaper. Assemble a bulletin board display around this theme: Paragraphs Are Everywhere.

Notice how each one of the sentences tells about why pigeons are good at living in the city. The sentences all work together to explain that one idea.

Exercises Studying Paragraphs

A. Here are five paragraphs. Tell what each paragraph is about. Then pick out any sentences that do not explain the main idea. Two of the paragraphs do not have any extra sentences.

1 Early days of ice hockey

Ice hockey has changed since its early days. Then, the game was played with seven rather than six players. Most of the games were played on outdoor rinks. The rinks did not have sideboards. This meant that players often went flying into the crowd of spectators. Goal judges were not protected either. They didn't wear special padding, and they didn't have goal nets.

2 Making a snack-sized pizza

To make a snack-sized pizza, first toast and lightly butter half an English muffin. Spread a thin layer of spaghetti sauce or canned pizza sauce on the muffin. Add extras such as hamburger, onions, olives, and mushrooms. ~~Food that is good for you can be tasty, too.~~ Lay a slice of mozzarella cheese on top. Broil from three to five minutes or until the cheese is melted.

3 Pet parakeet's behavior

Flapjack has strange habits for a parakeet. For instance, she likes to sleep late in the morning. In fact, she's crabby all day if someone wakes her before ten. Each morning she carefully inspects her cage. Then she settles down for her usual breakfast. It's always one pancake spread with a thin layer of peanut butter. ~~Melvin, our cat, has strange habits, too.~~

4 Buying sneakers

We went to the shoe store to buy some sneakers. Anthony chose white ones with blue stripes. Nick chose red ones with white stripes. When I chose blue ones with red stripes, the shoe man said, "We're all sold out." I had to buy plain old white ones.

5 Getting ideas for starting a business

The first thing you need to start your own business is some ideas. First, sit down and make a list of your own ideas. Then ask your relatives, neighbors, teachers, and friends for their ideas. ~~Beth Brown's cookie stand became very successful.~~ Don't worry about having too many ideas. Just get as many as possible on your list.

B. Here are five groups of sentences. Three of the groups are paragraphs. All of the sentences work together to explain one main idea. Two of the groups do not stick to one idea. Pick out the three good paragraphs. Be ready to explain why you think they are good paragraphs.

1 Unsatisfactory

Early in 1978 the United States released the names of its first women astronauts. All trips to other planets have so far been made without humans on board. The Space Center at Cape Canaveral has the world's longest runway. A Russian woman took part in one of her country's space missions.

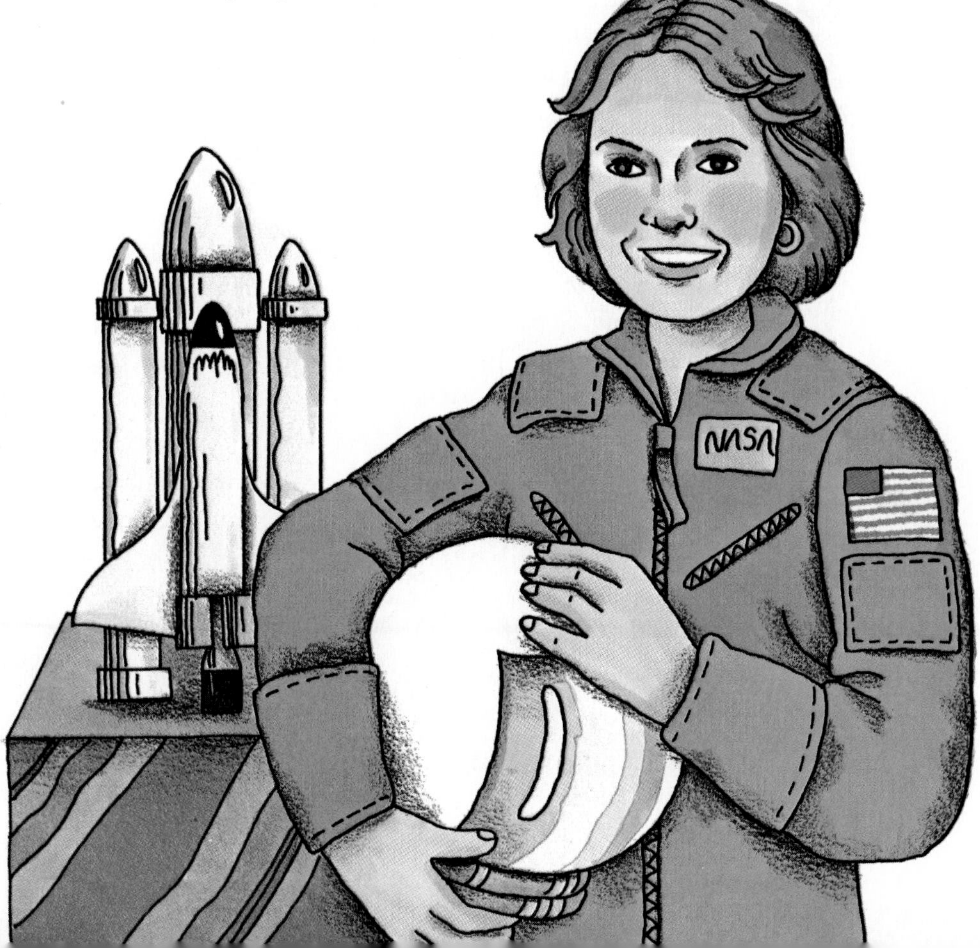

2 Good

The young boy turned over on the thin mattress as the summer sun edged its way over the East River. The sun moved slowly. It spread a soft, gray light down into the canyons between the buildings. It touched the boy's face, and he was awakened. His eyes opened quickly, hurrying sleep away. He lay still a moment, smelling and hearing the morning all around him.

3 Good

The Incredible Bulk is my favorite comic strip character. He's big and strong and smart. Week after week he gets into dangerous situations. He always figures a way out of them, though. He's also modest. He disappears before anyone can tell him what a great job he's done.

4 Good

Salmon are powerful fish. At spawning time they leave the ocean and swim upstream. Sometimes they swim for 2,000 miles. They battle swift currents and swirling rapids. They leap over waterfalls that are often ten feet high. When they reach their spawning grounds, they have no time to rest. They must dig holes for their eggs.

5 Unsatisfactory

Wearing braces on your teeth has some good points. Three students in Mr. Chen's math class got braces the same week. New metals and ways of putting on braces mean that they work better in a shorter time. People with braces often feel shy about them at first. My mom says it's better to have braces for a few years than to have crooked teeth your whole life.

Part 2

Objective

To identify a topic sentence in a paragraph by its function

Part 2 The Topic Sentence

As you know, a paragraph is a group of sentences. The sentences work together to explain one idea. A paragraph should have one sentence called a **topic sentence.** A topic sentence states the main idea. It tells what the entire paragraph is about.

Usually the topic sentence is the first sentence in a paragraph. It lets the reader know what the rest of the sentences are going to be about.

Seeing How Topic Sentences Work

Let's look at two examples of paragraphs. The first sentence is the topic sentence in each paragraph. In the first example, the topic sentence tells you that winter is staying too long. Notice how each sentence in the rest of the paragraph adds something to that main idea.

Example 1

Winter had come and was overstaying its welcome. January had borrowed the winds of March and was using them overtime. Ice spewed out of the ground. Rags and paper were wrapped around faucets to keep them from freezing. Broken window panes were stuffed with rags. Window cracks were jammed with paper. Beds were weighted down with homemade quilts and old overcoats and clothes. Men and boys wore two pairs of trousers. Girls and old ladies bundled up like babes.—SYLVESTER LEAKS

In this paragraph the second sentence tells about the wind. The third sentence tells about the ice. The fourth sentence tells how people used rags and paper to protect faucets. The fifth and sixth sentences describe other ways that people used rags and paper to keep out the cold. The seventh sentence describes the covers that people piled on their beds. The last two sentences tell about the clothes people wore to keep warm. All of these sentences work together to create a vivid picture of winter. They explain the main idea stated in the topic sentence.

Presenting the Lesson

1. Read pages 70, 71, and the first half of page 72. Discuss Examples 1 and 2. Emphasize that a topic sentence states the main idea of a paragraph and that the rest of the sentences develop the idea in the topic sentence.

2. Read pages 72 and 73. Demonstrate the process of checking each sentence in a paragraph against the topic sentence, using the sample paragraph.

3. Assign and discuss Exercise A. Paragraph 3 is about the match between Billie Jean King and Bobby Riggs. This idea is contained in the topic sentence. The fourth sentence, however, is not about the match; it is about King's first tennis game. Paragraph 5 describes thumbprints. However, it is split into two separate discussions. The first two sentences discuss thumbprint art, the last three the uniqueness of each thumbprint.

4. Assign and discuss Exercise B. This is the students' first opportunity to write a unified paragraph. Remind them to check each sentence against the topic sentence.

5. See Exercise B on page 81 for additional practice.

Extending the Lesson

Work in a small group with students who had difficulty writing a paragraph for Exercise B. Choose one of the three topic sentences. Ask the group to suggest information that might be included in the paragraph. List three or four ideas. Have the students write one sentence about each idea. Then put the sentences together into a paragraph.

Example 2

The next morning was a morning of no caterpillars. The world that had been full to bursting with tiny bundles of black and brown fur trundling on their way to green leaf and trembling grass blade, was suddenly empty. The sound that was no sound, the billion footfalls of the caterpillars stomping through their own universe, died. Tom, who said he could hear that sound, looked and wondered at a town where not a single bird's mouthful stirred.
—RAY BRADBURY

The topic sentence, "The next morning was a morning of no caterpillars," begins the paragraph. The next three sentences tell more about that morning. Each sentence adds something to the main idea.

Sticking to the Idea in the Topic Sentence

Here is another paragraph. It starts out with this topic sentence:

The removal of the Cherokees from Georgia during the winter of 1838–39 is called the Trail of Tears.

This sentence leads you to think that the whole paragraph is about the Trail of Tears. Read the other sentences in the paragraph to see if this is true.

The removal of the Cherokees from Georgia during the winter of 1838–39 is known as the Trail of Tears. That winter U. S. troops forced seventeen thousand men, women, and children to march through snow and bitter cold. Most were barefoot. All were hungry. One famous Cherokee named Sequoya invented a system for writing the Cherokee language. The California redwood trees are called sequoias in honor of this leader. Almost a fourth of the Cherokee people died on the Trail of Tears.

In this paragraph the second sentence does add to the main idea. It says that seventeen thousand Cherokees were forced to march through snow and cold. The third and fourth sentences add more information. The fifth sentence, however, has nothing to do with the Trail of Tears. It introduces a Cherokee leader named Sequoya. The next sentence is not about the Trail of Tears either. It also tells something about Sequoya. These two sentences do not work with the others to explain the main idea. The last sentence in the paragraph returns to the main idea. It tells how many Cherokee people died on the Trail of Tears.

A Topic Sentence Is Important

A topic sentence does three important things:

1. It states the main idea of the paragraph.

2. It helps you, the writer, to keep track of your ideas.

   You can easily check each sentence in your paragraph against the topic sentence. In this way, you can make sure that all the sentences stick to the main idea.

3. It helps the reader know what a paragraph is going to be about.

Exercises Studying Paragraphs

A. The topic sentence is the first sentence in each of the following paragraphs. In three of the paragraphs all of the sentences explain the main idea. In two of the paragraphs one or more sentences do not stick to the main idea. Pick out the three good paragraphs. Find the sentences in the other two paragraphs that do not belong with the others. Try to explain why they don't belong there.

1 Good

When Manolo was nine he became aware of three important facts in his life. First, the older he became, the more he looked like his father. Second, he, Manolo Olivar, was a coward. Third, everyone in the town of Arcangel expected him to grow up to be a famous bullfighter, like his father.

2 Good

No other dog had a voice like Sounder's. It came out of the great chest cavity and broad jaws as though it had bounced off the walls of a cave. It mellowed into half-echo before it touched the air. It was louder and clearer than any purebred's voice. Each bark bounced from slope to slope in the foothills like a rubber ball. It was not an ordinary bark. It filled up the night and made music.

3

In 1973 Billie Jean King beat Bobby Riggs in the most talked-about tennis match ever played. News reporters called it the Battle of the Sexes. King, a leader in the fight for women's equality in sports, played against Riggs, a critic of women athletes. ~~King had played her first tennis game when she was eleven years old.~~ King's victory over Riggs was witnessed by 30,000 fans in Houston and by millions of television viewers around the world.

4 Good

Before the crossing of the mountains, the Hobbits had already become divided into three breeds: Harfoots, Stoors, and Fallohides. The Harfoots were browner of skin, smaller, and shorter. They were beardless and bootless. Their hands and feet were neat and nimble. They preferred highlands and hillsides. The Stoors were broader, heavier in build. Their feet and hands were larger. They preferred flat lands and riversides. The Fallohides were fairer of skin and also of hair. They were taller and slimmer than the others. They were lovers of trees and woodlands.

5

You can turn a thumbprint into an insect, a face, a person, or a flower. All you need is a thumb, an ink pad, a pen, paper, and a lot of imagination. ~~Your thumbprint is unique. It is different from every other thumbprint in the world. Police officers often use thumbprints for identification.~~

B. Here are three topic sentences. Each contains a main idea. Choose one of the topic sentences. Then write three or four more sentences that tell about that main idea. Ask a classmate to read your completed paragraph. Make sure that all your sentences explain the main idea in the topic sentence.

1. Entertaining a four-year-old isn't as hard as you might think.
2. The paper bag is one of the most useful things ever invented.
3. Certain smells set autumn apart from the other seasons.

Part 3 Writing Good Topic Sentences

You now know what a topic sentence is. You also know that topic sentences help both writers and readers. The next thing to learn, then, is how to write good topic sentences.

Telling What the Paragraph Is About

A good topic sentence must tell what the entire paragraph is about. Look at these five sentences. See if you can pick out the one that tells what all of them are about.

1. She applied it to everything from making soup to planting her garden.
2. Sometimes she'd say it barely loud enough to hear, and I'd stop and think about what I was doing.
3. Other times she'd write it on a piece of paper and put the paper where I'd be sure to find it.
4. "An ounce of prevention is worth a pound of cure" was my great-grandmother's favorite saying.
5. I used to tease her about her "all-purpose" advice, but I never questioned the wisdom of that advice.

Part 3

Objective

To write good topic sentences

Presenting the Lesson

1. Read pages 75 to 77. Discuss the two functions of a topic sentence: to state the main idea and to catch the reader's attention. Emphasize that each sentence in a paragraph must relate to the topic sentence.

2. Read pages 77 and 78. Be sure that all students understand the concept of narrowing. A technique for helping students who have difficulty is given in Extending the Lesson.

3. Assign and discuss Exercises A, B, and C on pages 79 to 80. Give the class these four steps for use in doing Exercise C:

a. Decide what all the sentences are about.

b. Write a sentence that states the general idea of the paragraph.

c. Test the sentence by checking each sentence in the paragraph against the proposed topic sentence.

d. Revise and write a final topic sentence.

4. See Exercise C on page 81 for additional practice.

Extending the Lesson

For those students who need help in understanding the concept of narrowing, draw an inverted triangle. At the top write the name of your county or city. Below it, on a narrower part of the triangle, write the name of an area within the city, or the name of a street or road. Ask a student to write a specific address at the bottom of the triangle. Explain that narrowing involves breaking down a broad idea into its smaller parts.

Sentence 4, of course, is the one sentence that tells what all the rest of the sentences are about. Read that sentence first. Then read sentences 1, 2, 3, and 5. Each of these sentences tells about the main idea.

Here is another group of sentences. This time the topic sentence is missing. Read the sentences and decide what all of them are about.

1. ______(topic sentence)______
2. Three popular ways are in a dish, on a cone, or frozen on a stick.
3. A scoop of ice cream might be added to the top of a stack of pancakes or put into the hole of a doughnut or a melon half.
4. One favorite way is on a piece of pie.
5. Another is on a piece of cake or on a brownie.

All four sentences describe ways to serve ice cream. This main idea must be stated in the topic sentence. Here are two possible topic sentences for this paragraph:

There are many ways to serve ice cream.
Ice cream can be served in many ways.

When you are writing a topic sentence, try to think of it as an umbrella. It is the one sentence that covers, or takes in, all the other sentences in a paragraph.

Making Topic Sentences Interesting

A topic sentence should do more than just tell what a paragraph is about. It should make the reader want to read the rest of the paragraph. In other words, a topic sentence must *catch the reader's attention.*

Here are three pairs of topic sentences. Notice how the second sentence in each pair does a better job of making you want to read further.

1. I'm going to write about Samantha, who was good at solving mysteries.
   Samantha was a super sleuth.

2. We heard the sound of a werewolf.
   Part wolf, part man, the werewolf howled at the full moon.

3. CB language is very interesting.
   "Mama Smokey," "motion lotion," and "peanut butter in his ears" are all expressions used by CB radio operators.

The following paragraph needs a topic sentence. Below the paragraph are two sentences to choose from. Each one tells what the paragraph is going to be about. Read the paragraph, using the first sentence. Then read the paragraph again, using the second sentence. Which topic sentence is more interesting? Can you explain why?

> ______(topic sentence)______. Smooth, thick shakes are not really shaken. They are machine-mixed. At the soda fountain, the mixer looks like a long rod with a small ruffled disk on the end. At home, the small blades of the blender do the best job. They blend the shake and make it fluffy. The big blades of an egg beater can't make a good shake.—CAROLYN VOSBURG HALL

1. The secret of great shakes can now be revealed.

2. Here is how to make a good milk shake.

Narrowing the Topic

A topic sentence should state a main idea that can be covered adequately in one paragraph. Consider, for example, this topic sentence:

> Cereal makers have a responsibility to children.

You might wonder how the writer could possibly cover this idea in a few sentences. He or she would have to write about using less sugar in cereals, the safety of toys packed in cereal boxes, telling the truth in advertisements, and giving money to projects that help children. All these ideas would have to be covered in one paragraph!

The idea in the topic sentence, then, needs to be narrowed. Just one of those ideas would make a good paragraph. For example:

> Manufacturers should add less sugar to breakfast cereals.

The paragraph could then go on to explain why this would be a good thing to do.

Here is another topic sentence that needs to be narrowed:

> As a boy, Arthur Mitchell enjoyed many good times with his family.

All of these good times could not possibly be described in one paragraph. Notice how the writer of the following paragraph has narrowed the basic idea of good times. She tells only about the family's Sunday mornings.

> The best times in the Mitchell household were Sunday mornings. Arthur's father got up early and cooked. He made crisp fried chicken or juicy pork chops and cornmeal pancakes. Delicious smells filled the crowded apartment. Everyone sat around the kitchen table, talking and laughing together. Those were the times Arthur could really feel the love in his family.—TOBI TOBIAS

Points To Remember

As you write topic sentences, keep the following important points in mind:

1. A topic sentence should tell what the paragraph is about.
2. A topic sentence should be interesting enough to catch the reader's attention.
3. A topic sentence should present an idea that is narrow enough to be covered in one paragraph.

Exercises Working with Topic Sentences

A. Here are eight topic sentences. Five of them make you want to read the rest of the paragraph. The other three do not. Decide which sentences are interesting and which are not. Then rewrite the dull sentences to make them more interesting.

1. Half-crazed with hunger, the only survivor made his way through the dense jungle. Interesting
2. Merle stared out the window at the rain-swept street. Interesting
3. I'm going to tell you about my best friend.
4. *Incredible* is the only word to describe Kareem Abdul-Jabbar. Interesting
5. I have a pet dog that I'm going to tell you about.
6. The sudden silence was frightening. Interesting
7. This paragraph is about camping.
8. Down, down into the black depths the diver descended. Interesting

B. Here are eight more topic sentences. The main idea in some of them can be covered in one paragraph. The ideas in the rest are too broad. Find the sentences that are narrow enough. Rewrite those that are too broad so that they, too, can be covered in one paragraph.

1. The United States produces more food than it can use. Too broad
2. The tree-lined Paseo de la Reforma cuts through the heart of Mexico City. Satisfactory
3. The usefulness of computers is almost unlimited. Too broad
4. Sixth graders should take part in after-school activities. Satisfactory
5. The twelve-month school year has good points and bad points. Too broad
6. Many immigrants to the United States have become successful. Too broad
7. Pablo described the hunting trip to his cousin. Satisfactory
8. A deck of cards is made up of four suits. Satisfactory

C. Here are four groups of sentences. Make them into paragraphs by writing a topic sentence for each group. Be sure that each topic sentence tells what all the rest of the sentences in the group are about. On the next page are sample answers.

1. Mexico has influenced the United States. (topic sentence). The food of Mexico has become popular in all parts of our country. Many Mexican words have become part of the English language. Mexican music has influenced American music. Mexican designs have been used in American houses, especially in the Southwest.

2. Chesterfield was a magnificent horse. (topic sentence). His coat and mane were soft gold. He stood, straight and proud, looking over the grasslands. He gave a long, powerful roar. He was the master of his kingdom.

3. Kelly's life was food! (topic sentence). When she was happy, she ate. When she was sad, she ate. When she was angry, she ate. When she had something to celebrate, she had a party—with food, of course. When she had nothing to celebrate, she snacked alone.

4. Throughout history, jewelry has served many purposes. (topic sentence). Long ago the people of East Africa used jewelry as weapons. The Aztecs of Mexico used it to show a person's place in society. Certain jewelry has been worn for its magical powers. Other jewelry has been worn to remember people. For example, in the 1800's the British wore bracelets made of the braided hair of dead relatives.

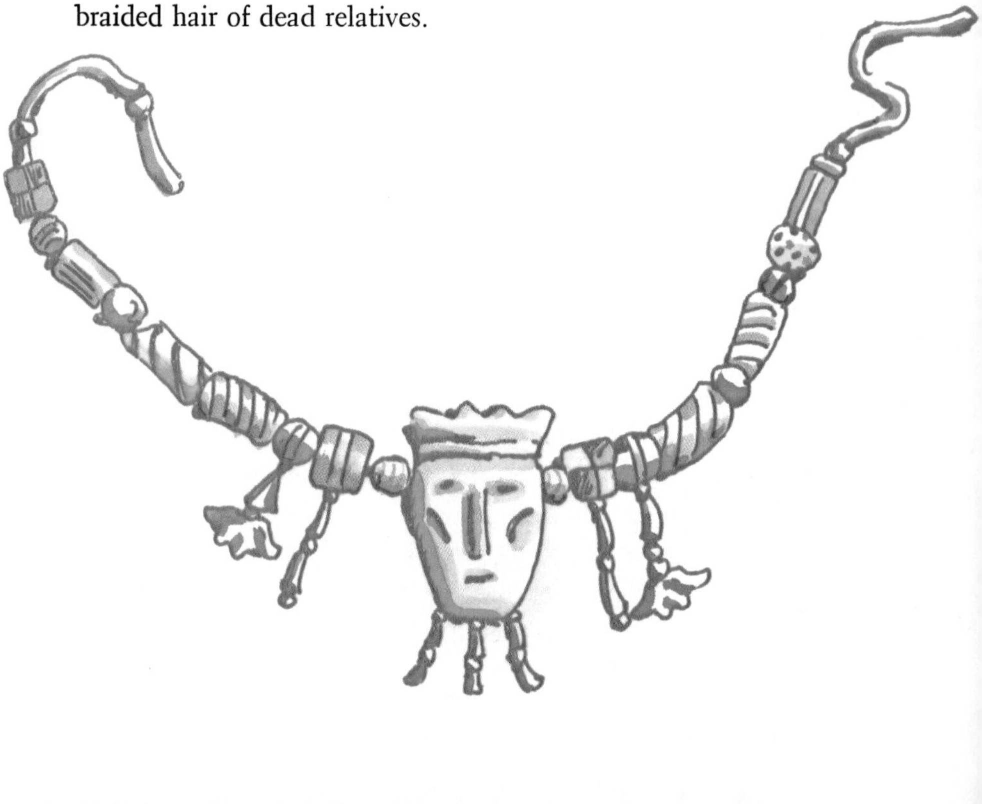

Additional Exercises

Writing Good Paragraphs

Use these two paragraphs to answer the questions below.

1. Pueblo boys learned many things from their fathers. They learned to grow corn, squash, and beans. The Pueblos lived on the desert lands of the West and Southwest. The boys learned to weave beautiful designs into cloth and to paint designs on pottery. They learned to weave baskets for harvesting corn.

2. One howl shows that a wolf wants to "talk". Another is a warning that danger is near. A much wilder, more primitive howl signals the beginning of a hunt. A wolf howls sadly when a loved one dies or is injured.

A. Studying Paragraphs (Use after page 68.)

What Pueblo boys learned from their fathers — Meanings of various wolf howls

1. What is the main idea of paragraph 1? of paragraph 2?

2. One of the paragraphs has a sentence that does not explain the main idea. Which paragraph has this sentence? Which sentence is it? Why doesn't it work with the others?
In paragraph 1, the third sentence doesn't fit. Reasons may vary.

B. Studying Paragraphs (Use after page 73.)

1. One of the paragraphs does not have a topic sentence. Which paragraph is it? Paragraph 2

2. What is the topic sentence of the other paragraph? List the ideas that explain the main idea.
In paragraph 1, the first sentence is the topic sentence.
Sentences 2, 4, and 5 explain sentence 1.

C. Working with Topic Sentences (Use after page 78.)

Suggested answer: A wolf uses different howls to say different things.

Write a topic sentence for the paragraph that does not have one.

Additional Exercises

If these Exercises were not used with each lesson, they may now be assigned for chapter review.

65

Chapter 5

Ways of Developing a Paragraph

You know that a good paragraph must have a topic sentence that presents the main idea. A topic sentence, though, is just a beginning. A good paragraph must also have sentences that explain the main idea. Adding "explaining" sentences to the topic sentence is called **developing the paragraph.**

There are many ways to develop a paragraph. One way is to add sentences with many details. Another is to give one example. Still another is to give several examples of what you are talking about. In this chapter you will learn three ways to develop a paragraph:

1. By using details
2. By using an example
3. By using several examples

Chapter Objectives

1. To recognize details and to appreciate their importance in paragraphs

2. To understand that details appeal to all five senses, and to develop a paragraph using sensory details

3. To develop a paragraph by using an example

4. To develop a paragraph by using several examples

Preparing the Students

Direct the class's attention to the photograph on page 82. Ask the students to note as many details as possible. Encourage them to notice textures, colors, and the expressions on the boys' faces. Ask them to imagine the sounds the boys are making. Explain that this chapter includes a study of how to use details in paragraphs.

Additional Resources

Mastery Test—pages 445 and 446 in this T.E. Recommended for use after teaching the chapter.

Additional Mastery Test—Recommended for use after any necessary reteaching. (In separate booklet, *Diagnostic and Mastery Tests, Gold Level,* pages 21 and 22.)

Skills Practice Book—pages 25–29

Duplicating Masters—pages 25–29

Part 1

Objectives

1. To recognize details and to appreciate their importance in paragraphs

2. To understand that details appeal to all five senses, and to develop a paragraph using sensory details

Presenting the Lesson

1. Read pages 83 to 85, through Adding Details. Note that the details used in the example sentences on page 84 are of three types:

words that tell *what kind* or *how* (the terms *adjective* and *adverb* will be presented in Chapters 14 and 15), including *lame, rain-swept, beautiful, perky,* and *wary,* and *haltingly, proudly, gaily,* and *quietly*

verbs with rich connotations, including *dragged* and *strutted*

phrases that add information, including *down the middle of the street, on the green lawn,* and *under the hedge*

Encourage students to develop several examples with different details, using the same sentence: The cat walked down the street.

2. Read pages 85 to 88. Emphasize the step-by-step approach taken by the writer of the paragraph about the painting and by the writer of the paragraph about popcorn. Both followed the steps listed on page 88. However, the writer of the painting paragraph concentrated only on sight details.

Part 1 Using Details

Details are the little things that make a person, place, or thing what it is. The excited shouts of boys playing basketball, the swishing sound of the ball as it flies through the net, the untiring energy of the boys as they play are all details.

Creating a Clear Picture

In a piece of writing, details are specific bits of information. They create a clear picture for the reader. For instance, the sentence "The cat walked down the street" doesn't create much of a picture in your mind. However, if the writer adds specific details about what the cat looks like, about how it walks, and about the place where it is walking, the picture comes alive.

The lame tomcat dragged haltingly down the rain-swept sidewalk.

With these details, the writer has even made you feel sorry for this sad-looking cat.

The writer might have used different details. Then your mental picture would have been different, too. Look at the following sentences:

1. The beautiful Angora strutted proudly down the middle of the empty street.
2. The perky white kitten rolled gaily on the green lawn.
3. The wary Siamese crept quietly under the hedge.

These sentences all describe the same thing—a cat. However, each contains a completely different set of details. Therefore, your mental picture is entirely different in each description.

Adding Details

When a paragraph is developed by using details, each sentence adds one or more details. Little by little, a complete picture is created. The writer of the following paragraph uses many details. Notice how they help you to get a clear mental picture of the man.

> He was rather fat but in a round, hard, not unpleasant way. His head was completely round. His teeth were very white under the trim mustache. His skin was darkish, and the features of his face formed a pleasant, round, cheerful image. He wore, naturally, a delivery boy's coat. Underneath he wore nice-looking gray flannel pants. His brown shoes were shined within an inch of their lives.
> —LOUISE FITZHUGH

The writer includes all these details:

1. That the man is fat in a round, hard way
2. That he has a round head and very white teeth
3. That he has a trim mustache and darkish skin
4. That he has a pleasant, round, cheerful face
5. That he is wearing a delivery boy's coat, gray flannel pants, and highly shined brown shoes

The writer has arranged these details so that she describes the man from head to toe.

Developing a Paragraph by Using Details

If you are going to develop a paragraph by using many details, it is a good idea to begin by getting a picture in your own mind. Think about what you are going to write about. Examine every part of your mental picture. Then make a list of details that you want to include in your paragraph.

3. Assign the Exercise on page 88. Remind students to follow the four easy steps.

4. See Exercise A on page 93 for additional practice in recognizing details.

Extending the Lesson

Assemble a box of items that have interesting shapes, textures, and colors. These might include rocks, bits of cloth, kitchen gadgets, and unusual beans and seeds. Have each student draw an item from the box, examine it by using all five senses, list details, then write a paragraph including the details.

Let's take a look at how one writer followed these steps. The assignment was to describe a painting. The writer chose to describe one called *Kid Stuff*. It showed a pile of old, worn tennis shoes. First, she studied the painting carefully. Later, she pictured it in her mind. She then made the following list of details:

20 worn-out tennis shoes in a pile
faded red
faded blue
gray-white
holes in soles
split seams
tattered edges
broken and knotted laces
frayed linings
grass green background
background paint that looks like blades of grass

Then she wrote the following paragraph.

> The painting called *Kid Stuff* uses tennis shoes to show the active life led by children. In the middle of the large, square painting is a pile of twenty worn-out tennis shoes. Some are faded red. Some are faded blue. The rest are a dirty-looking white. The shoes are piled every which way. You can see holes in soles, tattered edges, split seams, broken and knotted laces, and frayed linings. The area around the pile of shoes is grass green. The paint is put on so that, close up, it looks like blades of grass.

The writer first explains the main idea of the painting. She next gives the overall shape of the painting. She then describes the tennis shoes in detail. Finally, she talks about the background. She has arranged her details in the order in which she "sees" the painting in her mind.

Using All of the Senses

So far, all the examples have used details about what things *look* like. Suppose, though, that you were asked to describe something like eating popcorn. It wouldn't be enough to include only details about what popcorn looks like. You'd have to include details about how it smells, sounds, feels, and tastes. That's the only way a reader would get a clear idea of what eating popcorn is like. Here is a list of questions and answers about eating popcorn.

How does it look?	white, puffy, slightly yellow from butter, exploding from a shiny brown shell
How does it smell?	a little like corn, warm oil, butter
How does it feel?	light, warm
How does it sound?	crunches as it's bitten
How does it taste?	a little like corn, salty, buttery, becomes soft as it's chewed

Here is the paragraph that was written, using these details.

Eating popcorn is one of life's greatest pleasures. When I look at a bowl heaped with those white, exploded puffs of corn, my mouth begins to water. As I breathe in the warm, buttery smell, my hand is drawn to the bowl. I pick up a handful of the warm, light corn and ease it into my mouth. I make the first crunch, then another. As the heavenly corn, butter, and salt flavors blend, the popcorn softens. I sigh with happiness. Would you be surprised if I told you I never can stop at one handful, or two, or three?

Four Easy Steps

When you develop a paragraph by using details, try to follow these steps:

1. Get a clear picture in your mind of what you want to describe.
2. Examine your mental picture. You can do this in any order, such as from top to bottom or from left to right. Ask yourself: How does it look? How does it sound? How does it feel? How does it smell? How does it taste?
3. Make a list of details.
4. Write the paragraph. Keep in mind that you want the readers to see in their minds the same picture that you see in yours.

Exercise Writing a Paragraph Using Details

Here is a list of ideas for paragraphs. Choose an idea that interests you or use one of your own. Write a topic sentence that tells what the paragraph is about. Try to make it interesting, and narrow enough to be covered in one paragraph. Then develop a paragraph using details. Follow the four easy steps in this lesson.

1. The setting for a science fiction movie
2. The animal you'd least like for a pet
3. An unusual Halloween costume
4. Your best friend
5. Your favorite food
6. The most unusual place you've ever been
7. Your special hideaway
8. A cartoon character
9. A box full of something valuable
10. Your bike

Part 2 Using an Example

Some paragraphs can be developed by using an example. The topic sentence again presents the main idea. The rest of the paragraph explains the main idea by using an example.

Explaining the Main Idea

Let's say you're going to write a paragraph about Pecos Bill, the cowboy folk hero. You might begin with this topic sentence:

> Pecos Bill was totally fearless.

You might then describe an incident that shows his fearlessness. You would be giving an example of the idea in the topic sentence.

Sticking to One Example

One writer begins with this topic sentence:

> Even as a young girl, Maria Mitchell was a skilled astronomer.

She then developed the following paragraph about this famous nineteenth-century astronomer.

> Even as a young girl, Maria Mitchell was a skilled astronomer. One night a ship's captain arrived at the Mitchells' house. He wanted Maria's father to set his chronometer. This was a special clock used to tell time by the stars. Maria's father was away, and the captain needed the clock right away. Fourteen-year-old Maria offered to set it for him. The captain agreed to give her a chance. Maria worked long into the night. She measured the positions of the stars. She figured distances. By dawn she had fixed the chronometer. The amazed captain paid her the same fee he would have paid her father. He praised her for the fine work she had done.

Part 2

Objective

To develop a paragraph by using an example

Presenting the Lesson

1. Read pages 89 and 90. The paragraph about Maria Mitchell illustrates the idea that she was a skilled astronomer at a young age. It gives one incident, or example, of her early skill.

2. Assign the Exercise on page 90. In discussing some of the students' paragraphs, point out that the incidents should always be described as they happened, or in a time sequence.

3. See Exercise B on page 93 for additional practice.

Extending the Lesson

Those who had difficulty writing a paragraph might benefit from a more personalized type of practice. Help each student to complete the following topic sentence with a word that describes that student:

> I am ________.

Discuss incidents that have highlighted this quality. Then have the student choose one incident and complete the paragraph.

This paragraph sticks to one example. The example illustrates the main idea in the topic sentence.

Exercise Writing a Paragraph Using an Example

Here are five topic sentences. Choose one that interests you or one of your own. Then write a paragraph that uses one example to illustrate the main idea. You can use a personal experience or your imagination to develop your paragraph.

1. My younger brother (or sister) deserves to be called a menace.
2. My attempts at cooking have often been a disaster.
3. Some days it just doesn't pay to get out of bed.
4. Important lessons don't always come from books.
5. Some "firsts" are more memorable than others.

Part 3 Using Several Examples

You have learned that a paragraph can be developed by using one example to explain the main idea. Another type of paragraph can be developed by using several examples to explain the main idea. Here is a topic sentence:

> Jeannette Henry, a Cherokee, and her husband, a California Cahuilla, have worked tirelessly to gain rights for Native Americans.

You could develop this idea into a paragraph. You would probably want to include several examples of how this couple has helped Native Americans. These examples would illustrate the main idea that the Henrys have worked hard to assure the rights of Native Americans.

The following topic sentence could also be developed by using several examples.

> Several outstanding leaders of Mexican and Spanish descent have served in the Congress of the United States.

Part 3

Objective

To develop a paragraph by using several examples

Presenting the Lesson

1. Read pages 90 and 91. Emphasize that in developing a paragraph using examples, each example is given but not fully developed. In this way, the examples differ from those used to develop paragraphs in Part 2.

2. Read page 92. Discuss the meaning of *firsthand experience.* Ask the students to identify the examples that develop the main idea of the paragraph.

3. Assign the Exercise on page 92. Ask volunteers to share their completed paragraphs. Discuss the examples incuded in each paragraph.

You'd probably complete the paragraph by telling of the contributions of these leaders. You'd be giving examples to illustrate the main idea.

Developing a Paragraph by Using Several Examples

The following paragraph begins with the topic sentence, "The happiest and noisiest Jewish holiday is Purim." The rest of the paragraph gives several examples of what makes the holiday happy and noisy.

> The happiest and noisiest Jewish holiday is Purim. There are parties and plays, Purim songs and costume parades, and lots of *hamantashen*—delicious little triangular cakes. Sometimes gifts are given to friends. That is called *schlach manot*. Sometimes money is given to people in need. The old story of Queen Esther and wicked Haman is read aloud in the synagogue. Esther is the heroine of the Purim story. She protected her people, the Jews, when Haman was trying to hurt them. When the name *Haman* is read in the synagogue, children stamp their feet. They whirl or bang their noisemakers, called *graggers*, so no one can hear his name. The children dress up like characters in this story; and prizes are given for the best costumes. At Purim parties there are always *hamantashen*, so called because they are shaped like Haman's hat. —WENDY LAZAR

The paragraph gives several examples of why Purim is a happy, noisy Jewish holiday. It explains that the story of Queen Esther and Haman are read. It describes how the children stamp their feet and bang or twirl noisemakers during the reading. It tells about the plays and costumes and prizes. It describes the special food called *hamantashen*. All of these examples explain the main idea in the topic sentence.

4. See Exercise C on page 93 for additional practice.

Extending the Lesson

If students seem to need more practice in paragraph writing, ask them to choose one of the topic sentences in Additional Exercises, Exercise C, page 93, and to develop a paragraph using the appropriate method.

Using Examples in a Firsthand Experience

Often a paragraph written from firsthand experience will include many short examples. Look at the following paragraph.

> Martha Mae was the best at just about everything. She could send a ball farther than anyone on her team. She could weave a skateboard down a busy sidewalk and make it look easy. She could swim better and faster than anyone in the neighborhood. She could also make perfect dives off the high board. She could blow the biggest bubbles, draw the straightest lines, and sew on the tightest buttons. She won every card game, board game, and word game she played. To us, Martha Mae seemed unbeatable.

The writer has given many short examples of what Martha Mae did. These examples illustrate the main idea that Martha Mae was the best at just about everything.

Exercise Writing a Paragraph Using Several Examples

Here are ten topic sentences. Choose one or write one of your own. Then write a paragraph that uses several examples. You can use your own personal experience or your imagination to develop your paragraph.

1. Who says people aren't superstitious?
2. As winter changes to spring, lots of other things begin to change, too.
3. ______(name)______ is the bravest person I have ever met.
4. A carnival has something for everyone.
5. I am an incurable people-watcher.
6. I have a most unusual group of relatives.
7. Living in a city has many advantages.
8. Some people's names don't fit them at all.
9. My favorite places are all small.
10. It seems that most of the good TV programs are quickly taken off the air.

Additional Exercises

Ways of Developing a Paragraph

A. Writing a Paragraph Using Details (Use after page 88.)

Make a list of the things summer means to this writer. After each detail, tell the sense or senses that it appeals to.

> Summer is many things. Summer is birds singing. Summer is bare feet and daisies and dandelions and roses full on their stems. Summer is swimming at the beach and the sun hot and the sand hot from the sun. Summer is porches and cold lemonade and dogs sleeping in the shade. Summer is whirring lawn mowers on still afternoons and ice cream cones and watermelon. Summer is long nights and the stars low in the sky.—CHARLOTTE ZOLOTOW

B. Writing a Paragraph Using an Example (Use after page 90.)

Choose one of the following topic sentences. Develop a paragraph using an example from your own experience.

1. My best friend and I have often had arguments. One time . . . .
2. I've always admired __________. One day . . . .
3. I enjoy playing __________. During one game . . . .
4. I remember most of my birthdays. My favorite . . . .

C. Writing a Paragraph Using Several Examples (Use after page 92.)

For each topic sentence, explain whether you would develop the paragraph by using details, an example, or several examples.

1. I was alone in a dark, silent cave.
2. Alexander is the perfect pet.
3. A city is no place for a Great Dane.
4. Watch out for the poison ivy plant.

Additional Exercises

If these Exercises were not used with each lesson, they may now be used for chapter review.

Chapter 6

Different Kinds of Paragraphs

Most paragraphs have certain things in common. For one thing, they're made up of sentences. These sentences work together to explain the main idea in the topic sentence.

Sharing things in common, though, does not mean that all paragraphs are alike. In this chapter you will learn about different kinds of paragraphs. You will study paragraphs that tell about things that happened. They are called **narrative paragraphs.** You will study paragraphs that paint pictures in your mind. They are called **descriptive paragraphs.** You will also study paragraphs that explain how to do something, and paragraphs that explain why a writer holds a certain opinion. They are called **explanatory paragraphs.**

Chapter Objectives

1. To understand the term *narrative paragraph*

2. To recognize and use time sequence in the organization of narrative paragraphs

3. To understand the term *descriptive paragraph*

4. To recognize and use logical order in the organization of descriptive paragraphs

5. To understand the differences and uses of two types of explanatory paragraphs: the "how" paragraph and the "why" paragraph

6. To recognize time sequence and logical order in the organization of explanatory paragraphs, and to use the appropriate method of organization

Preparing the Students

Direct the class's attention to the photograph on page 94. Have students suggest possible topics for paragraphs related to the content of the photograph. Encourage them to think of a wide range of topics including these: how to make a windsail, why skating is a good sport, things you can do on skates, what we did last winter, and a winter day. Explain that different topics require different types of paragraphs.

Additional Resources

Mastery Test—pages 447 and 448 in this T.E. Recommended for use after teaching the chapter.

Additional Mastery Test—Recommended for use after any necessary reteaching. (In separate booklet, *Diagnostic and Mastery Tests, Gold Level,* pages 23, 24.)

Skills Practice Book—pages 30–37

Duplicating Masters—pages 30–37

Part 1 The Narrative Paragraph

If you read a paragraph that begins with "Once upon a time . . ." or "Something unexpected happened the day we went windskating," you expect the rest of the paragraph to tell you what happened. This kind of paragraph is called a narrative paragraph. In a narrative paragraph all the sentences work together. They tell about something that happened either to the writer or to someone else.

Telling Things in Order

The following is an example of a narrative paragraph. The writer is telling about something that happened to someone else. She describes what happened in the order that it happened.

> Tyrone took the flashlight and ran toward the darkest part of the alley. It opened into another, wider alley that was really a small street of vacant houses. On his way he stumbled over something round and hard. The flashlight dropped out of his hand and went out as he fell. He could tell his knees were skinned and probably bleeding, but he did not cry out from the pain. He lay there and felt around in the dark till he found the flashlight. It was lying near the piece of broken pipe that had tripped him. Fortunately it still worked. —KRISTIN HUNTER

You can make a list of what happened in this paragraph. Your list might look something like this:

1. Tyrone took the flashlight.
2. He ran toward the darkest part of the alley.
3. He stumbled and fell.
4. The flashlight dropped out of his hand and went out.
5. Tyrone felt around in the dark and found the flashlight.

These events form a **time sequence.** They tell what happened in the order that it happened. Time sequence is the way most narrative paragraphs are organized.

Part 1

Objectives

1. To understand the term *narrative paragraph*
2. To recognize and use time sequence in the organization of narrative paragraphs

Presenting the Lesson

1. Read pages 95 and 96. Emphasize that *narrative* means to retell something that happened. Ask students for examples from their own lives or from books, using questions such as these:

a. Has anything frightening ever happened to you?
b. What was your favorite fairy tale as a young child?
c. Have you ever been lost?
d. Have you ever read about a trick that one person played on another?

Point out the similarities between the students' oral accounts and the sample narrative paragraphs: both describe things that happened in the order that they happened.

2. Read page 97. Contrast the two first-person examples with the third-person example on page 96.
3. Read Using Details on pages 97 and 98. Ask students to point out the details in the sample paragraph. Note that the details include descriptive words (adjectives), rich verbs, and interesting phrases.
4. Assign and discuss the Exercise on page 98.
5. See Exercise A on page 109 for additional practice.

Describing Personal Experiences

The next paragraph is also a narrative paragraph. It, too, is organized in time sequence. The topic sentence tells you that the paragraph is about the writer's first experience with book knowledge. The word *I* lets you know that it is going to be about something that happened to the writer personally.

> The first thing I ever learned in the way of book knowledge was while working in a salt-furnace. Each salt-packer had his barrels marked with a certain number. The number given to my stepfather was *18*. At the close of the day's work the boss of the packers would come around and put *18* on each of our barrels. I soon learned to recognize that figure wherever I saw it. After a while I got to the point where I could make that figure. I knew nothing about any other figures or letters, though. —BOOKER T. WASHINGTON

Here is another narrative paragraph. The topic sentence, "We decided to write our own television show," begins the paragraph. The word *we* lets you know right away that the writer of the paragraph was personally involved. The rest of the paragraph tells what happened in the order that it happened.

> We decided to write our own television show. We called it "Dr. Sickbee at Your Service." It was the story of an orthodontist who moonlights in a rock band. He lives next door to a weird family and has a younger sister who ran away to join the roller derby. In his spare time he solves mysteries. We put the show on videotape and wrote some commercials to use with it. Some of the other English teachers let their classes see it.—PAULA DANZIGER

Using Details

Here is another narrative paragraph. It is a good example of a paragraph with many details.

Extending the Lesson

To help those students who have difficulty organizing events into a time sequence, draw (or have someone else draw) and duplicate a simple, six-frame cartoon that shows the following:

a. a girl walking along a sidewalk; she doesn't see an ornate bottle
b. she kicks the bottle by accident
c. she picks it up
d. she rubs it to look at the label
e. a genie emerges
f. she drops the bottle and runs

Help students to write a paragraph that describes what happens in the cartoon.

I remembered how much I used to like being alone. At times, instead of going home from school, I used to go into the bush to listen to pretty little birds quarrel in their harsh voices. One day I walked around the village. Then I climbed the highest hill. I lay looking down at people moving beneath me like so many insects. Soon I forgot time as I let my gaze play around the green of the trees, the bright reds of fruits, the pale blues and pinks of flowers. Then I watched as the wind wove everything into different patterns from one minute to the next. —ROSA GUY

The details are so vivid that you can almost hear the sounds of the birds. You can practically see the people moving around like insects, the green trees, the bright red fruits, the blue and pink flowers, and the changing patterns caused by the wind. These details help you, the reader, share the writer's experience.

Exercise Writing Narrative Paragraphs

Following is a list of topic sentences. Choose one or write one of your own. Then write a narrative paragraph. Remember to organize your paragraph in a time sequence. Use as many details as possible. You can either write from your own experience or create an imaginary experience.

1. I'll never forget the night my sister had her first date.
2. We took the wrong turn to the park.
3. One night the electricity went off in our apartment.
4. A group of us set out to decorate a wall.
5. ________________ was just about the happiest day of my life.
6. The day I changed my mind about ________________ is a day to remember.
7. I'll never forget the time my two-year-old sister took all the labels off the cans in the kitchen.
8. My first day of school was a nightmare.
9. We had a funny experience on our class trip.
10. My cat would not come down from the tree.

Part 2 The Descriptive Paragraph

You know that narrative paragraphs tell what happened. Descriptive paragraphs, however, have very little action. That's because the purpose of a descriptive paragraph is to paint a picture with words.

A descriptive paragraph appeals to one or more of the senses. It is written so that a reader sees what the writer sees, smells what the writer smells, hears what the writer hears, tastes what the writer tastes, or feels what the writer feels. In this chapter you will study only one type of descriptive paragraph. It is the type that appeals to the sense of sight.

Using Details

The writer of a descriptive paragraph must include many details. You have learned that details are the specific bits of information that create a clear picture for the readers. Without specific details, whatever the writer is describing never seems to come alive for the reader.

Let's take a look at a paragraph with many details. The topic sentence tells you that the paragraph is going to describe an ocean scene. The rest of the sentences contain many details. They work together to help you see the scene the way the writer sees it.

Example 1

The heaving ocean sprawled under the vast blue sky. Both sea and sky were shimmering with light. It seemed as if the sky poured it into the sea and the sea poured it back into the sky again so rapidly that they were both continually awash with light and never for a moment cold. The sun was tossed from sea to sky like a golden ball. The gulls ranged restlessly backward and forward, up and down, round and round. They searched endlessly, never finding, lighting a moment on the gleaming water, but never at peace.
—ROBERT AYRE

Part 2

Objectives

1. To understand the term *descriptive paragraph*
2. To recognize and use logical order in the organization of descriptive paragraphs

Presenting the Lesson

1. Read pages 99 and 100. For Example 2, have the students concentrate on identifying descriptive phrases rather than looking for specific adjectives, adverbs, and verbs.
2. Read pages 100 to 103. Emphasize that logical order is the order in which a person would examine something without consciously thinking about it. Discuss the organization of each sample paragraph, noting the details that have been included.
3. Assign and discuss Exercises A and B on page 103.
4. See Exercise B on page 109 for additional practice.

Extending the Lesson

Provide each student or group of students with an interesting photograph from a book or magazine, or project a slide for the entire class to use. Ask students to write a paragraph describing the entire picture or part of it. Remind them to examine the picture in some kind of order and to write a good topic sentence.

The writer of the paragraph includes many details that appeal to the sense of sight. He uses phrases like "heaving ocean," "vast blue sky," "shimmering with light," "awash with light," "golden ball," "ranged restlessly backward and forward," and "gleaming water." These specific details help to paint a vivid picture of the scene.

The next descriptive paragraph also includes many sight details. It paints a picture of a street scene. Pick out the specific details that help you see the street as the writer sees it.

Example 2

James stood for a while in front of his building. He looked at the street and the cars and the people walking or running or hobbling or moving like bits of paper in a high wind. He looked at the trash basket, a new silver one. It was sitting in the middle of the trash that was spread out all around it. He looked at two policemen walking down the middle of the street between the cars. He looked at a man with one arm. He was hurrying along the curb talking to himself and waving the stump of the other arm that was hidden in his sleeve. It looked like a puppet in the puppet show James had seen at a school assembly. What was the arm saying?

—PAULA FOX

Logical Order

In the lesson on using details in Chapter 5 you learned how to arrange them into logical order. You learned the four steps involved in developing a paragraph with many details:

1. Get a clear picture in your mind of what you want to describe.
2. Examine your mental picture.
3. Make a list of details.
4. Write the paragraph, keeping in mind that you want your readers to see in their minds the same picture that you see in yours.

Top-to-Bottom Order

When you do step 2, it is important to follow some order. For instance, if you are describing a person, the natural place to begin would be the person's overall size and shape. That's what you would probably notice first about someone. You would then examine the person's head and face and move downward, looking at arms, hands, and clothing. The following paragraph is arranged in top-to-bottom order. The writer describes a newly hatched creature from head to tail.

> I thought at first that it was a rat or something that had broken the egg and eaten it. After I got a good look, though, I could see that it wasn't any rat. It was about the size of a squirrel. It didn't have any hair, and its head—well, I couldn't believe my eyes when I saw it. It didn't look like anything I'd ever seen before. It had three little knobs sticking out of its head and sort of a collar up over its neck. It was a lizardy-looking critter. It kept moving its thick tail slowly back and forth in the nest. The poor hen was looking pretty upset. I guess she hadn't expected anything like this. Neither had I. —OLIVER BUTTERWORTH

Bottom-to-Top Order

Some paragraphs are organized so that a thing is described from bottom to top. The following paragraph is like that. It describes a skyscraper from bottom to top. This is the way you would most likely examine a tall building.

> The skyscraper was set in a cluster of buildings. Brightly painted benches, and trees and flowers in redwood pots surrounded the building at ground level. The display windows of elegant shops circled the first and second levels. The rest of the building was covered with huge, vertical slabs of gray stone. Between the slabs were long, narrow windows of tinted gray glass. Three antennas rose into the sky from the flat roof.

Moving from One Object to Another

This next descriptive paragraph is organized in yet another way. It moves from one main object to another in a room. This is a logical order. It is the way a person would probably examine a room.

> In the kitchen was an old-fashioned black stove, with six round iron lids and a chimney pipe going up to and through the ceiling. The sink was tin, now blackened with age, and there was a ridged wooden drainboard. Through a big hole in the rotting floor you could see to the cellar below. Things were piled high down there. There were wooden boxes with old, musty, mildewed dresses and hats spilling out. There were funny trunks with strips of tin and brass on top and leather handles on the sides. —MARY CHASE

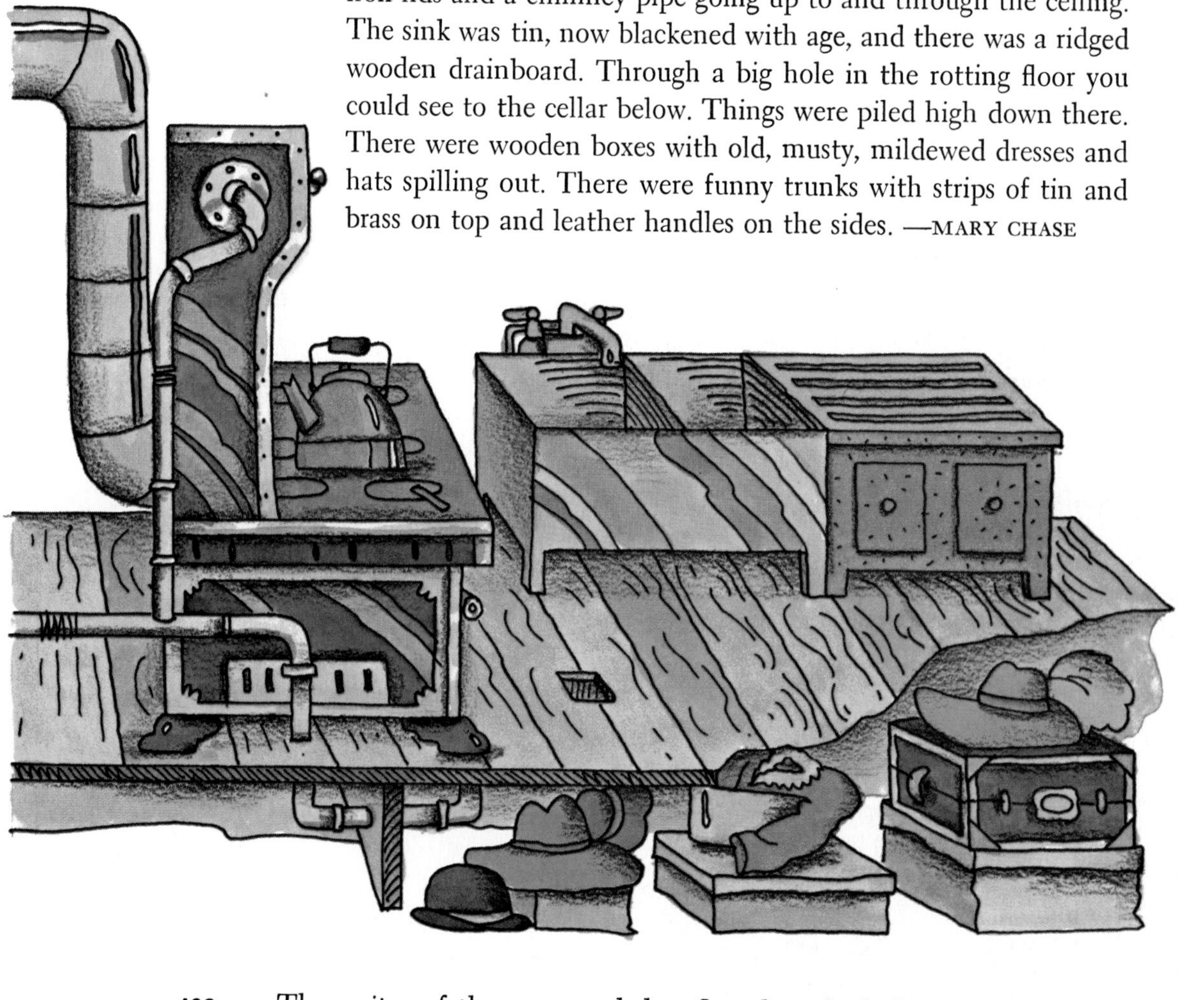

The writer of the paragraph has first described the stove and then the sink. She next describes the hole in the floor and the cellar under it. She has picked out these objects as the most important parts of the kitchen.

As you can see from the examples, a good way to arrange a descriptive paragraph is according to the way you would notice things. This is called a natural order. It is one of the most common, and easiest ways to organize a descriptive paragraph.

Exercises Writing Descriptive Paragraphs

A. Below is a list of topics. Write down some of the details you would include in a descriptive paragraph for each. Then decide on the way you would arrange the details. They could be in top-to-bottom order, in bottom-to-top order, or in an order moving from one object to another.

1. A person you like
2. Someone you have seen on TV
3. A basement recreation room
4. An unusual plant or flower
5. A tree

B. Here are eight topic sentences. Choose one or write one of your own. Then write a descriptive paragraph. Follow the four steps for developing a paragraph with many details. Be sure that all of your sentences work together to explain the main idea in the topic sentence.

1. Lake ______________ is one of the most beautiful places I've ever seen.
2. The decorating committee had changed the gym into an alien environment.
3. Tangled hedges enclosed a tiny, secret garden.
4. My new brother is a beautiful little baby.
5. Traug was an ugly creature.
6. On the table was every kind of food imaginable.
7. ______________ is the most impressive landmark in our town.
8. The room was a mess.

Part 3

Objectives

1. To understand the differences and uses of two types of explanatory paragraphs: the "how" paragraph and the "why" paragraph
2. To recognize time sequence and logical order in the organization of explanatory paragraphs, and to use the appropriate method of organization

Presenting the Lesson

1. Read pages 104 and 105. Emphasize the importance of a step-by-step approach to writing a "how" paragraph. Review the concept of *time sequence.*
2. Assign and discuss the Exercise on page 106.
3. Read pages 106 to 108. Some students may not understand the meaning of *opinion.* Work with these students in a small group until they understand that an opinion is one person's idea about something. Another person might hold the opposite opinion: Rocks make terrible pets. Objectively, neither person is right or wrong.
4. Assign and discuss the Exercise on page 108.
5. See Exercise C on page 109 for additional practice.

Part 3 The Explanatory Paragraph

The explanatory paragraph is one of the most useful paragraphs you will learn to write. You will most likely write more of them in your life than any other kind. The word *explanatory* means "to explain." That's exactly what these paragraphs do. They explain **how** or **why.**

The "How" Paragraph

The "how" paragraph explains how to do something. It is the most common type of explanatory paragraph. In fact, you've probably read hundreds of explanatory paragraphs. Every time you read directions for a card game, or for putting together a model, or for feeding a hamster, or for operating a radio, or for planting seeds, you are reading explanatory paragraphs.

Time Sequence

All "how" paragraphs have one important thing in common. They explain something in a step-by-step way. The steps are organized in a time sequence. They explain what should be done first, what should be done next, and so on. The language and organization of a good explanatory paragraph are so clear that a person reading the paragraph knows exactly what to do and when to do it.

Let's take a look at a paragraph that explains how to use an apple to print a T-shirt.

> You can create your own T-shirt design by using a plain T-shirt, a piece of cloth, an apple, a stiff paintbrush, and textile paint in any colors of your choice. Begin by slicing an apple in half lengthwise. Brush a thick layer of textile paint over the cut side of one of the apple halves. Press the apple, paint side down, on a piece of cloth. Keep practicing until you have it just right. Then print your T-shirt.

A person following these directions would be able to start out with a plain T-shirt and end up with a T-shirt printed with an unusual design. That's because the directions are clear. They are organized so that a reader can follow them step by step.

Organizing Ideas

The readers of the next paragraph will be confused. The writer is trying to explain how to do a simple trick with a pencil. Each sentence uses clear language. However, the sentences are so mixed up that the trick is just about impossible to do.

> This trick is called the rubber pencil trick. Move your hand up and down. Hold the pencil lightly between the thumb and forefinger of your right hand. To do it, all you need is one full-length sharpened pencil. The pencil will look as though it's bending, or made of rubber. The pencil should be parallel to your fingers. You should hold the pencil about a third of the way down from the eraser end.

In the next paragraph, see what a difference it makes when the sentences are organized in the right time sequence.

> This trick is called the rubber pencil trick. To do it, all you need is one full-length sharpened pencil. Hold the pencil lightly between the thumb and forefinger of your right hand. Hold it about a third of the way down from the eraser end. The pencil should be parallel to your fingers. Now move your hand up and down. The pencil will look as though it's bending, or made of rubber.

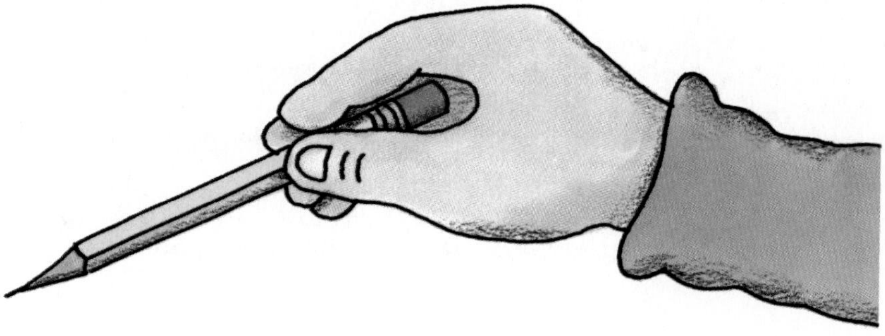

Extending the Lesson

Ask students to look in their homes for examples of directions. The examples might include recipes, directions on packaged and frozen foods, and maintenance instructions. Discuss the examples in class, emphasizing the importance of time sequence and clarity in explanatory writing.

Exercise Writing a "How" Paragraph

Following are some topics for "how" paragraphs. Choose one of them. Narrow the topic so that it can be covered in one paragraph. Then write an interesting topic sentence. After you have completed the paragraph, ask a friend to try out your directions. Rewrite whatever is necessary to make your directions work.

1. How to prepare a super special cat dinner
2. How to dress for subzero weather
3. How to get from ______________ to ______________
4. How to avoid ______________
5. How to plan a party
6. How to repot a plant
7. How to play ______________
8. How to grow ______________
9. How to cook ______________
10. How to make a mobile
11. How to pass a test
12. How to make a compost heap
13. How to make a puppet
14. How to turn a cardboard box into a ______________
15. How to choose a team mascot
16. How to teach a dog to sit up
17. How to win at ______________
18. How to make perfect ______________
19. How to save energy right at home
20. How to train for ______________

The "Why" Paragraph

A second type of explanatory paragraph is the "why" paragraph. It begins with a topic sentence that gives an opinion. The rest of the sentences give reasons to support that opinion.

Giving Reasons

A "why" paragraph might begin with a topic sentence like this:

> Every neighborhood needs a special place that's off-limits to adults.

This is an opinion. The rest of the paragraph would then give reasons to support that opinion. The reasons might include the following:

1. A special place would give kids a chance to take care of something on their own.
2. In a special place, kids could work or play or read without interruption.
3. A place like that would give kids a chance to plan surprises for adults.

The next paragraph is an explanatory paragraph that begins with the topic sentence, "Rocks make great pets." The rest of the paragraph explains why the writer believes that.

> Rocks make great pets. First of all, rocks are just about the cheapest pets to own. They don't need special food, clothes, beds, toys, or shots. Rocks are also clean and well behaved. They never leave half-eaten dog biscuits, scattered seeds, or old bones around. They wouldn't think of climbing on a bed, chewing a slipper, or running into the house with muddy paws. Rocks are independent, too. Their owners can leave them for days at a time and never have to worry about feeding or exercising them. Most important, though, is that rocks are always there when their owners need them. That's because they never get sick, run away, or get into bad moods. Rocks may be a little hard, but they're completely faithful.

Order of Importance

The writer of the paragraph on rocks has given four main reasons for believing that rocks are great pets:

1. Rocks are cheap.
2. Rocks are clean and well behaved.
3. Rocks are independent.
4. Rocks are there when their owners need them.

The writer has not organized these reasons in a time sequence. She has arranged them in their order of importance. The fact that rocks are cheap is the least important reason. The fact that rocks are there when you need them is the most important reason. The usual arrangement of a "why" paragraph is from the least important reason to the most important reason.

Exercise Writing a " Why" Paragraph

The following topic sentences give opinions. Choose one of these sentences. Revise it to make it as interesting as possible. Then develop it into a "why" paragraph. Be sure to arrange your reasons in an order from least important to most important.

1. ______________ is the best friend a person could possibly have.
2. Big cities are the best/worst places to live.
3. Rainy days are the worst kind.
4. ______________ is my favorite food.
5. It would save time if we could just take a pill every day and never have to eat.
6. Everyone should know how to swim.
7. No child should grow up without a pet.
8. ______________ is the best movie I've ever seen.
9. It's important for families to have traditions.
10. Taking part in class discussions is helpful for students.

Additional Exercises

Different Kinds of Paragraphs

A. Writing Narrative Paragraphs (Use after page 98.)

Rewrite the following paragraph so that it is in a time sequence.

[3]The present was a book all right, but it wasn't about secret codes. [1]The birthday present from Uncle Charlie was inside a small, flat box. [2]I eagerly ripped off the paper expecting to find a magic trick or a book about secret codes or a Superman T-shirt. [5]I thanked Uncle Charlie weakly and put it aside. [4]It was called *Me* and it contained nothing but blank pages. [6]I didn't know that that book would become my favorite present of all time.

B. Writing Descriptive Paragraphs (Use after page 103.)

Complete this paragraph by describing the dummy. Arrange the details in top-to-bottom order. Answers will vary.

The dummy sat stiff and straight on the ventriloquist's knee.

C. Writing an Explanatory Paragraph (Use after page 108.)

Reorganize these sentences so that they are in a time sequence.

[1]Here are five easy steps to great photographs. [4]Then examine the subject through your camera's viewfinder. [3]Put yourself at least four feet away from the subject. [6]Finally, press your shutter button, while holding the camera steady. [2]First you must choose an interesting subject. [5]Next aim your camera carefully.

Additional Exercises

If these Exercises were not used with each lesson, they may now be used for chapter review.

Chapter 7

Using Nouns

Part 1 What Are Nouns?

Who are you?

You are a person, a human being, a student. You are a girl or a boy, a daughter or a son, perhaps a sister or a brother. You may be a cyclist, a clarinet-player, a cook. You are a friend.

All of these answers are different names for you. They are all **nouns.**

Nouns are words that are used to name persons, places, or things. Here are a few more examples of nouns:

Naming Persons	Naming Places	Naming Things	
man	city	fence	spinach
woman	country	acorn	robot
dancer	ocean	dinosaur	Eiffel Tower
Juanita	Mexico	curb	boat
Paul	Africa	Peace Bridge	skateboard

Chapter Objectives

1. To understand the concept of the noun
2. To differentiate between common nouns and proper nouns
3. To differentiate between singular and plural nouns
4. To apply general rules for forming plural nouns
5. To form possessive nouns correctly

Preparing the Students

Ask students to examine the picture on the opposite page. How many different things in the picture can students name? Can they think of two different names for the same thing, for example, *clarinet* and *instrument?* Point out that all these words belong to one group of naming words.

Additional Resources

Diagnostic Test—page 427 in this T.E. Recommended for use before teaching the chapter.

Mastery Test—pages 449 and 450 in this T.E. Recomended for use after teaching the chapter.

Additional Mastery Test—Recommended for use after any necessary reteaching. (In separate booklet, *Diagnostic and Mastery Tests, Gold Level,* pages 25, 26.)

Skills Practice Book—pages 38–42

Duplicating Masters—pages 38–42

Part 1

Objective

To understand and to identify nouns

Presenting the Lesson

1. Read pages 111 and 112. Discuss the three types of nouns: those naming persons, those naming places, and those naming things. Make sure that students understand that nouns are not limited to physical objects. Ask students to supply additional examples of all types of nouns.

2. In addition to the definition of a noun given in this Chapter, there are other ways to identify a noun. The following chart, Ways To Identify Nouns, is based on what linguists have discovered about the structure of a word and the order of words in a sentence. It is suggested that the information in the chart be used to point out additional ways in which nouns function.

Ways to Identify Nouns

1. Look for words that have a singular, plural, or possessive form.

Singular	Plural	Possessive
girl	girls	girl's

2. Look for words that follow *a, an,* or *the.*

The *table* was made of pine.

3. Look for words that fit the blanks in one of these test sentences:

________ are very important.
That is a ________.
See the ________.
Put it near the ________.

3. Assign and discuss Exercises A and B on pages 111 and 113.

4. See Exercise A on page 124 for additional practice.

A **noun** is a word that names a person, place, or thing.

Nouns may name things you can see, such as *desk* and *bicycle.* There are many things we talk about that we cannot see or touch —such as *kindness, honesty, skill,* and *courage.* The words that name these things are also nouns.

Exercises Finding the Nouns

A. Number your paper from 1 to 10. Write the nouns in each sentence below.

Example: In the Arctic, reindeer live on lichen.

Arctic, reindeer, lichen

1. Texas is the second largest state.
2. The rules for this game are easy.
3. The tip of my ski is stuck under the log.
4. Mrs. Holmes kept her promise to the boys.
5. Which contest did the twins win?
6. An alert lifeguard sat on the platform at the beach.
7. Detroit has a problem with pollution.
8. My older sister moved to Massachusetts because of her job.
9. Three porpoises jumped out of the water beside Amy.
10. Does Betty know the title of that song?

B. Follow the directions for Exercise A.

1. Alaska and Hawaii are the newest states.
2. The cheese on this cracker tastes funny.
3. Pepper is a little dog with black spots.
4. A foil is a sword with a button on the point.
5. The prices of the coats are marked on the tags.
6. Sally was in Frontierland, looking at the old streets and houses.

7. People from Brazil speak the Portuguese language.
8. Buttercups and daisies were growing in the long grass.
9. The baby has the cutest smile.
10. Mr. Martin won't take any nonsense or excuses.

C. In this exercise, you will write only nouns. Answers will vary.

a. Write the names of four persons you know.
b. Write the names of four places you have visited.
c. Write the names of four things you can see at this moment.
d. Write the names of four things you cannot see or touch, such as *kindness, honesty,* and so on.

Part 2 Common Nouns and Proper Nouns

If you call yourself a student, you are giving yourself a name that you share with all the boys and girls in your class. If you call yourself a boy or a girl, you share that name with about half your classmates. *Student, boy,* and *girl* are names common to whole groups of people. They are **common nouns.**

Playground, town, and *lake* are words that name members of whole groups of places. They are common nouns. Many nouns name whole groups of things, like *book, tool,* or *animal.* These are all common nouns.

A **common noun** is the name of a whole class of persons, places, or things.

You are not simply any person. You have a name that is specifically yours. Alex Haley, Judy Blume, and Captain James T. Kirk are specific people. These names of specific people are called **proper nouns.**

Optional Practice

Have students try their answers to Exercises A and B in the test sentences in Presenting the Lesson. Do students discover any errors?

Extending the Lesson

Ask students to list as many nouns as they can that refer to themselves.

Example: Jim Davis
boy student
son friend
player

Part 2

Objective

To differentiate between common nouns and proper nouns

Presenting the Lesson

1. Read and discuss pages 113 and 114.
2. Ask students to think of additional examples of multi-word proper nouns.
3. It is recommended that Exercise A on pages 114 and 115 be done as a class activity. Assign and discuss the remaining exercises.
4. See Exercise B on pages 124 and 125 for additional practice.

Extending the Lesson

Ask students to bring short newspaper articles to class. Have them circle all proper nouns and underline all common nouns. If possible, duplicate one article for class discussion. Do students discover any capitalization errors in the newspapers?

Proper nouns can also name specific places, like Houston and Lake Erie, or specific things, like the Liberty Bell and a Big Mac.

> A **proper noun** is the name of a particular person, place, or thing.
> A proper noun always starts with a capital letter.

Common Nouns	**Proper Nouns**
Groups of Persons	**Particular Persons**
doctor	Dr. Jonas Salk
children	Jane Banks, Michael Banks
lawyer	Barbara Jordan
Groups of Places	**Particular Places**
street	Jefferson Street
park	Yosemite National Park
city	Richmond
Groups of Things	**Particular Things**
bridge	George Washington Bridge
country	Canada
religion	Christianity

You can see that a proper noun may be a group of words. *George Washington Bridge* is one noun because it is the name of one bridge. Capitalize all words in a proper noun. Do not capitalize the words *a*, *an*, or *the* before a proper noun.

Exercises Finding Common and Proper Nouns

A. Label two columns *Common Noun* and *Proper Noun*. Number from 1 to 20 down the left-hand margin of your paper. Opposite

each number, write its noun in the proper column. Be sure to capitalize proper nouns.

1. chair common
2. ᴹmaria proper
3. ᶜcolorado proper
4. mountain common
5. ᴿrocky ᴹmountains proper
6. ᴹmiss ᴾparsons proper
7. school common
8. ᵂwoolworth's proper
9. ᴴhudson ᴿriver proper
10. actor common

11. ᶜcountry common
12. ᴸlake ᴱerie proper
13. ᴱelizabeth proper
14. daughter common
15. cowboy common
16. ᴬatlantic ᴼocean proper
17. ᴳgreen ᴿriver proper
18. ᴹmartin ᴸluther ᴷking proper
19. ᴱelmwood ᴱelementary ˢschool proper
20. harbor common

B. Follow the directions for Exercise A.

1. bridge common
2. ᶠfrance proper
3. ᶜcleveland proper
4. man common
5. ᶜchicago ᴮblack ᴴhawks proper
6. ᴱeurope proper
7. ᴾphiladelphia proper
8. the ᵂwhite ᴴhouse proper
9. ᵂwindsor ᴾpalace proper
10. high school common

11. ᵂworld ᵂwar I proper
12. policewoman common
13. ˢsouth ᴬamerica proper
14. crossword puzzle common
15. lemonade common
16. ˢsaint ᵀtheresa proper
17. the ᴶjefferson ᴹmemorial proper
18. horse common
19. chess common
20. fortress common

C. Copy these sentences. Capitalize the first word in the sentence
and each proper noun.

1. ᴮbob ᴹmackey drove his car to ᶠflorida last winter.
2. ᴰdoctor ᴹmoore told us about islands in the ᴾpacific ᴼocean.
3. ᴬa great many potatoes are grown in the state of ᴵidaho.
4. ᴹmy uncle knew the famous actor ᴸlawrence ᴼolivier.
5. ᴮbrenda's birthday is in ᴶjanuary.

D. Write a proper noun to match each of these common nouns.
Answers will vary.

Example: island—Cuba

1. teacher	4. lake	7. school	10. country	13. canyon
2. street	5. city	8. ocean	11. doctor	14. supermarket
3. bridge	6. river	9. store	12. governor	15. actor

Part 3 Singular and Plural Nouns

Look at the two nouns in the picture above. They are exactly the same except for the last letter.

The noun *player* refers to one person. It is called a singular noun. A **singular noun** names just one person, place, or thing.

The noun *players* ends in *s*. It refers to several persons. It is called a **plural noun.** The word *plural* means more than one.

> A **singular noun** names one person, place, or thing.
>
> A **plural noun** names more than one person, place, or thing.

Part 3

Objectives

1. To differentiate between singular and plural nouns
2. To apply general rules for forming plural nouns

Presenting the Lesson

1. Read and discuss page 116. Make sure the students recognize the difference between singular and plural nouns, and between a singular noun and its plural form. Ask for examples of each class.
2. Read the rules on pages 117 and 118. Ask for additional examples to support each rule.

Here are seven rules for forming the plurals of nouns:

1. **To form the plural of most nouns, just add *s*.**

hats   streets   hamburgers   animals

tables   miles   shakes   movies

2. **When the singular ends in *s, sh, ch, x,* or *z,* add *es.***

gases   brushes   boxes

dresses   matches   buzzes

3. **When the singular ends in *o,* add *s.***

radios   solos   banjos   Eskimos

Exceptions: For the following nouns ending in *o*, add *es*:

echoes   heroes   potatoes   tomatoes

4. **When the singular noun ends in *y* with a consonant before it, change the *y* to *i* and add *es.***

pony—ponies   baby—babies

lady—ladies   daisy—daisies

5. **For most nouns ending in *f* or *fe,* add *s.* For some nouns ending in *f* or *fe,* however, change the *f* to *v* and add *es* or *s.***

belief—beliefs	thief—thieves	leaf—leaves
roof—roofs	knife—knives	half—halves
dwarf—dwarfs	wife—wives	shelf—shelves
cuff—cuffs	life—lives	elf—elves

6. **Some nouns are the same for both singular and plural.**

deer   sheep   trout   salmon   bass

3. Assign and discuss Exercises A, B, and C on page 118.

4. See Exercise C on page 125 for additional practice.

Optional Practice

Students may complete the following exercise for practice. Choose the correct plural form.

1. Three (mouse/mice) ate the cheese.
2. Those (leaves/leafs) blew into the gutter.
3. Give the (toyes/toys) to the small child.
4. The weather warning covers four (counties/countys).
5. The bells of all the (churchs/churches) rang at noon.

Extending the Lesson

Write the following nouns on the board. Students should identify the nouns that are singular, and be able to give the plural form of each. Then they should identify the plural nouns, and give the singular form for each.

pens	leaf
flower	banjo
half	cherry
faces	coaches
buggies	parades

7. **Some nouns form their plurals in special ways.**

mouse—mice	man—men	tooth—teeth
goose—geese	woman—women	foot—feet
	child—children	

Exercises Forming Plurals

A. Number your paper from 1 to 10. Write every plural noun in each sentence. After each noun, write the number of the rule that tells how the plural was formed.

Example: Representatives from three countries signed the treaty.
Representatives—1, countries—4

1. The children [7] heard echoes [3] in the cave.
2. The flies [4] were killed by the sprays [1].
3. On the fishing trip, I caught two bass [6] and several trout [6].
4. In some countries [4] even adults [1] believe in witches [2] and elves [5].
5. There are rushes [2] and bushes [2] in the marshes [2].
6. The farmer set the potatoes [3] and tomatoes [3] on the tables [1].
7. If I help you win the prize, will you go halves [5] with me?
8. Three deer [6] and some foxes [2] investigated the sheepfold.
9. Do mice [7] and geese [7] have teeth [7]?
10. The dairies [4] in the cities [4] suffered losses [2].

B. Write the plural form of these nouns.

1. watch (watches)	5. foot (feet)	9. leaf (leaves)	13. mouse (mice)	17. robot (robots)
2. city (cities)	6. sheep (sheep)	10. hero (heroes)	14. wife (wives)	18. porch (porches)
3. half (halves)	7. tomato (tomatoes)	11. potato (potatoes)	15. woman (women)	19. tooth (teeth)
4. company (companies)	8. life (lives)	12. candy (candies)	16. wish (wishes)	20. cry (cries)

C. Look around your room. In a column, write a noun for every object you see. Then write the plural of each noun in another column.

Answers will vary.

Part 4 How Nouns Show Possession

When you speak of a dog that belongs to Tom, you want a short way of expressing that relationship. You do not want to say, "The dog that belongs to Tom" every time you refer to it. In English, the shortcut is the **possessive form** of the noun. The possessive form of *Tom* is *Tom's*. The fast way to refer to the dog Tom owns is to say *Tom's dog*.

> **Possessive nouns** show possession of the noun that follows.

Forming Possessives of Singular Nouns

The difference between *Tom* and the possessive form *Tom's* is the ending. *Tom's* has an apostrophe and an *s*.

To form the possessive of a singular noun, add an apostrophe and *s*.

Singular Noun	Possessive Form
grandfather	grandfather's
baby	baby's
Charles	Charles's
Mrs. Wills	Mrs. Wills's

Part 4

Objective

To use the appropriate methods of forming possessive forms of nouns

Presenting the Lesson

1. Read and discuss pages 119 to 121.

2. Much popular journalism does not abide by the *'s* rule for singular words ending in *s*. Explain the importance of knowing formal English forms. Discuss possible reasons for changes in these rules.

3. Emphasize the importance of first deciding if a word is singular or plural before checking its possessive spelling.

4. Assign and discuss Exercises A, C, and D on pages 121 and 122. It is suggested that the class do Exercise B together.

5. See Exercise D on page 125 for additional practice.

Optional Practice

Have students rewrite the following words in their possessive forms. Cursive writing should be used.

Julie	player	lady
books	cities	oxen
window	king	child

Extending the Lesson

An important proofreading skill is knowing when a sentence requires a possessive form and when it does not. Ask students to select the correct word for each sentence.

1. Several (boys/boy's) played baseball in the park.
2. My (sisters/sister's) class went on a field trip.
3. The volume (control's/controls) are broken.
4. Seven (children/child's) won a prize in the contest.
5. Our (cats/cats') food dishes were empty.

Forming Possessives of Plural Nouns

There are two rules to remember for forming the possessive of a plural noun.

1. If the plural noun ends in *s*, simply add an apostrophe after the *s*.

Plural Noun	Possessive Form
teachers	teachers'
pirates	pirates'
cats	cats'
doctors	doctors'
students	students'

2. If the plural noun does not end in *s*, add an apostrophe and an *s* after the apostrophe.

Plural Noun	Possessive Form
men	men's
women	women's
children	children's
Hopi	Hopi's

Notice how changing the place of the apostrophe changes the meaning of the possessive.

The student's pencils means pencils belonging to one student.

The students' pencils means pencils belonging to two or more students.

If you are not sure how to write the possessive form of a noun, do this:

Write the noun first. Then follow the rules.

When writing *'s* in cursive, you should not connect the *s* following the apostrophe to the last letter before the apostrophe. The apostrophe should separate the two letters.

Peg's skates   James's mother

Exercises Writing the Possessive Form

A. Write the words in italics to show possession.

Example: That is *Curtis* music stand.
Curtis's

1. The trainer took the *runner* pulse. runner's
2. Is that the *manager* phone number? manager's
3. The new *girl* hair was long and curly. girl's
4. Follow your *mother* advice. mother's
5. A parade honored the *astronauts* homecoming. astronauts'
6. We could see the *raccoon* tracks. raccoon's
7. The *sailors* waterproofs protected them from the spray. sailors'
8. The *actress* smile looked real. actress's
9. My *dog* ears perked up. dog's
10. *Tess* butterfly collection has two dozen specimens. Tess's

B. Write the possessive form of each of the following nouns. Then write another noun after each possessive form to show what the first noun might possess.

Example: Thomas Edison
Thomas Edison's invention

1. a beaver 's
2. the mechanic 's
3. a pollywog 's
4. Louise 's
5. an Arab 's
6. Albert Jones 's
7. the fishermen 's
8. the secretaries '

9. some steel workers'
10. a chicken's
11. Ms. Lopez's
12. that cook's
13. the ducks'
14. your neighbors'
15. my aunt's
16. the whale's
17. the puppets'
18. an ostrich's
19. those babies'
20. the clown's

C. Copy these sentences. Underline each person, place, or thing that belongs to someone or something else. Place the apostrophe where it belongs to show who or what possesses the underlined noun.

1. The children's presents are in Noras closet.
2. Manuel's store sells maps.
3. The men's golf bags are in my fathers car.
4. That architect's designs for homes won an award.
5. Many campers' tents were destroyed in the forest fire.
6. We used Megan's scarf as a bandage.
7. Andrea's painting was sold!
8. The mice's whiskers twitched nervously.
9. The governor's mansion was lit by floodlights.
10. Ms. Conway's desk has a no-smoking sign.

D. Follow the directions for Exercise C.

1. The king's charger reared, his eyes flashing.
2. Ma Barrett's pies are known all over Grimsby County.
3. The boys' faces looked stunned.
4. Mr. White's garden always had sunflowers.
5. Aunt Fran's car has reclining seats.
6. Both wrestlers' muscles bulged and strained.
7. Those look like Anita's earmuffs.
8. Suddenly the referee's whistle stopped the game.
9. Barney's cats were yowling again.
10. A horned owl's feathers make points like ears.

Sentence Patterns The N V Pattern

Every sentence has a subject and a verb. The subject is usually a noun. In this chart, *N* stands for the noun in the complete subject. V stands for the verb in the complete predicate.

N	V
Margie	cheered.
Carl	ate quickly.
The baby	smiled.
The red balloon	popped.

The word order in these sentences follows a pattern. That pattern is noun-verb, or N V. This pattern is called the **N V pattern.**

Exercises The N V Pattern

A. Make a chart like the one above. Label one column *N* and the other *V*. Write these sentences on the chart.

1. Clouds | formed.
2. Jenny | skates every day.
3. The teams | struggled.
4. Strong winds | howled.
5. The dogs | barked loudly.
6. Alex | whistled.

B. Copy this chart. Complete each sentence in the N V Pattern.

Answers will vary.

	N	V
1.	________	shouted.
2.	The thunder	________.
3.	________	stood up.
4.	Nick	________.
5.	________	slept late.

C. Make a chart of your own for the N V pattern. Write five sentences in the N V pattern.

Sentence Patterns

Objective

To recognize the basic word order in the N V sentence pattern

Presenting the Lesson

1. Read and discuss page 123. As the chart indicates, the noun-part of each sentence includes not only the noun identified as the subject, but also all the modifiers of that noun. The verb-part includes the verb and its modifiers, if any (as in Carl *ate quickly).* The students should be able to identify the point at which a sentence can be divided into these two parts.

2. Assign and discuss Exercises A and C. It is suggested that the class do Exercise B together.

Extending the Lesson

The following lengthy sentences are basic N V pattern sentences. Ask students to identify the break between the noun-part and the verb-part.

1. My very funny Aunt Sarah jokes with us constantly.
2. Several gray squirrels ran across the yard and up the tree.
3. Those two players with green and white uniforms scored during the first half of the game.

Additional Exercises

If these Exercises were not used with each lesson, they may now be assigned for chapter review.

Additional Exercises

Using Nouns

A. Finding the Nouns (Use after page 112.)

Find the nouns in the sentences below.

1. The corn was stored in the silo.
2. My sister Tanya invited her classmates to a picnic in the park.
3. Robin Hood led the fight against the Sheriff of Nottingham.
4. Directions are on the back of the package.
5. A diesel uses oil for its fuel.
6. Barbara brought the class some delicious candy made from pecans and caramel.
7. Spring is my favorite season.
8. This thermometer is for the oven.
9. The librarian found the book about Tibet on the top shelf.
10. The chain on my bicycle keeps coming off.

B. Finding Common and Proper Nouns (Use after page 114.)

Copy these sentences. Capitalize the first word in the sentence and each proper noun.

1. a french explorer named cadillac founded detroit.
2. memorial day is a national holiday.
3. my cousin ellen can change that tire.
4. vickers' drive-in theater was showing a double feature.
5. walkerville public library is the biggest library in the county.
6. we visited carlsbad caverns.
7. morning glory pool in yellowstone national park looks like a blue morning glory.

8. we got this maple syrup from vermont. (W, V)

9. the drugstore was running a special on sunglasses. (T)

10. death valley in california receives less than three inches of rain yearly. (D, V, C)

C. Forming Plurals (Use after page 118.)

Write the plural form of these nouns.

1. party (parties)	6. goose (geese)	11. army (armies)	16. buoy (buoys)
2. witch (witches)	7. man (men)	12. trout (trout)	17. dress (dresses)
3. deer (deer)	8. radio (radios)	13. lobby (lobbies)	18. roof (roofs)
4. switch (switches)	9. lady (ladies)	14. day (days)	19. daisy (daisies)
5. thief (thieves)	10. knife (knives)	15. dwarf (dwarfs)	20. echo (echoes)

D. Writing the Possessive Form (Use after page 121.)

Write the words in italics in the correct possessive form.

1. *Darcy* math book was on the table. Darcy's
2. My *uncle* cabin is in New Jersey. uncle's
3. The bus *driver* left-turn signal was stuck. driver's
4. The *ladies* coats are in the next room. ladies'
5. My *dentist* office is on Shirley Street. dentist's
6. A goose was in the *magician* hat. magician's
7. Can you find your *puppy* leash? puppy's
8. My *grandfather* business is closed during July. grandfather's
9. The *boys* appetites were huge. boys'
10. *People* opinions vary. people's

Chapter 8

Using Verbs

Read the following words. Do you understand what they are saying?

Becky ________________ the cat.

The words above almost express a message. We can try to complete the message by putting various words in the blank.

Becky *pencil* the cat.

Does this set of words give you a complete idea? No, because *pencil* does not tell what Becky did.

Becky *orange* the cat.

Again, *orange* does not tell what Becky did. We still do not have a sentence.

Becky *petted* the cat.

Chapter Objectives

1. To identify verbs as either action words or state-of-being words

2. To recognize common helping verbs and their main verbs

3. To identify direct objects and to understand their relationship to verbs

4. To understand the concept of linking verbs

5. To identify both linking verbs and words they link to the subject in sentences

6. To understand the concepts of the three simple tenses of verbs: present, past, and future

7. To recognize and use the simple tenses

8. To choose the correct verb from verb pairs that are often confused

9. To use negatives correctly in sentences

10. To recognize the basic word order in the N V N sentence pattern

Preparing the Students

Chapter 3, especially in Parts 4, 5, and 6, has already introduced the verb. If much time has passed since the study of Chapter 3, you may wish to begin Chapter 8 with a review of subjects and predicates. Ask students to identify the complete subject and predicate for each of the following sentences.

1. The first five customers received prizes.
2. The thunder and lightning frightened our dog.
3. We found two small cracks in the vase.

Additional Resources

Diagnostic Test—page 428 in this T.E. Recommended for use before teaching the chapter.

Mastery Test—pages 451–454 in this T.E. Recommended for use after teaching the chapter.

Additional Mastery Test—Recommended for use after any necessary reteaching. (In separate booklet, *Diagnostic and Mastery Tests, Gold Level,* pages 27–30.)

Skills Practice Book—pages 43–54

Duplicating Masters—pages 43–54

Part 1

Objective

To identify verbs as either action verbs or state-of-being verbs

Presenting the Lesson

1. Read and discuss pages 127 and 128. Make a clear distinction between action verbs and state-of-being verbs. Action verbs are more easily understood and recognized. Additional practice with state-of-being verbs may be needed.

2. Ask students to identify the state-of-being verb in each of these sentences:

1. That award is a high honor.
2. We are happy with our new car.
3. The position was very important.
4. Lee's mother is a doctor.
5. My family is proud.

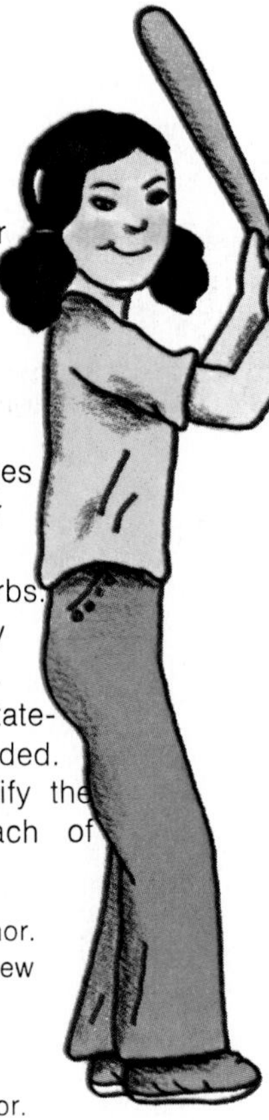

This time the words express a clear message. The word *petted* tells what Becky did, and gives the connection between her and the cat.

Are there any other words that could be placed in the blank to complete the sentence? Perhaps you thought of these:

Becky *fed* the cat.
Becky *held* the cat.
Becky *owned* the cat.

The words *petted, fed, held,* and *owned* all belong to a group of words called verbs. As you have seen, no sentence is complete without a verb. This chapter will tell you about verbs and how to use them.

Part 1 Kinds of Verbs

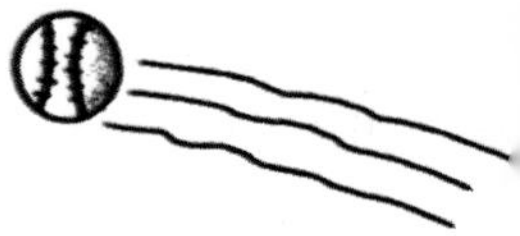

There are two kinds of verbs.
Some verbs tell about action. They are **action verbs.**

Sue *hit* the ball. Bill *ran* to the window.

Some verbs name action that you cannot see. That is, there is no physical movement taking place.

Barbara *thought* about pets. She *wanted* a puppy.

Some verbs are not action verbs. They simply state that something is. They express a state of being. They are **state-of-being verbs.**

Your book *is* on the table.
The slacks *were* the right size.

The most common state-of-being verbs are these:

is	are	were	being
am	was	be	been

Exercises Finding Action Verbs and State-of-Being Verbs

A. Copy these sentences. Draw two lines under each verb.

1. Our school held an art fair.
2. Students displayed their artwork.
3. Colorful ceramic pots lined the tables.
4. A band played music in the gym.
5. The mood at the party was joyful.
6. I took my dog to obedience school.
7. We reward Scamp with dog biscuits.
8. Sharon remembered her umbrella.
9. Last Sunday the weather was hot and humid.
10. Rosario missed the bus this morning.

B. Make two columns on your paper. Head one column *Action Verbs* and the other *State-of-Being Verbs*. Find the verb in each sentence and place it in the right column.

Examples: a. Willie plans (A) all our camping trips.

b. Debra was (SB) in my class during second grade.

Action Verbs	State-of-Being Verbs
a. plans	b. was

1. The rabbit's big, velvety ears twitched. (A)
2. This old dress is (SB) still in style.
3. Judy loves (A) dill pickles.
4. Listen (A) to the crickets.
5. The fourth question on the test was (SB) tricky.
6. Suddenly Sean's dark eyes flashed. (A)
7. I know (A) the names of all the lifeguards.
8. Valentina Tereshkova was (SB) the first woman in space.
9. The kingfisher swallowed (A) a frog and two fish.
10. Richard's bike accident happened (A) last June.

3. Point out the special use of these state-of-being verbs:

be—used only when preceded by a helping verb: *can, could, shall, should, would, may, might, must, will*

being—used only when preceded by a *be* word as a helping verb: *is, am, are, was, were*

been—used only when preceded by a *have* word: *have, has, had*

4. In addition to the general definition of a verb given in the text, there are other ways to identify a verb. These ways, listed in the following chart, are based on what linguists have discovered about the structure of a word and the order of words in a sentence. It is suggested that the information in the chart be used to point out additional ways in which verbs function.

Ways To Identify Verbs

1. Look for words that change their forms to show past time.

Present	Past
walk	walked
eat	ate

2. Look for words that follow helping verbs (forms of *be, do, have,* and helping verbs like *can, could, shall, will may, might,* and *must*).

3. Look for words with the following endings or suffixes:

-ify (*clarify*) *-ize* (*realize*)

4. Look for words that fit the blank in this test sentence:

Please ___________.

5. It is suggested that Exercises A and B on page 129 be done as a class activity. Assign and discuss Exercises C and D on page 130.

6. See Exercise A on page 151 for additional practice.

Optional Practice

Ask students to write sentences using each of the following words as a verb (use no helping verbs):

sing skates write thought take

Extending the Lesson

Collect a set of interesting action pictures from newspapers and magazines. Number the pictures. Pass them around the room and ask students to think of one verb suggested by each picture. When all students have finished their lists, write all the suggestions for each picture on the board. Can each be used in a sentence as a verb? Discuss them.

C. Follow the directions for Exercise B.

1. In 1927, Charles A. Lindbergh flew [A] from New York to Paris.
2. He was [SB] alone.
3. He faced [A] many hardships.
4. After many hours in flight, he was [SB] successful.
5. The French people welcomed [A] him.
6. He came [A] home on a United States cruiser.
7. The American nation gave [A] him many honors.
8. His solo flight was [SB] a great event.
9. It greatly aided [A] the development of aviation.
10. Lindbergh will [SB] always be [SB] an aviation hero.

D. Each of the following groups of words would be a sentence if a verb were added. Think of a verb to complete each sentence. Write your sentences and underline the verbs. Add the correct punctuation at the end of every sentence. Answers will vary.

1. A northwest wind
2. He the skateboard contest
3. The sleek car smoothly
4. Chris Evert tennis
5. The referee his whistle
6. During autumn the colors of the leaves
7. Three languages French, Spanish, and German
8. A snow skier poles, boots, and skis
9. Giraffes the tallest four-legged animals
10. The gardener the roses and marigolds

Part 2

Objective

To recognize common helping verbs and their main verbs

Part 2 Main Verbs and Helping Verbs

You already know that many verbs are made of more than one word. They are made up of the main verb and helping verbs.

Verb	Helping Verbs	Main Verb
am going	am	going
is going	is	going
can go	can	go
will go	will	go
has gone	has	gone
has been gone	has been	gone
could have gone	could have	gone

The most common of the helping verbs are these forms of *be, have,* and *do.*

be—am, is, are, was, were
have—have, has, had
do—do, does, did

These words can also be used by themselves as main verbs.

Used as Helping Verb	Used as Main Verb
Bob *is* going.	Bob *is* the pitcher.
Sally *has* gone.	Sally *has* a moped.

There are several other helping verbs that you will often use with main verbs:

be	may	would	will
being	can	should	shall
been	could	might	must

A **verb** tells about action or expresses a state of being. It may be a single word, or a group of words made up of a **main verb** and one or more **helping verbs.**

Presenting the Lesson

1. Read and discuss pages 130 to 132. Give special attention to the difference between the use of verbs as helping verbs and as main verbs. In the examples showing *is* and *has* as helping verbs, point out the main verb as well. Use the following sentences for practice. Have the students tell whether the italicized word is a helping verb or a main verb.

1. That tree *is* swaying in the breeze.
2. The winner *was* Mary Robertson.
3. Everyone *did* the lesson perfectly.
4. My new pen *is* already dry.
5. I *have* given that idea some serious though.

2. Assign and discuss Exercises A and B on pages 132 and 133.
3. See Exercise B on pages 151 and 152 for additional practice.

Extending the Lesson

Have students use each of the *be, have,* and *do* words listed on page 131 in two sentences. Use the word first as a helping verb and then as a main verb. Discuss the sentences.

Separated Parts of the Verb

The main verb and helping verbs are not always together. They may be separated by other parts of the sentence.

The batter *was* not *watching* for signals.
Andrea *has* never *missed* a band practice.
Did the kindergartners *make* popcorn today?
Frankenstein *couldn't control* his monster.

Notice that *not* and the ending *n't* in the contraction are not verbs.

Exercises Finding Main Verbs and Helping Verbs

A. Number your paper from 1 to 10. Make two columns. Head the first column *Helping Verbs*. Head the second *Main Verb*. Write the verbs for each of these sentences in the right column.

Example: The books could not be found anywhere.

Helping Verbs	Main Verb
could be	found

1. I was expecting a phone call.
 <small>HV MV</small>
2. The old chestnut tree was hit by lightning.
 <small>HV MV</small>
3. Where can we find a book about marine life?
 <small>HV MV</small>
4. You should have seen the flames.
 <small>HV HV MV</small>
5. This contest entry might be too late.
 <small>HV MV</small>
6. The beachball had completely collapsed.
 <small>HV MV</small>
7. Skip has never had the measles.
 <small>HV MV</small>
8. That bottle could have floated here from Greenland.
 <small>HV HV MV</small>
9. We have already eaten our sandwiches.
 <small>HV MV</small>
10. The team had been hoping for a sunny day.
 <small>HV HV MV</small>

132

B. Follow the directions for Exercise A.

1. The red wolf is becoming extinct.
 <small>HV MV</small>
2. Coach Perez had called a time-out.
 <small>HV MV</small>

3. The Bears are [HV] beating [MV] the Vikings, 7–0.
4. People should [HV] always eat [MV] a nutritious breakfast.
5. Cartoons can [HV] sometimes be [MV] violent.
6. Did [HV] Momoko bring [MV] her skateboard?
7. Have [HV] you ever written [MV] a poem?
8. Curt might [HV] be [HV] joining [MV] the hockey team.
9. Computers will [HV] soon be [HV] performing [MV] many household tasks.
10. The President may [HV] not be [HV] elected [MV] more than twice.

Part 3 Verbs and Direct Objects

In many sentences the thought is complete when there are only a verb and its subject:

Subject	Verb
The audience	applauded.
Mary Ann	coughed.
Donald	worked.

In other sentences the thought is not complete until other words have been added.

Paul polished ________________.
Lucy dropped ________________.

So far, you don't know *what* Paul polished and *what* Lucy dropped. We need to complete the sentences.

Paul polished the *silverware.*
Lucy dropped her *book.*

In the first sentence, the word *silverware* receives the action of the word *polished*. It is the **direct object** of the verb.

In the second sentence, *book* receives the action of *dropped*. It is the **direct object** of the verb.

Part 3

Objective

To identify direct objects and to understand their relationship to verbs

Presenting the Lesson

1. Read aloud and discuss pages 133 and 134. Most students will recognize that the word functioning as a direct object is usually a noun. Avoid discussion of pronouns as direct objects until after the study of Chapter 9.

2. Emphasize that the direct object receives the action of a verb. A verb that has a direct object must be an action verb, not a state-of-being verb.

3. It is suggested that you work with the class both the Adding Direct Objects Exercise A on pages 134 and 135, and the Finding Direct Objects Exercise A on page 135. Assign and discuss both Exercises B on pages 135 and 136.

4. See Exercise C on page 152 for additional practice.

Extending the Lesson

Use each of the following words in two sentences. In the first sentence, use it as the subject. In the second sentence, use it as the direct object.

pencil sled book lawn desk

The **direct object** tells what receives the action of the verb.

Recognizing Direct Objects

To find the direct object in a sentence, first find the verb. Then ask *what?* after the verb. If you cannot answer the question *what?* there is not a direct object.

Examples:

Christy likes math.
Christy likes *what? math*
The direct object is *math.*

Julio reads quickly.
Julio reads *what?*
You cannot answer the question *what?* so there is no direct object.

Julio reads magazines quickly.
Julio reads *what? magazines*
The direct object is *magazines.*

Exercises Adding Direct Objects

A. Number your paper from 1 to 10. Write objects that will complete each of the following sentences. Answers will vary.

1. Hamid planted ________ in his front yard.
2. The Cardinals scored a ________.
3. Newspapers littered the ________.
4. Jolita rode the ________ with ease.
5. The reporter wrote a sensational ________.
6. After the concert Andy Gibb left the ________.

7. Leroy wore a bright yellow ______________.
8. Kristin put the ______________ in her wallet.
9. My favorite radio station plays good ______________.
10. Did you close the ______________?

B. On a sheet of paper, write sentences using the following verbs. Put a direct object in each sentence. Draw a circle around the direct object that you have added. Answers will vary.

1. have caught
2. filled
3. would have stopped
4. was twisting
5. painted
6. will open
7. has invented
8. ruined
9. should limit
10. might use

Exercises Finding Direct Objects

A. Copy the following sentences. Underline the verb twice. Draw a circle around the direct object.

Example: The policeman stopped all (traffic.)

1. The scuba diver found a (shipwreck.)
2. Bruce Jenner won the (decathlon.)
3. The pilot steered his (craft) onto the airfield.
4. I am studying (science) now.
5. The children have built a huge (snowman.)
6. The Bureau of the Mint manufactures all (coins.)
7. Kathy will repair the (brakes) on her bike.
8. Delores likes (ice cream) with celery on top.
9. The United States exports (grains) to the Far East.
10. On Thanksgiving Day we eat (turkey) with gravy.

B. Number your paper from 1 to 10. Find and write the direct objects in these sentences.

1. A. J. Foyt drives racecars. racecars

2. Jody will answer the telephone. telephone
3. Our girls' basketball team won its first game. game
4. In 1785 Jean Pierre Blanchard invented the parachute. parachute
5. Tonia made pizzas for the party. pizzas
6. The sailors unfurled the mainsail. mainsail
7. The teacher wrote the assignment on the blackboard. assignmer
8. The zookeeper fed raw meat to the lions. meat
9. Did you drop the carton of eggs? carton
10. Beth placed the saddle on the horse's back. saddle

Part 4

Objectives

1. To understand the concept of linking verbs
2. To identify both linking verbs and words they link to the subject in sentences

Presenting the Lesson

1. Read and discuss pages 136 and 137.
2. Emphasize that linking verbs are not action verbs. They simply tell that something is, or exists. They are always followed by an adjective or a noun. Avoid the discussion of pronouns after linking verbs until after the study of Chapter 9. Carefully discuss the examples on page 137. Be sure that students can see the difference between direct objects and the predicate words that follow linking

Note that in the first two sample sentences, *feel* and *taste* indicate a state-of-being. No action is being performed. *Ill* merely describes *I*. *Delicious* merely describes *cookies*.

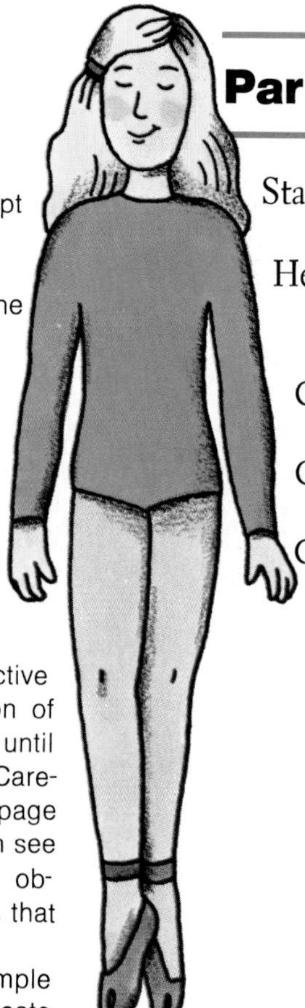

Part 4 Linking Verbs

State-of-being verbs are often called linking verbs.

Here are some examples.

Carrie *is* tall.

Carrie *is* hungry.

Carrie *is* musical.

Linking verbs connect the subject with a word in the predicate. In the examples, they connect *Carrie* with *tall*, with *hungry*, and with *musical*.

The words *is, am, are, was, were, be,* and *become* are often used as linking verbs. The words *seem, look, appear, smell, taste, feel,* and *sound* are sometimes linking verbs.

The words that follow linking verbs and tell something about the subject are either adjectives or nouns.

Examples of adjectives: I *feel* ill.
These cookies *taste* delicious.

Examples of nouns: Angela *is* my best friend.
A goat *became* the team mascot.

Do not confuse nouns following linking verbs with direct objects of verbs. In the examples just given, you can see that *friend* and *mascot* tell something about the subject of each sentence. They do not receive action of the verbs, and are not direct objects. To identify a linking verb, decide whether the noun following the verb tells something about the subject of the sentence. If it does, the verb is a linking verb.

Exercises Finding Linking Verbs

A. At the top of three columns write: *Subject, Linking Verb,* and *Word Linked to Subject.* Find the three parts in each sentence. Write them in the proper columns.

Example: The contestants in the marathon appeared weary.

Subject	Linking Verb	Word Linked to Subject
contestants	appeared	weary

1. Jane Fonda is an actress.
2. That clown's hat looks ridiculous.
3. The banana nut cake smells delicious.
4. A young kangaroo is a joey.
5. Don't bullfights seem brutal?
6. Samuel's story sounds unbelievable.

The text uses the term *adjective* here for the first time. Define it simply as a describing word; the adjective will be fully discussed in Chapter 14.

3. Assign and discuss Exercises A and B on pages 137 and 138. If students demonstrate problems in differentiating between direct objects and predicate words, have the class do Exercise C on page 138 together. Some students may need additional drill on identifying direct objects and predicate words.

4. See Exercise D on pages 152 and 153 for additional practice.

Extending the Lesson

Have students use each of the following verbs in two sentences. In the first sentence, they should use it as an action verb. In the second sentence, they are to use it as a linking verb.

taste	feel	look
grow	appear	sound

S LV W

7. That roller coaster looks scary.

 S LV W

8. Under water, straight lines will appear wavy.

 S LV W

9. Big Bird is a character on "Sesame Street."

 LV S LV W

10. Should we be quiet during the rehearsal?

B. Follow the directions for Exercise A.

 S LV W

1. The edge of this knife is dull.

 S LV W

2. My skates are becoming rusty.

 S LV W

3. The chili tastes fiery.

 S LV W

4. The fastest animal is the cheetah.

 S LV LV W

5. I don't feel sleepy.

 S LV W

6. The sequoia trees in California look huge.

 S LV W

7. Our country's oldest national park is Yellowstone.

 S LV W

8. The Vikings were Scandinavian pirates.

 S LV W

9. Mother must be very angry.

 S LV W

10. The most popular breed of dog is the poodle.

C. Some of the verbs in the following sentences are linking verbs and the others are verbs with direct objects. Copy each of the sentences. Draw a circle around the linking verbs. Draw two lines under the verbs with direct objects.

 Examples: a. Emmett Kelly (is) a famous clown.

 b. Congress approved the treaty.

1. The campers carried firewood to the campsite.
2. Bobby Orr (is) a famous athlete.
3. Vacations always (seem) too short.
4. The police detective felt the damp earth.
5. A down quilt (feels) very cozy.
6. The golfer was driving balls.
7. According to legend, Betsy Ross made the first flag.
8. The bill (may) soon (become) a law.
9. Mopeds use gas efficiently.
10. Mopeds (are) efficient vehicles.

Part 5 Verb Tenses

Verbs are time-telling words. They not only tell of an action or a state of being. They also tell *when* something takes place. By changing their forms, they tell whether the action or state of being is past, present, or future. These changes in form to show time are called **tenses.**

The **present tense** indicates an action or state of being happening now.

I *work* at school. I *am* a student.

The **past tense** indicates an action or state of being completed in the past.

I *worked* all last summer. I *was* a library aide.

The **future tense** indicates an action or state of being happening in the future.

I *will work* at the pool next year. I *will be* a lifeguard.

These three tenses are called the **simple tenses.** They are three of the most important tenses.

Tense changes are made in three ways:

1. By a change in spelling: *know, knew, known*
2. By a change in ending: *look, looked*
3. By a change in helping verbs: *did work, will work*

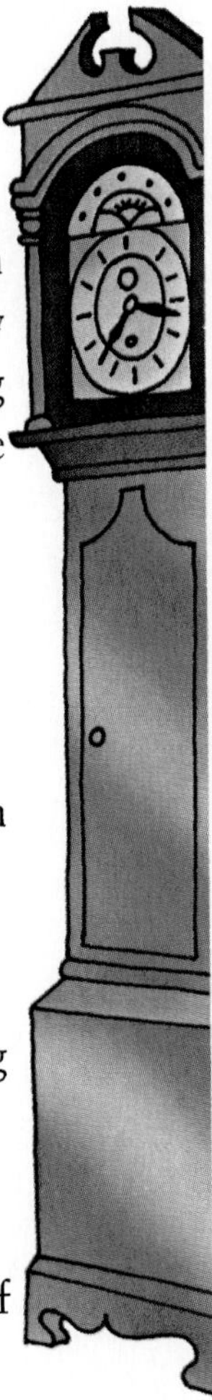

Part 5

Objectives

1. To understand the concepts of the three simple tenses of verbs: present, past, and future

2. To recognize and use the simple tenses

Presenting the Lesson

1. Read and discuss page 139. Provide additional examples for each of the simple tenses. Have students create sentences for each.

2. Ask students to add examples to each of the methods listed at the bottom of page 139?

3. Read aloud and discuss page 140. Be sure the students realize that the present tense has two forms: one used with singular subjects, that ends in *-s* or *-es*, and one used with plural subjects, that does not end in *-s* or *-es*. The future tense uses the second form.

4. Demonstrate the natural formation of regular verb past tense with a nonsense word example.

The teams *gronch* onto the field.
Yesterday the teams ___________.
(*gronched*?)

Most students will automatically

follow the regular *-ed* pattern. Point out that small children learning the language often naturally follow the regular verb form when the irregular verb form really applies. (*goed, eated, drinked, runned,* etc.)

5. Assign and discuss Exercises A and C on page 140 and 141. You may prefer to do Exercise B as a class exercise.

6. See Exercise E on page 153 for additional practice.

Optional Practice

Ask students to give the present (both forms), past, and future tense for all the verbs in Exercise C on page 141. When discussing them, have students use them in sentences.

Extending the Lesson

Ask students to design crossword puzzles that require knowledge of verb tenses for completion.

Example:

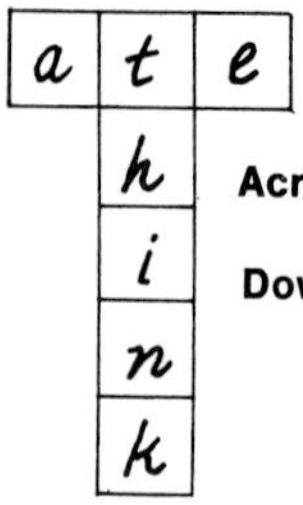

Across past tense of *eat*

Down present tense of *thought*

Forming the Tenses

Present Tense

In general, the **present tense** of the verb is the same as the name of the verb: *race, call, do, think.* An *-s* or *-es* is added to produce the form *he races, she calls, it does, she thinks.*

Past Tense

The **past tense** of most verbs is formed by adding *-d* or *-ed* to the present tense:

race call
rac*ed* call*ed*

These verbs are called **regular verbs.**

The past tense of other verbs, called **irregular verbs,** is usually shown by a change of spelling:

do think
did *thought*

Future Tense

The **future tense** is formed by using the helping verbs *will* or *shall* with the present tense:

will race *shall think*

Exercises Recognizing and Using Verb Tenses

A. Number your paper from 1 to 10. Write the verb in each of the following sentences. Name the tense of each verb.

Example: Clayton Moore played the Lone Ranger. *played, past*

1. Alison does crossword puzzles. does, present
2. Sir Edmund Hillary climbed Mount Everest. climbed, past

3. Our class will plan a school carnival. will plan, future
4. We saw a porpoise show. saw, past
5. The fans cheered Peter Frampton. cheered, past
6. "The Muppet Show" is hilarious. is, present
7. Students will take a bus home from school. will take, future
8. Tracy Austin plays fine tennis. plays, present
9. I will return this book to the library. will return, future
10. Indians first explored this wilderness. explored, past

B. Number your paper from 1 to 10. Write the form of the verb asked for in each of the following sentences.

Example: The runner (past of *cross*) the finish line. *crossed*

1. I (future of *read*) all of the Hardy Boys mysteries. will read
2. The lawyer (past of *argue*) her case. argued
3. We (present of *roast*) chestnuts in the fireplace. roast
4. Tyrone (past of *make*) a lamp for his room. made
5. The airplane (future of *land*) in a few minutes. will land
6. Scott O'Dell (past of *write*) *Island of the Blue Dolphins.* wrote
7. Evan and Teresa (past of *pick*) raspberries. picked
8. A cricket game (present of *confuse*) most American spectators. confuses
9. Sponges (present of *live*) in the deep seas. live
10. The track team (future of *run*) in a meet tomorrow. will run

C. Write a sentence for each of the verbs below. Use the verb in the tense indicated. Sentences will vary.

1. hurry (future) will hurry
2. think (past) thought
3. litter (present) litter (s)
4. develop (past) developed
5. remove (past) removed
6. frame (future) will frame
7. justify (past) justified
8. promote (present) promote (s)
9. drain (past) drained
10. bring (future) will bring

Part 6

Objective

To choose the correct verb from verb pairs that are often confused

Presenting the Lesson

1. This Part discusses six pairs of verbs, and provides an exercise for each pair and Review Exercises after each group of three. It is recommended that each pair be covered in a separate lesson, perhaps in conjunction with other review or enrichment material, so that each section gets individual attention. If you use this approach, assign the Exercises as suggested in the following steps.

If you prefer, you may present this Part in only two units: the first set of three verb pairs (through the Review Exercises on pages 144 and 145); and the second set of three verb pairs (through the Review Exercises on pages 147 and 148). If you use this approach, it is recommended that you do orally the Exercises in steps 3, 5, 7, 10, 12, and 14. Assign only the Review Exercises (steps 8 and 15) to be written.

2. Read and discuss page 142. Discuss the right meaning of the examples and the wrong meaning that occurs with the wrong choice.

3. Assign and discuss the Exercise on page 142.

4. Read and discuss page 143.

5. Assign and discuss the Exercise on page 143.

6. Read and discuss page 143. Students are unlikely to confuse *lie* in the sense of telling an untruth, with *lay*.

Part 6 Pairs of Verbs That Are Often Confused

Study the sentences to see how the following pairs of verbs are used. Study the difference in the meanings to avoid making mistakes when you use these words.

Can and *May*

1. Can you see me?	1. May I go with you?
2. Tina can swim like a fish.	2. You may go to the party.

1. Use ***can*** when you are talking about being able to do something.
2. Use ***may*** when you are asking or giving permission.

Exercise Using the Right Verb

Number your paper from 1 to 10. Choose the right verb from the parentheses. Write it on your paper.

1. (May, Can) you write backwards?
2. (May, Can) I blow the balloons up for the party?
3. You (can, may) turn the pancakes now.
4. (Can, May) that little stove heat this whole room?
5. (May, Can) Melina and I go out in the canoe?
6. (May, Can) you read the bottom line without glasses?
7. A catbird (can, may) imitate other birds.
8. (May, Can) I please be excused?
9. (Can, May) Eduardo go to the park with us?
10. Stevie (may, can) count up to forty-nine.

Leave and *Let*

1. Leave the room.
2. Did you leave a book?

1. Let me see your ring.
2. Don't let the puppy follow us.

1. ***Leave*** means to go away from.
2. ***Let*** means to permit or allow.

Exercise Using the Right Verb

Choose the right verb from the parentheses. Write it.

1. Betty (let, left) me see her stamp collection.
2. (Let, Leave) Jim have the spoon to lick.
3. (Leave, Let) Woof alone.
4. The fishing net (leaves, lets) all the minnows through.
5. Don't (let, leave) the baby fall backwards.
6. Who (let, left) the lid off the paint can?
7. (Leave, Let) your umbrella on the porch.
8. That licorice (lets, leaves) a nice taste in my mouth.
9. (Leave, Let) me take your coat.
10. Somebody must have (let, left) the light on.

Lie and *Lay*

1. I like to lie on the floor.
2. Is there a place where I can lay my books?

1. ***Lie*** means to rest in a reclining position.
2. ***Lay*** means to put.
   Lay also means to produce eggs. (A hen *lays* eggs.)

7. Assign and discuss the Exercise at the top of page 144.
8. Assign and discuss Review Exercises A and B on pages 144 and 145.
9. Read and discuss page 145.
10. Assign and discuss the Exercise on pages 145 and 146.
11. Read and discuss page 146.
12. Assign and discuss the Exercise on page 146.
13. Read and discuss page 147.
14. Assign and discuss the Exercise in the middle of page 147.
15. Assign and discuss Review Exercises A and B on pages 147 and 148.
16. See Exercise F on page 153 for additional practice.

Exercise Using the Right Verb

Number your paper from 1 to 10. Choose the right verb from the parentheses. Write it on your paper.

1. Elena likes to (lay, lie) on the rug.
2. My dad always (lays, lies) his ties over the doorknob.
3. (Lay, Lie) your cards face up.
4. The trainer can make the lions (lie, lay) still.
5. Those hens (lie, lay) only brown eggs.
6. (Lay, Lie) on the dock and get a good sun tan.
7. Alfalfa's cowlick wouldn't (lie, lay) down.
8. Don't ever (lie, lay) plastic dishes on the hot stove.
9. Mr. Ware was (laying, lying) on the sofa.
10. Papers were (laying, lying) all over the ball diamond.

Review Exercises Using the Right Verb

A. Number your paper from 1 to 10. Choose the right verb from the parentheses. Write it on your paper.

1. You're (laying, lying) on my towel.
2. (May, Can) Marcia and Fred really read that fast?
3. Certainly Jean (may, can) leave her bike in our garage.
4. (Leave, Let) the needle of the compass settle.
5. A sea turtle will crawl ashore and (lie, lay) her eggs in the sand.
6. (May, Can) we take Trudy to the boat races tomorrow?
7. Cindy always (lets, leaves) the icing till last.
8. Bricklayers never (lie, lay) bricks without a trowel.
9. The bus (lets, leaves) from Fountain Square every half-hour.
10. (May, Can) you hold all the groceries?

B. Follow the directions for Exercise A.

1. The explorers (left, let) their camp during the snowstorm.

2. (May, Can) we try shooting the Green River Rapids?

3. Are you (laying, lying) the spoons on the right side of the plates?

4. (Can, May) you see what's inside the box?

5. The brake will not (leave, let) the wheels spin freely.

6. You and she (may, can) take a copy of the play home.

7. My cat was (lying, laying) on top of the pumpkins.

8. You (can, may) often see forty miles from this lookout.

9. (Leave, Let) Wagger sleep.

10. Were you (lying, laying) in the sun?

Teach* and *Learn

1. I learned to do this trick after much practice.
2. Would you like me to teach you how to do it?

> **1.** You ***learn*** to do something with practice.
> **2.** You ***teach*** somebody how to do something.

Exercise Using the Right Verb

Number your paper from 1 to 10. Choose the right verb from the parentheses. Write it on your paper.

1. Can you (learn, teach) me to swim?
2. Fay is (teaching, learning) her parakeet to talk.
3. My little brother is (learning, teaching) the alphabet.
4. Jarilyn will (learn, teach) her nephew about traffic rules.
5. I am just (learning, teaching) to play chess.
6. Will you (learn, teach) me to braid my hair?
7. Juanita is (learning, teaching) us Spanish.
8. Patti would like to (teach, learn) to fly.

9. The pioneers (taught, learned) their children to be independent.

10. I can't (learn, teach) my puppy any tricks.

Rise and *Raise*

1. The rooster rises early to greet the sun.
2. She raised the baby from the floor.
3. The farmer raises many crops.

1. *Rise* means to get up.
2. *Raise* means to lift.
   Raise also means to grow something.

Exercise Using the Right Verb

Number your paper from 1 to 10. Choose the right verb from the parentheses. Write it on your paper.

1. All the ducks (raise, rise) into the air at once.
2. (Raise, Rise) your foot while I straighten the rug.
3. In every vampire movie, Count Dracula (raises, rises) from the dead once more.
4. Is the temperature in the engine room still (raising, rising)?
5. The Kellogg boys are (rising, raising) rabbits.
6. Turn off the burner when steam (rises, raises) from the kettle.
7. Marcy and Clare will (raise, rise) the curtain at eight sharp.
8. Is the moon (rising, raising) earlier or later?
9. It's not at all hard to (raise, rise) strawberries.
10. Did the drum major (raise, rise) his baton?

Sit and *Set*

1. Set the wheelbarrow down.
2. Then sit and rest awhile.

1. *Set* means to place or put.
2. *Sit* means to rest.

Exercise Using the Right Verb

Number your paper from 1 to 10. Choose the right verb from the parentheses. Write it on your paper.

1. Muffer perked his ears and (sat, set) up.
2. Elizabeth (sat, set) out the milk for the cats.
3. I found Jud (setting, sitting) in the Egyptian room.
4. (Set, Sit) the baby in his high chair, Jan.
5. The baby (set, sat) there chewing his spoon.
6. Mary climbed up the rock and (sat, set) down.
7. Billy Wong (set, sat) out food for the birds.
8. Come in and (set, sit) down for a while.
9. (Set, Sit) down the groceries and help me.
10. (Set, Sit) the fudge out in the snow to cool.

Review Exercises Using the Right Verb

A. Number your paper from 1 to 10. Choose the right verb from the parentheses. Write it on your paper.

1. (Teach, Learn) me how to make a real cake.
2. Jeff (sat, set) the alarm for 5 A.M.
3. Kathy should (rise, raise) next and take her place on stage.
4. (Set, Sit) still while I measure your arm.
5. I (learned, taught) the basic swimming strokes at the Y.

6. Do they (raise, rise) only corn in Kansas?
7. (Learn, Teach) Jessica and me how to throw a lasso.
8. The box was (sitting, setting) right where I left it.
9. He was (teaching, learning) us to eat with chopsticks.
10. Did Jill (raise, rise) the flag this morning?

B. Follow the directions for Exercise A.

1. In a standing ovation, the audience (raises, rises) up and applauds.
2. You have to (sit, set) still to fish.
3. (Set, Sit) the balance beam along this side of the gym.
4. The cardinal was (teaching, learning) its baby bird to fly.
5. Louise didn't even (rise, raise) her voice.
6. (Learn, Teach) the beginners how to hold their rackets.
7. The barometer is (raising, rising).
8. Uncle Frank (set, sat) up waiting for me.
9. (Raise, Rise) the hood and let's look at the engine.
10. Please (teach, learn) me how to ski.

Part 7 Using Negatives Correctly

Negatives are words that say "no." *Not, none, nobody, nowhere, nothing,* and *never* are negatives. Contractions such as *can't, don't, doesn't, wouldn't, won't, isn't,* and *aren't* are negatives. Each contains a shortened form of the word *not.*

Two "no" words used in the same sentence, when only one is needed, make what is called a **double negative.** Avoid double negatives in your talking and writing. Using double negatives can make you appear to be a careless user of the language.

Wrong: He doesn't have no paper.
Right: He doesn't have *any* paper.

Part 7

Objective

To use negatives correctly in sentences

Presenting the Lesson

1. Read and discuss pages 148 and 149.

2. Explain that in some sentences two negatives cancel each other out. If "He does *not* have *no* paper," then he does have paper. Usually a speaker using a double negative means to emphasize the negative. Point out that the meaning is much clearer when only one negative is used.

Wrong: He doesn't have none.
Right: He doesn't have *any*.

Wrong: Can't nobody work this puzzle?
Right: Can't *anybody* work this puzzle?

Exercises Using One Negative

A. Write the following conversation, or take turns reading it aloud. Choose the right word from the parentheses.

RUTH: Thank you, I can't eat (no, any) more pie.
JACK: Didn't you have (none, any)?
RUTH: Oh, yes. I couldn't eat (any, no) more.
PETER: Isn't it (no, any) good?
RUTH: Yes, it's good, but I don't (ever, never) eat more than one piece.
PAUL: I don't know (nothing, anything) I like better than pie. I have never heard (nobody, anybody) refuse pie before.
JANE: Can't (anybody, nobody) eat Ruth's pie?
PAUL: I wouldn't (never, ever) want to see any pie wasted. I'll eat it.

B. Number your paper from 1 to 10. Choose the correct word from the parentheses. Write it on your paper.

1. Gary can't think of (nobody, anybody) else.
2. Don't you want (any, no) pop?
3. Sue wouldn't have taken the album (nowhere, anywhere).
4. Albert won't climb (any, no) ladder more than three feet tall.
5. We aren't going (nowhere, anywhere) this summer.
6. I don't (never, ever) want to eat doughnuts again.
7. Sara doesn't go (anywhere, nowhere) without her bike.
8. I haven't heard (nothing, anything).
9. We haven't (no more, any more) string.
10. Nina wouldn't like (no, any) cake.

3. Assign roles and do Exercise A on page 149 aloud. Assign and discuss Exercise B.

Optional Practice

Have students choose the correct word from the parentheses.

1. The stranger won't tell (anybody, nobody) his name.
2. Meg has done (anything, nothing) about the cookie drive.
3. Couldn't you see (nothing, anything)?
4. Don't you have (none, any) of those green ribbons?
5. Doesn't the bakery have (any more, no more) bread for sale?
6. Can't (nobody, anybody) open that window?
7. Didn't you win (nothing, anything)?
8. Thunder doesn't hurt (anyone, no one).
9. Ted couldn't find (no, any) paper plates.
10. The girls didn't see (anybody, nobody) (anywhere, nowhere).

Sentence Patterns

Objective

To recognize the basic word order in sentences of the N V N sentence pattern

Presenting the Lesson

1. Read and discuss page 150. Make it clear that each of the three parts in the N V N pattern may have one or more than one word. Any words that describe the subject noun are grouped in the first noun-part. Any words that describe the verb are grouped in the verb-part. Any words that describe the object noun are grouped in the second noun-part.

2. Assign and discuss Exercises A, B, and C. It may be useful to write examples for Exercise C on the board.

Extending the Lesson

Point out that often an N V pattern sentence can be changed to an N V N pattern sentence by adding a single word, the direct object.

Example:

N V	He ate.
N V N	He ate lunch.

Have students write five pairs of sentences like those in the example. Use the words listed below:

won wrote plays
sang called

Sentence Patterns **The N V N Pattern**

The **N V N pattern** describes a sentence with three parts. The first N stands for the subject noun. The V stands for the verb. The second N stands for the direct object noun. Each of the sentences in the following chart is in the N V N pattern.

N	V	N
Rosa	ordered	waffles.
Henry	plays	chess.
The carpenter	pounded	the nails.
Birds	build	nests.
The class	presented	a play.

Exercises The N V N Pattern

A. Make a chart like the one above. Label the three columns *N, V,* and *N.* Write these sentences on the chart.

1. Diana collects seashells.
2. Plants need sunlight.
3. My brother loves chocolate.
4. Yuri climbed that peak.
5. The judges awarded prizes.
6. Eric bakes tasty bread.
7. NASA launched a rocket.
8. Our team won the game.

B. Copy this chart. Complete each sentence in the N V N pattern.
Answers will vary.

N	V	N
1. ________	shook	the house.
2. King Kong	grabbed	________.
3. ________	saw	________.
4. Tony	________	two hamburgers.
5. ________	called	Lou Ann.
6. The goat	rammed	________.

C. Make a chart of your own for the N V N pattern. Write five sentences in the N V N pattern.

Using Verbs

A. Finding Action Verbs and State-of-Being Verbs

(Use after page 128.)

Make two columns on your paper. Head one column "Action Verbs" and the other "State-of-Being Verbs." Find the verb in each sentence and place it in the right column.

1. The pens were^{SB} in my desk after all.
2. My dad considered^A the question carefully.
3. Were^{SB} you at the bicycle shop this morning?
4. Twenty years ago, my mother was^{SB} a high school student.
5. Big Ben struck^A eight o'clock.
6. Anita knows^A a lot about the battle of Saratoga.
7. Are^{SB} you Doctor Cleveland?
8. The village slept^A under the stars.
9. Were^{SB} the coyotes around last night?
10. The old man cupped^A his ear.

B. Finding Main Verbs and Helping Verbs (Use after page 132.)

Number your paper from 1 to 10. Make two columns. Head the first column "Helping Verbs." Head the second "Main Verb." Write the verbs for each of these sentences in the right column.

1. Were^{HV} you watching^{MV} TV last night?
2. A candy thermometer will^{HV} be^{HV} needed^{MV}.
3. The boys had^{HV} been^{MV} home for hours.
4. I may^{HV} have^{HV} pushed^{MV} the wrong button.
5. What else could^{HV} we say^{MV}?
6. Barbara Walters may^{HV} have^{HV} attended^{MV} that news conference.

151

Additional Exercises

If these Exercises were not used with each lesson, they may now be used for chapter review.

7. The children were (HV) just pretending (MV).
8. The fire could (HV) have (HV) destroyed (MV) the entire block.
9. Notebook prices have (HV) risen (MV) by fifteen cents this year.
10. Carol and Diane were (HV) often taken (MV) for sisters.

C. Finding Direct Objects (Use after page 134.)

Number your paper from 1 to 10. Find and write the direct objects in these sentences.

1. Carrie delivers newspapers. newspapers
2. The baby sucked his fingers. fingers
3. A snake can shed its skin. skin
4. The Bee Gees have released a new album. album
5. Spelunkers explore caves. caves
6. My aunt and uncle own a farm in Iowa. farm
7. I have been taking piano lessons for three years. lessons
8. Have you ever played soccer? soccer
9. The sixth graders were avidly studying Spanish. Spanish
10. Pony Express riders changed horses every ten miles. horses

D. Finding Linking Verbs (Use after page 137.)

Some of the verbs in the following sentences are linking verbs and the others are verbs with direct objects. Copy each of the sentences. Draw a circle around the linking verbs. Draw two lines under the verbs with direct objects.

1. A fire destroyed two houses.
2. The math test didn't seem very hard.
3. Is your sister an eighth-grader?
4. Lindsay smelled the lilacs.
5. Ocean breezes always smell delightful.
6. The workers are building a new library.
7. Yolanda collects shells of all kinds.
8. Hinduism is the common religion of India.

9. That noise in the attic sounds eerie.
10. Someone sounded the buzzer for a fire drill.

E. Recognizing and Using Verb Tenses (Use after page 140.)

Number your paper from 1 to 10. Write the form of the verb asked for in each of the following sentences.

1. The baby (past of *cry*) all night. cried
2. Charlie Brown always (present of *lose*) the game. loses
3. Amy (future of *laugh*) at even the dullest joke. will laugh
4. The choir (future of *sing*) popular folksongs. will sing
5. That pitcher (present of *throw*) curve balls. throws
6. The fog certainly (future of *clear*) before dawn. will clear
7. Charlayne (present of *go*) to the dentist twice a year. goes
8. Jenina (past of *catch*) a large salmon. caught
9. Balboa (past of *discover*) the Pacific Ocean. discovered
10. Sitting Bull (past of *fight*) in the Battle of Little Bighorn. fought

F. Using the Right Verb (Use after page 147.)

Number your paper from 1 to 10. Choose the right verb from the parentheses and write it on your paper.

1. (Raise, Rise) the lid and insert the tape.
2. (Lie, Lay) the baby in its crib, Stephen.
3. (Can, May) I come in?
4. Don't (sit, set) that brush on the wet paint.
5. I'll (leave, let) the can full of birdseed.
6. Who (taught, learned) you to throw a knuckleball?
7. The spray (raised, rose) high above the falls.
8. Rachel and the others are (laying, lying) out on the patio.
9. (Leave, Let) the huckleberries that aren't ripe yet.
10. My father (learned, taught) us how to cook spaghetti.
11. Mark can (lie, lay) tile as fast as his father.
12. (May, Can) Roosevelt sew well enough to make a shirt?

Chapter 9

Using Pronouns

Part 1 What Are Pronouns?

Read the two paragraphs below. Which paragraph sounds better?

1

Maria gets up at seven-thirty each morning. Maria eats breakfast. Maria goes to school. Maria opens Maria's English book and reads from Maria's book.

2

Maria gets up at seven-thirty each morning. She eats breakfast. She goes to school. She opens her English book and reads from it.

You probably decided that the second paragraph sounded better. Why did you think so? Perhaps you felt that using the name Maria over and over again became boring, or irritating. Perhaps you felt that the repetition made the first paragraph choppy.

Chapter Objectives

1. To understand the concept of the pronoun
2. To recognize the singular and plural personal pronouns
3. To use pronouns correctly as subjects of sentences
4. To use pronouns correctly after linking verbs
5. To use pronouns correctly as objects in sentences
6. To recognize and use the possessive pronouns
7. To distinguish between the possessive pronoun *its* and the contraction *it's*

Preparing the Students

Ask the students to look at the picture on page 154. Write this sentence on the board: The girl is holding the cup. Cross out the words *The girl* and ask for one word, not a name, that can be used instead to refer to the picture. (*She*) Then cross out the words *the cup* and ask for one word to replace the phrase. (*It*)

Point out that the sentence *She is holding it* is not clear by itself. It makes sense only when everyone knows who *she* and *it* stand for.

Additional Resources

Diagnostic Test—page 429 in this T.E. Recommended for use before teaching the chapter.

Mastery Test—pages 455 and 456 in this T. E. Recommended for use after teaching the chapter.

Additional Mastery Test—Recommended for use after any necessary reteaching. (In separate booklet, *Diagnostic and Mastery Tests, Gold Level*, pages 31 and 32.)

Skills Practice Book—pages 55–60

Duplicating Masters—pages 55–60

Part 1

Objectives

1. To understand the concept of the pronoun

2. To recognize the singular and plural pronouns

Presenting the Lesson

1. Read and discuss pages 155 and 156. Give special attention to the three uses of pronouns.

2. As an oral exercise, have students practice using each of the pronouns on page 156 in sentences.

3. Assign and discuss Exercises A and B on page 157.

4. See Exercise A on page 166 for additional practice.

Optional Practice

Ask students to rewrite the following paragraph, using pronouns in place of overused nouns.

> Sharon wrote a story about Sharon's cat. Sharon took the story to school. Sharon hoped that Sharon's teacher would like the story and would give Sharon an A.

Extending the Lesson

Ask students to bring short newspaper articles to class. Have them underline all of the pronouns in the article. On a separate sheet of paper they should then list every underlined pronoun and the noun that it stands for.

How did the second paragraph avoid that repetition? Did you notice how it used the pronouns *she* and *her* in place of the name *Maria?* Use of the pronouns didn't change the meaning of the paragraph, but it improved the sound.

> A **pronoun** is a word used in place of a noun.

You learned to use pronouns as soon as you learned to talk. You learned to use certain pronouns to do three things.

1. To refer to yourself:
   I invited *my* cousin to visit *me.*
2. To refer to the person you are talking to:
   You forgot *your* umbrella.
3. To refer to other persons, places, or things:
   Jack climbed *his* beanstalk.
   The cat blinked *its* eyes.

Singular Pronouns

Person Speaking:	I	my, mine	me
Person Spoken To:	you	your, yours	you
Other Persons, Places, and Things:	he	his	him
	she	her, hers	her
	it	its	it

Plural Pronouns

Persons Speaking:	we	our, ours	us
Persons Spoken To:	you	your, yours	you
Other Persons, Places, and Things:	they	their, theirs	them

Exercises Using Pronouns

A. Copy the following sentences. Underline the pronouns.

1. The bottle popped its cork.
2. Donna promised she would give me her old bike.
3. Take us to the car show, please.
4. Your tomatoes are much riper than ours.
5. We told them all about the walkathon.
6. You should find Ramon's marbles and return them to him.
7. He coaxed the chickens out of their coop.
8. I saw the birds as they flew over my yard.
9. A swan preened its snowy feathers.
10. We walked past her house.

B. In the following story, the pronouns are underlined in red. Read the story. Write all the pronouns in a list. After each pronoun, write the word it stands for.

Since Ted is eleven years old this year, he (1) can enter the Soap Box Derby. Mr. Williams gave him (2) a copy of the rules for the race. Ted is building the racer in the garage. Ted's father and mother are interested in it (3). They (4) often give him (5) advice. Ted paid $29.95 for the wheel and axle set, but the steering gear cost him (6) only $5.75. Ted hopes to win the race. He (7) thinks he (8) can win it (9) easily.

1. Ted
2. Ted
3. racer
4. mother and father
5. Ted
6. Ted
7. Ted
8. Ted
9. race

Part 2

Objective

To use pronouns correctly as subjects of sentences, particularly in compound subjects

Presenting the Lesson

1. Review the construction of complete sentences (subject plus predicate). Point out that in the sentences studied thus far, the subjects have been nouns. Pronouns, as substitutes for nouns, may take over the job of the subject.

2. Read and discuss page 158. Stress that the pronoun that is correct in a simple subject is also correct in a compound subject. Have students refer to the pronoun list on page 156, and try each pronoun by itself as the subject of a sentence. The students should have no trouble accepting the rule listing which pronouns should be used as subjects and which should not.

3. It is suggested that you do Exercise A on page 159 orally with the class. Encourage students to listen to the sound of the pronoun in the sentence. Assign and discuss Exercises B and C on page 159.

4. See Exercise B on pages 166 and 167 for additional practice.

Part 2 Pronouns in Subjects

Which of these sentences sounds right to you?

Her went to the party.
She went to the party.

You probably had no trouble in choosing the second sentence. Now let's add the name of someone else who went to the party.

Her and David went to the party.
She and David went to the party.

The second sentence is right. *She and David* is a compound subject. To figure out what pronoun to use in a compound subject, try each part separately.

David went to the party.
She went to the party.

Then put the two subjects together, using the same pronoun. Follow the same plan when there are two pronouns in the subject.

(He, Him) and (I, me) built a radio.
He built a radio. I built a radio.
He and I built a radio.

Here is another simple problem with pronouns. Which would you say: *We had a picnic* or *Us had a picnic?* As you probably know, the first sentence is right.

Now, which of these sentences is correct?

We girls organized a field trip. (Right. *We* is correct.)
Us girls organized a field trip. (*Us* is not a subject pronoun. It should never be used in the subject.)

The subject pronouns are *I, we, you, he, she, it,* and *they.*
Use only these pronouns in the subject of the verb.

Exercises Using Pronouns in the Subject

A. Choose the correct pronoun from the parentheses. Write it.

1. (We, Us) boys planted a four-foot pine tree.
2. Ms. Tandy and (we, us) came on the bus.
3. The third graders and (me, I) were drenched.
4. Did you find two blue mittens? (Them, They) are mine.
5. (They, Them) and the other cans are behind the garage.
6. The raft and (us, we) girls got stuck under Daw's Bridge.
7. My dog and (me, I) went out to take a look.
8. (He, Him) and (us, we) clocked the runners.
9. Bryan and (she, her) found the Little Dipper.
10. (We, Us) are in a hurry.

B. Follow the directions for Exercise A.

1. Susie and (I, me) ran the cold drink counter.
2. The fifth graders and (us, we) use the pool together.
3. (Us, We) girls and our big angora rabbit won.
4. (Him, He) and (her, she) both come from Louisville.
5. Those boots can't be the ones I lost. (They, Them) don't look like mine.
6. (We, Us) three got all the blame.
7. In the picture, Carla and (he, him) had no heads.
8. (He, Him) and (me, I) were talking to the prison guard.
9. Randy and (me, I) finished the cornflakes.
10. Kitty and (they, them) went up in the ski lift.

C. There are several subject pronouns in the picture below. Write five sentences using these pronouns. Answers will vary.

We

He

She

Optional Practice

Ask students to identify the subject of each sentence below. Then have them rewrite each sentence, substituting a pronoun for each subject.

1. The wooden fence blew down in the windstorm.
2. Two friendly police officers gave directions.
3. The talented actress won an Oscar.
4. My little brother lost his bicycle.
5. Nancy and Marty climbed Mt. Evans last summer.

Part 3

Objective

To use pronouns correctly after linking verbs

Presenting the Lesson

1. Review the definition of linking verbs as discussed in Chapter 8.

2. Read and discuss page 160. Because they are interchangeable, the pronoun following a linking verb must be able to sound right when used as a subject. Stress the sound of the pronoun when used as a subject to ensure the correct pronoun choice. Most students are not comfortable with the sound of the correct pronoun choice following a linking verb.

3. It is recommended that you do Exercise A on page 160 with the class. After each sentence, ask students to exchange the subject noun or pronoun with the predicate noun or pronoun. Assign and discuss Exercise B on page 161.

4. See Exercise C on page 167 for additional practice.

Optional Practice

Ask students to identify the nouns following each of these linking verbs. Have them rewrite each sentence, substituting pronouns for these nouns.

1. The contest winner was John.
2. My best friend is Pat.
3. Our choices were Margaret and Ralph.
4. It was Cleo who called last night.
5. The runners are Brian and Wally.

Part 3 Pronouns After *Is*, *Are*, *Was*, *Were*, and *Will Be*

Look at these two sentences.

The captain is he.   He is the captain.

They mean the same thing. As you see, the pronoun following *is* can be made the subject without changing the meaning of the sentence. The same is true with pronouns that follow the verbs *are*, *was*, *were*, and *will be*.

Change these sentences without changing their meaning.

The co-captains are Janet and he.
The tallest players are Andy and she.
The fastest runners were we Blues.

> Use subject pronouns after *is*, *was*, *are*, *were*, and *will be*.

Exercises Choosing the Right Pronoun

A. Choose the right pronoun from the two in parentheses.

1. The leaders are Valerie and (he, him).
2. It was (he, him) at the counter.
3. The guests of honor will be (we, us) girls.
4. Our club sponsors are Miss Martin and (he, him).
5. The runners-up were (we, us) boys.
6. The traffic managers for the talent show were Maria and (her, she).
7. The only people in that whole pool were Wayne and (me, I).
8. The earliest arrivals were (him, he) and Ron.
9. Was it (her, she) at the door?
10. The stage managers for our play are Paul and (them, they).

B. Follow the directions for Exercise A.

1. There were several adults and (we, us) girls waiting at the bus stop.
2. Our dinner guests were John and (she, her).
3. That's (he, him) on the pier by the submarine.
4. The fastest outfielders are George and (her, she).
5. The soloists are Wendy and (I, me).
6. My teammates were Isabella and (they, them).
7. The speakers at the assembly will be you and (he, him).
8. The funniest actress in our room is (her, she).
9. Faith's backup singers were Jenny and (they, them).
10. The only person with new skates was (he, him).

Part 4 Pronouns as Objects

A noun does not change its form when it is used as an object in a sentence. Pronouns, however, have special forms to be used when they are objects. These forms are called the **object pronouns.** The object pronouns are *me, us, you, him, her, it,* and *them.*

Pronouns After Action Verbs

These sentences will sound natural to you.

Dad drove *us* to the party. We met *him* later.

> Use the object pronouns *me, us, you, him, her, it,* and *them* as objects of verbs.

Be on guard when one or more pronouns are parts of a compound object.

Dad drove Jane and *us* to the party. We met *him* and *her* later.

Part 4

Objective

To use pronouns correctly as objects in sentences, particularly in compound objects

Presenting the Lesson

1. Review Part 3 in Chapter 8 (action verbs and direct objects).

2. Read and discuss Pronouns After Action Verbs on pages 161 and 162. Have the students refer once more to the pronouns listed on page 156, and try each one by itself as the object of a verb. Most students will naturally approve of each correct object pronoun by the way it sounds in the sentence.

3. Read and discuss Pronouns After Prepositions on pages 162 and 163. It is not important for students to completely understand prepositions at this time. (Prepositions are studied in Chapter 16.)

They should familiarize themselves with the use of prepositions and with the list of common prepositions on page 163. Again, stress the sound of the correct pronoun choice when used as the object of a preposition.

4. Assign and discuss Exercises A and B on page 163.

5. See Exercise D on page 167 for additional practice.

Optional Practice

Many students will insist on the incorrect pronoun choice *I* when selecting the first person pronoun used in a compound object. *Me* somehow seems less formal. Emphasize the choice of pronouns in a compound by the choice of each one separately. Few students who insist on "They chose he and I" will like the sound of "They chose I." Ask the students for original sentences using *me* correctly.

If you are not sure which pronoun to use, try each part separately.

Kay stopped (he, him) and (I, me).

Kay stopped him.
Kay stopped me.
Kay stopped him and me.

Pronouns After Prepositions

One kind of word always has a noun or pronoun after it, and shows a relationship between that noun or pronoun and the rest of the sentence. This kind of word is called a **preposition.** The noun or pronoun that follows a preposition is called the **object of the preposition.** Object pronouns are used as objects of prepositions.

	Preposition	Object
He called to Melina.	to	Melina
We waited for them.	for	them
I awoke at dawn.	at	dawn
Here is a letter from her.	from	her

In learning to talk, you learned to say *for me* rather than *for I*. You never say *to I*; you say *to me*.

Don't be fooled when there are a noun and a pronoun after a preposition. Don't be fooled when there are two pronouns after a preposition.

The presents are for Laura and *me*.
The presents are for *me*.

The driver called to *him* and *me*.
The driver called to *me*.

Use only object pronouns as objects of prepositions.

Here is a list of common prepositions:

of	with	under	over	along	below
in	at	about	across	around	beside
by	down	between	against	before	past
to	from	on	above	toward	behind
up	into	near	after	for	beneath

Exercises Choosing the Right Pronoun

A. Number your paper from 1 to 8. Write the verb. Choose the right pronoun to be used as the object of the verb.

Example: Help (we, us) and Nancy again, please. *help us*

1. Call (I, me) in the morning. call me
2. The sultan ruled (them, they) long and wisely. ruled them
3. Mom dropped Matt and (me, I) off at the City Hall. dropped me
4. The Kiwanis Club sponsored (he, him). sponsored him
5. Judy's dog led (them, they) to the lost child. led them
6. Ms. Lee complimented the class and (he, him) on the photos. complimented him
7. That owl scared Doug and (I, me) out of our wits. scared me
8. Don't you believe (she, her)? do believe her

B. Number your paper from 1 to 8. Write the preposition. Choose the right pronoun to be used as the object of the preposition.

Example: The flashlights are for Tina and (we, us). *for us*

1. You play against Lou and (he, him). against him
2. The choice is between (she, her) and Dorothy. between her
3. The dialogue was written by Kim and (I, me). by me
4. In the class picture, Pat's cousin Don is just above (she, her). above her
5. Dripping stalactites were all around (us, we). around us
6. The relay race depends on Francine and (he, him). on him
7. The skunk didn't even glance at Ross and (me, I). at me
8. The box for those envelopes is under (they, them). under them

Part 5

Objectives

1. To recognize and use the possessive pronouns

2. To distinguish between the possessive pronoun *its* and the contraction *it's*

Presenting the Lesson

1. Write this sentence on the board:

Here is Amy's sweater.

Ask students to identify the possessive noun. It may be necessary to review Chapter 7, Part 4, on possessive nouns. Ask students if they can suggest a pronoun to use in place of the noun.

2. Read and discuss page 164.

3. Assign and discuss the Exercise on page 164. Stress that each time a student adds an apostrophe, he or she should test the answer by substituting it is for *it's*. If the substitution does not fit, the answer is incorrect.

Optional Practice

Have students rewrite the following sentences, substituting possessive pronouns for the possessive nouns.

1. Ms. Walker's class is very busy.
2. The team's pennant is red and white.
3. Barry's hair is bright red.
4. The girls' pictures were in the newspaper.
5. The rabbit's leg was broken.

Part 5 Possessive Pronouns

To make the possessive form of a noun, you add an apostrophe or an apostrophe and an *s* to the noun. Pronouns have special possessive forms. These do not use apostrophes at all.

The possessive forms of pronouns are these:

my, mine	**our, ours**	**your, yours**
his, her, hers, its	**their, theirs**	

The only problem most people have with possessive pronouns is confusing the possessive *its* with the contraction *it's*. *Its* (without an apostrophe) is the possessive form of *it*. *It's* (with an apostrophe) means *it is* or *it has*.

The horse broke *its* leg. (The leg belongs to the horse.) *It's* having an operation tomorrow. (*It is* having an operation tomorrow.)

Exercise Using *Its* and *It's* Correctly

Copy the following sentences. Insert apostrophes where they are needed.

1. The rat lost its way in the maze. Correct
2. It's snowing throughout the Northwest.
3. Change the thermostat if it's set too low.
4. That stuffed dog lost a lot of its stuffing. Correct
5. Scoop up that groundball while it's fair.
6. K Mart ends its sale on school supplies next week. Correct
7. Leave the puzzle in its box. Correct
8. I hate gum when it's stuck in my hair.
9. The school started its basketball season last weekend. Correct
10. It's too late to go swimming now.

Sentence Patterns The N LV N Pattern

The **N LV N pattern** describes a sentence with three parts. The first *N* stands for the subject noun. *LV* stands for a linking verb. The second *N* stands for the noun that follows the linking verb.

N	LV	N
Chimpanzees	are	mammals.
Allen	is	my friend.
My favorite dessert	is	pudding.
The blizzard	was	a disaster.
Jade	is	a hard stone.

Exercises The N LV N Pattern

A. Make a chart like the one above. Label the three columns *N, LV,* and *N.* Write these sentences on the chart.

1. Dee is my sister.
2. Pumpkins are vegetables.
3. This chair is an antique.
4. The Tortugas are islands.
5. Pete is an artist.
6. Mushrooms are parasites.
7. The sun is a star.
8. My aunt is a jogger.

B. Make a chart like the one below. Complete each sentence in the N LV N pattern. Answers will vary.

N	LV	N
1. ________	is	a useful tool.
2. My best friend	was	________.
3. ________	are	reptiles.
4. The Riveras	________	my neighbors.
5. ________	are	________.

C. Make a chart of your own. Label the columns *N, LV,* and *N.* Write five sentences in the N LV N pattern.

Sentence Patterns

Objective

To recognize the basic word order in the N LV N sentence pattern

Presenting the Lesson

1. Read and discuss page 165. Review the meaning of linking verbs as presented in Chapters 8 and 9. Make it clear that, as with the N V and N V N patterns, each part of an N LV N sentence may have one or more than one word.

2. Assign and discuss Exercises A, B, and C on page 165. It may be helpful to write examples of N LV N sentences from Exercise C on the board for examination.

Extending the Lesson

Students have worked with Sentence Patterns on pages 123 and 150, as well as page 165. For practice with pronouns, have students work with these pages again, substituting pronouns for nouns wherever possible. For example, in the Exercises on page 165, the following substitutions can be made:

1. Dee is my sister.
   She is my sister.
2. Pumpkins are vegetables.
   They are vegetables.

Additional Exercises

If these Exercises were not used with each lesson, they may now be assigned for chapter review.

Additional Exercises

Using Pronouns

A. Using Pronouns (Use after page 156.)

Copy the following sentences. Underline the pronouns.

1. My aunt called them long distance in Alaska.
2. If your car won't start, take ours instead.
3. Tell Kevin to invite Mary when he sees her.
4. Mercury's winged sandals made his feet fly.
5. The Jacksons didn't take the trip. It was too expensive.
6. I saved my allowance but she spent hers.
7. Jonathan took his books with him.
8. Throw your best slider and watch me hit it.
9. The Plains Indians pitched their teepees near the waterhole.
10. You sound to me like an optimist.

B. Using Pronouns in the Subject (Use after page 158.)

Number your paper from 1 to 10. Choose the correct pronoun from the parentheses. Write it on your paper.

1. The boys and (them, they) made their skateboards.
2. (We, Us) kids vote for a picnic in Lion's Park.
3. (Them, They) and the rest of the parade lined up at 8:30.
4. (She, Her) and three boys from the science club organized the display.
5. Davy, (her, she), and (I, me) rode in the helicopter.
6. On Saturday, (they, them) and (me, I) cleaned out the Martins' garage.
7. (Her, She) and (he, him) were standing next to the door.
8. For our art project, (we, us) girls used yarn and cloth scraps.

9. (They, Them) and about twenty others hiked up Coconino Trail.
10. (Him, He) and his collie are always together.

C. Choosing the Right Pronoun (Use after page 160.)

Choose the right pronoun from the two in parentheses.

1. The volunteers were the boys and (they, them).
2. Your opponent will be Henry or (she, her).
3. The top students in math are Sally and (he, him).
4. The next contestants are you and (they, them).
5. The best storyteller in the school is (her, she).
6. The actors in the next scene are you and (he, him).
7. The caller at the square dance was (she, her).
8. Was it (he, him) who took the picture?
9. The only students absent today were Bonita and (him, he).
10. Is the next person (me, I) or (she, her)?

D. Choosing the Right Pronoun (Use after page 163.)

Number your paper from 1 to 10. Choose the right pronoun from the two in parentheses.

1. Lord Gascon ordered Mordleigh and (he, him) into a cold, dark dungeon.
2. Is the puzzle from (they, them) or Aunt Jill?
3. A beaver swam very close to Karen and (he, him).
4. The judges chose (she, her) and two other finalists.
5. Were you talking about (us, we) or (they, them)?
6. The ball didn't get past (her, she).
7. Here are some more strawberries for you and (they, them).
8. Did you count Delores and (I, me)?
9. Bayview isn't near (we, us).
10. The decision is up to (he, him) and (I, me).

Chapter 10

Using the Dictionary

What can you do when you come across a word you don't know? You can turn to a dictionary. The dictionary will tell you a lot about the word. It will explain its meaning, of course, but it will tell you much more. It will tell what other words have meanings like the word. It will also tell you the history of the word.

How can the history of a word help you? How can knowing other words with similar meanings help you? They will help you become familiar with the word. This means you can add another word to your growing vocabulary. You will be able to choose the best word to say what you want to say.

To make a dictionary help you, you must learn to use it. This chapter will show you how.

Chapter Objectives

1. To appreciate the uses of the dictionary
2. To develop skill in locating words in a dictionary
3. To recognize the various types of information found in a dictionary entry
4. To differentiate among the multiple meanings of a single word as presented in its entry
5. To use a synonymy

Preparing the Students

Ask students if they are familiar with the word game being played by the girl in the picture. (Scrabble) Have someone explain the procedure for playing Scrabble. Discuss the importance of knowing how to spell words correctly in playing the game. Ask them what they would do if they were unsure of the spelling of a particular word. They will undoubtedly suggest using a dictionary.

Have on hand as many different varieties of dictionaries as you can obtain, ranging from primary to unabridged. Include similar kinds from different publishers. Small groups of students should take turns examining the dictionaries. Have the students look at the arrangement of words on each page, the use of pictures, and the use of different kinds of type. Discuss the differences and similarities.

Additional Resources

Mastery Test—pages 457 and 458 in this T. E. Recommended for use after teaching the chapter.

Additional Mastery Test—Recommended for use after any necessary reteaching. (In separate booklet, *Diagnostic and Mastery Tests, Gold Level*, pages 33 and 34.)

Skills Practice Book—pages 61–65

Duplicating Masters—pages 61–65

Part 1

Objective

To arrange words in alphabetical order

Presenting the Lesson

1. Read and discuss pages 169 and 170. Be sure students understand how to alphabetize words, especially words that start with the same letters.

2. Assign and discuss the exercise on page 170.

3. See Exercise A on page 179 for additional practice.

Optional Practice

Prepare lists of words like those below. Have the students form teams. See how quickly the teams, or their representatives, can alphabetize each group of words. The first team that correctly alphabetizes the words earns points matching the difficulty of the list.

1	2
never	top
every	table
charity	terrible
zoo	turn
marble	tip

3	4
drain	chili
drown	chicken
drip	chill
dream	children
drug	Chicago

Part 1 Using Alphabetical Order To Find a Word

The words in a dictionary are listed in alphabetical order. The first words in a dictionary begin with *a*. The last ones begin with *z*. The words in between are also in alphabetical order. Words beginning with *p* come before words beginning with *q*, and so on.

Suppose two words begin with the same letter. Then they are alphabetized by the second letter. Suppose the second letters are the same. Then the words are alphabetized by the third letter, and so on.

The following groups of words are arranged in alphabetical order:

animal	man	chair
doll	mess	cherry
pocket	mitt	chill
rag	mop	chip

Exercise Using Alphabetical Order

Following are four groups of words. Arrange each group of words in alphabetical order.

	1		2		3		4
5	lemon	3	glue	8	players	5	Miami
4	grape	4	hammer	3	bat	1	Boston
6	lime	6	level	10	uniform	8	San Francisco
9	prune	8	saw	6	glove	7	New York
2	banana	1	chisel	7	helmet	2	Chicago
10	raspberry	5	lathe	1	ball	6	Montreal
1	apple	2	clamp	9	umpire	4	Los Angeles
8	peach	9	screwdriver	4	fans	10	Tulsa
7	nectarine	7	nails	2	base	3	Houston
3	cherry	10	wood	5	field	9	Toronto

Part 2 Using Guide Words

To find words quickly, learn to open the dictionary to the right spot. Open your dictionary at a spot that seems close to the middle. You should be in the *l*'s or *m*'s. If you are looking for a word that begins with a letter from *a* through *l*, look in the first half of the dictionary. If the word begins with a letter from *m* through *z*, look in the second half.

If you practice opening your dictionary to a specific letter, you will be able to find words more quickly.

Once you have opened to the right letter, look at the **guide words.** The guide words are found at the top of each page. The guide word on the left tells you the first word on the page. The guide word on the right tells you the last word on the page. Flip through the pages quickly. Look for guide words that come before and after the word you want.

On page 173 you will find the reproduction of a dictionary page. The guide words are *pliers* and *plumate.* Notice that all the other words fall between these two in alphabetical order.

Exercises Using Alphabetical Order and Guide Words

A. Working with a classmate, practice opening the dictionary as close as you can to a particular letter. Have your classmate say a letter. Try to open your dictionary to that letter. Then switch roles and say a letter for your classmate. Continue until you can open the dictionary close to a specific letter most of the time.

B. Do the same thing you did in Exercise A, but use words instead of letters. Use the guide words to help you find the word your partner names. Continue until you can find a word quickly.

Part 2

Objective

To understand the function of guide words

Presenting the Lesson

1. Read and discuss page 171. Stress that guide words are a useful aid for quickly locating words in the dictionary only if alphabetizing skills have been mastered.

The dictionary page reproduced on page 173 is taken from *Webster's New World Dictionary of the American Language,* Students Edition (William Collins & World Publishing Company, Inc., 1976). This edition is the source of every dictionary excerpt used in this chapter.

2. Students should work in pairs to do Exercises A and B on page 171. Circulate among the pairs to ensure that students stay at their task.

3. Exercise C on page 172 can be assigned for individual practice or can be used as material for a competition between two teams of students.

4. See Exercise B on page 179 for additional practice.

Optional Practice

Present the following word lists to the class. Instruct the students to assume that each pair of words serve as guide words on a given dictionary page. Have them decide whether each word listed in the group with the matching number would be found *on* that page, *before* that page, or *after* that page.

1. **huddle**	**humor**
2. **romance**	**room**
3. **calm**	**can**

1.	2.	3.
huge	roof	career
hurdle	rose	came
hymn	row	camp
humid	Rome	care
hose	robe	cane

C. Remember that the purpose of guide words is to help you find words more quickly. See how quickly you can find the following words in your dictionary. Copy the guide words from the page where you find each word. Answers depend on dictionary used.

ladybug	goat	falcon	gazelle	snake
kiwi	iguana	sailfish	narwhal	bat
pheasant	millipede	trawler	lamprey	cricket

Part 3 Getting Information About a Word

The information a dictionary gives about a word is called the **entry.** There is much information given in each entry. Let's take a dictionary entry apart and look at its different parts. We'll use the entry for the word *plot* on the dictionary page reproduced on page 173.

Entry Word

plot

The first part of an entry is the word. In most dictionaries it is divided into syllables. This is done with a space or a centered dot.

Pronunciation

(plät)

The next part of an entry is the pronunciation. In most dictionaries the pronunciation is printed in parentheses. When you pronounce a two-syllable word, one syllable gets a stronger emphasis than the other. You say PLIers and PLUMage. You put a heavier emphasis on the first syllable of each of these words. The emphasis is shown in a dictionary by using accent marks (ʹ).

pli·ers (plīʹərz)
plum·age (plo͞oʹmij)

Part 3

Objective

To recognize the various types of information found in a dictionary entry

Presenting the Lesson

1. Read and discuss each of the subdivisions of Part 3, on pages 172 to 175.

2. Entry and Entry Word: Clarify the difference between an entry and an entry word. Ask the students to count all of the entry words on page 173. How many are there in all? (32)

3. Pronunciation: Point out that the second syllable in *pronunciation* is *nun* and not *noun.* Many students say it incorrectly. Have the students read several of the words in the pronunciation key on page 172. After each word, point out the special marks or letters used in it. Ask for other words with the same sound.

Translation of the phonetic spelling is sometimes difficult for students. Write the following words on the board and ask the students to determine their pronunciation from the entries on page 173: *Pliocene, plisse, plough, ploy, plumage.*

pli·ers (plī′ərz) ***n.pl.*** [< PLY[1]] small pincers for gripping small objects, bending wire, etc.

plight[1] (plīt) ***n.*** [< Anglo-Fr. *plit*, for OFr. *pleit*, a fold] a condition or state of affairs; esp., an awkward, sad, or dangerous situation [the *plight* of the men trapped in the mine]

plight[2] (plīt) ***vt.*** [OE. *plihtan*, to pledge < *pliht*, danger] to pledge or promise, or bind by a pledge —**plight one's troth** to make a promise of marriage

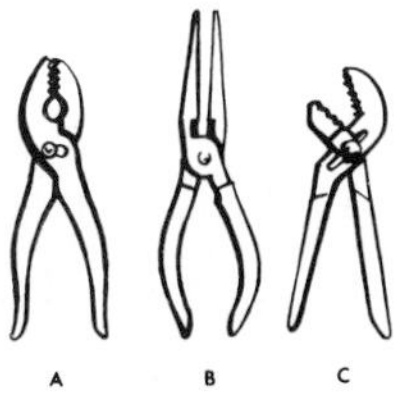

PLIERS (A, slip joint; B, needle nose; C, arc joint)

Plim·soll mark (or **line**) (plim′səl, -säl, -sôl) [after S. *Plimsoll* (1824–98), Eng. statesman] a line or set of lines on the outside of merchant ships, showing the water level to which they may legally be loaded

☆**plink** (pliŋk) ***n.*** [echoic] a light, sharp, ringing or clinking sound —***vt., vi.*** **1.** to make such sounds on (a piano, banjo, etc.) **2.** to shoot at (tin cans, etc.)

plinth (plinth) ***n.*** [< L. < Gr. *plinthos*, a brick, tile] **1.** the square block at the base of a column, pedestal, etc. **2.** the base on which a statue rests

Plin·y (plin′ē) **1.** (L. name *Gaius Plinius Secundus*) 23–79 A.D.; Rom. naturalist & writer: called *the Elder* **2.** (L. name *Gaius Plinius Caecilius Secundus*) 62?–113? A.D.; Rom. writer & statesman: called *the Younger:* nephew of *Pliny the Elder*

Pli·o·cene (plī′ə sēn′) ***adj.*** [< Gr. *pleōn*, more + *kainos*, new] designating or of the last epoch of the Tertiary Period in the Cenozoic Era —**the Pliocene** the Pliocene Epoch or its rocks: see GEOLOGIC TIME CHART

☆**Pli·o·film** (plī′ə film′) [< PLIABLE + FILM] *a trademark for* a sheeting of rubber hydrochloride used for raincoats, as a covering for packages, etc.

plis·sé, plis·se (pli sā′) ***n.*** [< Fr. < pp. of *plisser*, to pleat] **1.** a crinkled finish given to cotton, nylon, etc. with a caustic soda solution **2.** a fabric with this finish

plod (pläd) ***vi.* plod′ded, plod′ding** [prob. echoic] **1.** to walk or move heavily and with effort; trudge [the old horse *plodded* along the street] **2.** to work steadily and monotonously; drudge [to *plod* away at one's work] —***n.*** **1.** the act of plodding **2.** the sound of a heavy step —**plod′der *n.*** —**plod′ding·ly *adv.***

-ploid (ploid) [< Gr. *-ploos*, -fold + -OID] *a combining form meaning* of or being a (specified) multiple of the basic (haploid) number of chromosomes characteristic of a group of related organisms [*diploid*]

plonk (pläŋk, pluŋk) ***vt., vi., n.*** *same as* PLUNK

plop (pläp) ***vt., vi.* plopped, plop′ping** [echoic] **1.** to drop with a sound like that of something flat falling into water **2.** to drop heavily —***n.*** the act of plopping or the sound made by this —***adv.*** with a plop

plo·sive (plō′siv) ***adj.*** [< (EX)PLOSIVE] *Phonet.* produced by stopping and then suddenly releasing the breath, as the sounds of *k*, *p*, and *t* when used at the beginning of words —***n.*** a plosive sound

plot (plät) ***n.*** [OE., a piece of land] **1.** a small area of ground [a garden *plot*] **2.** a chart or diagram, as of a building or estate **3.** a secret, usually evil, scheme **4.** the plan of action of a play, novel, etc. —***v.* plot′ted, plot′ting** **1.** *a)* to draw a plan of (a ship's course, etc.) *b)* to mark the position or course of on a map **2.** to make secret plans for [to *plot* a robbery] **3.** to plan the action of (a story, etc.) **4.** *a)* to determine the location of (a point) on a graph by means of coordinates *b)* to represent (an equation) by joining points on a graph to form a curve **5.** to plan together secretly; scheme [to *plot* against the king] —**plot′less *adj.*** —**plot′less·ness *n.*** —**plot′ter *n.***

SYN.—**plot** is used of a secret, usually evil, project or scheme the details of which have been carefully worked out [a *plot* to keep him from getting his inheritance]; **intrigue**, implying more complicated scheming, suggests hidden, underhanded dealing often of an illegal nature [the *intrigues* of the royal court]; **machination** emphasizes trickery and slyness in forming plots intended to harm someone [the *machinations* of the villain]; **conspiracy** suggests a plot in which a number of people plan and act together secretly for an unlawful or harmful purpose [a *conspiracy* to seize the throne]; **cabal** suggests a small group of persons involved in a political intrigue

plough (plou) ***n., vt., vi.*** *chiefly Brit. sp. of* PLOW

plov·er (pluv′ər, plō′vər) ***n.***, *pl.* **plov′ers, plov′er:** see PLURAL, II, D, 1 [< OFr., ult. < L. *pluvia*, rain] a shore bird with a short tail, long, pointed wings, and a short beak

PLOVER (to 11 in. high)

plow (plou) ***n.*** [ME. *ploh* < Late OE.] **1.** a farm implement used to cut and turn up the soil ☆**2.** anything like this; specif., a SNOWPLOW —***vt.*** **1.** to cut and turn up (soil) with a plow **2.** to make furrows in with or as with a plow **3.** to make as if by plowing [he *plowed* his way through the crowd] **4.** to cut a way through (water) —***vi.*** **1.** to use a plow in tilling the soil **2.** to cut a way (*through* water, etc.) **3.** to go forward with effort; plod **4.** to begin work vigorously (with *into*) **5.** to strike against forcefully (with *into*) —**plow back** to reinvest (profits) in the same business enterprise —**plow up** **1.** to remove with a plow **2.** to till (soil) thoroughly —**plow′a·ble *adj.*** —**plow′er *n.***

plow·boy (plou′boi′) ***n.*** **1.** formerly, a boy who led a team of horses drawing a plow **2.** a country boy

plow·man (plou′mən) ***n.***, *pl.* **-men** **1.** a man who guides a plow **2.** a farm worker

plow·share (-sher′) ***n.*** the share, or cutting blade, of a moldboard plow

ploy (ploi) ***n.*** [? < (EM)PLOY] an action or maneuver intended to outwit or confuse another person in order to get the better of him

pluck (pluk) ***vt.*** [OE. *pluccian:* for IE. base see PILE[2]] **1.** to pull off or out; pick [to *pluck* an apple from a tree] **2.** to drag or snatch; grab [he *plucked* a burning stick from the fire] **3.** to pull feathers or hair from [to *pluck* a chicken, *pluck* eyebrows] **4.** to pull at (the strings of a musical instrument) and release quickly to sound tones **5.** [Slang] to rob or swindle —***vi.*** **1.** to pull; tug; snatch (often with *at*) [he *plucked* at his long mustache] **2.** to pluck a musical instrument —***n.*** **1.** a pulling; tug **2.** courage to meet danger or difficulty; fortitude —**pluck up** to stir up one's (courage); take heart —**pluck′er *n.***

pluck·y (pluk′ē) ***adj.* pluck′i·er, pluck′i·est** brave; spirited; determined —see ***SYN.*** at BRAVE —**pluck′i·ly *adv.*** —**pluck′i·ness *n.***

plug (plug) ***n.*** [MDu. *plugge*] **1.** an object used to stop up a hole, drain, etc. **2.** *a)* a cake of pressed tobacco *b)* a piece of chewing tobacco **3.** a device, as with prongs that stick out, for fitting into an electric outlet, etc. to make electrical contact **4.** *same as: a)* SPARK PLUG *b)* FIREPLUG **5.** [Colloq.] a defective or shopworn article ☆**6.** [Slang] an old, worn-out horse ☆**7.** [Colloq.] a boost, advertisement, etc., esp. one slipped into the entertainment part of a radio or TV program, a magazine article, etc. —***vt.* plugged, plug′ging** **1.** to stop up (a hole, etc.) with a plug (often with *up*) **2.** to insert (something) as a plug [he *plugged* the putty in the hole] **3.** [Colloq.] *a)* to promote (a song) by frequent performance ☆*b)* to promote with a plug (*n.* 7) **4.** [Slang] to shoot a bullet into —***vi.*** [Colloq.] to work or study hard and steadily; plod —**plug in** to connect (an electrical device) with an outlet, etc. by inserting a plug in a socket or jack —**plug′ger *n.***

☆**plug hat** [Old Slang] a man's high silk hat

☆**plug·o·la** (plug′ō lə) ***n.*** [PLUG, *n.* 7 + (PAY)OLA] [Slang] the paying of a bribe, or a bribe paid, for the dishonest promotion of something or someone on radio or TV

☆**plug-ug·ly** (-ug′lē) ***n.***, *pl.* **-lies** [Old Slang] a ruffian or gangster

plum (plum) ***n.*** [OE. *plume*] **1.** *a)* any of various small trees bearing a smooth-skinned fruit with a flattened stone *b)* the fruit eaten as food **2.** a raisin, when used in pudding or cake [*plum* pudding] **3.** the dark bluish-red or reddish-purple color of some plums **4.** something excellent or desirable [the new contract is a rich *plum* for the company]

plum·age (plo͞o′mij) ***n.*** [MFr. < L. *pluma*, a feather] a bird's feathers

plu·mate (-māt, -mit) ***adj.*** [< L. *pluma*, a feather] *Zool.* resembling a feather, esp. in structure

4. Parts of Speech: Remind the students that nouns and verbs are two large groups of words. Explain briefly that the other parts of speech are names of other groups of words. Complete explanations of the other parts of speech will be presented in later chapters.

5. Word origin: The original language is usually given in an abbreviation. Make sure students are familiar with the following abbreviations:

OE	(Old English)	L	(Latin)
ME	(Middle English)	Gk	(Greek)
OFr	(Old French)	Sp	(Spanish)

Make sure, also, that the students understand the meaning of the symbol < (is derived from).

6. Synonyms: Explain that synonyms are words that have similar meanings. Their meanings are never exactly the same, however. Read through the list of synonyms for *plot.*
Are students familiar with all the synonyms given there? Caution them against using synonyms whose specific meaning they do not fully understand.

Optional Practice

One of the most difficult tasks for students is to apply the information from a pronunciation key to the actual pronunciation of a new word. To help familiarize students with this process try the following exercise. Use the sample dictionary page on page 173.

Which word in the pronunciation key tells how to pronounce each of the following?

1. The *i* in *pliers* (bite)
2. The *u* in *plug* (up)
3. The *o* in *plop* (car)
4. The *oy* in *plowboy* (oil)
5. The *y* in *Pliny* (even)

Notice that in the pronunciations the words have been respelled. These respellings are slightly different from the normal spellings. This kind of spelling is a way of showing the sounds in the word. In the word *plot,* the letter *o* stands for the short *o* sound. The dictionary shows this sound as *ä.* At the bottom of the right-hand pages of most dictionaries there is a pronunciation key. This explains the respellings and tells you how to pronounce the words.

Part of Speech

After the pronunciation, the dictionary tells what part of speech the word is. Most dictionaries use abbreviations for this. Here is a list of the abbreviations and their meanings.

n. = noun	**pro.** = pronoun	**conj.** = conjunction
v. = verb	**adv.** = adverb	**interj.** = interjection
adj. = adjective	**prep.** = preposition	

Some words may be used as more than one part of speech. These words have more than one abbreviation. Each abbreviation for a part of speech is followed by the definition. For example, the word *plot* is first defined as a noun (**n.**). Then it is defined as a verb (**v.**).

Word Origin

[OE., a piece of land]

Next comes the origin of the word. This tells what language first used the word.

Definition

plot (plät) **n.** [OE., a piece of land] **1.** a small area of ground *[a garden plot]* **2.** a chart or diagram, as of a building or estate. **3.** a secret, usually evil, scheme **4.** the plan of action of a play, novel, etc. —**v. plot'ted, plot'ting 1.** *a*) to draw a plan of (a ship's course, etc.) *b*) to mark the position or course of on a map **2.** to make secret plans for *[to plot a robbery]* **3.** to plan the action of (a story, etc.) **4.** *a*) to determine the location of (a point) on a graph by means of coordinates *b*) to represent (an equation) by joining points on a graph to form a curve **5.** to plan together secretly; scheme *[to plot against the king]* —**plot'less** ***adj.*** —**plot'less·ness** ***n.*** —**plot'ter** ***n.***

The largest part of a dictionary entry is the definition. The definition is an explanation of the meaning of a word.

Synonyms

SYN:—**plot** is used of a secret, usually evil, project or scheme the details of which have been carefully worked out [a *plot* to keep him from getting his inheritance]; **intrigue**, implying more complicated scheming, suggests hidden, underhanded dealing often of an illegal nature [the *intrigues* of the royal court]; **machination** emphasizes trickery and slyness in forming plots intended to harm someone [the *machinations* of the villain]; **conspiracy** suggests a plot in which a number of people plan and act together secretly for an unlawful or harmful purpose [a *conspiracy* to seize the throne]; **cabal** suggests a small group of persons involved in a political intrigue

One last part is found in some entries. It is a list of synonyms. This is useful for choosing the best word to say what you want to say. In Chapter 2 you were using synonyms when you chose specific words to say exactly what you meant.

Part 4 The Multiple Meanings of a Word

Many English words have more than one meaning. When you look up a word, you will have to choose the meaning that fits what you are reading.

Look up the word *go* in your dictionary. How many definitions are given for it? The Student Edition of *Webster's New World Dictionary of the American Language* gives forty definitions for this one word!

Look at the definitions for the word *pluck* on page 173. Notice that for most of the definitions there is a sentence or phrase given as an example. These examples show how the word is used for a particular definition. Sometimes these examples are as much help to you as the definitions themselves. Also notice that each definition is numbered.

Extending the Lesson

Have students use the sample dictionary page on page 173 to answer the following questions.

1. What is the slang use of the word **pluck?**
2. Does the first syllable of **plumage** rhyme with the word *plum?*
3. Which synonym of **plot** implies complicated scheming and suggests hidden and underhanded dealings?
4. What is the meaning of the phrase "to plight one's troth"?
5. What entry word means the same as the word **plough?**

Part 4

Objective

To differentiate among the multiple meanings of a single word as presented in its entry

Presenting the Lesson

1. Read and discuss pages 175 and 176. Note the differences in the meaning of the word *pluck* in each of the sentences at the top of page 176.

2. Assign the Exercise on pages 176 and 177. Discuss when completed.

3. See Exercise C on page 179 for additional practice.

Optional Practice

Have the students explain the difference in the meaning of *run* in each of the following sentences.

He will *run* around the track three times.

The train *runs* from Chicago to Kansas City.

There was a *run* on the bank.

The player scored a *run* in the last inning of the game.

There is a *run* in the nylon material.

In each of the following sentences the word *pluck* is used with a different meaning.

John plucked at his long mustache.

I felt a pluck at my sleeve.

Sandy plucked an apple from the tree.

It is easy to pluck the strings of a guitar.

It took pluck to rescue the drowning girl.

Exercise The Multiple Meanings of a Word

Number a sheet of paper from 1 to 10. Use the following dictionary entry for *front.* Write the number of the definition that fits each sentence on page 177. Choose from the first fifteen definitions in the entry.

Dictionary Entry for *front*

front (frunt) **n.** [< OFr. < L. *frontis,* genitive of *frons,* forehead] **1.** outward behavior or appearance, esp. when merely pretended [to put on a bold *front*] **2.** the part of something that faces forward; most important side **3.** the first part; beginning [toward the *front* of the book] **4.** the place or position directly before a person or thing **5.** a forward or leading position or situation ☆**6.** the first available bellhop, as in a hotel **7.** the land bordering a lake, ocean, street, etc. **8.** the most forward area, where actual fighting is going on in a war **9.** a specified area of activity [the home *front*] **10.** a broad movement in which different groups are united in order to achieve certain political or social aims ☆**11.** a person who serves as a public representative of a business, group, etc., as because of his prestige ☆**12.** a person, group, etc. used to cover up some activity, esp. an illegal one [the barber shop was a *front* for the numbers racket] **13.** a stiff shirt bosom, worn with formal clothes **14.** a face of a building; esp., the face with the principal entrance **15.** *Meteorol.* the boundary between two masses of air that are different, as in density ***—adj.*** **1.** at, to, in, on, or of the front **2.** *Phonet.* sounded toward the front of the mouth [*i* in *bid* and *e* in *met* are *front* vowels] ***—vt.*** **1.** to face; be opposite to [our cottage *fronts* the ocean] **2.** to be before in place **3.** to meet; confront **4.** to defy; oppose **5.** to supply or be a front to [white stone *fronts* the building] ***—vi.*** **1.** to face in a certain direction ☆**2.** to be a front (senses 11 & 12) (with *for*) **—in front of** before; ahead of

1. The directions were in the front of the pamphlet. 3
2. She is at the front of all class activities. 5
3. He built his house on the ocean front. 7
4. The weather report said that a warm front is on the way. 15
5. When Martha was in the war, she was stationed at the front. 8
6. People on the home front joined Civil Defense. 9
7. The front of the church, including the steps, had caved in. 14
8. The senator is a front for the big oil companies. 11
9. The desk clerk called "Front!" when she saw my luggage. 6
10. He puts up a front to hide his nervousness. 1

Part 5 Synonyms

Synonyms are words that have similar meanings. The words *small* and *tiny* are synonyms. The words *tall* and *high* are also synonyms. However, synonyms do not have exactly the same meanings. They usually cannot be substituted for each other.

Look at the dictionary entry for *plot* on page 173. After the definition there is an abbreviation ***SYN.*** This abbreviation stands for *synonyms*. The list of synonyms for a word is called a **synonymy.**

Notice that the synonymy for *plot* does more than just list its synonyms. It also explains the special meaning and use of each of these words. Sometimes a synonymy will give sample phrases or sentences to help explain how each is used.

Often, a synonymy will help you choose the best word for what you want to say. Did Flight 766 *go, depart, leave,* or *withdraw* at midnight? A synonymy will explain the differences between each of these words. Then you can choose the best one.

Exercise Synonyms

A. Use your dictionary to find two synonyms for six of the following words. Use each synonym in a sentence to show its meaning. Answers will vary.

Part 5

Objective

To use a synonymy

Presenting the Lesson

1. Read and discuss page 177. Emphasize that even though synonyms have similar meanings, they are rarely interchangeable. Which word did students select to fit the sentence about Flight 766? Why did they make the choice they did?

2. Assign and discuss the Exercises on pages 177 and 178.

Optional Practice

Here is a second set of words to be used with the directions for Exercise A on page 177.

order	color	improve
root	division	notify
destroy	steal	thin

Extending the Lesson

Remind students that the specific meaning of a word is called its *denotation* and that the general meaning of a word is called its *connotation.* The connotation of a word often includes certain feelings about that word. Ask students to explain the difference in connotation for each of these pairs of synonyms.

house/home	punish/discipline
skinny/thin	crowd/mob

explain	fault	last	group
give	perform	use	large
strike	bait	anger	regard

B. Number your paper from 1 to 5. Use the following dictionary entry for *firm.* In each of the following sentences replace the word *firm* with one of its synonyms. Use the entry to choose the synonym that fits best.

Dictionary Entry for *firm*

firm[1] (furm) **adj.** [< OFr. < L. *firmus*] **1.** not giving way easily under pressure; solid [*firm* muscles] **2.** not moved or shaken easily; fixed; stable [he stood as *firm* as a rock] **3.** remaining the same; steady [a *firm* friendship] **4.** unchanging; constant [a *firm* faith] **5.** showing determination, strength, etc. [a *firm* command] **6.** formally settled; definite; final [a *firm* contract] —***vt., vi.*** to make or become firm; often with *up* [exercise will *firm* up flabby muscles] —**firm'ly** ***adv.*** —**firm'ness** ***n.***
SYN.—**firm** refers to something whose parts hold together so tightly that it does not give way easily under pressure or springs back into shape after being pressed [*firm* flesh]; **hard** is applied to that which is so firm that it is not easily cut into or crushed [*hard* as rock]; **solid** refers to something which is firm or hard and suggests that it is heavy or has its parts packed close together [*solid* muscle]; **stiff** is used of that which is not easily bent or stretched [a *stiff* collar]

---

1. Allyn's legs are very firm after running yesterday. solid
2. I assure you that the bank's vault door is quite firm. solid
3. Maple is the firmest wood sold at the lumber yard. hardest
4. Brand new clothes are sometimes so firm that they have to be washed before they can be worn. stiff
5. "This mattress is as firm as a rock!" complained Bill. hard

Additional Exercises

Using the Dictionary

A. Using Alphabetical Order (Use after page 170.)

Arrange the following words in alphabetical order.

5 Fiat	6 Ford	3 Datsun	1 Buick	13 Toyota
4 Dodge	8 Mercedes	11 Saab	14 Triumph	15 Volvo
12 Subaru	9 Pontiac	10 Porsche	2 Cadillac	7 Jaguar

B. Using Guide Words (Use after page 171.)

Below are the guide words for ten dictionary pages. Copy the guide words on your paper. Beside each pair, write a word that you would find on that page.

anther	**antidote**	**one**	**ooze**
drill	**drop**	**prize**	**procession**
fisher	**fix**	**rondo**	**rose**
immune	**impel**	**stir**	**stock**
matted	**maximum**	**vanilla**	**various**

C. The Multiple Meanings of a Word (Use after page 176.)

Read the sentences below. Each of the italicized words has an unusual meaning. Use your dictionary to find the meanings.

1. My mother allowed me to get a *hunch* of fudge. chunk, lump
2. People haven't worn *ruffs* since the seventeenth century. frilled collars
3. Aaron is Lauren's *spark*. beau, boyfriend
4. He tried to *cow* us by telling a scary story. frighten, intimidate
5. The magician did several good *wrinkles*. tricks
6. Because the ship was always *listing*, many of the passengers became sick. tilting to one side
7. In the attic was an old bear *fell* rug. hide or skin
8. We all agreed that John *jigged* well. danced

Additional Exercises

Assign these Exercises for chapter review if they have not already been used with each of the lessons.

Chapter 11

Using the Library

Libraries offer helpful and interesting information on thousands of topics. They offer books for enjoyment, reference books for facts and information, magazines and records, and many other useful materials.

This chapter will help you understand how books are arranged in a library. It will also describe the kinds of books usually found there. This information will help you become a more efficient library user.

Part 1 The Classification and Arrangement of Books

Since a library has so many books, finding one book among the hundreds or thousands may appear at first to be impossible. However, the job is not really difficult when you know what you are

Chapter Objectives

1. To understand the classification of books as fiction or nonfiction

2. To become familiar with the Dewey Decimal System of classifying nonfiction books

3. To understand the function of call numbers

4. To use the card catalog to locate books

5. To use the encyclopedia efficiently

Preparing the Students

The school library will be a valuable resource while teaching this chapter. Discuss your needs and expectations with the librarian. If possible, arrange to have your class meet in the library for one or more sessions. The librarian may wish to supplement your lessons with activities that pertain directly to your school's library and its procedures.

If you do not have access to a school library, or yours cannot accommodate your entire class, assemble a collection of library materials for use in your classroom. A trip to the nearest public library may be a reasonable consideration for a field trip.

Additional Resources

Mastery Test—pages 459 and 460 in this T.E. Recommended for use after teaching the chapter.

Additional Mastery Test—Recommended for use after any necessary reteaching. (In separate booklet, *Diagnostic and Mastery Tests, Gold Level,* pages 35 and 36.)

Skills Practice Book—pages 66–71

Duplicating Masters—pages 66–71

Part 1

Objectives

1. To understand the classification of books as fiction or nonfiction
2. To become familiar with the Dewey Decimal System of classifying nonfiction books
3. To understand the function of call numbers

Presenting the Lesson

1. This Part has three major divisions: alphabetical arrangement of fiction books; the Dewey system of arranging nonfiction books; and an explanation of call numbers. Each division is followed by two exercises. Because of the difficulty of the material, it is recommended that the Part be covered in at least three lessons.
2. Read and discuss pages 181 and 182. Ask students to name some fiction books they have read. Are they familiar with the works of Carolyn A. Adams, Betsy Byars, or Beverly Cleary?
3. Assign the Exercises on page 183.
4. Read the section on nonfiction on pages 183 and 184. Be sure that students see differences among the ten Dewey Decimal System categories.
5. Assign and discuss Exercise A on pages 184 and 185. Exercise B can be completed only if a visit to the school library is planned. It may be helpful to supply copies of the basic floorplan to be filled in with details during the visit.
6. Read and discuss pages 185 to 187. To help students understand the classes of books discussed (biographies and autobi-

doing. Books in the library are arranged in a certain way. Learning about the arrangement of books will help you locate any book quickly.

The Classification of Books

Books in the library are divided into two groups: *fiction* and *nonfiction*. Each group is arranged according to a different system.

Fiction

Fiction books are stories that were made up by a writer, or *author*. Since fiction comes from the author's imagination, it is not necessarily true. The writer of a fiction book may base a story on some real events or experiences, but then invent certain elements to make a good story. All fiction books are grouped together in the library.

Fiction books are arranged on shelves alphabetically according to the author's last name.

For example, books by an author whose last name is *Adams* are placed before books by an author named *Byars*. Books by *Byars* are placed before those by *Cleary*.

If someone has written more than one book, all of those books are placed together on the shelf. They are then arranged alphabetically by the first word in the title. Words like *a, an,* or *the* are not considered in arranging titles alphabetically. If a title begins with *a, an,* or *the,* it should be alphabetized by the second word in the title. For example, *The Good Master,* by Kate Seredy, would be alphabetized under G, rather than T.

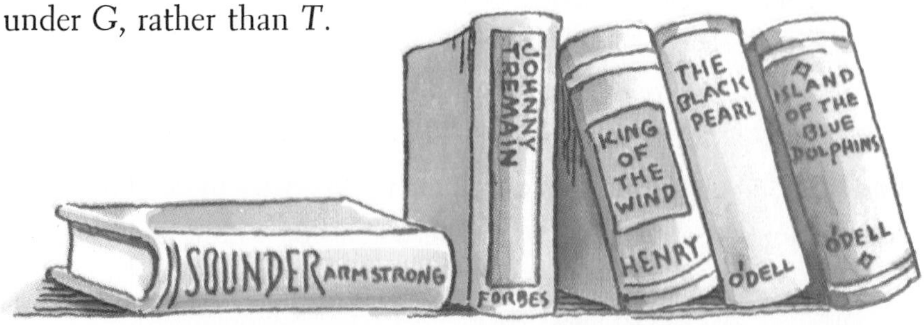

Exercises Arranging Fiction Books

A. On a separate sheet of paper, arrange these fiction titles and authors in the order in which they should appear on the shelves.

4	1. George, Jean	*My Side of the Mountain*
2	2. Burnford, Sheila	*The Incredible Journey*
12	3. Speare, Elizabeth	*The Witch of Blackbird Pond*
9	4. Neufeld, John	*Edgar Allan*
11	5. Sherburne, Zoa	*Jennifer*
8	6. Klein, Norma	*Mom, the Wolf Man, and Me*
7	7. Kjelgaard, Jim	*Outlaw Red*
3	8. Gault, William	*The Last Lap*
6	9. Kjelgaard, Jim	*Big Red*
1	10. Bonham, Frank	*Durango Street*
10	11. Pease, Howard	*The Jinx Ship*
5	12. Gilson, Jamie	*Harvey, the Beer Can King*

B. On a separate sheet of paper, alphabetize these titles of fiction books, all of which were written by Marguerite Henry.

4 1. *King of the Wind*
5 2. *Misty of Chincoteague*
3 3. *Justin Morgan Had a Horse*
2 4. *Brighty of the Grand Canyon*
1 5. *Benjamin West and His Cat Grimalkin*

Nonfiction

Nonfiction books are books reporting facts or ideas. They contain information on every subject you can think of. The books are classified and arranged according to their subjects. The classification system used most often is the **Dewey Decimal System.**

The Dewey Decimal System classifies all nonfiction books into one of ten major categories. The chart on the next page lists the ten Dewey categories:

ographies, short story collections, and reference books), provide samples of these kinds of books for students' examination.

7. Assign and discuss Exercises A and B on pages 187 and 188.

Optional Practice

1. The following fiction books were all written by Robert Newton Peck. Ask students to arrange them in the order that they would be found on the shelf.

Soup
Bee Tree and Other Stuff
Soup for President
Fawn
Soup and Me
Trig

Would books written by the author Richard Peck be found before or after those listed above?

2. When visiting the school library, ask students to locate one example of a book for each of the ten Dewey Decimal categories. They should list its title, author, and exact call number.

Extending the Lesson

1. Have a committee of students research the Library of Congress classification system. They should report their findings to the class.

2. Design a "Library Hunt," using materials in the school library. Students begin with instructions that lead them to a particular book. The next clue is on that book and leads to another location in the library. Create as many steps as can be handled in one class period. Discuss the results.

The Dewey Decimal System

000–099	**General Works**	(encyclopedias, almanacs, handbooks)
100–199	**Philosophy**	(conduct, ethics, psychology)
200–299	**Religion**	(the Bible, mythology, theology)
300–399	**Social Science**	(economics, law, education, commerce, government, folklore, legend)
400–499	**Language**	(languages, grammar, dictionaries)
500–599	**Science**	(mathematics, chemistry, physics)
600–699	**Useful Arts**	(farming, cooking, sewing, radio, nursing, engineering, television, business, gardening, cars)
700–799	**Fine Arts**	(music, painting, drawing, acting, photography, games, sports)
800–899	**Literature**	(poetry, plays, essays)
900–999	**History**	(biography, travel, geography)

All nonfiction books on the same subject are placed together in the same category, numbered by hundreds. For example, all science books are given the number 500.

Each category is divided into ten sections, numbered by tens. Those science books that are about animals, for example, are given the number 590.

Each section is divided into ten smaller sections, numbered by ones. Books about animals in the cat family have the number 599.

In this way, the books in each smaller section are closely related in subject.

Exercises The Dewey Decimal System

A. Using the ten major categories of the Dewey Decimal System, assign the correct category number to each of the following nonfiction books.

500 1. *The Rainbow Book of Nature* by Donald Peattie
300 2. *The Legends of Hawaii* by Padraic Colum
500 3. *Ecology* by Peter Farb
600 4. *Illustrated Motor Cars of the World* by Piet Olyslager
700 5. *Making Mosiacs* by Edmond Arvois
000 6. *Compton's Encyclopedia*
700 7. *The World of Ballet* by Anne Geraghty
900 8. *Ancient China* by John Hay
800 9. *Poetry Handbook* by Babette Deutsch
400 10. *The Story of Language* by Mario Pei

B. Draw a floor plan of your school library. Mark carefully each section that represents a classification of the Dewey Decimal System. Also, include the section where fiction books are shelved.

Call Numbers

In the Dewey Decimal System, a specific identification number is assigned to every nonfiction book. This identification number, known as the **call number** of the book, is like the address of the book. It tells exactly where each book in the library belongs on the shelves. The call number helps you locate books on the shelves.

Every nonfiction book has its call number on its spine.

Look at the call number of the following book. Notice how each part of the call number helps to identify the book:

Book: *Outdoor Survival*
Author: Charles Platt
Call Number: **796.5**
P422o

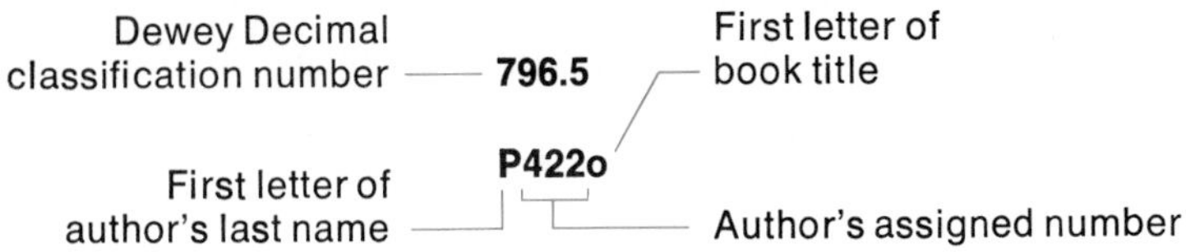

The top line of the call number identifies the subject of the book. The lower line identifies the author.

Among books classified by the Dewey system are three sections that deserve special attention.

Biography. A **biography** is the true story of a person's life written by another individual. An **autobiography** is the true story of a person's life written by the person himself or herself. Because biographies and autobiographies are true life stories, they are kept together among the nonfiction books. The Dewey class numbers for biography are 920 and 921.

920 This class number is reserved for collective biographies. These books contain the life story of more than one person. Collective biographies are arranged according to the author's last name. The call number of a collective biography is made up of 920 plus the first initial of the author's last name. For example, this is the call number of *Famous Underwater Adventurers* by Frederick Wagner:

920	Collective biography
W	First initial of Wagner

921 This class number is used for individual biographies and autobiographies. Such books contain the life story of a single person. These books are arranged on the shelf by the last name of the person about whom the book is written. For this reason, the call number of biographies and autobiographies is made of 921 and the initial of the person the book is written about. For example, this is the call number of *Laugh Clown, Cry: The Story of Charlie Chaplin* by Walter Oleksy:

921	Individual biography
C	First initial of Chaplin

Short Story Collections. Most libraries keep fiction books that contain several short stories in a special section. They are usually marked SC, for "Story Collection."

Such a book may be a collection of stories by one author. It may also be a collection of stories by several different authors. These stories were chosen and put into book form by an *editor*.

Books of short stories are usually arranged by the author's or the editor's last name. This is the call number of *Just So Stories*, all written by Rudyard Kipling:

SC
K

Reference Books. Reference books are special nonfiction books that are kept together in a certain section of the library. They are usually marked with an *R* above the classification number.

R
423.1
D56

Exercises Call Numbers

A. Each book below belongs in one of the special categories of biography, collective biography, or short story collections. Read the title carefully. Decide on the right category. Copy each title and author. Then assign the correct category number to each book.

921 *Jules Verne: The Man Who Invented the Future* by Franz Born
SC *O. Henry's Best Stories* edited by Lou P. Bunce
920 *People in History* by R. J. Unstead
921 *The Story of My Life* by Helen Keller
921 *Martin Luther King: The Peaceful Warrior* by Ed Clayton
SC *Stories Boys Like* compiled by Franklin M. Reck
921 *My Animals and Me* by Nan Hayden Agle
920 *Baseball's Greatest Pitchers* by Milton J. Shapiro
921 *Helen Keller* by Margaret Davidson
920 *Evel Knievel and Other Daredevils* by Joe Scalzo

B. Arrange the following call numbers for nonfiction books in correct order, the way they would appear on the library shelf.

7 **770 J15i**	9 **796.3 G34p**	10 **929 J36e**	8 **770 N76p**	5 **551.7 W49s**
6 **623.8 B18s**	1 **133.8 O26p**	2 **301 K45f**	4 **551.4 P78e**	3 **551.4 B46s**

Part 2

Objective

To use the card catalog to locate books

Presenting the Lesson

1. Read and discuss pages 188 to 190. Point out that some libraries have two separate card files, one for author and title cards and one for subject cards. Most school libraries have one master system of cards filed alphabetically.

2. Have students draw three rectangles on a piece of paper, each the approximate size of a catalog card. On each square they should copy an example of each kind of card: one author card, one title card, one subject card.

3. Assign and discuss Exercises A and B on page 190 and 191. Assign Exercise C only if the students have sufficient access to a library.

Optional Practice

Have the students use the card catalog in the school library to locate one card for each author, title, or subject listed below. What is the label on the drawer where

Part 2 Using the Card Catalog

The **card catalog** is a cabinet of small drawers filled with cards printed with information about every book in the library. The cards are arranged alphabetically according to the top line of each card. In the upper left-hand corner of each card in the catalog is the call number of the book listed on the card. This call number makes it easier to find the book on the shelves after you have found its card in the card catalog.

On the outside of each drawer there is a label that tells what letters of the alphabet are contained in that drawer. Inside each drawer there are **guide cards** that have tabs extending above the regular book cards. The tabs may have letters of the alphabet, complete words, or general subject headings printed on them. The guide cards separate the drawerful of cards into smaller groups. This makes it easier to find the exact card you are looking for.

There are usually three cards for the same book in the card catalog: the **author card,** the **title card,** and the **subject card.** All three cards give you the same information about the book, but in slightly different order. An author card has the name of the author of the book on the top line. A title card has the title of the book on the top line. A subject card has the general subject or topic of the book on the top line. All three cards for one book have the same call number in the corner.

Look carefully at the following examples of card catalog cards for the book *Wildlife in Danger* by Alan C. Jenkins.

The Author Card

When you know the author of a book you want to read, use the card catalog to look up the author's name. There will be an author card for each book in the library written by that author. All the cards for one author will be together, filed alphabetically under the author's last name (on the top line of each card). In the group of cards of one author, each card is also filed alphabetically by the first word in the title (on the second line of each card).

Here is an author card for the book *Wildlife in Danger.*

> 639 **Jenkins, Alan C.**
> **J41w**
>
> Wildlife in danger. Illus. with photos.
> N.Y., St. Martin's Press, © 1973

The Title Card

When you know the title of a book, but not its author, look for the title card of the book in the card catalog. Title cards are filed alphabetically by the first word in the title, which is on the top line of each title card. A, *An,* and *The* do not count as first words. Here is an example of a title card for the same wildlife book.

> 639 **Wildlife in danger.**
> **J41w**
>
> Jenkins, Alan C.
>
> Wildlife in danger. Illus. with photos.
> N.Y., St. Martin's Press, © 1973

each card is found? What are the headings on the guide cards that come before and after each card?

1. FOOTBALL
2. London, Jack
3. *Big Red*
4. Frost, Robert
5. *Tom Sawyer*

Extending the Lesson

Challenge the students to find the answers to each of the following questions, using only the card catalog:

1. Who is the author of the *Homer Price* series of books?
2. In what year was *Old Yeller* copyrighted?
3. Does your library have any books about the Loch Ness monster?
4. How many books by Robb White are in your library?
5. Are there any other books by the author of *The Lion, the Witch, and the Wardrobe* in your library? If so, list one title. Who is the author?

The Subject Card

If you were writing a report on wildlife, you would want to know the names and authors of several books on that subject in the library. The best way to find books on your topic would be to look in the card catalog under the subject heading WILDLIFE. The subject card for the book *Wildlife in Danger* would look like this.

> 639 **WILDLIFE—CONSERVATION**
> **J41w**
>
> Jenkins, Alan C.
> Wildlife in danger. Illus. with photos.
> N.Y., St. Martin's Press, © 1973

The subject on every subject card is frequently printed in capital letters, which helps you tell the difference between it and an author or title card. Notice, also, on the subject card for *Wildlife in Danger*, that the author's name is given next. Only the first letters and initials of his name are capitalized. The title of the book immediately follows the author's name. Only the first word and proper names in the title are capitalized. The title of the book in the example is *Wildlife in Danger*.

Exercises Using the Card Catalog

A. Each of the five words or phrases below is the first line of a card in a card catalog. Copy words or phrases in the order you would find them in the card catalog.

4	1. PHOTOGRAPHY	3	2. Wilder, Laura Ingalls
5	The Pigman	4	The Wizard Islands
1	Parlin, John	5	Workshops in Space
2	People Who Made America	1	White, Robb
3	Phoebe	2	The White Mountains

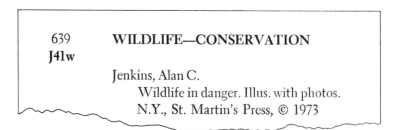

3 3. CAREERS

5 Careers in the Health Field

1 CAMERAS

4 Careers in Consumer Protection

2 Cameron, Eleanor

B. What subject cards would give you information about the following topics? Try to think of several subjects for each topic.

These are suggested answers.

Example: Development of the railroads
Railroads
American history
Transportation

1. How to study for a test Study (Method of), Tests, Examinations
2. Famous women athletes Athletes (Women), Sports
3. Rules of tennis Tennis, Sports (Rules)
4. History of the National Football League Football, Football History
5. How to grow a vegetable garden Gardening, Vegetable Gardening

C. Use the card catalog to find the title, author, and call number of a book on one of the following subjects: Answers will vary.

1. A book about skiing
2. A book of detective stories
3. A book about dinosaurs
4. A book of poems by Robert Louis Stevenson
5. A book about Pablo Picasso
6. A book about Harriet Tubman
7. A book about the Alamo
8. A book about U.S. presidents
9. A book about UFO's
10. A book of math games and puzzles

Part 3

Objective

To use the encyclopedia efficiently

Presenting the Lesson

1. Read and discuss the introduction to Part 3 on page 192. What kinds of reference books, other than encyclopedias, are students aware of? If they are not aware of others, it may be helpful to assign research on reference books. See Extending the Lesson, Exercise 1.

2. Read How To Use an Encyclopedia on pages 192 and 193. Discuss how guide words in an encyclopedia are like the guide words in a dictionary.

3. If possible, have a set of encyclopedias for use by the class. Divide the class into the same number of groups as there are volumes of the encyclopedia. Assign one volume to each group. Ask each to prepare a short oral presentation about the contents of their volume, based on the following set of questions:

1. What is the first article in the volume? the last?
2. Name an article that is at least four pages long.
3. Name at least one famous person discussed in the volume. Is there a picture of the person?
4. Is there an article on any foreign country in the volume? Is there more than one? Name the counties you found.
5. In this fast survey of the volume, which article looked most interesting to you? Which article would you like to read completely?

Part 3 The Encyclopedia

Every library has a special section of reference books. These special books offer you facts and information on every topic you can think of. They are called **reference books** because you *refer* to them to find some specific information you need. When you look up something in a reference book, you often read only one page, or even less. In this way reference books are different from regular fiction and nonfiction books, which you may read from cover to cover.

Another way in which reference books are different from regular library books is that reference books are usually not allowed to be checked out. They are to be used only in the library. In this way, they are always available for library users to look up information.

The reference works you are most likely to use are the encyclopedias. An **encyclopedia** is a reference book that contains general articles on many subjects. Most encyclopedias consist of several volumes, covering a wide variety of subjects. Sometimes, a whole set of encyclopedias is about one subject, such as art or biography. There are some encyclopedias that consist of one volume on a single subject, such as baseball or careers.

The following encyclopedias are used frequently by young people:

Britannica Junior Encyclopaedia (15 volumes)
Collier's Encyclopedia (24 volumes)
Compton's Encyclopedia (26 volumes)
Encyclopaedia Britannica (29 volumes)
Encyclopedia Americana (30 volumes)
World Book Encyclopedia (22 volumes)

How To Use an Encyclopedia

Encyclopedias are easy to use. Information is arranged in the volumes alphabetically by subject. Volumes are usually numbered to keep them in order. On the back, or spine, of each volume are letters or words to tell you what part of the alphabet is included in that volume. For example, in the *World Book Encyclopedia,* volumes are numbered in this way:

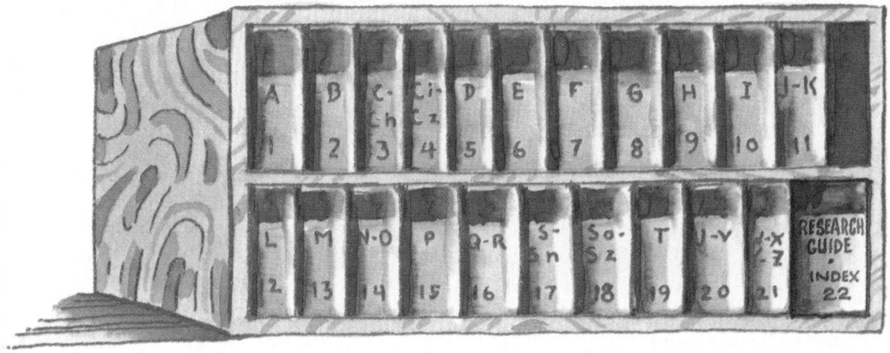

If you examine Volume 3 of *World Book Encyclopedia,* you will see that it begins with an article on "C," the alphabet letter, and concludes with an article on "churn"—the container in which cream or milk is stirred or beaten. Articles about people are usually alphabetized by the person's last name. Volume 4 begins with an article on John Ciardi, the American poet. The guides on the spines help you choose the volume that will have information on your topic.

At the top of each page of the encyclopedia are guide words. Like guide words in a dictionary, they help you locate the page that will have the article you seek. Most encyclopedias place guide words in both the upper left-hand and upper right-hand column of each two-page spread. For example, in Volume 2 of *Britannica Junior Encyclopaedia* (1976 edition), pages 252–253 cover "Angelico" to "Angola." Articles on those two pages deal with these topics:

Fra Angelico

Angkor, Cambodia

Anglo-Egyptian Sudan

Anglo-Saxon

Angola, Africa

4. Read and discuss The Encyclopedia Index on page 194. Stress that a single topic may be discussed in several different volumes, under different main headings. If necessary, review the basic skills of alphabetizing.

5. The section, The Encyclopedia Article, assumes the availability of a set of *World Book Encyclopedia.* If it is not available, use another set. Most encyclopedias have similar features. Emphasize the features highlighted on pages 194 and 195. Give special attention to the "See also" note about cross referencing.

6. Exercises A and B can be assigned without the need of reference materials. Note that there may be more than one correct answer for some questions in Exercise A. Exercises C and D require the use of an encyclopedia and might be assigned when the class visits the school library.

Optional Practice

1. Have students make a list of the multi-volume encyclopedias available in your school library. Which sets are the most recent?

2. Assign an encyclopedia. Have the students locate the article for each of the following topics. What is the volume number for each article? What are the guide words on the page where each is located?

Argentina	calcium
electricity	Boston
Harry S Truman	Nile River

Extending the Lesson

1. Ask more advanced students to find out which of the following books are in the reference section of your library. Each student should write a few sentences describing the contents of every reference book located.

1. *Current Biography*
2. *Who's Who in America*
3. *Guinness Book of World Records*
4. *Information Please, Almanac*
5. *Bartlett's Familiar Quotations*
6. *Roget's Thesaurus*
7. *Reader's Guide to Periodical Literature*
8. *American Heritage Dictionary*

2. Students may find it helpful to know the purpose of an encyclopedia yearbook. Have some more advanced students find out whether the encyclopedias in your school library have yearbooks. If so, the students should examine a recent yearbook, and report on their findings.

The Encyclopedia Index

Every set of encyclopedias has an **index.** The index may be a separate volume, or it may be part of the last volume. Always consult the index of an encyclopedia to help you find all articles on your topic. The index will direct you to every volume and page that contains information on your topic.

For example, if you were doing a report on the medication *terramycin,* you might look in the *World Book* Index and see this entry.

It directs you to four articles, appearing in volumes *T, A, D,* and *F.* The index also tells you what page to look at in each of the four named volumes.

The Encyclopedia Article

An article in an encyclopedia gives you brief, reliable information on any subject. Included in most encyclopedia articles are several aids to help you understand your topic. Find the article from *World Book Encyclopedia* on the subject of Hibernation. Notice these features as you read the article:

1. The subject title is in boldface type, using all capital letters.

2. Subheadings are in boldface type as well. They help you see at a glance what ideas or facts are discussed in the article.

3. Illustrations that accompany the article help you to see the main ideas presented. There may be photos, drawings, charts, maps, or graphs to help you visualize main ideas.

4. "See also" cross references are listed at the end of the article. They direct you to other articles in the encyclopedia that include information on your topic.

Exercises Using Encyclopedias

A. If you were looking for answers to the following questions, what key word in each question would you look for in the encyclopedia?

1. Who invented air brakes for trains?
2. What battle ended the Civil War?
3. How does a Polaroid instant camera work?
4. When did Richard Nixon resign from the presidency?

B. Refer to the *World Book Encyclopedia* volumes shown on page 193. In what volume would you find articles on each of these topics?

1. Aaron Burr Vol. 2
2. University of Chicago Vol. 3
3. Elizabeth II, Queen of Great Britain Vol. 6
4. Solar energy Vol. 18
5. The game of football Vol. 7

C. Choose one of the following topics and look it up in an encyclopedia index. List all articles on that topic. Give the titles of the articles, their volumes, and their pages. Answers will vary.

1. Mummies
2. Hercules
3. Dentistry
4. Soccer
5. Fashion

D. Look up one of the following topics in an encyclopedia. List the cross references appearing at the end of the article. Answers will vary.

1. The United States Post Office
2. Motion pictures
3. Ulcers

Chapter 12

Writing Compositions and Reports

By now you have learned to develop an idea in a paragraph. You have also learned to write different kinds of paragraphs. Sometimes, however, a paragraph just isn't long enough to explain an idea. You need several paragraphs joined together. This is called a **composition.**

Some compositions are called **reports.** When you plan to write a report, you first have to study and learn about your subject.

In the following pages you are going to learn how to write compositions and reports.

Part 1 What Is a Composition?

A composition is a group of paragraphs that work together to develop an idea. Does this definition sound familiar? It should. It's

Chapter Objectives

1. To understand the function and organization of a five-paragraph composition
2. To develop methods for finding a subject for a composition
3. To narrow a subject for adequate treatment in a composition
4. To develop methods for gathering information
5. To write a good introductory paragraph
6. To construct an outline to organize ideas
7. To write the body of a composition
8. To write a good ending paragraph
9. To complete a composition by revising, proofreading, and giving credit

Preparing the Students

Show students several examples of writing that is made up of several paragraphs. The examples might include an encyclopedia entry, a magazine article, and a news story or feature. Emphasize that each selection is about one subject and that several paragraphs are needed to cover the subject adequately. Explain that in this chapter students will learn to write a five-paragraph composition about one subject.

Additional Resources

Mastery Test—pages 461 and 462 in this T. E. Recommended for use after teaching the chapter.

Additional Mastery Test—Recommended for use after any necessary reteaching. (In separate booklet, *Diagnostic and Mastery Tests, Gold Level,* pages 37 and 38.)

Skills Practice Book—pages 72–79

Duplicating Masters—pages 72–79

Part 1

Objective

To understand the function and organization of a five-paragraph composition

Presenting the Lesson

1. Read pages 197 to 199. Emphasize that students have already mastered the basic unit of a composition—the paragraph. Discuss briefly the different kinds of reports that students have written. Explain that the method for writing a composition as explained in this chapter can be used for writing reports in subjects other than Language Arts. Remind students that each paragraph in a composition must begin with a topic sentence.

2. Read and discuss the sample composition on pages 199 and 200. The first sentence in each paragraph is the topic sentence. Review paragraph development by demonstrating how each sentence adds something to the main idea stated in the topic sentence. Ask the class to identify the title of the composition, to give the main idea (The purpose of many modern zoos is to study and preserve wildlife), to explain what each paragraph adds to the main idea, and to point out the three parts of the composition.

3. Assign and discuss the Exercise on pages 200 to 201.

Extending the Lesson

Work in a small group with those students who had difficulty with the exercise. Copy and duplicate the composition so that students can

almost like the definition of a paragraph. Both a paragraph and a composition are written to explain one idea. However, a composition is much longer than a paragraph. It gives more information about a topic.

The Introductory Paragraph

A paragraph begins with a topic sentence that tells what the paragraph is about. A composition begins with a whole paragraph that does the same thing. This paragraph is called the **introductory paragraph.** It tells the reader what the composition is going to be about.

Let's take a look at an introductory paragraph.

> Many modern zoos are planned and run with the purpose of studying and preserving wildlife. Scientists, animal keepers, dietitians, veterinarians, and other workers at these zoos work toward this goal. Even the animals' physical surroundings are built to help preserve their natural way of life.

The entire paragraph says that the composition is about modern zoos. It is going to describe these zoos as places where wildlife is studied and where animal life is protected. Like most good paragraphs, this paragraph has a topic sentence.

> Many modern zoos are planned and run with the purpose of studying and preserving wildlife.

The other two sentences in the paragraph add to the main idea.

The Body and Ending Paragraphs

Following is a five-paragraph composition about modern zoos. Each paragraph begins with a topic sentence. To help you, the topic sentences are underlined. A good composition is divided into three parts.

The Three Parts of a Composition

1. The **introductory paragraph** tells what the composition is about.
2. The **body paragraphs** develop the main idea given in the introductory paragraph.
3. The **ending paragraph** summarizes what has been said and ends the composition.

These paragraphs all work together to explain the main idea of the composition.

MODERN ZOOS

Many modern zoos are planned and run with the purpose of studying and preserving wildlife. Scientists, animal keepers, dietitians, veterinarians, and other workers at these zoos all work toward this goal. Even the animals' physical surroundings are built to help preserve their natural way of life.

Introductory paragraph

Modern zoos are places where scientists watch animal behavior and share what they learn. Many share their findings in books and magazine articles. Some help to plan programs for students, to produce television programs, or to teach zoo guides. Some work on special diets or care for sick animals. Others work with architects and planners to create healthy environments for the animals.

Zoo designers now try to create environments that are close to the animals' natural habitats. They use artificial rocks, trees, and flowers. They control heat and humidity for animals such as reptiles and snakes. They build shelters for animals like giraffes, who need protection in bad weather. They design large open spaces for birds and for large animals that need to roam over wide areas. They try not to use walls, cages, or fences. Instead, they use dry moats to confine the animals.

Zoos also help protect wildlife through their care of endangered species. Zoo scientists can now breed endangered species in captivity. In time, they even hope to send some of these

Body paragraphs

take notes as it is discussed. First analyze each paragraph. Help the group to identify the topic sentence and to explain how the other sentences develop the main idea. Then analyze the composition. Have the group identify the three parts. Discuss the function of the introductory paragraph and how each paragraph adds to the main idea of the composition.

animals back into the wild. This would turn around the old practice of capturing animals in the wild and keeping them in zoos.

Ending paragraph

Today's modern zoos are places where scientists study animal life. The natural life patterns of the animals are respected. Endangered species are protected and more of them are being bred. These zoos help to preserve the wildlife of the world. They will be even more important as people take over the animals' lands.

Exercise Studying the Parts of a Composition

Here is a five-paragraph composition about the game of basketball. First look at the introductory paragraph. Explain the main idea presented in that paragraph. Pick out the topic sentence of each paragraph. Finally, identify the three main parts of the composition.

THE GAME THAT ALMOST WAS BOXBALL

Introductory paragraph

Main idea: A game was invented.

Dr. James A. Naismith, a teacher at the International Y.M.C.A. Training School in Springfield, Massachusetts, invented a game in 1891. However, he had no name for it. He had simply made up a sport that all his students could enjoy.

Body paragraphs

It was a game that could be played indoors by both boys and girls and was not as rough as football. Dr. Naismith wanted his students to try out the new game, but he first had to find the right kind of ball. He also needed two boxes to use as goals. He decided to have the players use a leather soccer ball to toss into the goals.

He asked Mr. Stebbins, the building superintendent, to find two boxes that had openings about nine inches across. This would be wide enough for the soccer ball. Mr. Stebbins could not find the right-sized wooden boxes anywhere. As the time for the first game came near, there were still no goals hanging from the gym balcony. Dr. Naismith finally decided to use two peach baskets. After all, he thought, it was only a trial game. Boxes could always be found later to replace the baskets.

The peach baskets did present a bit of a problem, however. The players liked to shoot the soccer ball at the peach baskets. They earned a point each time the ball went into the basket. However, each time a goal was made, someone had to climb a ladder and take the ball out of the basket. After a few games, someone suggested that the bottoms of the baskets be cut out to allow the ball to fall through.

Ending paragraph

Naismith had simply called his invention "a new game." Because of the peach-basket goals, it soon became known as basketball. Those peach baskets were never replaced with wooden boxes as the inventor had first planned. What a difference it would have made if Mr. Stebbins had found wooden boxes for that very first game. Instead of basketball, boxball would be one of the most popular sports of all time.—MARY NELLE KAINER

Part 2 Finding a Subject

Have you ever sat down to write a composition and had your mind go as blank as the paper in front of you? If so, you're not alone. Almost everyone has trouble getting started.

The first thing you have to do is to find something to write about. This lesson is going to describe two ways to do this.

1. Do you want to write about something you have experienced first-hand?
2. Do you want to write about something you have studied and learned about?

A Composition Based on First-Hand Experience

Let's say you decide to write about a personal experience. However, you need an idea of what to write about. It might help to begin by doing some thinking about yourself. What do you like? What

Part 2

Objective

To develop methods for finding a subject for a composition

Presenting the Lesson

1. Read pages 201 and 202. Remind students that *first-hand experience* means something that actually happened to them. Give the class time to begin thinking and taking notes.

2. Study the model composition on pages 202 to 203. Identify the main idea of the composition and the three parts. Some classes may need further practice in identifying the topic sentence of each paragraph and in analyzing what each sentence contributes to the development of the paragraph. Discuss the writer's use of details and their importance in communicating a personal experience to a reader.

3. Assign the first Exercise on page 204.

4. Read page 204. Encourage students to explore their interests for possible subjects for compositions.

5. Assign the second Exercise on page 204.

Extending the Lesson

Some students may have been unable to make a list of subject ideas. Discuss some possibilities with them as a group, using the questions on page 202 as a starting point. You may also want to arrange for a trip to the school or local library during which time the students can look for further ideas in books and magazines.

don't you like? What do you feel? You will probably be surprised at how many ideas begin to pop into your head. In fact, for the next few days, you probably should carry a piece of paper and a pencil around with you. Then you can write down ideas as they come to mind. You'll end up with a whole list of possible subjects for compositions. Here are some questions to start your thinking:

Who is the person in your family you most admire?

What happened during your nicest summer?

What's your favorite color?

What's your favorite TV program?

If you could choose any time to live in all of history, when would you choose?

Why do you like animals?

What's your favorite way to spend Saturday morning?

What will be different in your life twenty years from now?

What's your idea of a perfect day?

If you could decorate your room any way, how would you do it?

What place have you most enjoyed visiting?

Who is the most unusual person you've ever met?

What has been your most embarrassing moment?

What's the most important quality in a friend?

Have you ever sent a fan letter?

A Model Composition

The following composition is written from first-hand experience. It is filled with details. They show that the writer is familiar with camp. The composition is divided into three parts: introductory paragraph, body paragraphs, and ending paragraph. Each paragraph begins with a topic sentence.

DAY CAMP

Yesterday brought back a vivid memory. My mild-mannered younger brother stamped his foot and yelled, "I refuse to go to that dumb old day camp." I'll never forget the summer, three years ago, when I, too, was dead-set against going to camp. I'll also never forget how, little by little, I came to love it.

The first day at camp was awful. I didn't know one person on the entire bus. I decided I would probably hate everyone anyway. That went double for Miss Priss, who sat next to me. After the bus had arrived at camp, we all played a "let's learn everyone's name" game. Miss Priss knew all the names the first time around. I, of course, couldn't remember one. After that we had relay races. Miss Priss was great! I finally learned her real name—Maggie.

The next day wasn't quite so bad. Miss Priss, I mean Maggie, sat next to me again. This time we had something to talk about. She asked me to call her Mag. She told me she had five brothers. I told her about my little brother, my gerbils, my cat Samantha, and my glass collection. Later that day we made terrariums out of pieces of glass and tape. We filled them with leaves, moss, and rocks from the woods. My terrarium was a little crooked, but OK. Mag's was perfect, of course.

The third day I decided that camp just might turn out to be kind of fun. For lunch we roasted hot dogs on sticks. We toasted marshmallows and spread the marshmallow goo on graham crackers. We put Hershey bars on top. No one felt much like running around after eating, so we learned camp songs. Mag, of course, already knew the words to all the songs. By then I was starting to like her too much to be jealous.

I guess the day of the marshmallow treats was the turning point. After that I stopped complaining about camp. I started to dread the day when it would be over. It finally was over, but never in my mind. I still can bring back the special sounds, sights, and smells if I close my eyes and think hard enough.

Exercise Choosing a Subject

By now you most likely have a different sort of problem—too many ideas. It's time to sort them out. Look closely at your list of possible subjects. Choose five and write them on a sheet of paper. Set the paper aside and go on to the next part of this lesson.

A Composition or Report Based on Learned Information

Let's say that you've decided to write, not about yourself, but about something you need to study and learn about. You might begin a list of possible subjects by going to the library. Look through your favorite magazines. Flip through some books from the shelves. Think about things you're interested in. Do you like to watch undersea adventures on TV? Do you like stories of knights and castles? Have you always wanted to know how to carve soap?

Over the next couple of days jot down as many ideas for compositions as come to mind. These should be subjects that you'd enjoy learning more about. That way it won't be hard to write an interesting composition. It will show that you know something about the subject.

Exercise Adding More Subjects to Your List

You now have even more ideas to work with. Look again at the list of things you'd enjoy learning more about. Choose five possible subjects for reports. Add these to your list of five subjects based on personal experience. Save this list for the next lesson.

Part 3 Planning the Composition or Report

You probably have decided what you're going to write about. Now you must be sure that your subject is narrow enough to be covered in a five-paragraph composition. Let's say that you've always been interested in history. You've decided to write about the history of the United States. This topic is, of course, much too broad to be covered in a few paragraphs. Whole books have been written about it.

Narrowing the Subject

You'd begin to narrow the subject by deciding what period of U.S. history interests you the most. Let's say it's the time when the pioneers were moving west of the Mississippi River. However, this subject is still too broad for a short composition. To cover it well, you'd have to describe the following:

Life on a wagon train

The role of scouts

The duties of a wagon master

How the territory was acquired by the United States

What happened to the Native Americans who had lived west of the Mississippi for centuries

You must narrow the subject further. You might decide to focus on life on a wagon train. However, you'd need to do still more narrowing. Your final subject might be something like, "Children on a Wagon Train."

Looking back, you can see that the original subject was narrowed in this way:

Part 3

Objectives

1. To narrow a subject for adequate treatment in a composition
2. To develop methods for gathering information

Presenting the Lesson

1. Read pages 205 and 206. Review the definition of *narrowing* as the process of reducing a broad subject to one of its smaller parts.
2. Assign and discuss Exercise A on page 206.
3. Assign and discuss Exercise B on page 206. Check students' subjects to be sure that they are narrow enough for a five-paragraph composition. Help each student to decide on a final workable subject.
4. Read pages 207 and 208. This discussion applies only to students who are going to write a composition based on learned information. However, the skill of note-taking should be studied by the entire class. Point out that the sample note cards are written in complete sentences and that each of the notes contains one item of information.
5. Assign the Exercise on page 208 to those students for whom reading and note taking are necessary.

Extending the Lesson

Provide each student with five 3" by 5" cards. Direct them to look in books and magazines for the following:

1. One fact about pet care
2. One fact about weather
3. One fact about sports
4. One fact about animals
5. One fact about a country other than the United States

One fact must come from a magazine; the rest can come from books other than encyclopedias. Students should record each fact on an index card, along with the source of information. Remind them to follow the format presented in this lesson.

The History of the United States

Pioneers Moving West

Life on a Wagon Train

Children on a Wagon Train

After narrowing the subject in this way, you would be ready to begin reading about children on a wagon train.

Subjects based on personal experience often need to be narrowed, too. For example, you might begin with a subject such as "Summer." After thinking about all the summers you've had, you might decide to write about last summer. That would still be too much for one composition. You could then narrow the subject to something about last summer. You could write about going to an art fair, helping with the harvesting, planting a garden, going to a carnival, or playing street games. You would have narrowed the subject from summer, to one summer, to one thing that happened during that summer. This would be the subject you would write about.

Exercises Narrowing a Subject

A. The following subjects are too broad for short compositions. Narrow each one until you reach one that can be covered in a five-paragraph composition.

1. Radios
2. Space Exploration
3. Books
4. Games
5. Holidays
6. Pets
7. Houses
8. Dreams
9. Movies
10. Friends

B. Take a look at the list of ten subjects you made for the previous lesson. Choose one you'd like to write about. Be sure that the subject can be covered in a five-paragraph composition. If not, narrow it. You will then be ready to begin work on your composition.

Reading About Your Subject

Perhaps you've decided to write about a subject you must study. The first thing you must do is to read about your subject. Use the card catalog and the *Abridged Reader's Guide to Periodical Literature*. They will help you find books and magazines that might have information about the subject. When you find something you want to include in your composition, write it down. Many writers like to use 3″ by 5″ cards to record information. They put different types of information on separate cards. They also include the source of the information on each card.

Sample Note Cards

Here are two sample note cards.

Note Card for a Book

This card includes the name and author of the book. It also includes the information you want to use.

Title

The First Book of the Oregon Trail

by Walter Havighurst   Author

Information

To go from Missouri to Oregon on the Oregon Trail was a five-month, 2000 mile trip.

Note Card for a Magazine

This card includes the name and date of the magazine, the title and author of the article, and the pages where the information was found. It also includes the information you want to use.

Magazine — Date — Title

Pet News, July/August 1978, "Pets and Vitamins"

Author — Pages

by Eldon W. Kienholz, Ph.D. pages 10-11

Information

Pets need vitamins. They should get them from a well balanced diet or their owners should give them vitamin supplements.

Exercise **Learning About Your Subject**

If you are going to write a composition or report based on learned information, it is now time to read about your subject. Take notes as you read. Save these notes to use when planning and writing your composition.

Part 4 Writing the Introductory Paragraph

The introductory paragraph is an important part of a composition. A good introductory paragraph lets the readers know what the entire composition is about. Even more important, it catches their interest. It makes them want to read the rest of the composition.

Telling the Main Idea

Here are three examples of good introductory paragraphs. Each one lets you know exactly what the composition is about. Each one makes you want to find out more about the subject. Each one also begins with a topic sentence. That sentence presents the main idea of the paragraph.

Part 4

Objective

To become aware of the qualities of a good introductory paragraph, and to write a good introductory paragraph

Presenting the Lesson

1. Read pages 208 to 210. Emphasize the two purposes of an introductory paragraph: to give the main idea of the composition and to catch the reader's attention. Discuss the examples on page 209 and the introductory paragraph to "Children on a Wagon Train" in terms of how the paragraphs fulfill the two purposes.

1

The Haida Indians had a ceremony for every stage of life. There was a ceremony for the newborn child and a ceremony for the naming of the child. There was a ceremony when a child was ready for marriage and one for the wedding. There was a ceremony when a new house was begun and when it was finished. There was a ceremony at death and one later to honor one who had died.

—MARION E. GRIDLEY

2

Mr. Mendelsohn sat in the lobby holding on to his cane and a cake box. He had told the nurse at the desk that his friends were coming to pick him up this Sunday. He looked eagerly toward the revolving doors. After a short while, he saw Ralphy, Julio, and Georgie walk through the lobby.—NICHOLASA MOHR

3

Sholiwe, the stick-dice game of the Zuñi Indians, was first played by priests to predict the outcome of a battle. The sticks they used were decorated to show the four quarters of the Earth. They pictured the seasons, fire, air, moisture, and the basic elements in nature. The sticks were made of split cane. They fitted into one another. Their pairing was an important factor in the game.

—SIGMUND A. LAVINE

Catching the Reader's Interest

Let's go back to "Children on a Wagon Train" on page 205. After reading about the subject and taking notes, one writer wrote the following introductory paragraph.

Thousands of children traveled west in the long wagon trains that lumbered over the grassy plains, burning deserts, and rugged mountains of the Oregon Trail. These children did their chores, studied their lessons, and played games, just as they would have done at home. This time, though, "home" was a wagon moving slowly across a 2,000 mile stretch of unknown and sometimes dangerous land.

2. Assign Exercise A on pages 210 and 211. The topic sentence begins each paragraph. Discuss the probable content of the compositions and the questions raised by the introductory paragraphs.

3. Assign Exercise B on page 211. Work with those students who have difficulty. Encourage the class to make first drafts and revised final copies of their introductory paragraphs.

Extending the Lesson

Ask each student to find one good example of an introductory paragraph to a magazine article. Suggest sources such as *Cricket* and *National Geographic World*. Provide time for students to share their examples.

The paragraph lets you know that the composition is going to be about the life of children on a wagon train. It also catches your interest in the subject. You begin to wonder what kinds of chores the children had. What games did they play? Who taught them their lessons? What did they do that was special? The paragraph has made you want to read the rest of the composition.

Exercises Working with Introductory Paragraphs

A. Here are five introductory paragraphs. Pick out the topic sentence in each. Explain what you think the rest of the composition is going to be about. Would each paragraph capture the reader's interest? Explain. ______ = topic sentence.

1

How fast can humans go on muscle power alone? Fifty miles an hour? Sixty? No one is sure, but people are trying to find out. In 1974, two Californians organized a contest called the International Human Powered Speed Championships. The contest has only one rule: "Anything that moves is legal, provided it is strictly human powered."—*National Geographic World*

2

Pretend you're a harbor seal named André, and you have a good friend named Harry. You haven't seen Harry all winter, so naturally you hurry home to greet him. That's what André did. He swam 175 miles in three days, a trip that usually takes a seal much longer. When André came home to Rockport, Maine, Harry Goodridge was there on the dock to welcome him.—*National Geographic World*

3

Last Saturday Mortimer Shortimer puzzled the entire neighborhood. He got out a shovel and started to dig a hole. He just dug and dug and dug. After an hour we began to wonder if he ever planned to stop.

4

People in Scotland celebrate the new year in a special way. On the night of December 31, called "Hogmanay," they have parties to welcome in the new year. Then, as soon as it's midnight, they go out to visit each other's homes. Even in the middle of the night the streets are as busy as day. All the people walk along wishing each other a happy new year.—SALLY E. WOOD

5

It was very quiet on the farm. Quiet and bright, for the moon was filtering through the lace curtains, making snowy patterns on the floor. Cynthia was staying with her grandmother. After living on the edge of a large, noisy city, she was not used to the cool moonlight and the sleepy silence of the country. She was afraid that this visit would be the same as the others—dull. But something seemed different about this night.—RONALD HUNT

B. Write the introductory paragraph to your composition. Make sure that it does the following:

1. It has a good topic sentence.
2. It tells what the composition is going to be about.
3. It catches the reader's interest.

Part 5 Planning the Body

You have written an introductory paragraph for your composition. It is now time to plan the body of the composition. This means making a list of the ideas you want to include. It also means arranging these ideas in some logical order.

Part 5

Objective

To construct an outline to organize ideas

Presenting the Lesson

1. Read pages 211 to 214. Review the concept of logical order. Point out that the main ideas for "Children on a Wagon Train" are arranged from the way the children spent most of their time to the way they spent the least. The ideas are in logical order. Review the meaning of *time sequence*. Explain that making a comprehensive outline simplifies the writing process immensely.

2. Assign and discuss Exercise A on pages 214 and 215. Note that numbers 1 and 4 should follow a time sequence.

3. Assign Exercise B on page 215. Provide individual help where needed.

Extending the Lesson

Review the mechanics of outlining with the class. (Rules for capitalization are on pages 356 to 359; rules for punctuation are on pages 363 and 364. Students should be advised to indent the steps of their outlines according to the model on pages 213 and 214.)

Compositions or Reports on Learned Information

If you are writing a composition based on learned information, you have taken notes. Read through them and choose the main ideas you would like to include in your composition. Make a list of these ideas.

Here is the introductory paragraph of the composition, "Children on a Wagon Train." Following it is the list of ideas that the writer made for the body.

CHILDREN ON A WAGON TRAIN

Thousands of children traveled west in the long wagon trains that lumbered over the grassy plains, burning deserts, and rugged mountains of the Oregon Trail. These children did their chores, studied their lessons, and played games, just as they would have done at home. This time, though, "home" was a wagon moving slowly across a 2,000 mile stretch of unknown and sometimes dangerous land.

I. The children had work to do each day.

II. At the end of the day the children were free to enjoy themselves.

III. Most of the children walked much of the way.

This was a list of the main ideas only. Each of these ideas will later be developed by adding details and specific examples.

Making an Outline

The next thing the writer did was to arrange the main ideas into a logical order. The writer was making an outline for her composition. Her final list of main ideas, or the skeleton of the outline, looked like this:

CHILDREN ON A WAGON TRAIN

Introductory paragraph

I. Most of the children walked much of the way.

II. The children had work to do each day.

III. At the end of the day the children were free to enjoy themselves.

She began with the activities that took up the most time. She ended with the activities that took up the least amount of time.

Adding Details to the Outline

The writer next filled in her outline with the details she wanted to include in each paragraph. Her outline then looked like this:

I. Introductory paragraph

II. Most of the children walked much of the way.

  A. Rode in the wagons on hot afternoons

  B. Walked 12–15 miles a day

  C. Some children herded the cow column. These were the milk cows and spare horses and oxen that followed the wagon train. These children rode horseback.

III. The children had work to do each day.

  A. Milked cows

  B. Fetched water

  C. Gathered wild fruits and berries

  D. Searched for prairie dog holes and alerted hunters

  E. Gathered buffalo chips, dried buffalo dung used for cooking and warmth

  F. Studied school lessons, using books that had been brought along

G. Learned how to hook rugs, make quilts, preserve meat in salt, start a fire from flint, and use an ax

IV. At the end of the day the children were free to enjoy themselves.

A. Played games like tag and hide-and-seek

B. Sang around campfire

C. Listened to adults talking

D. Went to bed early to be able to get up before dawn

After making this outline, the writer was ready to write three paragraphs. These would make up the body of the composition.

Compositions Based on First-Hand Experience

If you have decided to write a composition based on first-hand experience, you'll follow these same steps. You'll make a list of the main ideas for your composition. Then you'll arrange the ideas in a logical order. Finally, you'll fill in your outline with details and examples. However, you'll probably follow a different logical order. You'll be writing about an experience. Therefore, you'll follow a *time sequence*. You'll tell what happened first, what happened next, and so on.

Exercises Organizing Ideas

A. Here is a list of subjects followed by four main ideas. Arrange each set of ideas in a logical order. You can use a time sequence or any other order you think will work. There is no exact "right" order for numbers 2, 3, and 4. Be sure, though, that you can explain why you chose the order you did.

1. Skydiving

2 a. The plane ascends higher and higher until it is circling high above the target field.

4 b. The diver floats free for hundreds of feet, then pulls the rip cord.

1 c. Getting ready involves checking equipment.

3 d. The diver steps out onto the jump ramp, waits a minute, and jumps.

2. Hiccups
    a. Everyone seems to have a favorite cure for hiccups.
    b. Hiccups are downward jerks of a muscle.
    c. Nobody knows for sure why people get hiccups.
    d. Some hiccup cures are more drastic than others.

3. Scavengers, or nature's garbage collectors
    a. Fish and insects, as well as animals and birds, can be scavengers.
    b. Most animals scavenge, or eat dead animals, at one time or other.
    c. Scavengers help to maintain the balance of nature.
    d. Animals that scavenge for most of their meals have bodies that help them in this way of life.

4. The day the entire family picked out a car
    a. Arnie's Reliable Autos turned out to be the exact opposite of its name.
    b. We were all discouraged until we pulled into Taylor's Used Car Sales and saw THE CAR.
    c. All the cars in the first lot seemed to be black, gray, or dull brown.
    d. We pulled into Luxe Autos and pulled right out again.

B. List the main ideas you want to cover in your composition. Arrange them in a logical order. Then fill in your outline with the details you want to use in your paragraphs.

Part 6

Objective

To write the body of a composition

Presenting the Lesson

1. Read page 216. Emphasize the importance of following an outline when writing the body of a composition.

2. Read and study the composition on page 217 and the following paragraph of discussion on page 218. To show how closely the writer followed her outline, guide the students in checking the composition against the outline on pages 213 and 214. Note that the main ideas in the outline were incorporated into the topic sentences.

3. Assign the Exercise on page 218.

Extending the Lesson

Hold a "writing workshop" for those students who need help in writing paragraphs from an outline. Help each student to write one paragraph of their composition, based on a main idea and its related details. Then have the students work independently on the other two paragraphs.

Part 6 Writing the Body

The body is the main part of a composition. It develops the idea presented in the introductory paragraph. The body is usually several paragraphs long. Each paragraph has a topic sentence. It tells what the entire paragraph is about. The paragraphs of the body are arranged in some logical order. They are in a time sequence or some other order that fits the subject. All the body paragraphs work together to explain the main idea of the composition.

Following an Outline

You have studied an outline of a composition about "Children on a Wagon Train." You saw that the introductory paragraph was followed by three ideas. They were points II, III, and IV on the outline. You also saw how details were added to the outline.

The writer of the outline later wrote three paragraphs. Each paragraph included one idea plus details. When writing, she followed her outline closely. She made sure that she included the details that were listed. She also made sure that her paragraphs were in the order that she had decided on. This order was from activities that took the most time to activities that took the least.

Introductory and Body Paragraphs

Here is the introductory paragraph and the body of the composition, "Children on a Wagon Train."

CHILDREN ON A WAGON TRAIN

Thousands of children traveled west in the long wagon trains that lumbered over the grassy plains, burning deserts, and rugged mountains of the Oregon Trail. These children did their chores, studied their lessons, and played games, just as they would have done at home. This time, though, "home" was a wagon moving slowly across a 2,000 mile stretch of unknown and sometimes dangerous land.

Introductory paragraph

Most of the children's days were spent walking alongside the wagons. Only on the hottest desert afternoons did many ride in the shelter of the backs of the jolting wagons. Every day except Sunday the wagons covered—and the children walked—twelve to fifteen miles. One exception was a group of older children. They herded the "cow column," the milk cows and spare horses and oxen that followed the wagon train. These children spent most of the long journey on horseback.

The children had work to do each day. They milked the cows, fetched buckets of water from the creeks, and gathered wild fruits and berries. They searched for prairie dog holes and alerted the hunters in the train to their locations. One of their most important jobs was gathering "buffalo chips." They were the disks of dried buffalo dung that were burned for cooking and warmth. The children also studied their school lessons. They used books that had been packed into the wagons. In addition, they learned skills such as how to hook rugs, make quilts, preserve meat in salt, start a fire from flint, and use an ax.

When the wagons finally pulled up at the end of a long day and the supper dishes were done, the children were free to have some fun. They could then get together with the children from other wagons to play games like tag and hide-and-seek. They could join the singing around the campfires and listen to the adults share their dreams of a new life in Oregon. Recreation time ended early for those on a wagon train. Everyone had to be up before dawn to begin a new day.

Body paragraphs

Each of the three body paragraphs adds something to the main idea of the composition, the life of children on a wagon train. The first body paragraph explains how most of the children walked alongside the wagons. The second paragraph describes the children's work. The third describes how the children had fun. These three paragraphs work together. They give you, the reader, a good idea of what life was like on a wagon train.

Exercise **Writing the Body of the Composition**

Write the body of your composition. Follow the outline you made in Part 5. Be sure to use the main points of your outline in writing your topic sentences. Be sure also to include the details you listed. Arrange your paragraphs in the same order as you arranged the main points of your outline.

Part 7

Objectives

1. To become aware of various types of endings to compositions, and to write a good ending paragraph

2. To complete a composition by revising, proofreading, and giving credit

Presenting the Lesson

1. Read pages 218 and 219. The first two sample endings are not as structured as the other samples. Whatever structure students use, encourage them to follow the same rules for writing well developed paragraphs that they have used in writing the first four paragraphs of their compositions.

Part 7 Completing the Composition

Writing the Ending

The third main part of a composition is the ending. Some endings, like this one, are very short:

> We never went near that empty house again.

Others are longer. They end a composition by telling what happened later. The next paragraph is an example of this type of ending. It concludes a true story about a cat named Tom. Tom accidentally wandered onto a stage during a performance. He became a permanent part of the cast.

> Tom was glad when the play ended. Now he just sleeps in his box in the back of the theater. At night when no one is in the theater, Tom catches mice.—MARGUERITE P. DOLCH

Summarizing the Composition

A third type of ending summarizes the composition. This next example does just that. It summarizes the experiences of twenty-three teenagers from the Los Angeles area who climbed Mt. Whitney.

> For almost nine days we lived in the wilderness, under the skies, next to lakes and streams, in sight of the deer and raccoons, with only the things we could carry on our backs. There was no place to buy anything or get anything fixed. We couldn't even throw anything away. There was no garbage pickup. On our backs we had everything we needed—food, shelter, and clothing. We had Debbie, Chuck, and Kenny to guide us. Best of all, we had a great time! We made it to the top of the mountain, and we have a patch to prove it. It says, "I CLIMBED MOUNT WHITNEY." How many people can say that?—JEAN KEELAN

These three sample endings are very different. However, they do have one thing in common. They all signal the reader that the composition is over. They don't leave the reader waiting to find out what happens next.

Let's take a look at the ending of the composition "Children on a Wagon Train."

> The children on a wagon train did ordinary things. They worked, played, studied, ate, and slept. However, they also experienced out-of-the-ordinary things. They had hard wagon seats, tired feet, merciless heat, and long stretches of boredom as they crossed the vast West. These children were true pioneers, just like their parents.

Ending paragraph

This ending paragraph summarizes the idea that the children did many things they would have done at home. It also emphasizes the idea that the children on a wagon train had a very special kind of experience.

2. Read page 220. Note that students are directed to make a second revised copy of their compositions, then a third final copy.

3. Read page 221. Giving credit applies only to those students who have written compositions based on learned information. However, this section should be read by the entire class.

4. Assign the Exercise on page 221. Provide time for students to share their completed compositions.

Extending the Lesson

Make a list of the most commonly used proofreader's marks. These can be found in most college dictionaries. Ask a group of students (or several groups) to make a large poster illustrating the marks. Hang the poster (or posters) in the classroom for students to use when revising their compositions.

Revising

After completing a composition or report, you must go back over it to check your writing. You must make sure that everything is exactly as it should be. Ask yourself the following questions:

1. Does the composition have three parts—introductory paragraph, body, and ending?
2. Does the introductory paragraph present a main idea?
3. Do the body paragraphs develop that main idea?
4. Does the ending signal the reader that the composition is over?
5. Do all the paragraphs have topic sentences?
6. Do the sentences in each paragraph stick to the main idea of that paragraph?

Sometimes you will come across a word, a phrase, a sentence, or a paragraph that doesn't seem quite right. You can **revise,** or change, it to make it better. After you have revised your paper to make it better, make a new, clean copy.

Proofreading

After you have made a copy of your revised paper, go back over it once more to proofread it. Ask yourself these questions:

1. Is the capitalization correct?
2. Is the punctuation correct?
3. Are all the words spelled correctly?

You can check capitalization, punctuation, and spelling in Chapters 22, 23, and 24. After you have proofread carefully and made any necessary changes, make a final copy of your paper. Think about neatness, correct headings, straight margins, and good handwriting.

Giving Credit

If you have used information from books or magazines for a composition, you must name those sources. The writer of "Children on a Wagon Train" added these lines after her ending paragraph.

> Information taken from the following books:
>
> *The First Book of the Oregon Trail* by Walter Havighurst
>
> *Westward on the Oregon Trail*. American Heritage Junior Library

She "gave credit" to her two sources of information.

However, giving credit doesn't mean that you can copy the exact words from a book or magazine. You must always write your composition in your own words.

Exercise Finishing the Composition

Write the ending to your composition. Then go back and revise the entire composition. Make a revised copy and proofread it. Make any necessary changes. Make a final copy. If you have taken information from books, be sure to give credit at the end of the composition.

Chapter 13

Different Kinds of Compositions

In Chapter 12 you learned the important steps in developing a composition. Here are the steps:

1. **Find a subject.** It can be a first-hand experience or a subject you have learned about.
2. **Narrow the subject** so that it can be covered in a few paragraphs.
3. **Read about the subject.** This applies only to compositions based on learned information.
4. **Write an introductory paragraph.** It should tell what the entire composition is about. It should catch the reader's interest.
5. **Make a list of the main ideas** to be included in the composition.
6. **Arrange the main ideas in some logical order.**
7. **Add details** to your outline of main ideas.

Chapter Objectives

1. To recognize the steps for developing a composition

2. To identify and use time sequence in organizing a narrative composition based on personal experience

3. To identify and use logical order in organizing the descriptive composition

4. To identify time sequence and logical order in two kinds of explanatory compositions, the "how" composition and the "why" composition, and to use the appropriate method of organization in writing explanatory compositions

Preparing the Students

Review for the class the three different types of paragraphs studied earlier in the year: the narrative paragraph, the descriptive paragraph, and the explanatory paragraph, which includes the "how" paragraph and the "why" paragraph. Ask students to describe each type of paragraph. Explain that compositions, too, fall into these three catagories.

Additional Resources

Mastery Test—pages 463 and 464 in this T. E. Recommended for use after teaching the chapter.

Additional Mastery Test—Recommended for use after any necessary reteaching. (In separate booklet, *Diagnostic and Mastery Tests, Gold Level,* pages 39 and 40.)

Skills Practice Book—pages 80–87

Duplicating Masters—pages 80–87

8. **Write the body paragraphs** of your composition. Make sure that they work together to develop the idea presented in the introductory paragraph.
9. **Write an ending paragraph.** It should signal the reader that the composition is over.
10. **Revise** the composition where necessary. Make a new copy.
11. **Proofread** the new copy. Make any necessary corrections.
12. **Make a final copy** that includes the corrections you made in step 11.
13. **Give credit** to any books or magazines you used for information.

You can follow these steps in developing many different kinds of compositions. Three kinds are described in this chapter.

1. The narrative composition, or story
2. The descriptive composition
3. The explanatory composition

Part 1 The Narrative Composition or Story

You have studied narrative paragraphs. They relate something that happened either to the writer or to someone else. A narrative composition does the same thing. It is made up of several paragraphs that tell what happened. Like a narrative paragraph, a narrative composition relates events in the order in which they happened. It follows a time sequence. It tells what happened first, what happened next, and so on.

Writing About a Personal Experience

Here is an example of a narrative composition. It relates something that happened to the writer. You can tell that the composition is about a personal experience because the writer uses the word *I*.

Part 1

Objectives

1. To recognize the steps for developing a composition
2. To identify and use time sequence in organizing a narrative composition based on personal experience

Presenting the Lesson

1. Read pages 223 and 224. Remind students to use these steps as reminders when writing different kinds of compositions.
2. Read pages 224 to 226. Review the meanings of *time sequence* and *personal experience.* Discuss the details that Sterling North included. Emphasize the importance of details in making

RASCAL LEARNS A LESSON

I decided one day that Rascal the raccoon was clean enough and bright enough to eat with us at the table. I went to the attic and brought down the family highchair. I had used it when I was a baby.

Next morning while my father was fixing eggs, toast, and coffee, I went to get Rascal. I placed him in the highchair beside me at the table. On his tray I put a heavy stoneware bowl of warm milk. Rascal could reach the milk easily by standing in the chair and placing his hands on the edge of the tray. He seemed to like the new arrangement and chirred and trilled his satisfaction. Except for dribbling a little milk, easily wiped from the tray of the highchair, his table manners were excellent. They were much better than those of most children. My father was amused as usual. He even petted the raccoon as we finished our meal.

Breakfast for three became part of the daily plan, and we had no trouble until I offered Rascal a lump of sugar. Rascal felt it, sniffed it, and then began his usual washing ceremony. He swished it back and forth through his bowl of milk. In a few moments, of course, it melted entirely away. A more surprised little raccoon you have never seen in your life. He felt all over the bottom of the bowl to see if he had dropped it. He turned over his right hand to assure himself it was empty. He examined his left hand in the same way. Finally he looked at me and trilled a shrill question. Who had stolen his sugar lump?

Recovering from my laughter, I gave him a second sugar lump. Rascal examined it carefully. He started to wash it, but stopped. A shrewd look came into his bright black eyes. Instead of washing away a second treat, he took it directly to his mouth. He began to munch it with complete satisfaction.

When Rascal had learned a lesson, he had learned it for life. Never again did he wash a lump of sugar.—STERLING NORTH

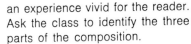

an experience vivid for the reader. Ask the class to identify the three parts of the composition.

3. Assign the Exercise on pages 226 and 227. Help those students who have difficulty getting started. Remind the class to make sure that their subjects are narrow enough for a five-paragraph composition.

Extending the Lesson

Read selected incidents from *Rascal* by Sterling North. Ask students to describe humorous or unusual experiences they have had with pets. If the students seem interested enough, assign a composition on the subject. Gather the completed compositions into a booklet for class reading.

Following a Time Sequence

In the introductory paragraph, the writer tells you that the composition is about Rascal the raccoon, eating with the family. In the body paragraphs, the writer tells what happened. You could list the events he has described. Your list might look like this.

1. Rascal was placed in a highchair.
2. A bowl of milk was put in front of him.
3. Rascal reached the milk.
4. Rascal showed excellent manners.
5. The writer's father was amused and petted the raccoon.
6. Rascal began eating with the writer and his father every day.
7. The writer offered Rascal a lump of sugar.
8. Rascal "washed" the sugar and it melted away.
9. Rascal looked for the sugar and couldn't figure out what had happened to it.
10. The writer gave Rascal a second sugar lump.
11. Rascal put the lump right into his mouth.

The writer ends the composition by stating the lesson that Rascal has learned. Notice how the writer has related all the events in the composition in a time sequence. He tells about what happens first, what happens next, and so on.

Exercise Writing a Narrative or Story

Go back to Chapter 12, Part 2. Use the way described there for finding a subject based on personal experience. Then write a five-paragraph narrative composition. Follow the steps listed at the beginning of this chapter. In case you have trouble finding a subject, here are a few suggestions.

1. The day my dog almost lost his happy home
2. Trapped in a ____________________
3. Learning how to ____________________
4. Moving day
5. The most memorable birthday I've ever had
6. Stung!
7. Nobody's perfect
8. The time I felt totally alone
9. Opening day at the ____________________
10. The hardest thing I've ever done

Part 2 The Descriptive Composition

A descriptive composition, like a descriptive paragraph, paints a picture with words. It is made up of several paragraphs. They work together to create a vivid picture in the mind of the reader.

A descriptive composition includes many details. They appeal to one or more of the senses. These details help the reader to see what the writer sees, smell what the writer smells, hear what the writer hears, taste what the writer tastes, and feel what the writer feels. In this lesson we will work only on descriptive compositions that appeal to the sense of sight.

Using Details

Let's look at a composition that paints a word picture of the monster Ubir. The details used are so specific that you could probably draw a good picture of the monster.

UBIR

In the forests of eastern Asia there once lived a monster named Ubir. She was one of the greediest monsters around. Day and night

Part 2

Objective

To identify and use logical order in organizing a descriptive composition

Presenting the Lesson

1. Read the introduction to Part 2, and Using Details, on pages 227 to 229. Review the definition of *detail.* Ask students to note the details included in the composition "Ubir." Emphasize the importance of details in descriptive writing. Ask the students to identify the three parts of the composition and the topic sentence in each paragraph.

2. Read Following a Logical Order, on pages 229 and 230. Review the meaning of *logical order.* Remind students that when they prepare to write a descriptive composition, they should first get a clear picture of what they are going to describe. They should then examine their mental pictures in a step-by-step manner, noting details as they do so. This process is described in Chapter 6, Part 2, The Descriptive Paragraph.

3. Assign the Exercise on pages 230 to 231. Remind the class to include as many specific details as possible and to arrange the details in logical order. Ask volunteers to share their completed compositions with the class.

Extending the Lesson

To encourage an awareness of details in descriptive writing, have the students draw pictures of the stage set described in the sample composition "Life Star 101."

she prowled the forests, gobbling up the unfortunate men and cattle that crossed her path. Ubir was also very, very ugly.

Ubir wasn't especially tall for a monster, but what she lacked in height she made up in width. Her great stomach measured fifteen feet around. Like most of her body, it was covered with flat, fish-like scales. They changed from blue to green with the shifting light.

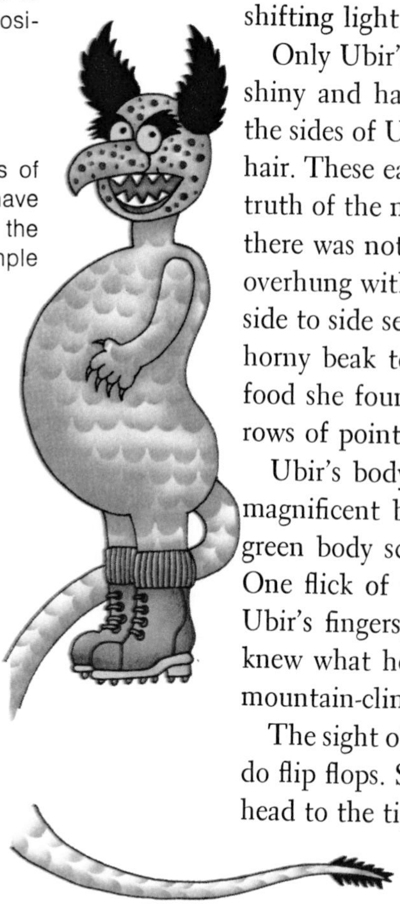

Only Ubir's head and face were without scales. They were both shiny and hairless and were colored with mud-brown spots. On the sides of Ubir's head were large pointed ears covered with black hair. These ears were certainly large enough to hear anything. The truth of the matter is that Ubir was just a little bit deaf. However, there was nothing wrong with her sight. Her bulging yellow eyes, overhung with fierce black brows, never blinked. They swept from side to side searching for tasty morsels. She would often lower her horny beak to sniff the ground for the scent of food. Whatever food she found went immediately into a huge mouth lined with rows of pointed teeth.

Ubir's body was equipped with several weapons. One was her magnificent but deadly tail. It was long and covered with blue-green body scales. Near its end were a dozen razor-sharp points. One flick of that tail meant death to whatever was in its path. Ubir's fingers, too, were tipped with sharp points. No one ever knew what her toes looked like. Ubir always wore heavy, spiked mountain-climbing boots.

The sight of Ubir was enough to make knees shake and stomachs do flip flops. She was the stuff of nightmares, from the top of her head to the tip of her tail.

The writer begins her composition by giving a few facts about Ubir. She lived in eastern Asia. She was greedy. She ate men and cattle. The writer ends her introductory paragraph by stating that Ubir was very ugly. This makes the reader want to know more about Ubir's appearance. The next three paragraphs supply this information. The second paragraph gives details about Ubir's size, shape, and body covering. The third describes Ubir's head and face. The fourth describes her natural weapons. A topic sentence at the beginning of each paragraph lets the reader know what that paragraph is going to be about.

Following a Logical Order

The writer has arranged the details about Ubir's appearance in a logical order. She has started with the monster's overall size and shape. This is a natural place to begin. It's what you usually notice first about someone. She then goes on to Ubir's head and moves down. She describes the monster's ears, eyes, nose, mouth, tail, fingers, and feet. She has arranged the entire composition in top-to-bottom order.

The writer of the next composition has followed a different order. He describes a stage set. He focuses first on the left-hand side of the stage, next on the background, and finally on the right-hand side. This is a natural order. An audience would be likely to examine a set from left to right.

LIFE STAR 101

The set for *Space Dog Saves Life Star 101* was finally finished. The carpenters had pounded the last nail. The painters had finished the last bit of scenery. The furniture movers had shoved everything into place. The curtain hangers had hung the side drapes in perfect pleats. The stage of the J. B. Norton Middle School had been changed into the spaceport and meeting area on Life Star 101.

On the left-hand side of the stage was a large, round space ship. From its shiny silver surface projected six movable observation tubes. A large *D* with an *S* inside it was painted on the top third of the ship.

The backdrop of the set showed the stars and planets surrounding Life Star. Against a background of pale blue were twelve stars —bright silver disks of different sizes. Among the stars floated three planets and their moons. The first planet had a purple-and-white-striped surface and seven pale yellow moons. The second planet was bright yellow and had three black moons. The third was different shades of green, blue green, grass green, and a green so dark it was almost black. It was circled by a large orange moon and by swirls of wispy pink clouds.

The right-hand side of the stage was the meeting area. It was the site of the Life Star peace conference. A white plastic table with six low stools stood ready. At each place was a dish of water. Space Dog's dish was marked with the same *D* and *S* design that was painted on the space ship.

The setting was ready and waiting for the action to begin.

The writer starts this composition by catching your interest. As you read the opening sentences, you probably began to wonder just what the set looks like. In the next three paragraphs the writer tells you.

As he describes the main parts of the set, the writer uses many color words. He uses "shiny silver," "purple-and-white-striped," "bright yellow," "blue green," "grass green," "green so dark it was almost black," and "wispy pink clouds." These help you, the reader, to form a vivid mental picture of the set.

It's now time for you, the reader, to become you, the writer. In developing a descriptive composition, you'll follow the same steps as you did in developing a narrative composition. These stages are listed at the beginning of the chapter. When you make a list of the main ideas in step 5, be sure to have a clear mental picture of what you want to describe. This will help you remember that you want your readers to see in their minds the same thing that you see in yours.

Exercise Writing a Descriptive Composition

Here are some possible subjects for descriptive compositions. Choose one of the subjects or make up one of your own. Then develop a five-paragraph composition. Follow the thirteen steps listed at the beginning of the chapter.

1. A veterinarian's office on a busy afternoon
2. A perfect island
3. A recreation room after a party
4. A classroom
5. A shopping center
6. A park after a rainstorm
7. A tree house
8. A junk yard
9. An imaginary character in a story
10. An interesting looking person you have seen.

Part 3 The Explanatory Composition

The explanatory composition, like the explanatory paragraph, explains something. There are many different types of explanatory compositions. This lesson focuses on two:

1. Those that explain how something is done
2. Those that state an opinion, with reasons to support that opinion.

The "How" Composition

The "how" composition is a group of paragraphs that explain how to do something. A "how" composition gives step-by-step directions in a time sequence. It tells what to do first, what to do second, and so on.

Here is an example of a "how" composition. It tells how to make candles from old crayons. The directions are clear and specific. You would have no trouble following them if you decided to use your old crayons in this way.

Part 3

Objective

To identify time sequence and logical order in two kinds of explantory compositions, the "how" composition and the "why" composition, and to use the appropriate method of organization in writing explanatory compositions

Presenting the Lesson

1. Read the introduction to Part 3 and The "How" Composition, on pages 231 to 233. Emphasize the importance of organizing a "how" composition in a time sequence. Have the class list the main steps given in the sample composition.

2. Assign and discuss the exercise on page 233.

3. Read pages 233 to 235. Review the meaning of *opinion.* Emphasize that the body paragraphs of a "why" composition give reasons that support the opinion in the introductory paragraph. Ask students to identify the topic sentence in each body paragraph. Note that each topic sentence states a main reason. The rest of the sentences explain that reason.

4. Assign the Exercise on page 235. Work in a small group with the students who have difficulty in developing a composition. Take them through each step for writing a composition.

Extending the Lesson

Make copies of the students' "how" paragraphs. Distribute a set to each member of the class. Have the students demonstrate the directions they explained in their paragraphs. After each demonstration, discuss places where the directions should be clarified or expanded. Provide time for students to revise their compositions, based on the class's suggestions.

CANDLES FROM CRAYONS

Have you ever wondered what to do with old, half-used crayons? Have you ever needed an inexpensive gift for someone? Here's a solution to both of these problems. You can make candles out of crayons.

Begin by getting your supplies together. To make one candle, you'll need a pound of paraffin, which you can buy at a supermarket; cotton twine or candlewick, which you can get at a hobby store; and crayons. You'll need a one-pint cardboard juice can with a peel top. If the can has a metal rim, you'll have to cut it off. You'll also need a double boiler or a coffee can in a pan of water, a wooden spoon, a pencil or stick, a small metal weight such as a washer, scissors, and potholder mitts.

Next get your paraffin and wick ready. Break the pound of paraffin into chunks. Melt the chunks in the top of a double boiler, over water, or in a coffee can set in water. Do not melt paraffin directly over heat. It may catch fire. After the paraffin has melted, color it by breaking up a crayon and putting the pieces into the hot wax. For a medium shade, use half a crayon to a pound of paraffin. Stir the melting crayon into the paraffin with a wooden spoon. Then cut a piece of cotton twine or candlewick two inches longer than your juice-can mold. Dip the string into the melted paraffin. Set the wick aside to dry. After it dries, tie one end to the center of a pencil or stick. Tie a weight to the other end to keep the wick straight. Place the stick across the top of the mold. Make sure that the wick hangs down into the container.

You're now ready to pour the candle. Using potholder mitts to protect your hands, pour the paraffin mixture into the mold. The wax may splash, so keep your face away. If you want to make a striped candle, fill only part of the mold. Prepare another paraffin mixture using a different color of crayon. Let each layer harden before adding another color. Let the candle cool overnight. Then untie the stick and cut the wick about half an inch above the top of the candle. Peel off the mold.

Step back and admire your creation. You have made an original gift out of something you'd ordinarily have thrown away.

—*National Geographic World*

The introductory paragraph immediately catches the reader's interest by suggesting a good use for old crayons. The body paragraphs then explain the steps for making a candle in a time sequence. Words like *begin, next, then, now,* and *after* help to move the reader along through the paragraphs. The ending reminds the reader that making candles from crayons is a useful skill.

Exercise Writing a "How" Composition

Make a list of things that you know how to do well. Do you make super special pancakes? Can you oil a bike like an expert? Do you know the best way to mow a lawn? Are you good at entertaining four-year-olds? Do you know all the steps to a popular dance? Choose a subject. Then write a five-paragraph "how" composition. Follow the steps listed at the beginning of this chapter.

The "Why" Composition

The introductory paragraph for a "why" composition states an opinion or idea that the writer believes to be true. The writer of the following opening paragraph, for example, believes that students should take part in making the rules for their school.

STUDENTS MAKING RULES

Every school has rules and regulations. In most schools students have to be in their rooms at a set time. Students have to follow lunch room, learning center, and playground rules. Most of the time these rules are made by the school board, the principal, the teachers, and sometimes by a group of parents. I think it would be better for everyone if the students helped to make the rules.

Introductory paragraph

The topic sentence of the paragraph lets you know that the paragraph is about school rules and regulations. The entire paragraph tells you that the composition is about why students should help to make the rules.

Giving Reasons

The body paragraphs give the reasons why the writer believes as she does.

STUDENTS MAKING RULES

Working with the principal and teachers would help the students to see problems from a different point of view. Most students have a hard time understanding the reasons for some rules. They often think that rules are made to keep them from having fun. They forget about reasons like the safety of younger children or getting along better as a group. If students helped to make the rules, they could explain the reasons behind them to their friends and classmates.

Body paragraphs

Students would be more likely to follow rules that they understand and that they had a part in making. The rules would be their rules, not just the teachers' rules or the principal's rules. Therefore, the students would be more likely to see that the rules were followed by everyone.

Most important, by helping to make the school rules, students would learn to accept responsibility for their actions. They would have to think about how the rules they suggested would affect everyone in the school. They would have to decide whether to be for or against suggested rules and to have good reasons for their choices. They would have to answer to all of the students for the success or the failure of the rules they helped to make.

Arranging the Reasons

The writer has given three main reasons to support her opinion:

1. Students would see problems from a different point of view.
2. Students would be more likely to follow rules they helped to make.
3. Students would learn to accept responsibility.

She has arranged these reasons from the least important to the most important. She has then developed each of them into a paragraph.

The Ending Paragraph

The writer ends the composition by explaining how, if her suggestion were carried out, school would be improved for everyone.

STUDENTS MAKING RULES

Including students in making rules would be good for the entire school. The students who worked on the rules would be better able to see problems from different points of view. They would learn to think about how their actions would affect other people. All the students would have either a direct or an indirect part in making the rules. Therefore, they would be more likely to follow these rules. The teachers and the principal would not have to waste a lot of their time in seeing that rules were followed. They could spend that time in planning interesting projects or in helping students.

Ending paragraph

Exercise Writing a "Why" Composition

Following are ten opinion statements. Each one could be developed into a "why" composition. Choose one or write an opinion statement of your own. Then write a five-paragraph composition giving reasons to support the opinion. Be sure to follow the steps for writing a composition that are listed at the beginning of this chapter.

1. Decisions affecting everyone in a family should be made at a family conference.
2. No one should be allowed to have an exotic pet.
3. Apartment buildings are interesting places to live.
4. Students should help make up school cafeteria menus.
5. Everyone in a family should share in the chores.
6. Everyone should have a private place.
7. Every town should have a curfew.
8. Every child should have to work for an allowance.
9. Every child should have a fixed allowance.
10. Students should have to take part in an after-school activity.

Chapter 14

Using Adjectives

Part 1 What Are Adjectives?

Look at the horse in the picture. Does the sentence below tell you what kind of horse it is?

Brian owns a horse.

Can you tell what kind of horse Brian owns when you read the following sentence?

Brian owns a brown horse with a white blaze on its nose and forehead.

What words are added in the second sentence to tell you which kind of horse Brian owns? *Brown* and *white* make the meaning more exact. They are **adjectives.** Adjectives are words that are used with nouns and pronouns. They are called **modifiers** because they change, or modify, the meaning of the word they go with.

Chapter Objectives

1. To understand the function of the adjective, and to identify adjectives in sentences

2. To identify and use articles

3. To understand and to use predicate adjectives

4. To recognize the formation of proper adjectives, and to use proper adjectives with correct capitalization

5. To use the demonstrative adjectives (*this, that, these, those*) correctly

6. To differentiate between *those,* used as either a demonstrative adjective or pronoun, and *them,* used only as a pronoun

7. To form the comparative and superlative forms of adjectives, and to choose the correct form.

Preparing the Students

Ask students to examine the picture on page 236 and to list ten things in the picture that can be named with nouns (*boy, hat*). Then ask students to add one word before each of the nouns on their list that helps to describe it (*blond* boy, *straw* hat). Discuss how much more specific the communication is when the second word is added. Explain that these words are called adjectives and that their use will be further explored in this chapter.

Additional Resources

Diagnostic Test—page 430

Mastery Test—pages 465 and 466

Additional Mastery Test—Recommended for use after any necessary reteaching. (In separate booklet, *Diagnostic and Mastery Tests, Gold Level,* pages 41 and 42.)

Skills Practice Book—pages 88–94

Duplicating Masters—pages 88–94

Part 1

Objective

To understand the function of the adjective, and to identify adjectives in sentences

Presenting the Lesson

1. Read and discuss the introduction to Part I on pages 237 and 238. Make sure the students are conscious of how the meaning of the sentences at the top of page 238 changes with the substitution of different adjectives. How many more adjectives can students think of to fit the basic sentence?

2. Read Some Adjectives Tell *What Kind.* Ask students to change the meaning of the four sample sentences by changing the adjectives in italics. Note the adjective endings listed at the bottom of the page. Can students think of additional adjectives with these endings?

3. Read Some Adjectives Tell *How Many.* Discuss how the four sample sentences can be changed by changing the adjectives in italics. Point out that adjectives can tell "how many" in countable amounts (one, sixteen) or in general amounts (few, several).

4. Read Some Adjectives Tell *Which Ones.* Point out that these adjectives do not describe the nouns they modify, but serve to point them out.

Specific information on demonstrative adjectives, and practice in their use, will be presented in Part 5 of this chapter. At this time it should not be necessary to go into detail.

5. In addition to the definition of an adjective presented in Chapter

Only the adjectives differ in the following sentences. How does the adjective change, or modify, the picture you have in your mind as you read each sentence?

1. Kathy drove along the *crowded* highway.
2. Kathy drove along the *deserted* highway.
3. Kathy drove along the *narrow* highway.
4. Kathy drove along the *bumpy* highway.

An **adjective** is a word that modifies a noun or pronoun.

One or more adjectives may be used before the noun or pronoun being modified. Very often, when we use two or more adjectives together, we separate them with commas.

The *hot, thick, sticky* topping smothered the ice cream.

Adjectives may also follow the noun or pronoun being modified.

I met Al, *tired* and *hungry,* at the top of the canyon trail.

Some Adjectives Tell What Kind

We use adjectives to describe what we are talking about. They tell *what kind* of thing we have in mind.

1. Henry wore *furry* gloves and a *colorful* scarf.
2. The alligator's *sharp* teeth are *dangerous* weapons.
3. Lately we have had *warm, rainy* weather.
4. Goldilocks found a *comfortable* bed.

Many adjectives that tell *what kind* are formed by adding an adjective ending to a noun. Here are some examples:

Noun		Adjective Ending		Adjective
rain	+	y	=	rainy
color	+	ful	=	colorful
danger	+	ous	=	dangerous
comfort	+	able	=	comfortable

Some other adjective endings are *-less*, *-ible*, and *-al*.

careless driving　　*terrible* storms
experimental model

Some Adjectives Tell How Many

We use adjectives to tell *how many* we are talking about.

1. Mr. and Mrs. Ellsworth own *twenty* trucks.
2. Their trucks travel across *several* states.
3. Some trucks have *many* license plates.
4. They have *frequent* repairs but *few* accidents.

Some Adjectives Tell Which Ones

Some adjectives tell *which one* or *which ones* we are talking about.

1. *These* trucks hold nine rooms of furniture.
2. *Those* trucks transport new automobiles.
3. *This* truck is used for hauling coal or dirt.
4. *That* truck is used to tow away wrecks.

Exercises　Using Adjectives

A. Copy these sentences. Draw a line under each adjective that tells *what kind.*

Example: Karen has long, curly hair.

1. Tina complained of stiff knees.
2. Bonnie scraped sticky gum from her shoe.
3. Do you know how to do artificial respiration?
4. An unearthly howl made Rich tremble.
5. These green darts are for Tim.
6. Peculiar rhythmic noises came from the closet.
7. The sky was filled with white, puffy clouds.
8. The boys looked for small starfish.

14, there are other ways to identify an adjective. These ways, listed in the following chart, are based on what linguists have discovered about the structure of a word and the order of words in a sentence. It is suggested that the information in the chart be used to point out additional ways in which adjectives function.

Ways To Identify Adjectives

1. Adjectives have more than one form. They change form to show comparison. Adjectives of more than two syllables usually show comparison by using the words *more* and *most*.

new	newer	newest
good	better	best
awful	more awful	most awful

2. Adjectives are often preceded by words such as *very*, *quite*, or *much*.

very bright　quite good
much better

3. Adjectives usually occur before nouns.

Rosa has a *beautiful* ring.
Juan has the *best* idea.

6. It is suggested that you do both Exercises A and B on pages 239 and 240 with the class.

7. See Exercise A on page 249 for additional practice.

Optional Practice

Ask students to supply three different adjectives to modify each of the following nouns. Write a sentence using each noun with one of the adjectives.

dress	flowers	lawn
table	dinner	horse

B. Number your paper from 1 to 8. Make two columns. Head one column *Which Ones.* Head the other *How Many.* Find the adjectives in these sentences and place them in the right column.

Example: Those trees have grown two feet this year.

Which Ones	How Many
those, this	two

WO = Which Ones
HM = How Many

1. That (WO) light flashed a signal to some (HM) men on the shore.
2. Many (HM) people prefer this (WO) brand of frozen dinners.
3. Look at this (WO) odometer now.
4. Mr. Harvey had several (HM) boxes of cartridges.
5. Is this (WO) saddle for Sara?
6. These (WO) cards belong to that (WO) game.
7. Janet has used this (WO) saw many (HM) times.
8. We have ordered several (HM) cakes from that (WO) bakery.

Part 2 The Articles

The words *a, an,* and *the* are called **articles.** Since they always modify nouns, they are also adjectives.

Use *a* before words beginning with consonant sounds.

a box *a* hat *a* horse *a* moth

Use *an* before words beginning with vowel sounds:

an apple	*an* engineer	*an* island	*an* ostrich	*an* umbrella
an ape	*an* eagle	*an* icicle	*an* overcoat	*an* uncle

Some words begin with a silent *h.* In these words, you do not say the *h* sound. Instead, you begin the word with the vowel sound after the *h.* Therefore, you follow the rule given above, and use *an:*

an honor *an* hour *an* honest person

Part 2

Objective

To identify and use articles

Presenting the Lesson

1. Read aloud The Articles on page 240. Point out that *the* can be used with either beginning consonant or vowel sounds. If students bring up the question, explain that the long *u* sound is grouped with the consonants. The article *a* is used before the long *u* sound. (*a* uniform, not *an* uniform)

2. Point out that articles are special adjectives that specify nouns but do not describe them. They are never used with pronouns.

3. It is suggested that Exercise A on page 241 be done orally. Assign and discuss Exercise B.

4. See Exercise B on page 249 for additional practice.

Exercises Using Articles

A. Copy the following sentences. Fill in the blanks with *a* or *an*.

1. I just peeled __an__ onion.
2. __An__ acrobat could do that.
3. Carlos was riding __a__ bicycle.
4. Is that __an__ iceberg near the horizon?
5. Can you ride __a__ horse?
6. Dennis is known as __an__ honest person.
7. Mom's gone to __an__ important meeting.
8. Does the car have __an__ undercoating to prevent rust?
9. Our national bird is __an__ eagle.
10. The boat drifted in __an__ aimless pattern.

B. There are twelve nouns below. Write six sentences, using two of the nouns in each sentence. Place an article and another adjective before each noun. Answers will vary.

1. man	4. rocks	7. brook	10. stream
2. trees	5. leaves	8. bushes	11. flowers
3. valleys	6. dog	9. mountains	12. path

Part 3 Predicate Adjectives

When an adjective follows a state-of-being verb like *is* or *seemed*, it is part of the predicate. However, it often modifies a noun or pronoun in the subject. Look at these examples.

He is right. The patient seemed dazed.

When an adjective following a state-of-being verb modifies the subject, it is called a **predicate adjective.**

Optional Practice

Have students decide whether *a* or *an* should be used with each of the following words or phrases.

______box
______eggplant
______jar
______usual day
______unusual test
______hourglass

Extending the Lesson

Explain that the article *the* is called a definite article because it specifies a particular item.

the envelope (a specific envelope)
the book (a specific book)

A and *an* are indefinite articles because they do not indicate a specific item.

an envelope (any one)
a book (any one)

Ask students to identify each article they used in Exercise B as definite or indefinite.

Part 3

Objective

To understand the function of predicate adjectives, and to use predicate adjectives

Presenting the Lesson

1. Briefly review linking verbs (Chapter 8, Part 4). Remind students that linking verbs connect the subject with a word in the predicate.

2. Read Predicate Adjectives on page 241. Be sure that students understand that the adjective in the predicate must modify the subject, and not any other noun. Here is a sample sentence:

The flower is a yellow daisy.

The adjective *yellow* modifies the noun *daisy* and not the subject *flower. Yellow* is not a predicate adjective. Here is another sentence:

The flower is yellow.

The adjective *yellow* modifies the subject *flower.* In this sentence, *yellow* is a predicate adjective.

3. It is suggested that you do Exercise A, page 242, on the board with the class. Assign and discuss Exercise B.

4. See Exercise C on page 250 for additional practice.

Optional Practice

Have the students tell whether the underlined adjective is a predicate adjective. If it does not modify the subject, what noun does it modify?

1. My favorite sweater is beige.
2. The dog was a gray poodle.
3. Bill's uncle is friendly.
4. The explorers were restless travelers.
5. Several parents were present.

Part 4

Objective

To recognize the formation of proper adjectives, and to use proper adjectives with correct capitalization

Exercises Using Predicate Adjectives

A. Copy these sentences, putting an adjective in the blank. Draw an arrow from the adjective to the word it modifies.

Answers will vary.

1. Lemons are ________.
2. Before a test, we are very ________.
3. The boys were ________ after their victory.
4. Every day at noon, I am ________.
5. The sky was ________ this morning.
6. With the new addition, the house will be ________.
7. You are ________ than any other student here.
8. This rose is ________.
9. Ann will be ________ when she sees your present.
10. From far away, the bell sounded ________.

B. Follow directions for Exercise A.

Answers will vary.

1. The plane to Omaha will be ________.
2. The early settlers were very ________.
3. Your new suit looks ________.
4. That book was ________.
5. The week-old milk smells ________.
6. Without water, the plants will become ________.
7. Vincent's violin sounds ________.
8. This apple tastes ________.

Part 4 Proper Adjectives

In this chapter, you have already used many adjectives formed from common nouns, for example, *rainy, dangerous, comfortable.* **Proper adjectives** are adjectives formed from proper nouns.

You know that a proper noun names a particular person, place, or thing. By adding adjective endings to some proper nouns, we change them into proper adjectives. Here are some examples:

Proper Noun	**Proper Adjective + Noun Modified**
Arthur	Arthurian legend
Britain	British royalty
Japan	Japanese yen
Mexico	Mexican jewelry

Very often a proper name is used as an adjective without the addition of an adjective ending. Here are some examples of the second kind of proper adjective:

Hitchcock thriller   Cinderella story   Ford engine

1. A **proper adjective** is an adjective that has been made from a proper noun.
2. A proper adjective begins with a capital letter.

Exercises Using Proper Adjectives

A. Number your paper from 1 to 10. Write each proper adjective in these sentences. Capitalize correctly.

1. Is that an irish setter?
2. The austrian ski team won the downhill competition.
3. My sister bought a japanese stereo set.
4. This delicatessen sells polish sausages.
5. When was the alaskan pipeline started?
6. The jewish community is celebrating Rosh Hoshana.
7. We had kentucky fried chicken.
8. The canadian Rockies are higher than the american Rockies.
9. Napoleon's army was defeated by the russian winter.
10. The museum just purchased a picasso painting.

Presenting the Lesson

1. Review proper nouns (Chapter 7, Part 2). Emphasize that all proper nouns are capitalized. (Be sure that students do not confuse the words *proper nouns* with the word *pronouns*.)

2. Read Part 4 on pages 242 and 243. Ask students for examples of both types of proper adjectives: those formed by adding adjective endings to proper nouns, and those formed by using proper nouns in adjective positions.

3. Assign and discuss Exercises A and B.

4. See Exercise D on page 250 for additional practice.

Extending the Lesson

1. Ask students for the proper adjective that corresponds with each of the following proper nouns.

Alaska	Wales	Canada
America	Ireland	France

2. Have students use each of the words below in two sentences; first, as a proper noun, and then as a proper adjective.

Muppet   Chevrolet   Dr. Seuss

B. Follow the directions for Exercise A.

1. When was the gregorian calender developed?
 _G
2. Valerie had a siamese kitten and a persian cat.
 _S _P
3. Cleopatra ruled the egyptian people.
 _E
4. I like italian dressing better than french dressing.
 _I _F
5. Lawrence is taking german lessons.
 _G
6. My aunt bought some real indian turquoise.
 _I
7. Mrs. Haas was a dutch immigrant.
 _D
8. It is hard to add roman numerals.
 _R
9. The bantu chief greeted the travelers with dignity.
 _B
10. Eduardo drove an italian car across the canadian border.
 _I _C

Part 5

Objectives

1. To use the demonstrative adjectives (*this, that, these, those*) correctly

2. To differentiate between *those,* used as either a demonstrative adjective or pronoun, and *them,* used only as a pronoun

Presenting the Lesson

1. Read pages 244 and 245. Ask students to suggest phrases using the four demonstratives. Make sure the students realize that *this* and *these* refer to objects that are close at hand, while *that* and *those* refer to objects that are at a distance.

2. Some students will need more emphasis on the *them/those* usage than others. Plan the discussion to suit the needs of your class.

3. It is suggested that you do Exercises A and B as a class activity. What are the common errors?

4. See Exercise E on page 251 for additional practice.

Part 5 Demonstrative Adjectives

Four adjectives that tell which one, or which ones, are *this, that, these,* and *those.* When they modify nouns or pronouns, they point out specific things.

> *This* cake tastes sweeter than *that* one.
> *These* notebooks cost a quarter each. *Those* notebooks cost a dollar.

This, that, these, and *those* are called the **demonstrative adjectives.**

We use *this* and *that* with singular nouns. We use *these* and *those* with plural nouns.

this Frisbee	these Frisbees
that field	those fields

The nouns *kind* and *sort* are singular. Therefore, we say *this kind* and *this sort.* We use *these* and *those* only with the plurals: *these kinds* or *those sorts.*

Using *Those* and *Them*

Those is a word with many uses. It may be used as an adjective:

> Where did you find *those* skates?

Those may also be used as a pronoun. As a pronoun it can be the subject of a verb or it can be an object.

Those are my books. (subject)

We'll clean these shelves today. Leave *those* for tomorrow. (object of verb)

Them is always an object pronoun. It is never used as an adjective. As a pronoun, it is never used in the subject.

Right: My uncle gave me *those* stamps.

Right: *Those* are my stamps. He gave *them* to me.

Exercises Using Demonstrative Adjectives and *Them*

A. Number your paper from 1 to 10. Choose the correct pronoun.

1. Bill needs (that, those) kind of car to finish his train set.
2. (Them, Those) flowers across the street are snapdragons.
3. Do you like (this, these) kind of coat?
4. (These, Them) girls with me are my cousins.
5. (Those, These) swimming lessons last summer were fun.
6. Lois often buys (them, these) sorts of rings.
7. Can you see (those, them) geese flying south?
8. I think (those, them) kinds of cookies are the best.
9. These cookies have chopped walnuts in (those, them).
10. (Them, These) illustrations are by Wanda Gag.

B. Copy these sentences. Use *them* or *those* in the blanks.

1. You can't ask __them__ for all __those__ labels.
2. Are __those__ posters dry yet?
3. Tell __them__ to come back tomorrow.
4. __Those__ slacks fit me better than these.
5. Joan took the boxes and painted __them__.
6. Where did you get all __those__ old magazines?
7. __Those__ missions were built by the Spaniards.
8. I want those posters. How much do you charge for __them__?

Optional Practice

Ask students to add a demonstrative adjective to each sentence below. They should be able to tell whether the modified noun is singular or plural.

1. ______ birthday card will make her happy.
2. Can you bring ______ paper with you?
3. ______ trees are covered with apple blossoms.
4. I read ______ books.
5. Did you find ______ dictionary?

Extending the Lesson

Discuss the difference between the use of demonstratives as adjectives and their use as pronouns. As adjectives they must modify nouns. Have students decide whether each of the underlined words is a demonstrative adjective or a demonstrative pronoun. They should give reasons for their answers.

1. *This* is very important.
2. *These* answers are correct.
3. *That* is not funny.
4. *That* cheerleader is full of school spirit.
5. *These* are mine.

Part 6

Objective

To form the comparative and superlative forms of adjectives, and to choose the correct form in sentences

Presenting the Lesson

1. Read pages 246 and 247. Make sure the students see the difference between the comparative form (used to compare two things) and the superlative form (used to compare three or more things).

Part 6 Making Comparisons with Adjectives

A bear is big. An elephant is big. A dinosaur was big.

Are all three animals the same size? Certainly, the answer is no. If we want to say the animals are of different sizes, will the word *big* do the job? Again, the answer is no. However, we can change the word *big* so that it will show the differences in the group.

We use the word *bigger* to compare two persons or things.

An elephant is *bigger* than a bear.
A dinosaur was *bigger* than a bear.

We call *bigger* the **comparative form** of *big*.

We use *biggest* to compare three or more persons or things.

A dinosaur was the *biggest* of the three.
A dinosaur was the *biggest* of all animals.

We call *biggest* the **superlative form** of *big*.

Use the **comparative form** of an adjective to compare *two* things.

Between the history and spelling tests, the history test was harder.

Use the **superlative form** of an adjective when you are concerned with *three or more* things.

The math exam was the hardest test of all.

Usually, we form the comparative form of a short adjective by adding *-er*, and the superlative form by adding *-est*.

Adjective	Comparative Form	Superlative Form
long	longer	longest
old	older	oldest
funny	funnier	funniest

For longer adjectives, we form the comparative by using the word *more*, and the superlative by using the word *most*.

Adjective	**Comparative Form**	**Superlative Form**
difficult	more difficult	most difficult
noticeable	more noticeable	most noticeable
careful	more careful	most careful

Use only one form of comparison at a time. Do not use *more* and *-er* with the same word, or *most* and *-est* with the same word.

Wrong: This pillow is *more softer* than that one.
Right: This pillow is *softer* than that one.

Wrong: That painting is the *most prettiest* of all.
Right: That painting is the *prettiest* of all.

The Forms of *Good* and *Bad*

A few adjectives do not change their forms by adding *-er* or *-est*. The comparative and superlative forms of the adjectives are completely new words. Here are two important ones to remember:

good better best   bad worse worst

Exercise Making Comparisons with Adjectives

Choose the correct form of the adjective from the parentheses.

1. Claire is the (carefulest, most careful) bike rider I know.
2. Tomorrow will be (colder, more colder) than today.
3. Who is the (most old, oldest) in your family?
4. I was wearing my (bestest, best) jeans.
5. The Sky Harbor weather is (badder, worse) than ours.
6. Have you heard the (latest, most late) news?
7. Superman is (stronger, strongest) than ordinary humans.
8. Cindy has the (most, mostest) beautiful guitar.
9. The snow was (worse, worser) in the parking lot.
10. That is the (best, better) picture in the whole book.

2. Point out that long adjectives would be difficult to pronounce with *er* or *est* added. It is easier to say and understand a long adjective with *more* or *most* before it.

3. Ask students to suggest sentences using the comparative and superlative forms of *good* and *bad*. Can students give both forms for these adjectives:

little (less, least, or littler, littlest)
much (more, most)
many (more, most)
ill (worse, worst)

Tell students that the dictionary will provide comparative and superlative forms of adjectives that do not follow the regular patterns.

4. Point out that only adjectives that describe (tell *what kind*) can be used in comparisons. Demonstratives, articles, proper adjectives, and adjectives that tell *how many* do not have forms for comparison.

5. It is suggested that you do the Exercise on page 247 orally. Discuss reasons for each answer.

6. See Exercise F on page 251 for additional practice.

Optional Practice

Have students choose the correct form of the adjective from the parentheses.

1. A balanced meal is (gooder, better) for your health than junk food.
2. Name brands are usually (expensiver, more expensive) than generic foods.
3. My fever is (worse, more worse) today.
4. That is the (funnier, funniest) show of the season.
5. Between Andrea and Luis, Luis is the (taller, tallest).

Sentence Patterns

Objective

To recognize the use of adjectives in the N LV Adj sentence pattern

Presenting the Lesson

1. Read and discuss page 248. If students raise the question, let them know there may be more than one word in the adjective-part of an N LV Adj sentence.

N	LV	Adj
Peter	is	very friendly.
This melon	tastes	even sweeter.

2. Assign and discuss Exercises A, B, and C.

Extending the Lesson

Have students decide which of the sentences below fits the N LV Adj pattern. Which sentences fit the patterns previously studied (N V, N V N, N LV N)?

1. She is friendly.
2. Lions roared.
3. Those pirates buried the treasure.
4. The children seem busy.
5. Kittens are cute baby animals.

Sentence Patterns — The N LV Adj Pattern

There are three parts to sentences that have the **N LV Adj pattern.** The *N* stands for the subject noun. *LV* stands for a linking verb. *Adj* stands for the predicate adjective. Each of the sentences in the following chart is in the N LV Adj pattern.

N	LV	Adj
Peter	is	friendly.
The water	looks	murky.
Evonne	was	sunburned.
Your voice	sounds	hoarse.
This melon	tastes	sweet.

Exercises The N LV Adj Pattern

A. Make a chart like the one above. Label the three columns *N, LV,* and *Adj.* Write these sentences on the chart.

1. Lottie (N) | seems (LV) | cautious (Adj).
2. This ice (N) | is (LV) | slippery (Adj).
3. Cherry pie (N) | is (LV) | delicious (Adj).
4. Skydivers (N) | are (LV) | adventurous (Adj).
5. Jeff (N) | seemed (LV) | lucky (Adj).
6. The Cubs (N) | were (LV) | victorious (Adj).
7. The sky (N) | looked (LV) | gloomy (Adj).
8. My father (N) | will be (LV) | late (Adj).

B. Make a chart like the one below. Complete each sentence in the N LV Adj pattern. Answers will vary.

	N	LV	Adj
1.	________	is	cheerful.
2.	The snow	became	________.
3.	Clowns	look	________.
4.	The Soos	________	busy.
5.	________	was	________.

C. Make a chart of your own. Label the columns *N, LV,* and *Adj.* Write five sentences in the N LV Adj pattern.

Additional Exercises

Using Adjectives

A. Using Adjectives (Use after page 239.)

Number from 1 to 10. Make three columns. Head the columns *What Kind, How Many,* and *Which Ones.* Find those kinds of adjectives in these sentences and place each in the right column.

WK = What Kind
HM = How Many
WO = Which Ones

1. That [WO] lake has a sandy [WK] beach.
2. There are nine [HM] planets in the solar [WK] system.
3. Those [WO] coins fell out of my back [WK] pocket.
4. For several [HM] miles, we drove in dense [WK], soupy [WK] fog.
5. That [WO] heavy [WK] rain saved many [HM] farmers.
6. Babe Zaharias won several [HM] important [WK] tournaments.
7. These [WO] four [HM] months are named for ancient [WK] gods.
8. Strong [WK] west [WK] winds bent those [WO] trees.
9. During the evening, Kim killed twenty [HM] mosquitoes.
10. That [WO] experimental [WK] model made many [HM] trial [WK] flights.

B. Using Articles (Use after page 240.)

Copy the following sentences. Fill in the blanks with *a* or *an*.

1. Mary Poppins always carried ____an____ umbrella.
2. I feel a draft from ____an____ open window.
3. ____A____ huge crowd turned out for the fireworks.
4. A figure with eight sides is ____an____ octagon.
5. The governor's visit is ____an____ honor for our school.
6. The lab did ____an____ analysis of the patient's blood sample.
7. This fairy tale is about ____an____ enchanted princess.
8. Evelyn saw ____a____ cardinal in her back yard.

Additional Exercises

If these exercises have not been previously assigned, use them now for chapter review.

9. That terrible shipwreck was caused by __an__ iceberg.
10. You will never find __a__ mastodon in the zoo.

C. Using Predicate Adjectives (Use after page 241.)

Copy these sentences, putting an adjective in the blank. Draw an arrow from the adjective to the word it modifies.

1. That pie was __Answers will vary.__.
2. The water under the ice is ________.
3. Most of your answers are ________.
4. The ambulance siren sounded ________.
5. That radio station is not ________.
6. After the parade, the streets were ________.
7. Some toothpicks are ________.
8. Courtney will look very ________ on those stilts.
9. This candy is too ________.
10. The toaster is ________, but it still works.

D. Using Proper Adjectives (Use after page 243.)

Number your paper from 1 to 10. Write each proper adjective in these sentences. Capitalize correctly.

1. Tomorrow is the japanese firefly festival.
2. Those long loaves are french bread.
3. Vanya has a strong russian accent.
4. My favorite paintings are rembrandt portraits.
5. We had chinese chop suey at the restaurant.
6. Some african countries are very small.
7. The spanish language is spoken in latin american countries.
8. "The Entertainer" is a scott joplin rag.
9. Those gloves are italian imports.
10. They were weighing california oranges.

E. Using Demonstrative Adjectives (Use after page 245.)

Number your paper from 1 to 10. Choose the correct pronoun from the parentheses.

1. Mr. Redlin gave the students' papers back to (those, them).
2. Did Alice find (them, those) missing keys?
3. Many people like (that, those) kind of music.
4. (Those, Them) melons are almost ripe.
5. Dan grew (this, these) sort of peppers in his garden.
6. Joanne listened to (those, them) records all afternoon.
7. These windows look streaked. I'll wash (those, them) again.
8. (That, Those) kinds of shoes are not good for hiking.
9. Barbara will buy (those, them) skates with her savings.
10. I can eat all (them, those) pieces of pizza.

F. Making Comparisons with Adjectives (Use after page 247.)

Number your paper from 1 to 10. Choose the correct form of the adjective from the parentheses.

1. Of the two sisters, Jean sings the (better, best).
2. Elena is the (goodest, best) swimmer on the team.
3. Is Bill (stronger, strongest) than you?
4. Mr. Jensen is the (most honest, most honestest) man I know.
5. This is the (better, best) of the three shows.
6. My alarm clock has a (more loud, louder) buzzer than yours.
7. You should use a (lighter, more light) bowling ball than that one.
8. Teresa's ice skates are (newer, more new) than mine.
9. Sean has the (baddest, worst) temper in the family.
10. Mother bought the (softer, softest) pillows she could find.

Chapter 15

Using Adverbs

Part 1 What Are Adverbs?

Adjectives modify nouns and pronouns. **Adverbs** modify verbs, adjectives, and other adverbs.

Adverbs Modify Verbs

Jo kneeled.

How? Jo kneeled *carefully*.

Where? Jo kneeled *outside*.

When? Jo kneeled *immediately*.

Adverbs Modify Adjectives

That is a bright light.

How bright? That is a *very* bright light.

This stunt is dangerous.

How dangerous? This stunt is *too* dangerous.

Chapter Objectives

1. To understand the function of the adverb, and to identify adverbs in sentences
2. To form the comparative and superlative forms of adverbs, and to use the correct forms in sentences
3. To differentiate between adverbs and adjectives, and to make the correct choice in sentences

Preparing the Students

Ask the students to look at the picture on page 253 and to describe the picture using details. List their descriptive phrases on the board. Most (if not all) phrases will use adjectives: *pink* dress, *green* grass, *tiny* flower. Ask the students what class of word is modified by these adjectives. In most cases, the answer will be nouns.

Then write the sentence *Jo kneeled.* Point out that the sentence has not only a noun, but also a verb. Refer to the phrases already listed. Do any of the descriptive words modify a verb? Explain that this Chapter will present the group of words that can be used to describe words other than nouns and their substitutes, pronouns.

Additional Resources

Diagnostic Test—page 431

Mastery Test—pages 467 and 468

Additional Mastery Test—Recommended for use after any necessary reteaching. (In separate booklet, *Diagnostic and Mastery Tests, Gold Level,* pages 43, 44.)

Skills Practice Book—pages 95–100

Duplicating Masters—pages 95–100

Part 1

Objective

To understand the function of the adverb, and to identify adverbs in sentences

Presenting the Lesson

1. Read pages 253 and 254. Discuss the sentences in the examples. Can students offer other adverbs for each example?

2. Ask students to form adverbs by adding *-ly* to the adjectives in this list:

sure fair slow joyful correct

3. In addition to the definition of an adverb given in Chapter 15, there are other ways to identify an adverb, based on what linguists have discovered about the structure of a word and the order of words in a sentence. The following chart lists these ways. You may use the information in the chart to point out additional ways in which adverbs function.

Ways To Identify Adverbs

1. Adverbs are often difficult to separate from adjectives. One of the best ways to identify adverbs is by their positions in sentences. They are most often found at the end of a sentence.

She walked *slowly*.
He worked *quickly*.

2. Adverbs can also be found in other places in a sentence.

AT THE BEGINNING
Now I will hurry.
BETWEEN SUBJECT AND VERB
The people *here* are honest.

Adverbs Modify Other Adverbs

John dances well.

How well? John dances *extremely* well.

The horse ran away.

To what extent? The horse ran *far* away.

As the above examples show, adverbs usually tell *how, when where,* or *to what extent* about the words they modify. If you are not sure whether a word is an adverb, ask yourself if it answers one of these questions. Generally, an adverb that modifies an adjective or another adverb comes before the word it modifies, as in *very* bright, *extremely* well. An adverb that modifies a verb may often be placed in more than one position in the sentence: He watched TV *often*. *Often* he watched TV. He *often* watched TV.

Many adverbs are formed by adding -ly to an adjective:

bad — badly	slow — slowly	careful — carefully
quick — quickly	happy — happily	suspicious — suspiciously

> **Adverbs** modify verbs, adjectives, and other adverbs.

Exercises Finding and Using Adverbs

A. Number from 1 to 20. Copy each adverb below. Write *how, where, when,* or *to what extent* to show what each adverb tells.

1. angrily (how)	6. quite (to what extent)	11. well (how)	16. soon (when)
2. meekly (how)	7. now (when)	12. almost (to what extent)	17. often (when)
3. slowly (how)	8. too (to what extent)	13. always (when)	18. afterward (when)
4. quickly (how)	9. never (when)	14. very (to what extent)	19. sometimes (when)
5. outside (where)	10. ever (when)	15. there (where)	20. early (when)

B. Write five sentences. Use a different one of these adverbs in each sentence.

very now here never often

C. Number your paper from 1 to 10. Write every adverb used in each sentence.

1. Roberto was there yesterday.
2. Suddenly Jill looked up.
3. Soon the sun came out.
4. Because of his cold, Dennis can hardly talk.
5. When the fire alarm rang, the class filed outside quickly.
6. Fortunately I didn't slide on the ice too often.
7. Those two boys are never sleepy.
8. The explosion happened so quickly.
9. Did you ever hear Louisa play?
10. Soon afterward the mist cleared.

Part 2 Making Comparisons with Adverbs

Since adverbs, like adjectives, are words that describe, they can be changed to comparative and superlative forms. You use the **comparative form** when you consider two persons or things:

Jack ran *faster* than the giant.

You use the **superlative form** when you consider three or more persons or things:

The cheetah runs the *fastest* of all animals.

The comparative and superlative forms of adverbs are formed in three different ways.

Some short adverbs add *-er* for the comparative and *-est* for the superlative.

WITHIN VERB PHRASES

You can *often* see that star.

BEFORE AN ADJECTIVE

David was *unusually* quiet.

3. Look for words that fit the blank in this test sentence:

He did it ________.

4. Look for words with the ending *-ly:*

adjective + *ly* = adverb

bad + ly = badly

quick + ly = quickly

4. Assign and discuss Exercises A, B, and C on pages 254 and 255.

5. See Exercise A on page 260 for additional practice.

Optional Practice

Have students use each of the adverbs in Exercise A in original sentences. Discuss what words they modify.

Part 2

Objective

To form the comparative and superlative forms of adverbs, and to use the correct form in sentences

Presenting the Lesson

1. Read pages 255 and 256. Discuss the similarities between the adjective and adverb forms of comparison.

2. Assign and discuss Exercises A and B on pages 256 and 257.

3. See Exercise B on pages 260 and 261 for additional practice.

Optional Practice

Have students use each of the words in Exercise A on page 256 in a sentence. They should identify whether the adverbs tell *how, when, where,* or *to what extent.*

Adverb	Comparative Form	Superlative Form
fast	faster	fastest
hard	harder	hardest

Most adverbs that end in *-ly* form the comparative with the word *more.* They form the superlative with the word *most.*

Adverb	Comparative Form	Superlative Form
easily	more easily	most easily
carefully	more carefully	most carefully

Some adverbs make their comparative and superlative forms by complete word changes.

Adverb	Comparative Form	Superlative Form
well	better	best
much	more	most
little	less	least
badly	worse	worst

Exercises Making Comparisons with Adverbs

A. Number your paper from 1 to 12. Make three columns. Copy the words below in the first column. Write the comparative form in the second column and the superlative in the third.

more often, most often 1. often	more quickly, most quickly 5. quickly	worse, worst 9. badly
more heavily, most heavily 2. heavily	better, best 6. well	earlier, earliest 10. early
more peacefully, most peacefully 3. peacefully	more easily, most easily 7. easily	more strongly, most strongly 11. strongly
more carefully, most carefully 4. carefully	more slowly, most slowly 8. slowly	sooner, soonest 12. soon

B. Number from 1 to 8. Choose the right word from the parentheses. Write it on your paper.

1. Sheila pitches (most fast, fastest) when the pressure is greatest.
2. Gayle skates (more carefully, most carefully) than Kenneth.

3. That stunt driver is driving (more recklessly, most recklessly) than ever before.

4. This lid came off (more easily, most easily) of all.

5. Push the car (more hard, harder) if you want to get it out of the snowbank.

6. I did (worse, more badly) than you in the test.

7. Power brakes will stop a car (more quickly, quicklier) than standard brakes.

8. Nora is the (less, least) noisy person in the room.

Part 3 Adjective or Adverb?

Some adverbs are made by adding *-ly* to an adjective:

Adjective	**Adverb**
careful	carefully
happy	happily

Because these words are so much alike, it is sometimes hard to know whether to use the adjective or adverb form. Which would you say?

Anita worked very *careful.*
Anita worked very *carefully.*

In this example, *carefully* is right. It tells *how* Anita worked. It goes with, or modifies, *worked,* which is a verb. *Carefully* is the adverb.

Which of these two sentences would you use?

Snow Treasure is a *real* good book.
Snow Treasure is a *really* good book.

You want the word you choose to modify *good,* an adjective. Therefore you need an adverb. *Really* is the adverb.

Part 3

Objective

To differentiate between adverbs and adjectives, and to make the correct choice in sentences

Presenting the Lesson

1. Read and discuss the first section of Part 3, pages 257 and 258. Place particular emphasis on the different questions answered by adjectives and adverbs.

2. Use these sentences for practice. Ask students to fill in the blanks, and to tell whether the word supplied is an adjective or an adverb. The students should be able to tell which word is being modified.

1. That music is ________ loud.
2. Jogging is ________ than running.
3. Please find the answer ________.
4. She ________ raised her hand.
5. The swallow flew away________.

3. It is suggested that you do the Exercise on page 258 with the class.

4. Read Using Good and Well on pages 258 and 259. Make sure the students understand the meaning and use of each word. Use the following sentences for practice. Ask students to choose the correct word in parentheses. They should be able to identify the word being modified.

1. That is a (good, well) answer.
2. The skater performed (good, well) at the Olympics.
3. After eating the third candy bar, I don't feel so (good, well).
4. Their dog is a (good, well) hunter.
5. That band played (good, well).

5. It is suggested that the Exercise on page 259 be done as a class activity.

6. See Exercise C on page 261 for extra practice.

Optional Practice

Point out that when *well* is used as an adjective to describe a state of health (I feel well), the verb in such sentences is a linking verb. Only linking verbs are followed by predicate adjectives.

Decide whether the verb in each sentence below is an action verb or a linking verb. Tell if *well* is used as an adjective or an adverb.

1. The trained seal performed well.
2. I don't feel too well.
3. She dresses well.
4. She seems well today.
5. The athlete ran well today.

Remember:

Adjectives tell *which one, how many,* or *what kind* about nouns and pronouns.

Adverbs tell *how, when, where,* or *to what extent* about verbs, adjectives, and other adverbs.

Exercise Choosing the Right Word

Number from 1 to 10. Choose the right modifier, and write it on your paper. Next write the word it modifies. Then write *Adjective* or *Adverb* to show how the modifier is used.

Example: The choir sang (good, well).
Well, sang, adverb.

1. Karen didn't look (really, real) sure. Adv.
2. Dan pitched (wild, wildly). Adv.
3. The team felt (bad, badly) about losing the game. Adj.
4. The actor sang too (poor, poorly) to get the role. Adv.
5. The barn looked (dim, dimly) in the moonlight. Adj.
6. The edge of the paper was (real, really) crooked. Adv.
7. I go to the library (regularly, regular) on Friday. Adv.
8. The sun set (slow, slowly). Adv.
9. The teams were matched fairly (even, evenly). Adv.
10. Our telephone rang (promptly, prompt) at ten. Adv.

Using *Good* and *Well*

The words *good* and *well* are often confused. They form their comparative and superlative forms in exactly the same way:

good	better	best
well	better	best

Good is always an adjective that describes a noun or pronoun. It is never used as an adverb.

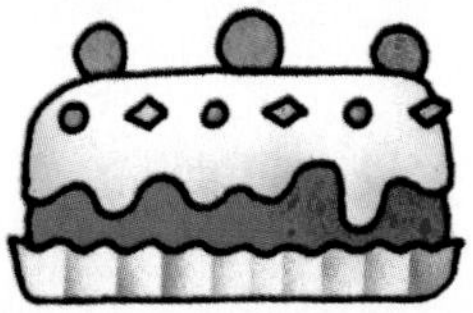

You are a good student. (*Good* modifies *student.*)

That cake looks good.
(*Looks* is used as a linking verb here, so *good* modifies *cake.*)

Well is an adjective when it describes a noun or pronoun and means healthy.

If you take your medicine, you will be well. (*Well* modifies *you.*)

I feel well. (*Feel* is a linking verb here, so *well* modifies *I.*)

Well is an adverb when it modifies a verb, adverb, or adjective, and tells *how* something is done.

You cook well. (*Well* modifies *cook.*)

Exercise Using *Good* and *Well* Correctly

Number your paper from 1 to 10. Write *Adjective* or *Adverb* to tell how each word in italics is used. Then write the word or words that the word in italics modifies.

Example: Carey is the *best* jumper in our room.
Adjective, modifies *jumper*

1. The witness had a *good* look at the robber. adjective, modifies *look*
2. In training camp, the football players eat *well.* adverb, modifies *eat*
3. Ted takes *good* care of his kitten. adjective, modifies *care*
4. Can you see *better* without sunglasses? adverb, modifies *see*
5. Dana gave the *best* answer. adjective, modifies *answer*
6. These shoes fit me *best.* adverb, modifies *fit*
7. Kelly is *good* at tennis. adjective, modifies *Kelly*
8. You are *better* at soccer. adjective, modifies *You*
9. Andy writes *good* reports. adjective, modifies *reports*
10. These ski boots don't fit *well.* adverb, modifies *fit*

Additional Exercises

Use pages 260 and 261 for chapter review if they have not been previously assigned.

Additional Exercises

Using Adverbs

A. Finding and Using Adverbs (Use after page 254.)

Number your paper from 1 to 10. Write all the adverbs used in these sentences.

1. The mail has already arrived.
2. Lately the creek has been very low.
3. The bowl of onion dip was almost empty.
4. The toast popped up quickly.
5. We are almost sure to win.
6. The rain came down hard.
7. Then the tall man turned around.
8. The letter was obviously addressed incorrectly.
9. The solution was perfectly simple.
10. The terribly loud claps of thunder frightened the baby.

B. Making Comparisons with Adverbs (Use after page 256.)

Number from 1 to 10. Choose the right word from the parentheses. Write it on your paper.

1. Tip performs (worse, worst) than the other dog in the act.
2. Sarah runs (faster, more faster) than any other girl here.
3. The wind blew more and more (fiercely, fiercer).
4. The pigeon pecked at the bell more (cautiously, cautious).
5. Do you feel (weller, better) than yesterday?
6. Of the two players, Chico works (harder, the hardest) to improve.
7. A smart detective could solve that mystery (easier, easily).
8. Tina is the (less, least) selfish person I know.

9. On this path you have to go (more slowly, slowlier) to avoid chuckholes.

10. Among all the songbirds, which one sings (more sweetly, most sweetly)?

C. Choosing the Right Word (Use after page 259.)

Number from 1 to 10. Choose the right modifier, and write it on your paper. Next write the word it modifies. Then write *Adjective* or *Adverb* to show how the modifier is used.

Example: The soloist sang very (soft, softly).

softly, sang, adverb

1. The actors and actresses knew their parts (perfect, perfectly). Adv.
2. The goal line was drawn (uneven, unevenly) across the field. Adv.
3. That hailstorm started very (sudden, suddenly). Adv.
4. Was the baby sleeping (sound, soundly)? Adv.
5. Betsy can spell (well, good). Adv.
6. The mountains are (real, really) gigantic. Adv.
7. Red Hawk and his brothers work (good, well) as a team. Adv.
8. After eating five hot dogs, Dale didn't feel too (good, well). Adj.
9. Lillian copied the instructions (careful, carefully). Adv.
10. Mr. Steven's lesson was very (good, well). Adj.

Chapter 16

Using Prepositions and Conjunctions

Earlier chapters of this book have discussed **nouns, verbs, pronouns, adjectives,** and **adverbs.** A word may be placed in one of these groups according to its use in a sentence.

Besides the five groups listed above, there are three other classifications of words. They are **prepositions, conjunctions,** and **interjections.** All together, these eight groups are called the **parts of speech.** Grouping our words in this way makes it easier to study them and the rules for using them.

This chapter discusses prepositions and conjunctions. These are two groups that do not have meaning in themselves. They are used only to connect and relate other words in a sentence to each other.

Chapter Objectives

1. To understand the function of the preposition, and to identify prepositions in sentences

2. To identify nouns and pronouns as objects of prepositions, and to use the correct pronoun forms as objects of prepositions

3. To identify prepositional phrases in sentences

4. To differentiate between the use of a word as a preposition and its use as an adverb

5. To understand the function of the conjunction

6. To use conjunctions to combine sentences

7. To avoid run-on sentences

8. To recognize the use of a word as various parts of speech

Preparing the Students

Have the students look at the photograph on page 262. Point out that the two boys are not doing anything together, but in several ways they are related to each other. For example, one boy is *above* the other; one boy has his back *to* the other. They are also related to the tree: they are *in* the tree. Ask the students to suggest other sentences that show relationships between things in the photograph. Explain that the words that show relationships form a special word group, which will be studied in this Chapter.

Additional Resources

Mastery Test—pages 469–472

Additional Mastery Test—In separate booklet, *Diagnostic and Mastery Tests, Gold Level,* pages 45–48.

Skills Practice Book—pp. 101–111

Duplicating Masters—pp. 101–111

Part 1

Objective

To understand the function of the preposition, and to identify prepositions in sentences

Presenting the Lesson

1. Read and discuss pages 264 and 265. Can students suggest other ways to change the sample sentences "I took a photo of ________" and "The pencil is ________ the notebook"? Make sure the students realize that in the first sentence, the object of the preposition is being changed. In the second sentence, the preposition is being changed.

2. As a class exercise, have students take turns making up sentences with the words at the top of page 265. Be sure that they use the words as prepositions and not as adverbs.

3. Assign and discuss Exercise A on page 265. It is suggested that you do Exercise B on pages 265 and 266 as a class.

4. See Exercise A on page 280 for additional practice.

Optional Practice

Ask students to copy each of the following sentences and label each word according to its part of speech.

1. That clock rang early in the morning.
2. We ran around a track.
3. My dog chased after a rabbit.
4. The sandwich was on the plate.
5. I like days without rain.

Part 1 What Are Prepositions?

Read these sentences and notice what is changed:

I took a photo of the boys.
I took a photo of the class.
I took a photo of the evening sky.

In these sentences, the subject, verb, and object remain the same: *I took a photo*. However, your understanding of the photo changes as the words following *photo* change: photo *of the boys;* photo *of the class;* photo *of the evening sky*.

Each of these phrases begins with the word *of*. *Of* relates the words following it (*boys, class, sky*) to the word before it, *photo*. The phrase beginning with *of* modifies *photo*, telling you *what kind* of photo.

The word *of* is a preposition. The noun or pronoun following a preposition is called the **object of the preposition.** A **preposition** is a word that stands before its object and shows a relationship between that object and another word in the sentence.

The pencil is near the notebook.
The pencil is on the notebook.
The pencil is inside the notebook.
The pencil is under the notebook.

The prepositions *near, on, inside,* and *under* give four different ways of relating the notebook to the pencil.

> A **preposition** is a word that relates its object to some other word in the sentence.

Here is a list of words we often use as prepositions:

about	before	down	of	to
above	behind	during	off	toward
across	below	for	on	under
after	beneath	from	onto	underneath
against	beside	in	out	until
along	between	inside	outside	up
among	beyond	into	over	upon
around	but (except)	like	past	with
at	by	near	through	without

Exercises Finding Prepositions

A. Number your paper from 1 to 10. Write the preposition in each of the following sentences.

1. Jeff opened his book to the index.
2. There is gum stuck on my shoe.
3. Under the new rules, our team can't compete.
4. This portrait of George Washington is two hundred years old.
5. Louisa May Alcott wrote about her own times.
6. All the cans under that sign are dented.
7. Mom's tire was sliced by some broken glass.
8. The Plains Indians depended primarily upon the buffalo.
9. The pinch hitter drove the ball deep into left field.
10. Everybody in my family has blue eyes.

B. Complete the sentences that follow. How many different prepositions can you find for each blank space? You may refer to the list above. Answers will vary.

Example: Pick up the ball ________ the table.
on, under, beside, behind

1. B.J.'s dog was playing ________ the house.
2. Cornelia heard a strange noise ________ the hall.

Part 2

Objective

To identify nouns and pronouns as objects of prepositions, and to use the correct pronoun forms as objects of prepositions

Presenting the Lesson

1. Read and discuss page 266.

2. It is suggested that you do the Exercise on page 266 orally.

3. Remind students that pronouns are substitutes for nouns, so objects of prepositions can be nouns or pronouns. Read Using Pronouns as Objects of Prepositions and discuss how sentences in the preceding exercise could be changed by substituting a pronoun for each noun object.

4. Read Using Pronouns in Compound Objects. Remind the class that *compound* means "more than one." Stress the choice of pronouns in compounds by first considering the pronoun as a single object. Carefully discuss the sample sentences.

5. Read Using *Between* and *Among*. Make sure that students understand the difference in their use. For practice, ask students to decide whether each of the following sentences is correct as is, or if it needs to be corrected.

3. A flock of birds flew ________ the river.
4. Who put the butter ________ the oven?
5. An American flag flew ________ the house.
6. We found these coins ________ the bookcase.

Part 2 Objects of Prepositions

Using Nouns as Objects of Prepositions

You have seen that nouns may be used as subjects or objects of verbs. You will now study nouns used as objects of prepositions. Here are some examples of objects of prepositions:

The Indians pitched their tents near the *river*.
Micky left his gym shoes in his *locker*.
The winning run was scored by *Bonita*.
The movie was about the *arrival* of *aliens* on *earth*.

Exercise Finding Nouns Used as Objects of Prepositions

Number from 1 to 10. Head one column *Preposition* and another *Object*. For each sentence write the preposition and its object.

1. Kathy cleared the dishes from (Prep.) the table (Obj.).
2. These Civil War photographs are by (Prep.) Matthew Brady (Obj.).
3. Nobody in (Prep.) that movie (Obj.) is well known.
4. Elizabeth Blackwell began the study of (Prep.) medicine (Obj.) here.
5. The new couch will be delivered before (Prep.) Friday (Obj.).
6. The temperature went below (Prep.) the freezing point (Obj.) last night.
7. Around (Prep.) the Christmas tree (Obj.) were piled numerous presents.
8. Later that year, gold was discovered in (Prep.) California (Obj.).
9. The lid on (Prep.) this jar (Obj.) won't budge.
10. The football sailed over (Prep.) the goal posts (Obj.).

Using Pronouns as Objects of Prepositions

When a pronoun is used as the object of a preposition, its object form must be used. The object forms are these:

me us you him her it them

Examples: The prize was awarded *to us.*
Was there a message *for me?*
Laura's mother was looking *for her.*

Using Pronouns in Compound Objects

You will probably make few mistakes in using the object form of pronouns in the object of a preposition. But you may become confused when the object of a preposition is compound.

Simple Object	**Compound Object**
Play with *her.*	Play with *Darren* and *her.*
We stood near *him.*	We stood near *Jackie* and *him.*
Give that to *me.*	Give that to *her* and *me.*

If you are not sure which form to use, say the sentence with the pronoun alone following the preposition. Then say the complete sentence.

Example: We're waiting for James and (she, her).
We're waiting for *her.*
We're waiting for James and *her.*

Using *Between* and *Among*

We use *between* when we speak of two persons or things. We use *among* when we speak of three or more. Here are examples:

Choose *between* these two programs.
The next game is *between* the Jefferson High team and us.
We will divide the jobs *among* Nancy, you, and me.

1. They had to choose among pie or ice cream.
2. That is a problem between all the nations of the world.
3. There is little difference between this one and that one.
4. We will divide the candy among all six boys.

6. It is suggested that Exercise A on page 268 be done orally. Assign and discuss Exercise B.

7. See Exercise B on page 280 for additional practice.

Exercises Using Pronouns as Objects of Prepositions

A. Choose the correct pronoun from the two given in parentheses. Write it with the preposition.

Example: The villain shot at Marshall Dillon and (he, him).
at him

1. The coach called on Leo and (I, me).
2. The roof over Marcia and (them, they) started to leak.
3. Vote for one person among Loretta, Jorge, and (she, her).
4. Will you sit beside your mother and (me, I)?
5. The car traveling behind Beverly and (us, we) broke down.
6. A firecracker exploded near Timothy and (we, us).
7. My advice to Norita and (him, he) was ignored.
8. The howling of wolves came from all around Thompson and (they, them).
9. The album by James Taylor and (her, she) went on sale today.
10. The rivalry between Ohio State and (them, they) started years ago.

B. Follow the directions for Exercise A.

1. On your cue, turn toward Mr. Bennett and (she, her).
2. As Paula hurried past Brian and (him, he), she tripped.
3. Miss Washington was looking right at Jason and (I, me).
4. The softball championship will be between the Blues and (we, us).
5. Terrence's kite flew above the other boys and (he, him).
6. That car almost bumped into Gayle and (they, them).
7. I ordered a cheese and mushroom pizza to be split among Susan, me, and (her, she).
8. Everyone but Peter and (us, we) has already had a turn.
9. The paper carried an article about the marching band and (they, them).
10. My pet duck likes to waddle after my friends and (I, me).

Part 3 Using Prepositional Phrases

The group of words that includes a preposition and its object is a **prepositional phrase.** Words that modify the object are also part of the phrase.

Examples:

Mary Kay's house is *on the corner.*

We rode *in an old, broken-down bus.*

The prepositional phrases in these sentences are *on the corner* and *in an old, broken-down bus.*

If a preposition has a compound object, all the parts of the object are included in the prepositional phrase.

Example: Weeds grew *in the lawn, the flower garden, and the vegetable garden.*

Part 3

Objective

To identify prepositional phrases in sentences

Presenting the Lesson

1. Read and discuss page 269. Ask the students for original prepositional phrases. They may refer to the list of prepositions on page 265.

2. It is suggested that the class do Exercise A on page 270 orally. Assign and discuss Exercise B.

Optional Practice

Play a game of Prepositional Phrase Charades. Make a set of cards with a prepositional phrase on each. One student draws a card and acts out the phrase. No talking is allowed. The first student to identify the phrase correctly gets the next turn.

Example phrases:

under the desk
beside the table
in the doorway

Extending the Lesson

Have each student bring to class a magazine or newspaper ad that contains one or more prepositional phrases (the more the better). Ask them to circle each phrase. They should be prepared to present their findings to the class. The ads can then be used to create an interesting "real world" bulletin board display.

Exercises Finding the Prepositional Phrases

A. Number your paper from 1 to 10. Write all the prepositional phrases in each of the following sentences.

Example: The yarn was stuck to the paper with glue.
to the paper, with glue

1. The doll beside the teddy bear has a dress with red buttons.
2. Everybody in the classroom could hear the accident down the street.
3. Draw a line under the word that begins with a vowel.
4. Maria and her little brother played on the swings for hours.
5. Donald plays clarinet in the orchestra at school.
6. The acrobat fell from the tightrope stretched between two buildings.
7. Mary Ann waited near the school door until four o'clock.
8. Alone in the room, Shawn listened to his stereo.
9. The apartment across the hall has been empty for a month.
10. Mother hung a clock with a flower design above the door.

B. Follow the directions for Exercise A.

1. During its journey, the space probe will travel past Mars, Jupiter, and Saturn.
2. Rosa tied a ribbon around the present for her cousin.
3. The team from El Paso plays against us before Thanksgiving.
4. Janet finished her painting of the willow trees along the river.
5. Tell me about the characters in the soap opera.
6. After the hurricane, the river spilled over its banks and the nearby streets.
7. The squirrel ran up the maple tree outside my window.
8. You may choose among the last three dinners on the menu.
9. Dave shopped at the drugstore beside the restaurant.
10. The child climbed onto the table and knocked a plate to the floor.

Part 4 Preposition or Adverb?

Several words that are used as prepositions are also used as adverbs.

Examples:

We looked *up*. (adverb)
We looked *up* the chimney. (preposition)

The children ran *around*. (adverb)
The children ran *around* the track. (preposition)

If you aren't sure whether a word is an adverb or a preposition, look at how it is used. If it begins a phrase, it is probably a preposition. If it is used alone, it is probably an adverb.

Exercise Finding Prepositions and Adverbs

In each pair of sentences that follows, one word is used both as an adverb and as a preposition. Number your paper from 1 to 10. After each number, write *a.* and *b.* After each letter, write the word that is used two ways in the two sentences. Then write the way the word was used in that sentence.

Example: a. Look out! b. Look out the window.

a. out, adverb b. out, preposition

1. a. There was litter all around the store. b. There was litter all around. a. around, prep. b. around, adv.
2. a. Don't come near! b. Don't come near the cliff! a. near, adv. b. near, prep.
3. a. Can you get past the barrier? b. Can that big Cadillac get past? a. past, prep. b. past, adv.
4. a. Those cans should be stored underneath the cabinet. b. Those cans should be stored underneath. a. underneath, prep. b. underneath, adv.
5. a. Miguel will soon be coming along. b. Miguel is coming along the path. a. along, adv. b. along, prep.
6. a. Please stand by. b. Please stand by the window. a. by, adv. b. by, prep.

Part 4

Objective

To differentiate between the use of a word as a preposition and its use as an adverb

Presenting the Lesson

1. Review the definition and functions of adverbs in Chapter 15.
2. Read and discuss page 271. Stress that a preposition must be followed by an object (noun or pronoun). Prepositions must be part of a phrase.
3. You may prefer to do the Exercise on page 271 as a class. Students should be able to explain reasons for each answer.
4. See Exercise C on page 281 for additional practice.

Optional Practice

Have students use each of the following words in two sentences, first as the first word in a prepositional phrase, and second as an adverb.

under	by	off
above	across	in

7. a. Above the party room, the lights burned brightly. b. Above, the lights burned brightly. a. above, prep. b. above, adv.

8. a. Two skaters fell through. b. Two skaters fell through the ice. a. through, adv. b. through, prep.

9. a. We've met before today. b. We've met before. a. before, prep. b. before, adv.

10. a. Puffs of white smoke drifted up. b. White smoke drifted up the chimney. a. up, adv. b. up, prep.

Part 5 What Are Conjunctions?

How is the word *and* used in each of these sentences?

A. Tracy *and* Deborah went to the movie.
B. Allen's puppy barked loudly *and* chased the squirrel.
C. Yastrzemski hit a double *and* two singles in the game.

Did you see that in each sentence, *and* connected words or groups of words? Did you notice that those words or groups of words were of the same type? In Example A, two subjects were joined. In B, two predicates were joined. In C, *and* connected two objects of the verb.

We call *and* a conjunction.

Part 5

Objective

To understand the function of the conjunction

Presenting the Lesson

1. Read and discuss pages 272 and 273. Analyze each of the five sentences on page 273. Make sure the students can identify the words being connected by the italicized conjunction, and the role of those words in the sentence.

2. Students who have mastered the parts of sentences studied thus far should have little difficulty with the various kinds of compound structures shown on page 273. Some students, however, may have difficulty understanding these compounds. Such students should review sentence parts studied in previous chapters, and should be asked only to identify conjunctions in sentences. They should not be required to write compound sentences and sentences with compound parts at this time.

3. It is recommended that the class do Exercise A on page 273 as an oral exercise. Assign Exercise B only to those students who

A **conjunction** is a word that connects words or groups of words.

Two other conjunctions that are often used are *but* and *or*. Like *and*, they may be used to connect sentence parts.

Andrew *or* Ginny will bring the potato chips. (compound subject)
The forward shot for the basket *but* missed it. (compound predicate)
Buy some raisin bread *or* some sweet rolls. (compound direct object)
The package was bulky *but* light. (compound predicate adjective)
The orchestra performed for the faculty *and* parents.
(compound object of a preposition)

Exercises Using Conjunctions

A. Number your paper from 1 to 10. In each sentence there is a compound subject, a compound predicate, or a compound object. Write which of the three you find. Write the compound subject, predicate, or object with its conjunction. Underline the conjunction.

Example: The Mets survived that season and gradually improved.

compound predicate, survived that season and gradually improved

1. (Tecumseh and his brother) led their forces against the U.S. Army. comp. subj.
2. For breakfast, Lorraine likes (poached eggs or oatmeal.) comp. obj.
3. The wind (shook the roof and whistled down the chimney.) comp. pred.
4. Glue (the string and the toothpicks) to the cardboard. comp. obj.
5. (Our neighbor's TV and our stereo) were stolen last night. comp. subj.
6. Gerald (takes piano lessons but doesn't practice.) comp. pred.
7. The puppy (yawned and shook himself.) comp. pred.
8. (Football and soccer) are Lennie's favorite sports. comp. subj.
9. Trudy splashed (Doug and me) with her paint. comp. obj.
10. (The snow and ice) made the roads impassable. comp. subj.

showed competence on Exercise A. Discuss Exercise B when it is completed. Students who had difficulty with Exercise A should do the Optional Practice Exercise in place of Exercise B.

4. See Exercise D on pages 281 and 282 for additional practice.

Optional Practice

In the sentences below, one part is underlined. Have the students tell whether the underlined part is a compound subject, a compound predicate, or a compound object. They must also identify the conjunction.

1. Singers and dancers auditioned for the musical.
2. The car needs repairs but still runs.
3. Phyllis repaired her vase and the old pitcher.
4. Henry wanted a mystery or an adventure story.
5. I wrote a letter but need a stamp.
6. Iced tea or lemonade tastes good on a hot day.

B. Write sentences with compound subjects, predicates, or objects as the directions ask for. Use *and, but,* or *or.* Answers will vary.

Example: Compound direct object. Use a noun and a pronoun.
Please take Amy and me to the library.

1. Compound subject. Use two nouns.
2. Compound predicate.
3. Compound direct object. Use two nouns.
4. Compound subject. Use a noun and a pronoun.
5. Compound direct object. Use two pronouns.

Part 6

Objective

To use conjunctions to combine sentences

Presenting the Lesson

1. Read and discuss page 274. Stress that a compound sentence is two complete thoughts joined together with a conjunction. Students should be able to name the subject and predicate of each part of the compound sentence.

2. It is suggested that you do Exercise A on page 275 orally. Students should identify the kind of compound in each sentence. Assign and discuss Exercise B.

3. See Exercise E on page 282 for additional practice.

Part 6 Combining Sentences

The conjunctions *and, but,* and *or* can do more than connect parts of sentences. Sometimes they can combine whole sentences.

Using Conjunctions To Combine Sentences

Sentences combined by *and, but,* or *or* must express ideas that are closely related. Here are some examples that use conjunctions correctly to combine sentences:

The rain started, *and* everyone ran for cover.
We wanted another ride on the Double Loop, *but* the line was too long.
The princess had to guess the little man's name, *or* he would take her first-born child.

Notice that a comma is used at the end of the first sentence, before the conjunction. The comma alerts the reader to the end of one idea and prepares him or her for a second idea. This makes it easier to understand the long sentence. You may leave out the comma only when the two sentences that you join are very short.

Sit down and I'll help you.

Exercises Combining Sentences

A. In six of the following sentences, conjunctions are used to combine sentences. Commas are needed. In the others, they combine parts of sentences. Commas are not needed. Number your paper from 1 to 10. If the conjunction in an example joins two sentences, copy that example and put in the comma. If the conjunction joins parts of sentences, write *Correct.*

1. The day was warm, but the old woman wore a heavy sweater.
2. Margaret and Hal went to the park. Correct
3. Gloria is on a diet, and she won't eat candy.
4. Phil must put his dog on a leash, or it will run away.
5. For my partner, I want Beverly or Wanda. Correct
6. Dominic ordered a hamburger and a Coke for lunch. Correct
7. We might spend a few days at Niagara Falls, or we might camp at the Finger Lakes.
8. The classroom window was open, and a bee flew inside.
9. The grandfather clock in the hall and the alarm clock in my room stopped this morning. Correct
10. This suit was expensive, but I can use it for a long time.

B. Rewrite the following sentences, combining each pair with *and, but,* or *or.* Choose the conjunction you think is best. Use commas where needed.

1. The yard is covered with leaves. [, and] I have to rake them.
2. Jerry might play centerfield. [, or] He might pitch.
3. Deanna got up late. [, and] She missed the bus.
4. The window isn't open. [, but] I feel a draft.
5. Harriet would have come on time. [, or] She would have told us that she would be late.
6. The wind was high. [, and] The forest fire spread quickly.
7. Ramon worked hard all day. [, but] He didn't finish cleaning the basement.
8. Lena called the office. [, but] There was no answer.

Part 7

Objective

To avoid or correct run-on sentences

Presenting the Lesson

1. Read and discuss page 276. Since run-on sentences are a common problem in sixth-grade writing, it may help to combine the study of this lesson with some short composition work.

2. It is suggested that you do Exercise A on page 276 with the class. Assign and discuss Exercises B and C on page 277.

3. See Exercise F on pages 282 and 283 for additional practice.

Extending the Lesson

Ask students to write a paragraph on one of the following topics:

1. My favorite food
2. The best show on TV
3. Why I love vacations

Have students exchange papers for the purpose of editing. They should be particularly sensitive to run-on sentence problems. Allow time for short editor/writer conferences. Students should make necessary corrections and prepare a final copy.

Part 7 Avoiding Run-on Sentences

Often students combine sentences that do not belong together. When you combine sentences that are not related, you form a **run-on sentence.** Here is an example:

I visited my cousin he is sixteen years old.

There are two complete and separate ideas in this sentence. They should be in two separate sentences:

I visited my cousin. He is sixteen years old.

When you are writing, be careful to use only one complete idea in each sentence. Mark the end of each idea with a period, question mark, or exclamation point. Begin each new idea with a capital letter.

Exercises Avoiding Run-On Sentences

A. Six of the following sentences are run-on sentences. Four are correct. Number your paper from 1 to 10. For each sentence write either *Run-on* or *Correct.*

1. We had art class today we worked with chalk. Run-on
2. All of the books in that part of the library are nonfiction. Correct
3. Lou and Bruce went to the game there was a long line. Run-on
4. May I use your scissors I lost mine. Run-on
5. Scientists are developing ways to predict earthquakes. Correct
6. Brazil is a large country people speak Portuguese there. Run-on
7. Terry has his own calculator he got it for his birthday. Run-on
8. During colonial times, children went to school for only a few years. Correct
9. Valerie and Susan took lessons in ballet and tap dancing. Correct
10. Anita got an A on the science test she had studied for it all weekend. Run-on

B. Four of the following sentences are correct. Six are run-on sentences. Number your paper from 1 to 10. If the sentence is correct as it is, write *Correct.* If it is a run-on, rewrite the sentence as two sentences, with correct capitalization and punctuation.

1. John bought a sandwich it had beef, pickles, and tomatoes in it.
2. Last summer I went swimming it's too cold now.
3. Balboa discovered the Pacific Ocean and claimed it for Spain. Correct
4. Betsy has a garden she grows flowers.
5. The strong wind across the deck made my eyes water. Correct
6. Have you ever read this book by Madeleine L'Engle I like it.
7. Tabitha kept careful records of all her experiments. Correct
8. Two companies of firemen fought the fire it was on my street.
9. Edith and her family visited Idaho they went in a camper.
10. Bill "Bojangles" Robinson was a popular dancer and appeared in movies. Correct

C. The following book report is one long run-on sentence. Break it into shorter sentences, using correct punctuation.

> Carlo Collodi wrote a book about a wooden puppet named Pinocchio Pinocchio acts like a real boy he promises to be good but forgets his promise he runs away from home and gets into trouble there is an exciting ending to the story you will enjoy reading it.

Part 8 Using Words as Different Parts of Speech

In Part 4 of this chapter, you learned that the same word could be used as either an adverb or a preposition. For example, *up* is an adverb in *Come up* and a preposition in *Come up the ladder.*

Other words also may be used as several different parts of speech. For example, the word *book* may be used in these three ways:

Part 8

Objective

To recognize the use of a single word as various parts of speech

Presenting the Lesson

1. Read and discuss pages 277 and 278.

2. Encourage students to use a dictionary for examples of words used as more than one part of speech. Have them look especially for sample sentences in entries for such words.

3. Assign and discuss the Exercise on page 279. Note that in the third pair of sentences, the word *house* has two different pronunciations.

4. See Exercise G on page 283 for additional practice.

Optional Practice

Have students use each word below in at least two different sentences, each time as a different part of speech.

1. picture	3. down	5. wish
2. cup	4. flower	6. fish

Used as a noun

This is my English *book*.

Used as a verb

The officer will *book* the suspect.

Used as an adjective

Trudy gave a *book* report in class today.

When a word is used as a certain part of speech, it follows the rules for that part of speech. For example, when you use *book* as a noun, you form the plural by adding *s*: *books*. When you use it as a verb, you form the past tense by adding *ed*: *booked*.

There is only one sure way to decide what part of speech a word is. You must see how the word is used in the sentence. Here are several examples:

The farmer will *plant* the seedlings next spring.

In this sentence, *plant* means an action. Also, the helping verb *will* comes just before it. We can be sure it is used as a verb.

The *plant* grows best in light, sandy soil.

Here, *plant* is the name of a thing. It is used as a noun.

My father is a *plant* foreman.

In this sentence, *plant* tells *what kind* of foreman. It modifies a noun, so it is used as an adjective.

I feel very *well*.

Here, *well* modifies the pronoun *I*. It is used as an adjective.

You skate very *well*.

Now, *well* modifies the verb *skate*. It is used as an adverb.

Exercise Telling the Part of Speech

In each pair of sentences that follows, one word is used as two different parts of speech. Number your paper from 1 to 10. After each number, write *a.* and *b.* After each letter, write the word in italics and tell how it is used. It may be a *noun, verb, adjective, adverb,* or *preposition.*

Example: a. Open a *can* of beans. b. My mother *cans* tomatoes.

a. can, noun b. cans, verb

1. a. The class president *chaired* the meeting. b. This *chair* is too hard. a. chaired, v. b. chair, n.
2. a. A lyric soprano sings *high* notes. b. The team's fortunes have reached a new *high.* a. high, adj. b. high, n.
3. a. My family is moving to a new *house.* b. The university will *house* the visiting athletes in a dormitory. a. house, n. b. house, v.
4. a. Vince went *outside* for a walk. b. We saw several deer *outside* the cabin. a. outside, adv. b. outside, prep.
5. a. Ms. Taylor made a *pencil* sketch of the waterfall. b. I have to sharpen my *pencil.* a. pencil, adj. b. pencil, n.
6. a. Carla built a roof *over* the patio. b. Those thunderclouds will soon blow *over.* a. over, prep. b. over, adv.
7. a. My brother usually *drives* to work. b. Nellie enjoys *drives* in the country. a. drives, v. b. drives, n.
8. a. The king had a *fool* to entertain him. b. A good magician *fools* the audience. a. fool, n. b. fools, v.
9. a. Turn off the *light,* please. b. The store has a wide variety of *light* bulbs. a. light, n. b. light, adj.
10. a. Look *up!* b. Alice urged her horse *up* the steep hill. a. up, adv. b. up, prep.

Additional Exercises

Assign pages 280 to 283 as chapter review if they have not been used already.

Additional Exercises

Prepositions and Conjunctions

A. Finding Prepositions (Use after page 265.)

Complete the sentences that follow. How many different prepositions can you find for each blank space? Answers will vary.

1. Martha put the notice ________ the door.
2. Christopher saw a snake ________ that rock.
3. The mug ________ that box is broken.
4. Please dust the table ________ the window.
5. Nels sat down and talked ________ Sara.
6. Juanita moved the chair ________ the wall.
7. A potted plant would look attractive ________ that ledge.
8. The ball flew ________ the shortstop.

B. Using Pronouns as Objects of Prepositions (Use after page 267.)

Choose the correct pronoun from the words given in parentheses.

1. The sales department is under Ms. Hyman and (he, him).
2. There was a strong friendship between Helen Keller and (her, she).
3. Are you coming with Benjamin and (me, I)?
4. Radiation from space is constantly passing through our atmosphere and (we, us).
5. Give your new address to Alice and (I, me).
6. The novel tells of (they, them) and their families.
7. A blackbird swooped over Tim and (she, her).
8. The waves crashed against Gladys and then (him, he).

C. Finding Prepositions and Adverbs (Use after page 271.)

In each pair of sentences that follows, one word is used both as an adverb and as a preposition. Number your paper from 1 to 10. After each number, write *a.* and *b.* After each letter, write the word that is used two ways in the two sentences. Then write the way the word was used in that sentence.

1. a. Sam likes to ramble on the beach. b. Sam likes to ramble on. a. on, prep. b. on, adv.
2. a. The parade has gone by. b. The parade has gone by the reviewing stand. a. by, adv. b. by, prep.
3. a. You can crawl under. b. You can crawl under the wire. a. under, adv. b. under, prep.
4. a. Cut the cake into two layers and spread the filling between. b. Spread the filling between the two layers. a. between, adv. b. between, prep.
5. Beyond, the sea stretched to the horizon. b. Beyond the rocky shore, the sea stretched to the horizon. a. beyond, adv. b. beyond, prep.
6. a. We must walk up the stairs. b. We must walk up. a. up, prep. b. up, adv.
7. a. We played outside. b. We played outside the fence. a. outside, adv. b. outside, prep.
8. a. When will this poster be taken down? b. Will this poster slide down the wall? a. down, adv. b. down, prep.
9. a. Several geese flew over us. b. Several geese flew over. a. over, prep. b. over, adv.
10. a. What lies beyond this galaxy? b. What lies beyond? a. beyond, prep. b. beyond, adv.

D. Using Conjunctions (Use after page 273.)

Number your paper from 1 to 10. In each sentence, there is a compound subject, a compound predicate, or a compound object. Write which of the three you find. Write the compound subject, predicate, or object with its conjunction. Underline the conjunction.

1. At dinner, Spencer had (ribs and sweet potato pie.) comp. obj.
2. (Unicorns and dragons) are imaginary animals. comp. subj.
3. Lydia (concentrated on her bowling form and rolled a strike.) comp. pred.
4. You can check out (books, magazines, and records) from the library. comp. obj.

5. A contestant (quits the game after one turn or goes on for a bigger prize.) comp. pred.

6. (Madeline and Hal) played six games of checkers. comp. subj.

7. Bruce collected (spiders and unusual insects.) comp. obj.

8. I (want a taco but don't have enough money.) comp. pred.

9. (Ms. Burke or Mrs. Mitchell) will go on the field trip with us. comp. subj.

10. The choir sang (two spirituals and several folk songs.) comp. obj.

E. Combining Sentences (Use after page 274.)

Rewrite the following sentences, combining each pair with *and, but,* or *or.* Choose the conjunction you think is best. Use commas where needed.

1. The letter on the eye chart may be an E. [, or] It may be an F.
2. I sprayed insect repellant on my arms. [, but] Mosquitoes bit me anyway.
3. Jarita has several assignments. [, and] They are all difficult.
4. You may have cookies for dessert. [, or] You may have an orange.
5. The car had engine trouble. [, and] We had to call a tow truck.
6. Rhea's arm is still in a cast. [, but] She played baseball today.
7. The pies from that bakery are delicious. [, but] The prices are high.
8. You can wait in the car. [, or] You can come into the store with me.
9. The weatherman predicted rain. [, but] The sun is shining.
10. The herd of buffalo moved north. [, and] The hunters followed.

F. Avoiding Run-on Sentences (Use after page 276.)

Four of the following sentences are correct. Six are run-on sentences. Number your paper from 1 to 10. If the sentence is correct as it is, write *Correct.* If it is a run-on, rewrite the sentence as two sentences, with correct capitalization and punctuation.

1. My favorite holiday is Christmas. [T]the best part is the presents.
2. A forest fire destroys an important natural resource. [I]it takes many years for new trees to grow.

3. The sun rises later during the winter. The temperature of the air drops.

4. Staple the blue sheets of paper and the art projects to the bulletin board. Correct

5. In the story, Katherine wishes on a magic coin and gets into a tournament with Sir Lancelot. Correct

6. Give me more cake, please. I'm still hungry.

7. None of the apples in that basket is ripe yet. Correct

8. Mother bought some hamburger, a dozen buns, and a watermelon at the supermarket. Correct

9. Craig tried on six different jackets. They were all too tight.

10. The producer held auditions. He chose some schoolchildren for small parts in the movie.

G. Telling the Part of Speech (Use after page 278.)

In each pair of sentences that follows, one word is used as two different parts of speech. Number your paper from 1 to 8. After each number, write *a.* and *b.* After each letter, write the word in italics and tell how it is used.

1. a. Ron bought *paper* cups for the party. b. Dad will *paper* the dining room walls this weekend. a. paper, adj. b. paper, v.

2. a. I'd like a push-button *phone* in my room. b. The store accepts *phone* orders. a. phone, n. b. phone, adj.

3. a. Coke *bubbles* up when you pour it. b. Gloria blows huge *bubbles* with her gum. a. bubbles, v. b. bubbles, n.

4. a. The ducks swam in the *water*. b. Cypress Gardens presents a famous *water* show. a. water, n. b. water, adj.

5. a. The dogs *chased* the fox for several miles. b. Almost every Keystone Cops film had a *chase* scene. a. chased, v. b. chase, adj.

6. a. Please stand in the light *near* the window. b. The end of the story is *near*. a. near, prep. b. near, adj.

7. a. Edith works very *hard*. b. This bread has a *hard* crust. a. hard, adv. b. hard, adj.

8. a. Snow *covered* the city. b. Put a *cover* on the baby. a. covered, v. b. cover, n.

Chapter 17

Writing Letters

Did you visit an unusual place last summer? Maybe you went on a vacation or visited relatives. If so, you probably met some new people or renewed old friendships. The best way to continue these friendships is by writing letters. Writing letters can also help you order materials and request information.

This chapter will explain the correct form to use for various kinds of letters. It will also help you make your letters more interesting and easier to write.

Chapter Objectives

1. To become familiar with the organization and correct form of a friendly letter

2. To differentiate between friendly letters and social notes in purpose and form, and to use each form where it is appropriate

3. To differentiate between the form of the friendly letter and the form of the business letter, and to use each form where appropriate

4. To understand the purpose of the letter of request, the order letter, and the letter of complaint

5. To use the correct form for addressing envelopes

Preparing the Students

Orally sharing experiences will help students to remember events that they can write about in a letter. Encourage students to talk about their vacation trips, new friends they have met, new experiences they have had, or new places they have seen. You may wish to put some of the ideas on the chalkboard and have students copy them. They can then refer to the list when they need ideas for the letter writing assignments in this chapter.

Additional Resources

Mastery Test—pages 473 and 474

Additional Mastery Test—In separate booklet, *Diagnostic and Mastery Tests, Gold Level,* pp. 49, 50.

Skills Practice Book—pp. 112–117

Duplicating Masters—pp. 112–117

Part 1

Objective

To become familiar with the organization and correct form of a friendly letter

Presenting the Lesson

1. Read and discuss pages 285 and 286. Emphasize particularly the importance of using natural expression. Ask different pairs of students to hold a conversation about what they did last weekend as an example of conversational tone.

Point out that different topics in a letter should be arranged in separate paragraphs.

2. Read the sample letter on page 287. Have students point out the specific parts of the letter that follow the guidelines on page 286.

3. Read Using Correct Letter Form on page 288. After each part, have the students locate that part in the sample letter on page 287. Discuss how the purpose of each part is achieved in the letter.

4. Review the rules on page 289 for capitalization and punctuation in letters. Again, refer to the sample letter as an illustration of correct usage.

5. Before students write the paragraph for Exercise A on page 289, it would be helpful to get their imaginations working by talking about the possibilities for each subject. Assign and discuss Exercises A, B, and C on pages 289 and 290.

Part 1 Writing Friendly Letters

When you have had an experience that you want to share with a friend, you first have to organize your ideas so the reader can follow them easily. The following guides will help you to organize your ideas:

Guides for Organizing Your Ideas

1. Write as naturally as if you were speaking to the person.
2. Begin by answering the other person's questions or by commenting on the information in his or her last letter.
3. Write about things that are interesting to both you and the person to whom you are writing.
4. Describe a new or interesting experience you have had. Add vivid details, strong verbs, and a variety of adjectives and adverbs to make your description come alive.

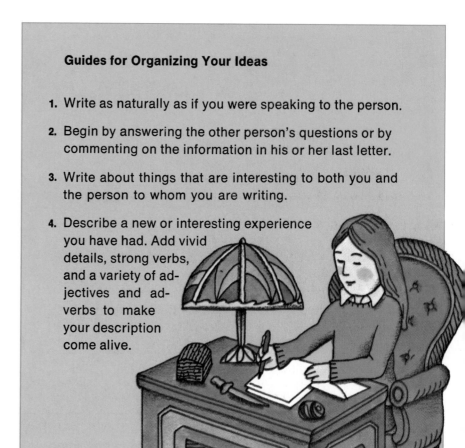

A Sample Letter

Read the following friendly letter. Notice that each part has a specific form and purpose.

1201 West Leonard Street

Heading Pensacola, Florida 32501

October 5, 1980

Salutation

Dear Miguel,

Body

Today our class went to a wooded area for a science lesson. We had to find specimens of different leaves. When I found some poison ivy, I thought of you right away! Remember when we went on that hike at camp and the poison ivy found you! Boy, did you itch.

I've been pretty busy so far this fall. We formed a neighborhood skateboarding team. Every Saturday a different person is in charge of making a new obstacle course. It's my turn this week. I'm using cones and a small ramp that Dad helped me build. I'm sending you a copy of the design for the course. Does it look difficult to you? Have you been doing a lot of skateboarding? You have much better hills in Georgia, so I bet you're really good.

I would like to know what you've been doing. If you can, send me a picture of your dog doing one of his famous tricks. Also, have you added any new albums to your collection?

Closing Your friend,

Signature Jerry

Extending the Lesson

1. Students may enjoy making an anthology of letters about themselves, the school, or the community for a real or imaginary newcomer to the class.

2. Have students write a letter to a real or imaginary friend about a parade. They can write about a parade they have seen or been a part of, or they can write about an imaginary parade.

Using Correct Letter Form

Each part of a letter has its own specific form and purpose. This organization makes it easier for you to write a letter. Review each of these parts in the following chart:

Part	Place	Purpose
Heading	The **heading** is written in the upper right-hand corner.	The **heading** tells where you are and when you are writing. It consists of three lines: house number and street name city, state zip code month, day, year
Salutation	The **salutation** is written on the line below the heading and begins at the left margin.	The **salutation,** or greeting, is the way you say "hello" to your friend. It can be casual, such as *Hi, Dear Mary,* or *Greetings.*
Body	The **body** begins on the line below the salutation. Each paragraph is indented.	The **body** of a letter is for talking to your friend. Arrange the body in paragraphs for each subject you discuss.
Closing	The **closing** should line up with the first line of the heading.	The **closing** is a simple way of saying "goodbye." Some common closings are *Love, Sincerely, Always,* or *Your friend.*
Signature	After the closing, skip a line. Your **signature** should line up with the first word in the closing.	In a friendly letter, only your first name is needed unless you don't know the person well.

Using Correct Capitalization and Punctuation

Using correct capitalization and punctuation will make your letter much easier for your friend to read. Review the following rules for letter writing:

Heading

1. Capitalize all proper names.
2. Place a comma between the name of the city and state.
3. Put the zip code after the state. No comma is necessary to separate the state and the zip code.
4. Place a comma between the day and the year.

Salutation

5. Capitalize the first word and any proper nouns in the salutation.
6. Use a comma after the salutation.

Closing

7. Capitalize only the first word of the closing.
8. Use a comma after the closing.

Exercises Writing Friendly Letters

A. Choose two of the following subjects. Write an interesting paragraph about each that could be used in a friendly letter. Include vivid details:

getting a new pet	going to a party
winning an event or contest	seeing a movie
moving to a new town	going on a field trip
receiving a birthday present	making something new

B. In your best handwriting, copy the following parts of a letter, using the correct capitalization and punctuation. Use separate lines where necessary. Label each section.

1. 336 old mill road / phoenix , arizona 85040 / august 7, 1980 (O M R P A A)
2. dear mary anne , (D M A)
3. 852 busse avenue / mount prospect , illinois 60056 / june 3, 1980 (B A M P I J)
4. missing you, / laura (M L)
5. dear aunt sarah and uncle ted , (D A S U T)

6. sincerely yours, jeff parker

7. 71 south madison avenue mapleton, iowa 51034 september 11, 1980

8. your friend, michelle

C. Write a friendly letter to a real or an imaginary friend. Follow the Guides for Organizing Your Ideas on page 286. Use the proper form for each part of your letter. Use correct capitalization and punctuation. Make the main subject of your letter about one of the following ideas. You may choose your own subject if you wish.

1. An interesting person you have met
2. An interesting place you have visited
3. Something unusual you have seen or done

Part 2 Writing Social Notes

Everyone enjoys receiving gifts, giving parties, and going to parties. These kinds of occasions require the writing of **social notes.** Writing social notes is a form of courtesy that people appreciate. These notes have the same forms as a friendly letter except that they are much shorter and generally use only the date in the heading.

You will use the following social notes most frequently.

1. Thank-you notes
2. Invitations
3. Notes of acceptance or regret

The Thank-You Note

After you have received a gift, or someone has done you a special favor, you should write a thank-you note as soon as possible. This will let the person know that you appreciate his or her thoughtfulness.

Part 2

Objectives

To differentiate between friendly letters and social notes in purpose and form, and to use each form where appropriate

Presenting the Lesson

1. Read the introduction to Part 2 on page 290. Stress the two main differences between friendly letters and social notes: the length, and the use of the date only in the heading. These differences are illustrated in the thank-you note on page 291 and the bread-and-butter note on page 292. Courtesy should also be emphasized as the purpose of social notes.

2. Read the Thank-You note and the samples on pages 290 to 292. Most students will be familiar with the thank-you note. In discussing

Another occasion for writing a thank-you note is when you have spent the night at someone's home. This kind of thank-you note is sometimes called a "bread-and-butter" note. It helps to show that you appreciate the person's hospitality.

The following are examples of the two types of thank-you notes. Notice that these notes are both courteous and friendly.

A Sample Thank-You Note

April 6, 1980

Dear Aunt Loretta,

It was nice of you to remember my birthday. I especially like the pillow you stitched for my bed, and so does my new kitten, Pepper. He curled up next to it and made himself right at home. The colors in the pillow match my bedroom perfectly.

I had a good time on my birthday and your gift made it even better.

Thank you again.

Love,
Marsha

the samples, point out that punctuality in writing the note is necessary or the note will lose its effectiveness. Both samples illustrate the need to use specific details in making reference to a gift or to a visit. These details help to make a short letter more interesting.

3. Read and discuss The Invitation on pages 292 and 293. Students will already be familiar with invitations, but mainly with the packaged kinds sold in stores. Have students bring in examples of packaged invitations to illustrate the similarities between the information asked on them and the details listed on page 293. Students should be aware that a handwritten invitation is much more personal and friendly.

4. The sample invitation on page 293 includes the address in the heading. Ask students why this information should be included on an invitation. A discussion of RSVP would be appropriate with this example. You may wish to write the actual French translation on the board: *Répondez s'il vous plaît* (Respond, if you please).

5. Read and discuss Notes of Acceptance or Regret on pages 294 and 295. Students may think that a note of acceptance is not really necessary when they can just tell the person they are coming to the event. Point out that with a note, the person planning the event will have a record of who is coming in order to make plans. In addition, it is a courtesy to write a response to the person who took the time to invite you to a party.

6. The example of a note of regret on page 295 illustrates the need to include the reason why he or she cannot attend. Again, point out that the person planning the event needs a record of who is and is not coming. The note of regret also prevents hurt feelings when someone doesn't show up the day of the event.

7. Assign and discuss Exercises A, B, and C on pages 295 and 296. It is important that students write a note from each of the three Exercises, as each Exercise represents a different type of social note. They may want to write the notes to each other, especially the invitations. Working with a partner may be helpful.

Extending the Lesson

The class may want to write a joint letter inviting someone to speak to the class on a topic they have been studying.

A Sample Bread-and-Butter Note

July 18, 1980

Dear Mr. and Mrs. Johnson,

Thank you for inviting me to your summer cottage last weekend. It was great to visit with Jack again.

Riding in your boat was exciting, and now I can say I know how to water-ski. I've been wanting to learn for a long time. The cookout on the beach was fun, and the food was delicious.

Thank you again for inviting me. I really enjoyed myself and hope that Jack can visit me soon.

Sincerely,
Todd Monroe

The Invitation

Everyone enjoys receiving invitations, so be sure that yours are written clearly and carefully. Invitations should include the following information:

1. Type of activity
2. Purpose of activity
3. Where the activity will take place
4. The day, date, and time of the activity
5. How the person should reply

An invitation should include all the necessary details and should be written in a friendly tone. It is also a good idea to include your return address in the heading so people can easily respond. Use the following example as a model.

An Invitation

4402 Nancy Lane
Phoenix, Arizona 85040
October 17, 1980

Dear Ellen,

You are invited to attend a Halloween party at my house on Saturday, October 31, at 7:30 P.M. This is going to be a costume party, so start thinking of something original.

Sincerely,
Bruce

R.S.V.P.

Notes of Acceptance or Regret

Suppose you have been invited to attend an event such as the party in the sample invitation. You should reply as soon as you know if you can go. The *R.S.V.P.* at the end of an invitation is an abbreviation for a French phrase that means "please respond." Sometimes there will be a phone number included so you can just telephone your response. It is much better, however, to write a note of acceptance or regret.

Use the following examples as guides for responding to an invitation.

A Note of Acceptance

October 20, 1980

Dear Bruce,

Your Halloween party sounds like great fun. I already have an idea for a surprise costume, so you can count on my being there.

Thanks for inviting me.

Yours truly,
Ellen

A Note of Regret

October 20, 1980

Dear Bruce,

I would really like to come to your party but my family is going out of town that weekend to visit my sister. I hope that your party is a success and that you take some good pictures of the costumes.

Thanks for the invitation.

Sincerely,
Ellen

Exercise Writing Social Notes

Choose one situation from each of the following categories. Write the appropriate form of social note for each situation. Label each kind of note you write. Use your best handwriting.

A. 1. A note to your aunt and uncle for taking you skiing (or somewhere of your own interest).

2. A note to your grandmother for letting you spend the weekend.

3. A note to your best friend, who recently moved, for the birthday present he or she sent. You decide on the present.

B. 1. A note asking your friends to go on a camping trip.

2. A note asking the members of a club to come to a special meeting.

3. A note asking your cousin to watch you in a swimming meet or some type of performance.

C. 1. A note telling your friend you will attend a surprise birthday party for a mutual friend.

2. A note telling your aunt you can't spend the weekend at her house.

3. A note telling your cousin you will be attending the play she is in.

Part 3

Objectives

1. To differentiate between the form of the friendly letter and the form of the business letter, and to use each form where appropriate

2. To explain the purpose of the letter of request, the order letter, and the letter of complaint

Presenting the Lesson

1. Survey students to find out if any have ever written a business letter. Have those who have written a business letter explain their reason for writing one.

Part 3 Writing Business Letters

The most common types of business letters you will need to write are the following:

1. Letters requesting information
2. Letters ordering materials
3. Letters complaining about merchandise

A business letter is written for a specific purpose. The letter should be written clearly and to the point so that you achieve your purpose.

Business letters follow a specific form and include exact information. The following guidelines will help you write successful business letters.

Parts of a Business Letter

The parts of a business letter are similar to those of a friendly letter except that they are written more formally. A business letter also has one additional part, the **inside address.** Review the following parts of a business letter. Notice the exact information that is included in each part.

1. **Heading.** The heading of a business letter is the same as the heading for a friendly letter. Write your street address on the first line. Write your city, state, and zip code on the second line. Write the date on the third line. Use correct capitalization and punctuation, and try not to abbreviate.

2. **Inside Address.** In a business letter, the name and address of the organization to which you are writing appear in the letter itself. This address follows the same punctuation and capitalization rules as the heading. The inside address comes below the heading and begins at the left margin. The inside address should be exactly the same as the address on the envelope.

3. **Salutation.** The salutation of a business letter is more formal than that of a friendly letter. If the letter is being written to a specific person, use *Dear* followed by the person's name:

Dear Ms. Hopkins: *Dear Mr. Steinberg:*

Many times you don't know the name of the person to whom you are writing in a business letter. In this case, you use a general greeting such as the following: *Dear Sir or Madam:*

Dear Ladies and Gentlemen:

All salutations begin two lines after the inside address at the left margin and end with a colon (:).

4. **Body.** The body of a business letter is usually short. It should be courteous and state clearly the subject you are writing about.

2. Read and discuss pages 296 to 298. Have students find each part in the sample letter on page 299. Particular attention should be paid to the following:

Punctuation, especially the use of the colon
The inside address
The formal salutation and closing

Point out that the body should include a discussion of specific details as opposed to the vivid details of a friendly letter. Students should be aware that not all of the information listed in the guidelines, especially for the order letter, may be applicable for every letter.

3. Have students read the sample business letter on page 299 and compare it with the sample friendly letter on page 287. Discuss the differences.

4. Emphasize that neatness and organization are necessary in a business letter if the writer expects to receive a response.

5. Assign and discuss the Exercise on page 300. Remind students to use the guidelines concerning body information. You may wish to encourage the use of plain white paper, and ink, not pencil.

Extending the Lesson

The business letter section provides the opportunity for students to request information for reports or to exercise their rights as consumers. Every company cares about consumers, regardless of age. Students may be encouraged to write directly to advertisers about commercials on TV or to networks about television shows.

Use the following checklist for the body of different types of business letters:

Letter of Request

1. Tell *what* specific information you need.
2. Tell *why* you need that information.
3. Tell *when* you need the information.

Order Letter

1. Tell the name of the product and how many you want.
2. Tell the name of the publication where you saw the ad.
3. Tell the catalog number, size, and color.
4. Tell the price. List postage and handling separately.
5. Compute the total price of the order.
6. Tell what you are enclosing with the letter, such as a check, subscription form, or coupon.

Letter of Complaint

1. Tell the name and model of the order.
2. Tell where and when the product was purchased.
3. Tell the nature of the problem.
4. Ask for instructions for having the problem corrected.

5. **Closing.** The closing appears on the first line below the body. The closing should line up with the heading. The most common closings for a business letter are these:

Sincerely, *Respectfully yours,*

Very truly yours, *Yours truly,*

6. **Signature.** Print or type your name four spaces below the closing. Write your signature in the space between. This way the reader will have no trouble reading your name so that he or she can reply to you. It is best to make a copy of your business letters so that you will have a record of what you wrote and when you wrote it. You can do this easily by using carbon paper. Mail the original and keep the copy.

Study the following business letter to see how all of the parts work together to form a well organized, clearly stated letter.

A Business Letter

Heading
51 Bank Street
Stamford, Connecticut 06901
September 22, 1980

Inside Address
Tropical Shell Institute
Dept. BH-8
Box 21490
Fort Lauderdale, Florida 33335

Salutation
Dear Sir or Madam:

Body
In the August issue of _Better Homes and Gardens_, I read your advertisement for your shell collection offer and catalog. I would like to order both of these items. Please send me the following order as soon as possible.

1 shell collection (150 shells)	$12.95
1 catalog	1.00
postage	3.00
total	$16.95

I am enclosing a money order for the amount of $16.95.

Closing Sincerely,

Signature Laurie Douvris

Laurie Douvris

Exercise Writing Business Letters

Choose one of the following items and write the letter described. Supply any names and facts needed to complete the letter. Use your own name and address and your best handwriting.

1. Your family will be vacationing in California this spring. Write to ABC Guest Relations, 41–51 Prospect Avenue, Hollywood, California 90027, and ask for tickets to your favorite TV show. Consider when you will be there and how many tickets you will need.

2. You need information about basketball for a report you are writing. Write to Basketball Hall of Fame, P.O. Box 175, Highland Station, 460 Alden Street, Springfield, Massachusetts 01109, for the free booklet *Basketball Was Born Here*. Include a self-addressed stamped envelope.

3. You finally received your address labels, but the zip code is wrong. The 1,000 labels cost $1 plus 25¢ for handling from Imprint Products, 482 Sunrise Highway, Rockville Centre, New York 11570.

4. Your string art kit arrived, but the instruction booklet is missing. Write to Kelly's String Art Division, Dept. BH-88, Box 36195, Cincinnati, Ohio 45236.

Part 4 Addressing Envelopes

Addressing the envelope correctly is an important part of writing letters. If you want your letter to reach its destination, you must be sure you have the correct address and zip code. If you're not sure of a zip code, call your local post office.

Use the following checklist when addressing envelopes:

1. Make sure the envelope is right-side up.
2. Put your return address on the envelope.
3. Make sure all numbers are in proper order.

Part 4

Objective

To use the correct form for addressing envelopes

Presenting the Lesson

1. Read and discuss pages 300 and 301.
2. Assign and discuss the Exercise on page 301.
3. Additional practice can be provided by having students draw blank envelopes on paper and addressing letters to their doctor, dentist, or any other person.

4. Include the correct zip code.
5. Write as neatly as possible.

Look carefully at the following example.

Miss Faith Copeland
510 South Fulton
Mt. Vernon, New York 10550

Mr. Miles Kimball
2244 Bond Street
Oshkosh, Wisconsin 54901

Envelopes for social notes are often smaller in size. In this case, the return address may be put on the back of the envelope.

Exercise Addressing Envelopes

Write each of the following addresses in proper order as it should appear on an envelope. Capitalize and punctuate correctly and use your best handwriting.

1. hobbit house p.o. box 12684 dallas, texas 75225
2. ms. jan bleeker lincoln junior high school 700 west lincoln street mount prospect, illinois 60056
3. national wildlife federation 1412 16th street washington, d.c. 20036

8
7

Chapter 18

Making Subjects and Verbs Agree

Do these sentences sound correct to you?

The rides is exciting.
One cloud float in the sky.
Our friends is watching us.
We calls down to them.

If you have been speaking English all your life, the four sentences may sound unusual to you. Each one of them puts together words that don't normally fit together. Each one of them breaks a basic rule in our language: the subject and verb in a sentence must agree.

Chapter Objectives

1. To become aware of the importance of subject and verb agreement

2. To be alert to tricky subjects in sentences, and to use the correct verb form with each of these subjects

Preparing the Students

Ask the students to look at the photograph on page 302, and to describe the girls and the car in which they are riding. Write *car* and *girls* on the board. Under each subject, write the verbs used in suggested sentences about that subject. (List even nonstandard verbs used.) When there are about six verbs in each list, ask the students to examine the lists for patterns in word endings. They should be able to notice that most (if not all) action verbs under *car* end in *s*, while those under *girls* do not. Explain that the purpose of this chapter is to help the students recognize some important speech patterns and to apply them in their speech and writing.

Additional Resources

Mastery Test—pages 475 and 476 in this T. E. Recommended for use after teaching the chapter.

Additional Mastery Test—Recommended for use after any necessary reteaching. (In separate booklet, *Diagnostic and Mastery Tests, Gold Level,* pages 51 and 52.)

Skills Practice Book—pages 118–123

Duplicating Masters—pages 118–123

Part 1

Objective

To become aware of the importance of subject and verb agreement

Presenting the Lesson

1. Read and discuss page 303. Ask students to correct each sample sentence. If they change the subject, point out that the intended meaning of the sentence is changed. Help them see that the verb must be changed to agree with the subject. Be sure that when the verb is changed, the new form is in the present tense. Students often try to solve agreement problems by changing to the past tense.

2. Read and discuss page 304. Emphasize the *s* ending as the mark of the singular form of most verbs. Let the students know that another term for "making the subject and verb agree" is *agreement of subject and verb.*

3. Read and discuss page 305. (Note that understanding of this section is crucial to Exercise B.)

Point out that it is helpful to read the sentence, leaving out the prepositional phrase; this should clearly indicate which word is the subject.

4. Assign and discuss Exercises A and B on page 305. It may also be helpful to develop Exercise A further as a class activity. Ask students to supply a possible verb that agrees with each subject. Use each subject and verb in a sentence.

Part 1 Rules for Making the Subject and Verb Agree

When a noun stands for one thing, it is **singular.**

student fox penny

When a noun stands for more than one thing, it is **plural.**

students foxes pennies

Verbs, too, have singular and plural forms. In a sentence, the verb must always agree in number with its subject. The word *number* refers to singular and plural.

Notice these examples:

Singular	Plural
She *sings* in the next act.	Many girls *sing* soprano parts.
The baby *crawls* everywhere.	Babies *crawl* before they can walk.
That boy *speaks* in the program.	Those boys *speak* clearly.

When we talk about one girl, we say she *sings.* When we talk about more than one girl, we say the girls *sing.* One baby *crawls* but many babies *crawl.* One boy *speaks,* but many boys *speak.*

The *s* at the end of verbs like *sings, crawls,* and *speaks* shows that the verbs are used with singular nouns. In the examples, the singular nouns *girl, baby,* and *boy* were the subjects. When the subject is plural, the *s* is dropped. Look again at the sentences above.

1. If the subject is singular, use the singular form of the verb.
2. If the subject is plural, use the plural form of the verb.

Prepositional Phrases after the Subject

Be careful with prepositional phrases that come after the subject and before the verb. Do not let yourself confuse the subject of the verb with the object of the preposition.

Example:

The children on my block (rides, ride) a school bus.

Who rides? *The children.*

On my block is a prepositional phrase describing the *children.* The verb must agree with *children,* not *block,* so we use the plural form *ride.*

Exercises Studying Singular and Plural Forms

A. In each complete subject, find the subject of the verb. Write it and tell whether it will take the singular or the plural form of the verb.

1. the apples Pl.
2. a carnival Sing.
3. Sheila Sing.
4. the wristwatch Sing.
5. autumn leaves Pl.
6. the mice Pl.
7. the passengers in the car Pl.
8. a box of pencils Sing.
9. the men on the moon Pl.
10. wild geese Pl.
11. the Johnson twins Pl.
12. umbrellas in the rain Pl.

B. Number your paper from 1 to 6. Find the subject and the verb in each sentence below. Write the subject and verb.

Example: The dogs in the yard barked at us. *dogs, barked*

1. The men in the truck work with my father.
2. The three customers at the counter need service.
3. My friends on the next street visit me often.
4. Many new recruits for the Army are women.
5. The girl on stilts walks very quickly.
6. Those students in the hall will audition for the talent show.

5. Read page 306. Put the following chart on the board and discuss it.

	Singular	Plural
Present Tense	is has does	are have do
Past Tense	was had did	were had did

Discuss also the negative contractions of the words on the chart: (*isn't, hasn't,* etc.) Ask the students which of the verbs and negative contractions may be used with *he, she, we,* and *they.*

6. It is suggested that Exercise A on page 306 be done orally. Assign and discuss Exercise B, pages 306 and 307.

7. See Exercise A on page 311 for additional practice.

Special Forms of Certain Verbs

A few verbs have special forms that you should keep in mind.

Is, Was, Are, Were. The verb forms *is* and *was* are singular. The forms *are* and *were* are plural.

Singular: Carlos *is* here. Carlos *was* here.
Plural: The boxes *are* here. The boxes *were* here.

Has, Have. The verb form *has* is singular. The form *have* is plural.

Singular: Pam *has* a plan.
Plural: They *have* a plan.

Does, Do. The verb form *does* is singular. The form *do* is plural.

Singular: Joe *does* the cooking.
Plural: They *do* the cooking.

Exercises Using the Right Verb Form

A. Choose the right form of the verb from the parentheses.

1. Two ski poles (was, were) standing in the drift.
2. Bob's teeth (has, have) never had a cavity.
3. The locker rooms (is, are) newly painted.
4. My cousin (has, have) been singing in the choir this year.
5. At high tide, those boats (is, are) floating on the water.
6. (Is, Are) the Boy Scouts coming?
7. The noises in this cave (has, have) weird echoes.
8. Toni's swollen knee (is, are) getting better.
9. Rico (doesn't, don't) waste time.
10. The two stores on Central Street (is, are) closed.

B. Follow the directions for Exercise A.

1. Our bus (has, have) a flat tire.
2. My feet (is, are) too big for these shoes.

3. The girls (was, were) diving for oysters.
4. How many people (is, are) in your family?
5. Some friends of my sister (is, are) coming for dinner.
6. (Isn't, Aren't) the cookies for dessert?
7. All along the street (was, were) Japanese lanterns.
8. (Does, Do) the canary ever sing?
9. The brakes on this bike (is, are) not working properly.
10. In *Peter Pan*, all of the children (is, are) lost.

Part 2 Tricky Subjects To Watch

Certain Pronouns

The words listed below are singular. Each is used with a singular verb form.

each	either	everyone	anyone
one	neither	everybody	nobody

Everybody is hungry.
Either of the answers *is* right.
Nobody leaves after eight o'clock.

Watch out for these words when they are used as subjects and followed by a prepositional phrase. If the object of the preposition is plural, you may make the mistake of using a plural verb form.

Is the verb correct in this sentence?

Neither of the dogs *was barking.*
What is the complete subject? *Neither of the dogs*
What is the prepositional phrase? *of the dogs*
What is left? *Neither*

Neither is the subject of the verb.
Neither is singular, so the singular form *was barking* is correct.

Part 2

Objective

To be alert to tricky subjects in sentences, and to use the correct verb form with each of these subjects

Presenting the Lesson

1. Read and discuss page 307.
2. Assign and discuss the Exercise on page 308. Some students may need to review prepositional phrases (Chapter 16).
3. Read and discuss *There Is, Where Is,* and *Here Is* on page 308.
4. Assign and discuss the Exercise on page 309.
5. Read and discuss Compound Subjects on page 309. Stress the difference between *and* and the other conjunctions used in a subject.
6. It is suggested that the Exercise on pages 309 and 310 be done orally.
7. Read and discuss The Words *I* and *YOU* on page 310.
8. Assign and discuss the Exercise on page 310.
9. See Exercise B on page 311 for additional practice.

Extending the Lesson

Tell the students that the pronouns listed on page 307 are called *indefinite pronouns.* Ask if they can explain that name.

Exercise Choosing the Right Verb Form

Copy these sentences, leaving a space for the verb. Draw a circle around the prepositional phrase. Then, choose the right form of the verb and write it.

Example: Neither of the bolts (fits, fit).

Neither (of the bolts) fits.

1. Nobody (in our class) (swim, swims) a full length under water.
2. One (of the propellers) (was, were) bent.
3. Each (of you girls) (is, are) allowed five minutes for your act.
4. Neither (of the cats) (has, have) been fed.
5. One (of the bathroom taps) (are, is) leaking.
6. Each (of the uniforms) (has, have) the sponsor's name on it.
7. Either (of the digital clocks) (tell, tells) perfect time.
8. Everybody (from both classes) (was, were) invited.
9. Each (of the displays) (is, are) on a different country.
10. (Has, Have) either (of you) brought the hammock?

There Is, Where Is, Here Is

Many of our sentences begin with *There*, *Where*, or *Here*. These words are never subjects. In sentences beginning with these words, the subject usually comes after the verb.

Before you can choose the right verb form, you have to know what the subject is. You have to know whether it is singular or plural.

There are your books. (*Books* is the subject; the plural form *are* is correct.)

Here is the path. (*Path* is the subject; the singular form *is* is correct.)

Where do the pencils belong? (*Pencils* is the subject; the plural form *do belong* is correct.)

Exercise Choosing the Right Verb Form

Choose the right form of the verb for each sentence.

1. Where (does, do) this road go?
2. Here (is, are) your paper and pencil.
3. There (was, were) no salt in the salt shaker.
4. (Was, Were) you waiting long?
5. Where (is, are) everybody?
6. Here (is, are) four more pieces for the puzzle.
7. Where (are, is) that cushion with the stripes?
8. There (was, were) many reasons for the president's action.
9. Here (is, are) one of the oars.
10. Where (does, do) the books on the table belong?

Compound Subjects

When two or more parts of a compound subject are joined by the conjunction *and*, use the plural form of the verb.

The mayor and the police chief *were* in the parade.

When the parts are joined by *or*, *either-or*, or *neither-nor*, use the form of the verb that agrees with the nearer subject.

Carol or Janet *is* singing.

Neither Mathew nor his brothers *are* coming.

Either six pencils or one pen *costs* a quarter.

Exercise Choosing the Right Verb Form

Choose the right form of the verb for each sentence.

1. Duchy and her pups (sleeps, sleep) on the back porch.
2. Kermit the Frog or Miss Piggy (is, are) my favorite Muppet.
3. Ted and Victoria (has, have) Kodak cameras.
4. Either Mrs. Lunt or her son (walks, walk) the dog every day.

5. Neither the girls nor the boys (has, have) the right answer.
6. Everyone and his dog (was, were) there.
7. Seven oranges or one melon (weighs, weigh) three pounds.
8. The swimmers and their coach (practices, practice) every day.
9. Neither the lights nor the phone (works, work).
10. Either Ed or the other boys (is, are) setting up the chairs.

The Words *I* and *You*

Although *I* stands for a single person, the only singular verb forms used with it are *am* and *was*.

I *am* in my room. I *was* here yesterday.

Otherwise, the verb form is the same as the plural form.

I *do* my work. I *have* a cold. I *throw* a good fastball.

The word *you* can stand for one person or for several persons. It may be either singular or plural. Whether it is singular or plural, always use the plural verb form with the pronoun *you*. For example, never say or write *you was*. Always say or write *you were*.

Exercise Choosing the Right Verb Form

Choose the right form of the verb for each sentence.

1. You (was, were) ready, (wasn't, weren't) you?
2. I (am, is, are) going for a walk.
3. In that closet (is, are) the roller skates.
4. With your new bike, you (rides, ride) faster than before.
5. Among the library aides, I (is, am, are) the youngest.
6. You or anyone else (is, are) welcome at the party.
7. (Has, Have) you brought in the flag?
8. I or my friend Lucy (am, is, are) the best speller in the class.
9. (Was, Were) you afraid?
10. My mother and I (am, is, are) going to the supermarket.

Additional Exercises

Making Subjects and Verbs Agree

A. Using the Right Verb Form (Use after page 306.)

Choose the right form of the verb from the parentheses.

1. (Was, Were) the three of you too hot?
2. Moles by nature (is, are) almost blind.
3. The equipment (has, have) been moved to the attic.
4. The guests (is, are) being shown the doll collection.
5. In the summer all the sheep (huddle, huddles) in the shade.
6. How (do, does) Corinne get to school?
7. All the girls on the team (has, have) been practicing their shots.
8. When (is, are) Uncle Bert arriving?
9. Many trout usually (hide, hides) by this old log.
10. (Isn't, Aren't) there any brownies left?

B. Choosing the Right Verb Form (Use after page 310.)

Choose the right form of the verb for each sentence.

1. Dan and Joanie (take, takes) turns for Saturday chores.
2. Over the door (was, were) carved two huge swords.
3. My pet fish (doesn't, don't) need a lot of attention.
4. Here (is, are) some bigger pieces of pizza.
5. Neither of us boys (has, have) ever shot the rapids.
6. Where (are, is) the cord for this radio?
7. Between the bricks (are, is) a small metal handle.
8. Where (have, has) Maria's hammer and nails been put?
9. Behind the door (was, were) an old umbrella stand and some model planes.
10. Everyone usually (crowd, crowds) into the kitchen.

Additional Exercises

Use this page for chapter review if it has not been previously assigned.

Topper

Chapter 19

Using Irregular Verbs

Part 1 Principal Parts of Verbs

Every verb has many different forms. You have seen and used the forms *talked, have talked, had talked, will talk, would have talked,* and others. All of these different forms of a verb are made from just three parts. For this reason, the three parts of any verb are called its **principal parts.**

The principal parts of a verb are the following:

1. **present**	2. **past**	3. **past participle**
talk	talked	talked

Chapter Objectives

1. To understand the function of the principal parts of verbs

2. To form the principal parts of regular verbs

3. To differentiate between regular and irregular verbs

4. To become familiar with the principal parts of common irregular verbs

Preparing the Students

Ask students to examine the picture on the opposite page and write five sentences that deal with it in some way. Have them identify the predicate in each sentence, and the verb. What is the tense of each verb?

If necessary, review verb tenses. See both the student material and the Teacher's Manual suggestions for Chapter 8, Part 5.

Additional Resources

Mastery Test—pages 477 and 478 in this T. E. Recommended for use after teaching the chapter.

Additional Mastery Test—Recommended for use after any necessary reteaching. (In separate booklet, *Diagnostic and Mastery Tests, Gold Level,* pages 53 and 54.)

Skills Practice Book—pages 124–127

Duplicating Masters—pages 124–127

Part 1

Objectives

1. To understand the function of the principal parts of verbs
2. To form the principal parts of regular verbs

Presenting the Lesson

1. Read and discuss pages 313 and 314. Have students practice using the principal parts of the verbs listed at the top of page 314 in sentences. Make sure that the students realize that the only difference between the past and past participle forms of regular verbs is the use of helping verbs with the past participle.
2. Remind students that as early learners of the language, children often use the regular form for all verbs, even when it might not be appropriate: *goed, runned, bringed.* This indicates how common the regular form is.
3. Assign Exercises A and B on page 315. Discuss the answers for Exercise A. Have some examples of sentences for Exercise B put on the board before discussion.

Here are some examples:

Present	**Past**	**Past Participle**
call	called	called
hurry	hurried	hurried
look	looked	looked
paste	pasted	pasted
stop	stopped	stopped
walk	walked	walked

The **present** part of the verb is its present tense. (Add *s* to form the singular.) The present part used with *will* or *shall* forms the future tense.

The **past** part of the verb is its past tense.

The **past participle** is used with helping verbs to make other forms of the verb. Here are some examples of these other forms:

has called	was being called
have called	shall be called
had called	has been called
was called	will have called
were called	should have been called

Regular Verbs

In the list of principal parts given above, the verbs are called **regular verbs.** Every verb that is *regular* forms its past tense by adding *-ed* (*call**ed***) or *-d* (*paste**d***) to the present form. The past participle is the same as the past form and is always used with a helping verb. Most English verbs are regular.

Exercises Forming Principal Parts

A. Number your paper from 1 to 10. Write the verb form indicated for each of the following regular verbs. Use one or more helping verbs with each past participle.

1. print (past) printed
2. decorate (present) decorate
3. paste (past participle) HV pasted
4. carry (past) carried
5. use (past participle) HV used
6. help (past participle) HV helped
7. confuse (present) confuse
8. list (past) listed
9. cover (past participle) HV covered
10. like (future) Will like

B. Write a sentence for each of the verbs below. Use the verb form indicated. Sentences will vary.

1. introduce (future) will introduce
2. protect (past) protected
3. wobble (present) wobble
4. add (past participle) HV added
5. trade (past) traded
6. sound (past participle) HV sounded
7. develop (past) developed
8. need (future) will need
9. improve (past) improved
10. organize (past participle) HV organized

Part 2 Irregular Verbs

Some verbs do not form their second and third parts in a regular way. These five verbs are examples:

Present	**Past**	**Past Participle**
feel	felt	felt
go	went	gone
know	knew	known
see	saw	seen
think	thought	thought

These verbs are not regular verbs. They are called **irregular verbs.**

Part 2

Objectives

1. To differentiate between regular and irregular verbs
2. To become familiar with the principal parts of common irregular verbs

Presenting the Lesson

1. Read and discuss pages 315 and 316. Be sure that students have a clear understanding of the difference between regular and irregular verbs.

2. Students should learn the forms of the common irregular verbs on page 317.

3. Practice and discussion is the best method of mastering the use of irregular verb forms. Sixteen special pages on irregular verbs are located on pages 407 to 422 of the teacher's edition. The pages provide practice with these verbs:

begin/began/begun
choose/chose/chosen
come/came/come
do/did/done
eat/ate/eaten
freeze/froze/frozen
give/gave/given
go/went/gone
grow/grew/grown
know/knew/known
ride/rode/ridden
run/ran/run
see/saw/seen
take/took/taken
throw/threw/thrown
write/wrote/written

Before assigning these pages, administer the diagnostic test (page 406). Assign only those practice pages a student demonstrates need for. Assign and discuss each of the practice pages individually. They should not be presented as an uninterrupted unit.

Optional Practice

Do a class oral activity with the words on page 317. Have the students take turns creating sentences with each of the principal parts of each irregular verb. Discuss any errors as they arise.

There are about sixty of these irregular verbs in English. The best way to learn about them is to memorize their three principle parts. A list of the most commonly used irregular verbs is given on page 317.

When you are using irregular verbs, you should remember these two rules:

1. The past form is always used by itself, *without* a helping verb.

   We *went* to the library.

2. The past participle is always used *with* a helping verb.

   We *have gone* to the library.

Helping Verbs

The word's most often used with the third principal part of all verbs are the forms of *be* and *have*. Here they are, so that you can refer to them when you need to.

	Be		**Have**
I	am	*I, we, you, they*	have
we, you, they	are were		
he, she, it	is was	*he, she, it*	has
Each of these must be used with one or more additional helping verbs.	be been being	(any subject)	had

Principal Parts of Common Irregular Verbs

Present	Past	Past Participle
begin	began	begun
break	broke	broken
bring	brought	brought
choose	chose	chosen
come	came	come
do	did	done
drink	drank	drunk
eat	ate	eaten
fall	fell	fallen
fly	flew	flown
freeze	froze	frozen
give	gave	given
go	went	gone
grow	grew	grown
have	had	had
know	knew	known
lay	laid	laid
lie	lay	lain
ride	rode	ridden
ring	rang	rung
rise	rose	risen
run	ran	run
say	said	said
see	saw	seen
sing	sang	sung
sit	sat	sat
speak	spoke	spoken
steal	stole	stolen
swim	swam	swum
take	took	taken
teach	taught	taught
throw	threw	thrown
wear	wore	worn
write	wrote	written

Extending the Lesson

The following irregular verbs are not included on page 317. Have students find the principal parts for each.

beat	hurt
bite	lose
burst	shake
draw	sting
drive	tear

Can students think of still other irregular verbs? What are the principal parts?

Chapter 20

Improving Your Speaking Skills

Everywhere you go you hear people talking. They may be talking about their hobbies or planning a trip. They may be asking about an assignment or just talking with a friend. There are many reasons for talking. Here are some of them:

To fill a need to share our feelings

To communicate our ideas

To control the things around us

To get a response from others

To gain understanding

To satisfy our physical needs

However, most people talk just because they like to talk. They seldom stop to think about all the things that make human speech

Chapter Objectives

1. To distinguish between verbal and nonverbal communication
2. To use the voice for different effects
3. To interpret volume, rate and articulation, and stress and phrasing
4. To prepare and select material for oral reading
5. To recognize the structure of good conversation

Preparing the Students

Ask students to examine the picture on page 318. What might the girls be saying to each other in this situation? Have two students pretend to be these girls and stage a conversation. Read the introduction on pages 319 and 320. Which of the reasons for talking were used by the two students in the role-playing situation? Can students add any other reasons for talking to the list?

more than just a mixture of sounds. This chapter will discuss some of the basics of spoken language. It will give you a chance to improve your speaking skills.

Part 1 Verbal and Nonverbal Communication

Much of what we say to each other comes out in words or sounds called **verbal** messages. Sometimes, however, all or part of our message is sent through silent but visible signals. These signals are called **nonverbal** communication. Look carefully at these pictures:

What messages do you receive from each picture? What gives you the message?

You can also say things with body movements. While riding your bike down the street, you might say hello to a friend with the wave of a hand. While listening to someone tell a story, you might show you understand by nodding your head. Expressions on your face give messages, too. A smile tells your aunt you're glad to see her. A frown tells your mom that salmon is not your favorite meal.

As you can see, an important part of your daily communication is completely silent. Can you think of other examples of nonverbal messages you use or see every day?

Part 1

Objective

To distinguish between verbal and nonverbal communication

Presenting the Lesson

1. Read page 320. Discuss possible interpretations of the three pictures in the center of the page.

Do Exercises A, B, C, and D on page 321 either as a class or in small groups.

2. Read and discuss The Whole Message on page 321. Make a clear distinction between verbal and nonverbal communication. What verbal messages might each of the characters in the pictures on pages 320 give to match their nonverbal message?

3. Discuss other examples of nonverbal messages that students use or see every day. Ask volunteers to demonstrate these messages for the class.

4. Divided the class into small groups of four or five students. Assign the Exercises on page 322 to the groups. Shy students are more likely to do the activities if they don't have to perform for an entire class. At a later time, the more outgoing students from each group can then be asked to demonstrate their group's interpretations to the class. Compare the interpretations of the groups but do not place value judgments on any serious contributions. Allow students to become confident with their own interpretations.

Exercises Sending Nonverbal Messages

A. Show these sounds but don't make them.

shout growl laugh whisper
sneeze cheer scream cry

B. Show these emotions on your face.

fear anger happiness
sorrow confusion excitement

C. Act out these short nonverbal messages.

Wait for me! Where are you?
Come on. I don't understand.
Get out! Forget it!
Who cares? Stop.
Isn't it hot? What do you want?

D. Walk into a room and sit down in a chair as each of these characters might.

a fashion model a heavyweight wrestler
a four-year-old an old person with a cane

The Whole Message

Most communication is a mixture of verbal and nonverbal signals.

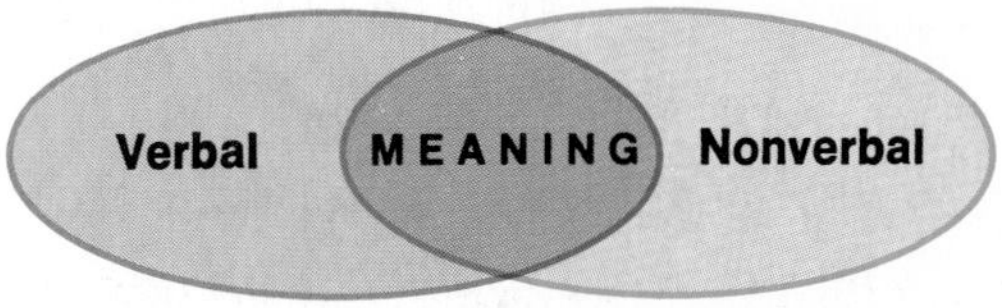

A good speaker tries to be sure that the message sent verbally is the same as the message sent nonverbally. If you pat your teammate on the back as you say "Good play," your message is clear. Try not to confuse your listener by saying one thing verbally and something else nonverbally. For example, saying "This is a really interesting movie" and yawning at the same time send opposite messages.

Optional Practice

Play a pantomime game with the class. Students form a circle, sitting on chairs or on the floor. The first player is handed an imaginary glob of "magic clay." He or she is to mold it into some imaginary object and then pantomime the use of that object. When finished, he or she mashes the object back into the glob and passes it to the next player. No talking is allowed. Students should try to guess what object is being formed by each player, but they are not to share their thoughts until the conclusion of the game. They may take notes to help them remember. When each player has had a turn, discuss the interpretations of each pantomime. What helped to identify each object? Were any objects not able to be identified?

Extending the Lesson

Ask students to research the art of mime and famous mime performers such as Marcel Marceau, and Shields and Yarnell. Have them share their findings with the class. Volunteers may wish to try some simple mimes.

Exercises Sending the Whole Message

A. Count to ten these ways:

Measuring teaspoons of sugar and adding them to a cake mix
Counting pennies on a table
Doing a physical exercise
Counting out a fighter like a referee
Counting people in a room

B. Give these messages, using verbal and nonverbal signals together:

Hurrah!	No.	Not me!
Ouch.	Who cares?	This doesn't make sense.

C. Say each of the following messages verbally but give the *opposite* message nonverbally:

This is delicious.
Just what I wanted!
Sure, you can come with me.
Oh, that's terrible.
This movie isn't scary at all.

D. Choose a partner and act out the following situations. Be sure to communicate both verbally and nonverbally.

You are in a movie theater saving a seat for a friend who went to buy popcorn. Someone comes, pays no attention to you, and tries to take the seat.

You are in the dentist's waiting room with a toothache. You don't feel like talking to anyone. A very chatty person sits down next to you and starts to drive you crazy.

You answer the door to a pushy salesperson who won't take your polite "No, thank you" and go away.

E. Give examples of times when you have said one thing in words and meant just the opposite.

Part 2 Using Your Voice Effectively

Volume

While you are watching your favorite TV show, your brother turns on the vacuum cleaner. Your dog begins to bark. You can no longer hear the program. What can you do? You probably go to the set and turn the knob labeled "Volume." Ah! That's better. Now you can enjoy the show.

Volume is the strength or power of a sound. When you are speaking, you must be sure that your volume is at the right level for others to understand you. It must not be too high or too low. Practice speaking with reasonable volume.

Exercises Controlling Your Volume

A. Make a list of things that have a volume control. When are you likely to adjust them to a low or soft level? When might you have them at a higher or louder level?

B. Practice volume control with a partner. One person repeats the sentence, "I am learning to control my volume." The other person controls the speaker's volume by raising (louder) or lowering (softer) a hand. Take turns being a speaker and volume controller.

C. Whisper this sentence: "Can you hear me?" Can you make the whisper louder but still keep it a whisper? What happens when you reach the highest volume of a whisper? What is the next higher level? How is it different from a whisper?

D. Say, "Go all the way down" to someone next to you. Ten feet away. Fifty feet away. One hundred feet away.

Part 2

Objectives

1. To use the voice for different effects
2. To interpret volume, rate and articulation, and stress and phrasing

Presenting the Lesson

Volume

1. Read Volume on page 323. Ask students to demonstrate several levels of volume: one too low for class discussion, one too high for class discussion, and one that seems appropriate for class discussion. What conditions might occur to warrant a change to lower or higher volume in a normal classroom discussion?
2. Assign Exercise A to all students and then compare lists.
3. Have students do Exercises B. C, and D with partners. When they are finished, discuss with the students what they have learned by doing these volume activities.

Rate and Articulation

1. Read Rate and Articulation on page 324. Be sure that students understand the definitions of rate and articulation. Discuss their individual importance for effective speaking.

2. How many dialects are students aware of? Can they demonstrate any of them? Have any students in the class recently transferred from an area where a different dialect was spoken? What comparisons can be made between their speech patterns and those of the rest of the class?

3. All of the Exercises on pages 324 and 325 can be done with partners. Discuss the results of poor articulation after completion of the Exercises.

Optional Practice

Make a collection of tongue twisters for use by the class. Encourage students to create some of their own.

Rate and Articulation

Have you ever put a record on a record player and when it started to play, discovered it was at the wrong speed? The result is a strange listening experience. To enjoy the record, you must play it at the correct rate of speed.

To communicate in the best way you can, you must pay attention to your **rate** of speaking. How quickly or slowly you speak can affect your meaning. If you speak too slowly, your listener may become bored. If you speak too quickly, your listener may have trouble understanding you.

Articulation is the forming of sounds into separate words. To be able to articulate clearly, you must first know how to pronounce the words you use. A good dictionary will provide the standard American pronunciation of a word. However, people in different parts of the country or of different backgrounds may pronounce words in other ways.

These variations are called **dialects.** As a speaker, use the speech that you are most comfortable with and that your audience will best be able to understand. At all times, speak clearly and distinctly.

Exercises Rate and Articulation

A. Read the following tongue twisters slowly. Then increase your rate. What begins to happen as the rate gets faster?

Please paint the post purple, Polly.
Much whirling water makes the water wheel work.
She makes a proper cup of coffee in a copper coffee pot.
Six thick thistles stick through the fence.

B. Say the following word pairs several times, starting at a slow rate and gradually increasing your speed. What happens if each word is not carefully articulated?

my trip my twin my crushes I scream great rain

C. Choose a partner. Ask your partner to listen to you talk for a minute. Any subject will do. As you talk, experiment with different rates of speaking. Ask your partner to tell you what the best rate seems to be for you. Continue talking for another minute, trying to maintain your best rate.

D. Practice careful articulation with these word pairs:

can't you   let me   don't you   give me   want to

E. Say these tricky tongue twisters slowly and distinctly:

Penny picked the peppers perfectly.
Pearl joined the boys and girls.
Brown bears wandered around the park grounds.
Tent tops and ten tops are tip top.

Stress and Phrasing

As you have learned, it is important to say individual words distinctly. To get your meaning across to your listener, you must also emphasize words of importance. **Stress** is emphasis. Read the following sentences aloud. Emphasize each underlined word.

I want some ice cream.   I want some ice cream.
I want some ice cream.   I want some ice cream.

Did you notice that the meaning of each sentence is slightly different? What situation might suggest each of the above responses?

Phrasing is putting words together into meaningful groups. Read the following two sentences aloud. Group the words as the punctuation suggests.

The boy says his sister is a fool.
"The boy," says his sister, "is a fool."

If you read each sentence correctly, you should have discovered that the meaning of the second is the opposite of the first. Who is the fool, according to each sentence?

Stress and Phrasing

1. Read and discuss Stress and Phrasing on page 325. In what way do these two techniques blend to give expression to speech?

2. Divide the class into small groups to do the Exercises on page 326. Ask for volunteers from each group to demonstrate the findings for each activity.

Optional Practice

How many different ways can the word *oh* be expressed? What are the different meanings conveyed by each? Ask students to demonstrate them for the class.

Exercises Stress and Phrasing

A. Show the difference in meaning as you say these pairs of sentences.

"You hope," she said, "too much."
You hope she said too much.

What do you think? I will invite you to my party.
What? Do you think I will invite you to my party?

Ms. Sanders, our teacher, was late.
Ms. Sanders, our teacher was late.

B. Use the statement, "You're my friend." Say it three times, each time placing the stress to give the following different meanings:

But she's not.
You're not his friend.
You're not my enemy.

Do the same with each of the following statements.

"José walked to school."

Not Alice.
He didn't run.
Not to the park.

"She found the money."

Not he.
She didn't earn it.
She didn't find the wallet.

C. Stress the underlined words and explain why the phrases have different meanings.

green house—greenhouse
singing teacher—singing teacher
playing cards—playing cards
sailboats—sail boats
White House—white house

Part 3 Reading Poems and Stories Aloud

An excellent way to practice the effective use of your voice is reading aloud. Everyone enjoys hearing an interesting story or a good poem. With some planning you can share some of your favorites with your friends.

Preparing To Read Aloud

> I took a deep breath and ran right up to the diving board and jumped into the swimming hole. This time I held my breath and kept my mouth shut as I paddled and kicked my way to the surface. Then I began paddling furiously with my arms and kicking my legs. The next thing I knew I had reached the river bank. All the kids ran up to congratulate me. It was the proudest moment of my life. I wasn't afraid of the water anymore. As soon as I got my wind I ran and jumped off the diving board again.
>
> —JOHN D. FITZGERALD

This paragraph is a good selection for sharing. Prepare it for reading aloud. Follow these simple steps for preparing a selection:

1. Silently read the selection *twice*.
2. Copy the selection on paper, leaving space between the lines.
3. Look up the meaning and pronunciation of any unfamiliar words.
4. Decide on the meaning of each phrase, sentence, paragraph, or stanza.
5. On your own copy, make any marks that will help you to remember particular pronunciations, stresses, or pauses needed to get the meaning across to the listener.
6. Practice reading the selection aloud many times. Think about the nonverbal signals you convey. Be sure they add to the reading.

When several members of the class are ready, take turns reading the selection aloud. How well has each reader followed the steps?

Part 3

Objective

To prepare and select material for oral reading

Presenting the Lesson

1. Read page 327. Depending on the ability of the class, it is suggested that page 327 be read silently. Students should note the procedure for preparing a selection and then actually prepare the Fitzgerald selection for reading aloud.

2. Ask several volunteers to read the prepared selection. Discuss the effectiveness of each speaker.

3. Read the first paragraph of page 328. Assign the rest of Choosing a Selection on pages 328 and 329 to be read silently. Each student should prepare one of the four selections for the class.

4. The following Rating Guide can be used by the students or the teacher for evaluating the oral performances of the class members:

Rating Guide

Score each item on a scale of 1 (lowest) to 5 (highest).

1. Voice

Pronounced words correctly
5 4 3 2 1

Articulated carefully
5 4 3 2 1

Used helpful stress and phrasing
5 4 3 2 1

Controlled volume and projection
5 4 3 2 1

2. Nonverbal

Used helpful facial expressions and gestures

5 4 3 2 1

Had good posture

5 4 3 2 1

3. Overall Effectiveness

Showed concern for doing a good job

5 4 3 2 1

Achieved a good, finished performance

5 4 3 2 1

5. Do Exercise B on page 330 as a class activity. Assign Exercises A, C, and D on pages 329 and 330 for individual completion by students. Then have the students report and discuss their results.

Choosing a Selection

When you choose material to read aloud, choose a selection you enjoy. Also consider who will be listening to you. If your audience is going to be young children, you may want to select something different from what you would read to your classmates.

Select one of the following story excerpts or poems. Prepare it for presentation to the class.

> There was no trace of the fog now. The sky became bluer and bluer and now there were white clouds hurrying across it from time to time. In the wide glades there were primroses. A light breeze sprang up, which scattered drops of moisture from the swaying branches and carried cool, delicious scents against the faces of the travelers. The trees began to come fully alive. The larches and birches were covered with green, the laburnums with gold. Soon the beech trees had put forth their delicate, transparent leaves. As the travelers walked under them, the light also became green. A bee buzzed across their path.—C. S. LEWIS

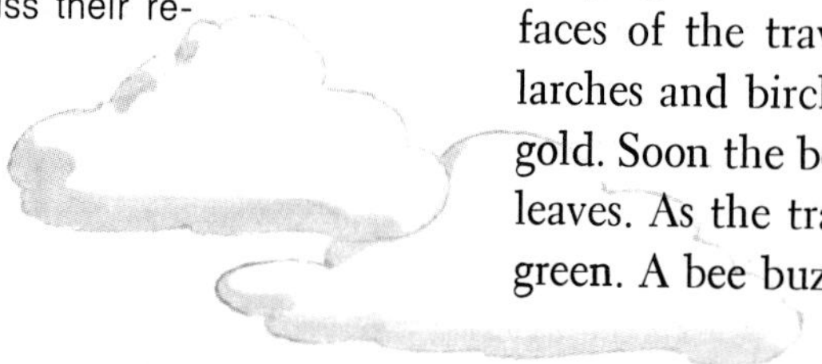

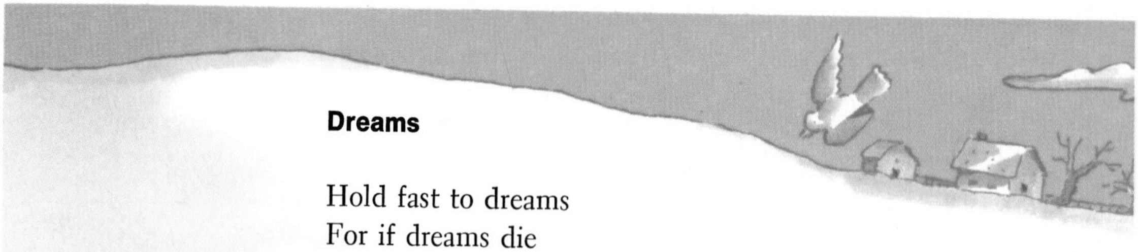

Dreams

Hold fast to dreams
For if dreams die
Life is a broken-winged bird
That cannot fly.

Hold fast to dreams
For when dreams go
Life is a barren field
Frozen with snow.

—LANGSTON HUGHES

Spaghetti

Spaghetti, spaghetti, all over the place,
Up to my elbow—up to my face,
Over the carpet and under the chairs,
Into the hammock and wound round the stairs,
Filling the bathtub and covering the desk,
Making the sofa a mad mushy mess.

The party is ruined, I'm terribly worried,
The guests have all left (unless they're all buried).
I told them, "Bring presents." I said, "Throw confetti."
I guess they heard wrong
'Cause they all threw spaghetti!

—SHEL SILVERSTEIN

The big bear swerved to one of the strong gray barns, and pushed his head against the door. Within he heard cattle stamping nervously, and the threatening rumble of a chained bull that scented danger to the herd. The big bear inserted a front claw in the crevice where the two barn doors rolled shut, and with all his tremendous strength tried to pry them open. But they were stoutly built, and the most he could do was force them an inch apart. Then the oaken doors sprang right back together again. The bear champed his jaws angrily, and slapped the earth in senseless fury. A shower of pebbles leaped up to strike him in the face. His jaw curled in a snarl.—JIM KJELGAARD

Exercises Reading Poems and Stories Aloud

A. A person who is reading aloud should help the listeners understand and enjoy the selection. Make a list of some of the ways a reader can do this. Compare your list with those of others in your class.

Extending the Lesson

Prepare a class presentation of oral reading to be shared with another class or with a group of younger children.

B. Most newscasters read the news on their programs. Listen to several different newscasters. Compare the way they read aloud. Do some sound better to you than others? Does there seem to be any difference between the way local and national newscasters read aloud? Discuss your observations with the class.

C. Find a poem or story that you think a young child might enjoy. Prepare it for reading aloud. If you can, actually read it to a child.

D. Collect a notebook of selections you think you would enjoy sharing aloud with others. Include both poetry and story material. Plan a reading-aloud day in class.

Part 4 Taking Part in Conversation

Probably the most common use of talking in our daily lives is in conversation. However, good conversation is more than just talking. It has three parts:

1. **Thinking**—What are you going to talk about? How will you say it? What are possible reactions to your ideas? How do you judge the response you get?

2. **Talking**—Use your voice effectively. Don't forget the nonverbal signals you send.

3. **Listening**—Pay attention to what others are saying. Be sure your part of the conversation fits with the other parts.

Part 4

Objective

To recognize the structure of good conversation

Presenting the Lesson

1. Read pages 330 and 331. Ask for volunteers to play the roles in the sample conversation on page 331. Emphasize the importance of being both a speaker (initiating a message) and a listener (answering with a response) while taking part in a conversation.

2. Read aloud the Guide for Taking Part in Conversations on page 332. Discuss each point and ask for examples or suggestions to elaborate on each. Does the sample conversation on page 331 follow the guidelines? Why or why not?

3. Do Exercise A with the class as suggested. Exercises B and E can be done with small groups or partners. Exercises C and D may be assigned for individual completion.

A good conversation is something like a game of catch. In catch, the ball should always keep moving from one player to the next. If one or two players hold the ball for too long, the game is no fun for the others. In conversation it is just as important to keep things moving from person to person. One or two long-winded speakers can take the sharing out of the process.

Remember that in conversation a speaker is a speaker only part of the time. The rest of the time the speaker should be listening and thinking of his or her response to others.

Read the following conversation. Notice how each member helps to keep things going.

JOHN: I wish you could have seen my crazy dog Bif last night.

BETH: Why, what did he do?

JOHN: Well, he was sound asleep on the floor in his usual position —on his back with all four paws in the air. I turned on the TV and the sound was really loud. Old Bif jumped up, gave me a dirty look, and pushed the "Off" button with his nose!

KARL: Did you teach him to do that?

JOHN: Nope. It was a complete surprise.

BETH: Karl, doesn't your cat do some funny things, too?

Extending the Lesson

For the next few days, ask students to practice good conversational skills and to take note of problems in conversations in which they take part. Discuss those items from Guides for Taking Part in Conversation that are most often not followed. What are some of the ways students tried to improve the conversations?

The only way to improve speaking skills is to use them. Encourage continuation of oral practice even after the completion of Chapter 20.

In your own conversations, try to follow these simple guides:

Guides for Taking Part in Conversations

1. Think of topics to interest others.
2. When you don't agree with another's point of view, don't interrupt.
3. Wait your turn to speak and then tell your reasons for disagreeing and your point of view. For example:

   LISA: *Wasn't that electronic music Mr. Van played for us in music class just awful? It sounded like the screeching of car brakes.*

   MICHAEL: *Well, I liked it. It reminded me of the theme music from that new science fiction movie we saw last week.*

4. Avoid remarks that might hurt someone's feelings.
5. Ask questions for the sake of clear understanding. For example:

   LEROY: *Please bring your records when you come to my party on Saturday.*

   ALICE: *Do you want 45's or just albums?*

6. Ask questions to encourage others to speak. For example:

   MARCIA: *What do you think about that new rule, Murray?*

7. Listen carefully to what others are saying.
8. Give everyone a chance to speak

Go back and re-examine the conversation on page 331. Did it follow the guides?

Exercises Taking Part in Conversations

A. Choose three speakers to read the roles of John, Beth, and Karl in the conversation on page 331. At the end, they should continue the conversation on their own for a few minutes. Discuss how well the speakers followed the Guides for Taking Part in Conversations.

B. In groups of two or three, practice good conversation techniques. Use one of the following topics, or choose one of your own. After a short time, discuss common group successes or problems.

A favorite TV show	A recent sports event
A funny happening	An embarrassing moment
How school could be better	

C. Make a list of several topics that might be appropriate for conversation with each of the following groups:

A few close friends	The parents of a friend
Several elderly relatives	A stranger on a bus
A new neighbor	Your teacher

D. Listen to conversations in the school cafeteria, on the bus, or in the classroom. Decide whether these conversations follow the Guides for Taking Part in Conversations.

E. Choose a partner. Act out examples of each of the following conversation problems. Demonstrate how you might try to aid the conversation in each case.

1. One person has been talking for several minutes.
2. One person has listened carefully but has not talked.
3. You and another person begin to speak at the same time.
4. Someone makes a statement you know to be incorrect.
5. Someone begins to change the topic before the original topic has been completed.

Chapter 21

Improving Your Listening Skills

"What did you say?"
"I didn't hear that."
"Sorry, I wasn't listening."

These words are probably familiar to you. Why? The reason is that most people like to talk more than they like to listen. Look at the time people spend communicating. You can see that they spend more time listening than speaking.

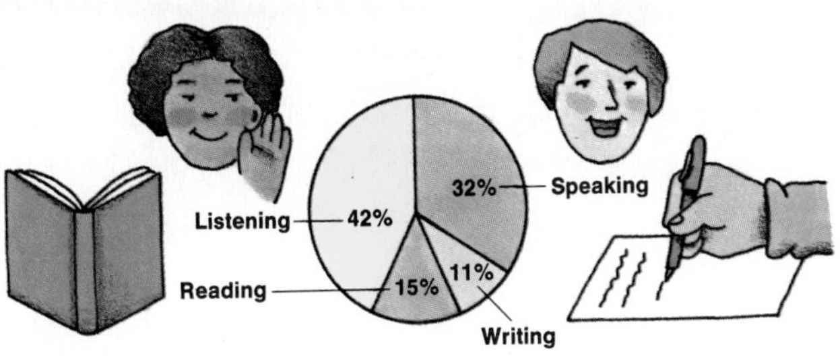

Chapter Objectives

1. To appreciate the importance of good listening

2. To gain awareness of various barriers to communication and to develop approaches to deal with each

3. To develop habits of careful listening when receiving directions

Preparing the Students

Administer the following Listening Test orally. Give the following instructions to the students:

> To do this test you will need one sheet of lined notebook paper with margin lines on the sides. You will also need a pen or pencil. I will read aloud all of the directions only once. Follow them carefully but quickly to avoid confusion. Do not put any marks on the paper unless I tell you to do so.
>
> Write your first and last name on the top line of your paper. Start as close to the left margin as you can.
>
> Write the words *Listening Test* on the second line, in the center of the page.
>
> Skip two lines and number each of the next lines from one to nine. Put the numbers just to the left of the left margin line. Circle each number.
>
> Write the answers to the following nine questions after each number.
>
> 1. Write the name of the day before yesterday.
> 2. Write your teacher's last name.
> 3. What letters are missing from the following alphabet? Write them. a b d f g h k l m o p t u v y z
> 4. Print the name of this month backwards.
> 5. If 3 × 2 equals 8, make an X. If not, make a circle.

6. Write the wrong answer to this question: "Are you now in the United States?
7. Write the numbers 4 2 7 9 5. Underline the largest.
8. If you underlined 7 in the last question, make a square here. If not, go on to the next question.
9. Write the words *the end.*

Have students correct their own papers. What are some of the common errors that the students made? Discuss the importance of good listening skills.

Read aloud and discuss the introductory material on pages 335 and 336. Do the students agree with the reasons for improving listening skills? Can they add any others to the list?

Part 1

Objective

To appreciate the importance of good listening

Presenting the Lesson

1. Obtain several sound effects records from the public library. Play selections for the class and ask the students to identify as many sounds as they can. If recording equipment is available, have groups of students create their own sound effects tapes and test other students on them.

2. Read and discuss page 336. Emphasize the difference between listening and hearing.

3. Ask students to answer the four questions on page 337 by raising their hands in response to

Here are some good reasons for improving your listening.

1. **You can learn more.** All around you, exciting, educational, and entertaining things are happening. Good listeners are able to make more of this outside world a part of their own.
2. **You will be popular with talkers.** Remember that most people prefer talking to listening. They are always looking for someone to pay attention to them. Good listeners make good friends.
3. **You will be more dependable.** The more you know, the more you can share with others. Good listeners try to get correct information to share.
4. **You will be spared embarrassment.** If you don't hear something, you can't respond to it. If you are supposed to be somewhere or to do something, you need the right information. It really pays to be a good listener.

Part 1 Listening or Hearing?

Most people use the words *hearing* and *listening* to mean the same thing. Actually, they are not the same. *Hearing* is knowing that sounds are entering your ears. *Listening* is thinking about those sounds so that they have meaning. The number of things you hear at any given moment is very great. To how many of those sounds do you pay close attention? Do you think about every sound you hear? Of course not. You wouldn't even want to. For example, as your favorite record plays, you probably ignore other sounds such as that of a lawn mower outside or even a fly buzzing near you.

Listening is not always easy. It means paying attention to some of the things you hear even if they don't seem interesting or important to you at the time. You must put your mind on the important sounds and blot out the other noises around you. You may need to practice concentrating.

True or False?

Read the following statements and decide if each is true or false.

1. Good listeners are smarter than poor listeners.
2. Better readers are better listeners.
3. Only a small part of your time is spent taking in information.
4. Most people are good listeners.

Believe it or not, all four of the above statements are false. Here's why.

1. Good listeners are not smarter than poor listeners. Listening skills must be taught to people of all levels of intelligence. Good listeners *are* able to take in more information. They are able to increase their knowledge. Those who don't listen don't learn as much.
2. Good listening and good reading have some of the same requirements. However, they are different skills. Being good at one doesn't make you good at the other.
3. Much of your time is spent taking in information. At least seventy percent of the time you are awake you spend in gathering facts and details. The amount of information you are able to use depends on how well you have listened.
4. Most people are *not* good listeners. Many other activities steal time and energy. To become a good listener, you must want to be a good listener.

your reading them aloud. Read and discuss the answers provided by the text. Make sure students are aware of the meaning of being a good listener.

4. To encourage listening skill, use several of the following lists. Have students listen as you read a complete list. Then ask them to write down as many of the items as they can remember. Note that lists with abstract words are more difficult to remember than lists of objects, and that lists of related objects are the simplest to recall.

run	sandwich	apple
cloud	cookie	pear
love	apple	grape
finger	cheese	orange
receive	candy	banana
bell	ice cream	peach
suggest	milk	plum
travel	cake	apricot
pencil	raisins	melon
want	potato chips	berries

5. Do Exercises A and B on page 338 with the entire class. Discuss the results. Do the remainder of the Exercises in small groups. Compare the findings of the groups.

Optional Practice

Read aloud a short story that is rich in sound-effect suggestion. Ask students to supply orally the right sound effect on cue. It is wise to prearrange some control of sound length and volume.

Exercises Listening or Hearing?

A. Close your eyes and spend the next few minutes listening carefully only to certain sounds you hear. As your teacher directs, do this for each of the following:

Sounds outside the building
Sounds in the hallway
Sounds in the room
Your own sounds (heartbeat, breathing)

Is it hard to concentrate on only one set of sounds? Did you become aware of sounds you don't remember hearing before?

B. Close your book while your teacher or a student reads the following list of words. See how many you can remember.

table	couch	lamp	shelf	clock
chair	mirror	rug	television	drapes

Make lists of your own and try them with the class.

C. Explain why you don't give full attention to all the sounds you hear. What kinds of sounds do you usually ignore?

D. Play a game of "telephone." The class lines up and a message is whispered down the line. No one may say the message more than once. Compare what the last person thinks the message was with the original. Everyone heard. Who listened?

E. In conversations, you concentrate on your own thoughts. You tend to tune out what others are saying. Here is an exercise to help you stretch your ability to concentrate.

Do the exercise with a partner. Face each other. One person begins by saying a simple sentence. The partner then repeats what he or she has just heard and adds a new sentence. Speakers continue to say two sentences each, the partner's added one and a new one. Speakers never repeat their own sentences. Continue for an agreed length of time or until your teacher tells you to stop.

Part 2 Becoming a Good Listener

Many things stand in the way of good listening. These are called **communication barriers.** Some of these barriers cannot be controlled by the listener. Some can. If you want to become a good listener, you need to practice concentration. Zero in on the message and ignore the things that try to get in the way.

What a speaker says is not always what the listener hears. What the listener understands may be only one half of what the speaker tries to communicate. How does this happen? What things get in the way of communication? In Chapter 20, you learned the importance of effective speaking and of controlling nonverbal signals. Poor speakers create some communication barriers. Poor listeners create or fail to deal with barriers of other kinds. Let's look at how good listeners differ from poor ones.

Are You a Poor Listener or a Good One?

Paying Attention

Poor listeners let their thoughts drift to other things.	Good listeners pay attention to the information. They save daydreaming for other times.

Concentrating on the Speaker

Poor listeners are easily distracted.	Good listeners make the best of any situation. They concentrate on the speaker.

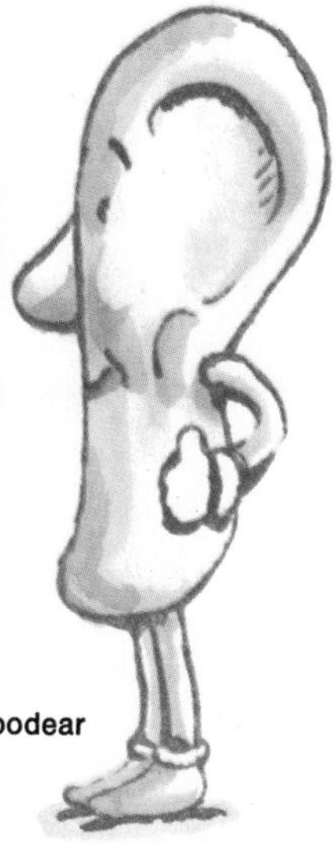
Mr. Goodear

Part 2

Objective

To gain awareness of various barriers to communication and to develop approaches to deal with each.

Presenting the Lesson

1. Read the introduction to Part 2 on page 339. Discuss different kinds of communication barriers that students are aware of. Why do they cause a problem for both speakers and listeners? What adjustments must be made by both the speakers and the listeners when barriers exist?

2. Read and discuss each item in the chart Are You a Poor Listener or a Good One? on pages 339 and 340. Ask students to rate themselves in each area, using this scale:

1—always a poor listener
2—often poor
3—sometimes poor, sometimes good
4—often good
5—always a good listener

Discuss practical ways to become a better listener in each situation. Read the final paragraph of Part 2 on page 341.

3. Assign Exercises A, B, and E on page 341, and discuss the results with the class. Do Exercises C and D with the whole group. Assign Exercise F on page 342 to a small group of interested students.

4. Ask students which of the following behaviors show good listening skills and which are barriers. Discuss how the barriers might be overcome.

1. Taking notes
2. Watching a fly buzz around
3. Asking questions at an appropriate time
4. Thinking about how nice the speaker looks
5. Reconsidering a conclusion previously made

Optional Practice

Read aloud short stories or excerpts from longer works. Prepare questions for students to answer at the conclusion of the reading. Be sure to include questions concerning main idea, sequence, and details.

Listening to the Message

Poor listeners pay too much attention to nonverbal signals.

Good listeners tune out extras and listen to the main message.

Getting the Main Ideas

Poor listeners pay too much attention to details. They miss the important ideas.

Good listeners get the main ideas and try to keep them in order.

Listening and Thinking

Poor listeners don't try to listen.

Good listeners work hard to get new information.

Making Judgments

Poor listeners get carried away with certain words or ideas. They tune out the main idea.

Good listeners don't jump to conclusions. Judgments are saved for the end of the presentation.

Learning

Poor listeners decide they aren't interested before they even know if they are.

Good listeners plan for listening. They prepare for the speaker and are eager to learn new things.

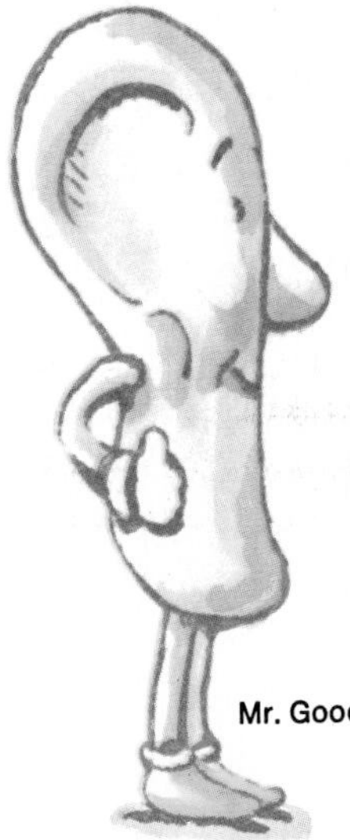
Mr. Goodear

Did you see yourself in any of the listening situations? Are you more often a good listener or a poor one? Practice being a good listener. Don't let nonverbal, emotional, or other barriers get in your way. Remember that being a good listener requires effort and energy. The results are worth it.

Extending the Lesson

Play selections of various types of musical compositions. Which do students like best? Why? Discuss emotional response as a barrier to good listening.

Exercises Becoming a Good Listener

A. List five things you can do to become a better listener in the classroom. Compare your list with those of your classmates. Can you add more ideas to your list?

B. What barriers to listening have you experienced? Discuss the ways you might have dealt with those barriers and improved your listening.

C. In pairs, act out the following situations. After a few moments, discuss the communication barriers that you notice in each situation.

a. A student comes home from school two hours late and meets a parent at the door.

b. Brother and sister both believe it is the other's turn to do the dishes.

c. One student has lost another student's book. The second student did not even know the first had borrowed the book.

D. Create a class story. The first student begins with a few sentences. The second student repeats the first student's ideas and adds more to the story. Continue until everyone has had a chance to add ideas. How well do students listen to one another?

E. List five topics for discussion that would interest you. List five more that would tempt you to tune out. Compare lists with those of your classmates. Discuss why a speaker has problems communicating with all the members of an audience.

F. Find out the meaning of the term *noise pollution.* Give some examples of noise pollution. Are you ever guilty of creating noise pollution? Ask your teacher if you may put up an anti-noise pollution bulletin board in the classroom.

Part 3

Objective

To develop habits of careful listening when receiving directions

Presenting the Lesson

1. Read the introduction to Part 3. Discuss students' experiences with directions that resulted from poor listening skills.

2. Use the map and the Practice in Following Directions activities on pages 342 to 344 for a class exercise. Discuss the barriers to listening that occur during the exercise. What ways of dealing with the barriers are the responsibility of the speaker? What ways are the responsibility of the listener?

3. Assign the direction writing in Exercise A, on page 344, to all students. Form small groups to test the accuracy of the directions and the listening skill of the group members. Do Exercise B on page 345 in small groups, also. Do Exercises C and D as a class.

Part 3 Following Directions

Juanita had collected newspaper articles all week for a current events project. She had carefully pasted each article to a sheet of paper. Then she made an attractive cover for the notebook she had assembled. As she placed it on her teacher's desk, she noticed that Jerry had only put his clippings into an envelope.

"Where's your current events notebook, Jerry?" asked Juanita politely.

"What notebook?" replied Jerry with a surprised look.

"The one Mr. Navin assigned last Thursday," stated Juanita.

"Oh, no," moaned Jerry. "I didn't know we were supposed to make a notebook. I must not have been listening to directions."

Has anything like this ever happened to you? Most students have had an experience like Jerry's. They didn't follow directions because they weren't listening.

As you get older, your world becomes more complicated. It is important for you to listen carefully while something is being explained. You may want to learn a new game or take a message for someone. You may wish to try a new recipe or find a new park. Like other types of listening, following directions takes concentration.

Practice in Following Directions

One good way to practice following directions is to use a map. Take a moment to examine the imaginary neighborhood map on the next page. Notice the names of the streets, the locations of landmarks, and the compass direction marker. Ask someone to read aloud the sets of directions on page 344 while you try to follow them. Compare results with others.

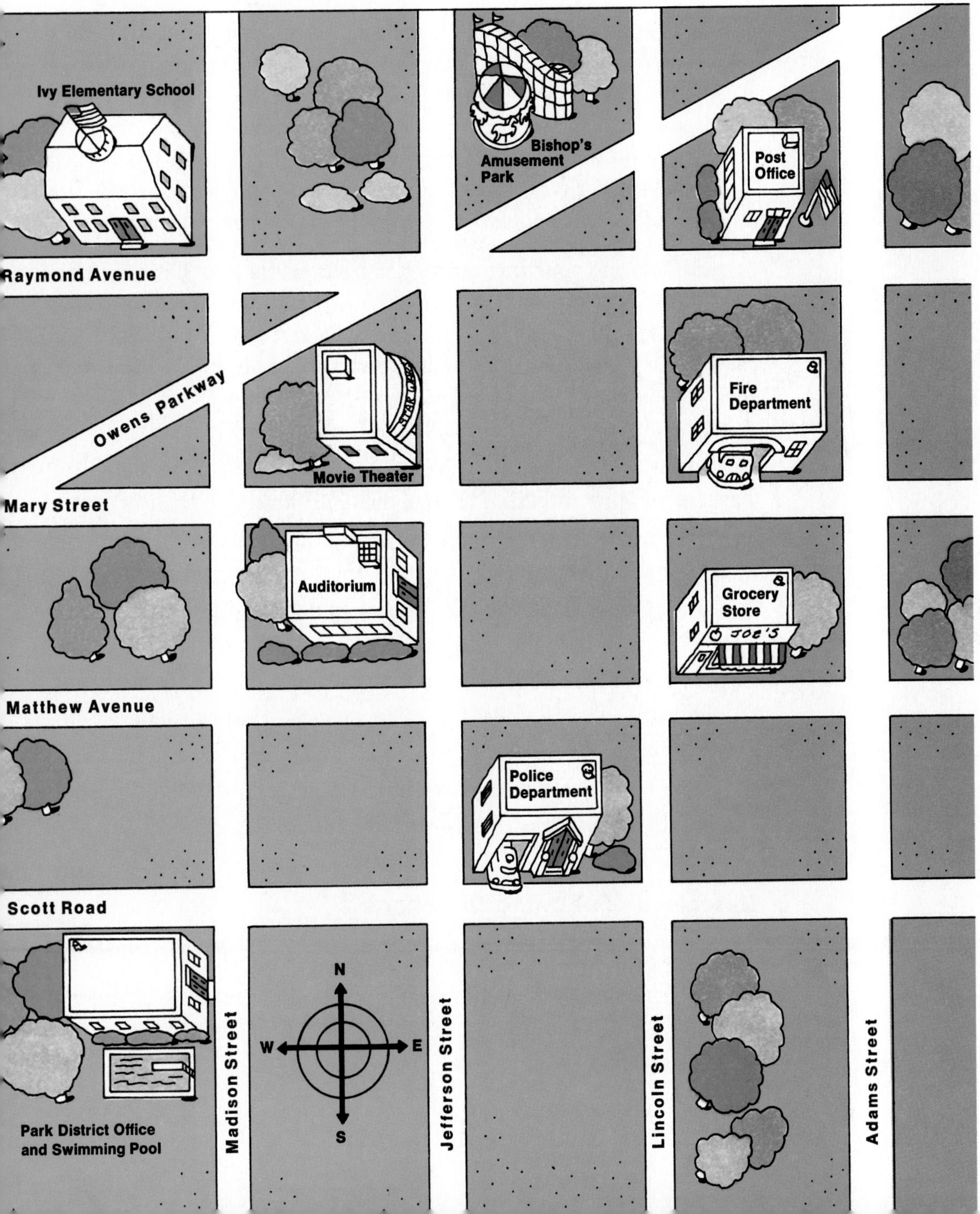

Optional Practice

1. Choose a leader and play the old game of "Simon Says. . . ." Students are to follow the directions of the leader only when the directions are preceded by the phrase "Simon Says. . . ."

2. Students will take more interest in direction-following exercises if maps of their own community or town can be used. Check local Chamber of Commerce offices or tourist bureaus for copies of maps for your class. Work out varying sets of directions for the class, using the maps.

1. You are at the corner of Adams and Scott. You travel north two blocks and make a left turn. You continue two blocks and then turn north again. After walking one half block more, where will you be? In front of the Movie Theater

2. You leave Ivy Elementary School to go home, but must do a few errands on the way. You walk east three blocks and stop to mail a letter. You then turn around and go back one block. You go south on Lincoln for two blocks. After buying a loaf of bread, you walk west on Matthew one block and then turn left. When you reach the northwest corner of Scott and Jefferson you are home. What landmark is across the street from where you live? The Police Department

3. You and your friends meet in front of the Park District Office on Scott. You walk to the corner of Scott and Madison and go north until you get to the Owens Parkway. You turn right and continue one block. You turn left on Jefferson Street. After walking about one half block north, where will you be? In front of Bishop's Amusement Park

How well were you able to follow directions? Were there any barriers to your listening? What did you do about them? Was it necessary for the direction-giver to repeat any part of the directions?

Sometimes the listener can help the speaker or direction-giver to do a better job. If the speaker's volume is too low, the listener should politely ask the speaker to talk more loudly. If some part of the speaker's message is unclear, the listener should ask questions.

Following directions is an active process. If the listener is not concentrating, the information will be lost or confused. The speaker's time and energy will be wasted. Try to follow the good listening habits suggested earlier in this chapter.

Exercises Following Directions

A. Make a set of directions, using the map on page 343. Have classmates practice their listening skills while you read the directions aloud. As a direction-giver, be sure you are polite and clear, and your directions are complete.

B. Place two chairs back to back. In one chair the speaker gives directions for drawing one of the suggested figures. In the second chair, the listener tries to draw the figure. The listener may not ask the speaker to repeat any directions. When the drawing is finished, compare it with the original. Is the drawing accurate? If not, what might have been the problem? If it is accurate, what helped it to be that way?

Suggested figures:

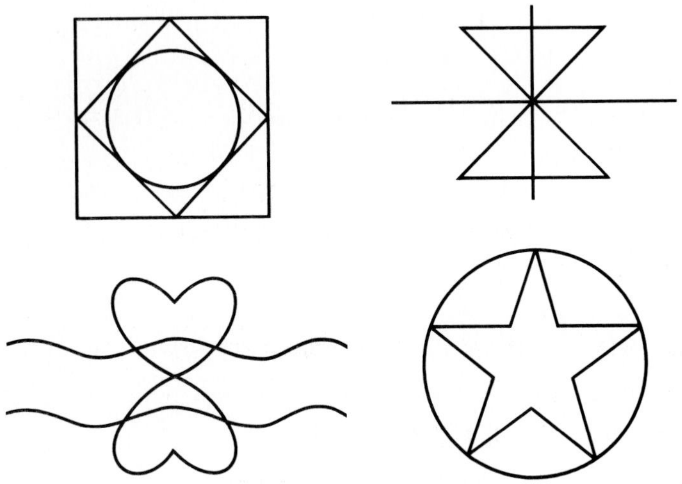

C. Demonstrate how a listener might nonverbally show these messages to a speaker:

I'm tired of sitting in this chair.
This sure is complicated.
Oh no! Not this again!
I don't understand.
This is very interesting.

D. Bring to class examples of written directions. These might be recipes, model kit instructions, or washing instructions for an article of clothing. Write two or three questions about the directions. Read the directions to a classmate and see if he or she can answer the questions.

Chapter 22

Capitalization

The use of capital letters is called **capitalization.** When you use a capital letter at the beginning of a word, you **capitalize** the word.

Capital letters are used to make reading easier. They call attention to the beginnings of sentences and to certain special words.

Part 1 Proper Nouns and Adjectives

Capitalize **proper nouns** and **proper adjectives.**

A **common noun** is the name of a whole group of persons, places, or things.

girl country book

A **proper noun** is the name of a particular person, place, or thing.

Queen Victoria Sweden Bible

Chapter Objectives

1. To understand and apply the rules for capitalizing proper nouns and adjectives

2. To capitalize first words of sentences, poems, and other writings, where appropriate

Preparing the Students

Students have been familiar with the use of capitalization since they first began to read and write. Two kinds of errors occur frequently in student writing: the use of capitals where not needed, and failure to capitalize necessary words. The following paragraph contains both kinds of errors.

Write the paragraph on the board or distribute copies of it. Ask students to circle all the mistakes.

> all the trees on Oliver street are Elm Trees. dr. lang, a Biology Teacher at wallis high school, says it's lucky none of them have caught dutch Elm disease. i hope they don't. it would be a shame to lose the cool Summer Shade and the beautiful Fall Colors.

Are students able to find all the errors? (Prepare a similar paragraph for use as review at the conclusion of this chapter.)

Additional Resources

Diagnostic Test—page 432
Mastery Test—pages 479 and 480
Additional Mastery Test—In separate booklet, *Diagnostic and Mastery Tests, Gold Level,* pp. 55, 56.
Skills Practice Book—pp. 128–132
Duplicating Masters—pp. 128–132

Part 1

Objective

To understand and apply the rules for capitalizing proper nouns and adjectives

Presenting the Lesson

1. Read and discuss pages 347 and 348. Stress the difference between common and proper nouns. Point out the progression in the examples from general terms (the common nouns *girl, country,* and *book*) to specific terms (the proper nouns *Queen Victoria, Sweden,* and *Bible*), and then to the adjective form of the specific terms (the proper adjectives *Victorian, Swedish,* and *Biblical*).

2. Encourage students to supply additional examples for each item discussed.

3. Assign and discuss Exercises A and B on page 349. (The Exercises in this Part are cumulative; for best results, cover the material in the order in which it is presented.)

4. Read and discuss page 350.

5. Assign and discuss Exercises A and B on page 351.

6. Read and discuss pages 351 and 352. Be sure that students understand the meanings of the terms *race, religion, nationality,* and *language.*

7. Assign and discuss Exercises A and B on pages 352 and 353.

8. See Exercise A on page 358 for additional practice.

Extending the Lesson

Ask students to make a collection of examples of capitalized

A **proper adjective** is an adjective formed from a proper noun.

Victorian   Swedish   Biblical

There are many different kinds of proper nouns. The following rules will help you recognize many proper nouns which need to be capitalized.

Capitalize the names of people.

Begin every word in a person's name with a capital letter. An initial stands for a name. Write initials as capital letters. Put a period after every initial.

Examples: Susan B. Anthony   A. J. Foyt

Capitalize a title used with a person's name.

Examples:

In assembly today, Dr. Martin and Coach Brown talked about food, rest, and exercise.

Have you seen Ms. Gray or Mr. Townsend?

Capitalize words referring to God and to religious scriptures.

Examples:

the Deity	the Bible	the Gospel
Allah	the Talmud	the Book of Genesis
the Lord	the Koran	the New Testament

Capitalize the word *I*.

Example: Mary and I planted sunflower seeds.

Exercises Using Capital Letters Correctly

A. Number your paper from 1 to 10. Copy the following sentences. Change small letters to capital letters wherever necessary.

1. A television series was based on books by laura ingalls wilder.
2. The names linda ann rigby and spencer a. marks were engraved on the plaque.
3. Some people think that thomas edison was a genius.
4. The name nadine means "hope."
5. This famous scientist, dr. george washington carver, was born a slave.
6. In church last week, i heard a reading from the book of genesis.
7. Stacy and i played tennis against kenny and maria.
8. We live next door to mr. and mrs. torres.
9. The best teacher i ever had was professor eileen black.
10. My sister annette made an appointment with our dentist, dr. means.

B. Follow the directions for Exercise A.

1. The Indian chiefs william brant and red jacket signed a treaty with moses cleaveland.
2. Tomorrow i will cut miss quinlan's lawn.
3. Years later, president lincoln met harriet beecher stowe.
4. The twins, sandy and dennis, went to the store with their father, mr. cage.
5. The leader of althea's Bluebird group is mrs. hartley.
6. After adopting the Muslim religion, the boxer cassius clay changed his name to muhammed ali.
7. For years, researcher jane goodall lived with a band of apes.
8. One of the speakers was the artist, andrew wyeth.
9. Either lottie or i can take you to ms. franklin's office.
10. When did marian anderson begin her career?

proper nouns and adjectives found in various printed sources, such as magazines, newspapers, direct mail advertising, church bulletins, etc. They should assemble their findings into a notebook. Make a bulletin board or display of the student work.

Capitalize the names of months, days, and holidays.

Do not capitalize names of seasons (spring, summer).

Examples:

On Friday, December 16, our Christmas vacation begins.

My favorite season is winter.

Capitalize the names of particular places and things.

a. Cities, states, and countries.

Examples:

Which is larger, Portland, Oregon, or Detroit, Michigan?

Brazil is the largest country in South America, and Canada is the largest country in North America.

b. Streets, bridges, and buildings.

Examples:

The Chambers Building is at the corner of Greenlawn Avenue and High Street.

c. Geographical names. Capitalize all geographical names. Also capitalize the words *north*, *south*, *east*, and *west* when they refer to a section of a country. Do not capitalize them when they refer to a direction.

Examples:

Most of the area between the Rocky Mountains in the West and the Appalachian Mountains in the East is drained by three rivers, the Mississippi, the Ohio, and the Missouri.

The boat sailed west, toward the island.

Exercises Using Capital Letters Correctly

A. Number your paper from 1 to 10. Copy the following sentences. Change small letters to capital letters wherever necessary.

1. If you can't come at easter, come next summer.
2. We could see long island and new jersey from the top of the empire state building.
3. Is the amazon river in brazil or in argentina?
4. Dean's dairy bar isn't open on holidays.
5. Doreen was in the west, visiting relatives in arizona.
6. We rode north from the lazy l ranch just before sunset.
7. The first king of hawaii was king kamehameha.
8. Interstate highway 80 carries heavy traffic.
9. The famous irwin hospital is in the east.
10. Five states border the gulf of mexico.

B. Number from 1 to 10. Copy each of the following groups of words. Wherever necessary, change small letters to capitals.

1. in the twentieth congressional district
2. the most powerful tribes in the west
3. ten miles east of pike's peak
4. in houston on tuesday
5. the altitude of denver, colorado
6. the golden gate bridge in san francisco
7. the spring holidays in florida
8. special thanksgiving celebrations at plimoth plantation
9. on cathedral square in the kremlin in moscow
10. in puerto rico on thursday, july 12

Capitalize the names of races, religions, nationalities, and languages.

Modern American Indian artists often use traditional designs in their work.

Judaism, Christianity, and the Muslim religion share a belief in one God.

The Russians and the Chinese have frequent arguments about their border.

Does this junior high school offer French?

Capitalize the names of clubs, organizations, and business firms.

My aunt belongs to the Centerville Garden Club.

Where is the headquarters of the Boy Scouts of America?

Don's father works for General Motors.

Exercises Using Capital Letters Correctly

A. Number from 1 to 10. Copy each of the following groups of words. Wherever necessary, change small letters to capitals.

D
1. a dutch windmill
A
2. african art
J
3. a jewish temple
C S
4. the cub scouts
P
5. polish sausage
A
6. an anglican minister
F
7. filipino traditions
C G
8. the campfire girls
B T C
9. bell telephone company
A
10. the arab oil fields

B. Number from 1 to 10. Copy each of the following sentences. Wherever necessary, change small letters to capitals.

F I
1. Some of the Romance languages are french, italian, and
S
spanish.

2. The olmecs were an ancient indian tribe in mexico.

3. Gabriel joined the united states marine corps.

4. Were those tourists speaking japanese?

5. Many people of india practice hinduism.

6. Dolores's mother tests computers for digital equipment company.

7. The elmwood photography club meets every monday in the carnegie library.

8. Roberto became an officer of a junior achievement business.

9. The museum exhibits include an egyptian mummy and several roman statues.

10. The irish writer jonathan swift wrote a great english novel about a man named gulliver.

Part 2 First Words

Sentences

Capitalize the first word of every sentence.

Workers digging the foundation found a mastodon bone.

When will the eclipse begin?

Look out!

Poetry

Capitalize the first word in most lines of poetry.

I'll tell you how the sun rose
A ribbon at a time,
The steeple swam in amethyst,
The news like squirrels ran.

EMILY DICKINSON, "I'll Tell You How the Sun Rose"

Part 2

Objective

To capitalize first words of sentences, poems, and other writings, where appropriate

Presenting the Lesson

1. Read and discuss pages 353 and 354.

2. Assign Exercises A and B on pages 354 and 355. Have students exchange papers and proofread each other's work. Discuss the answers after corrections have been made.

3. Read and discuss pages 356 and 357. Do not dwell on capitalization in outlines unless actual outlining is to be assigned to the class at this time. Give attention to capitalization, underlining, and quotation marks in titles.

4. Assign and discuss the Exercise on page 357.

5. See Exercise B on pages 358 and 359 for additional practice.

Optional Practice

Ask students to bring copies of daily newspapers to class. Divide the class into groups and assign the following tasks. The written lists must be correctly capitalized, underlined, or punctuated.

1. Locate and list the titles of five television shows that will appear on the evening of the date of the paper.
2. Locate and list the titles of three television movies that are scheduled for that date.
3. Locate and list the titles of three movies that are playing at local or area theaters.
4. If the paper has a book review section, locate and list the titles of three books discussed there.

Extending the Lesson

Assign an outline of a section of the students' history or science book.

Sometimes, especially in modern poetry, the lines of a poem do not always begin with a capital letter.

so much depends
upon

a red wheel
barrow

glazed with rain
water

beside the white
chickens.

WILLIAM CARLOS WILLIAMS, "The Red Wheelbarrow"

Exercises Using Capital Letters Correctly

A. Number your paper from 1 to 10. Find the words in the following sentences that should be capitalized. Write the words after the proper number, using the necessary capital letters.

1. the third sunday in june is father's day.
2. is cotton still an important crop in the south?
3. a bird came down the walk:
   he did not know i saw;
   he bit an angleworm in halves
   and ate the fellow, raw.

   EMILY DICKINSON, "A Bird Came Down the Walk"
4. last year we had a dry summer and a rainy fall.
5. do you like italian food? we can get pizza at tina's restaurant.
6. there is a program on television tonight about japan.
7. dr. frances gilbert teaches english literature at carroll university.
8. this month has five saturdays.
9. have you seen any movies by d. w. griffith?

10. whose woods these are i think i know.
his house is in the village though;
he will not see me stopping here
to watch his woods fill up with snow.

ROBERT FROST, "Stopping by Woods on a Snowy Evening"

B. Follow the directions for Exercise A.

1. the school orchestra will play two works by wolfgang amadeus mozart.

2. whenever richard cory went down town,
we people on the pavement looked at him:
he was a gentleman from sole to crown,
clean favored, and imperially slim.

EDWIN ARLINGTON ROBINSON, "Richard Cory"

3. on wednesday i'll be late for dinner. the girl scouts are having a meeting at four o'clock.

4. what is the spanish word for *table?*

5. brown and furry
caterpillar in a hurry;
take your walk
to the shady leaf or stalk.

CHRISTINA GEORGINA ROSSETTI, "The Caterpillar"

6. we celebrate flag day on june 14.

7. are you visiting montreal, in quebec? there, canadians speak french.

8. the Rhino is a homely beast,
for human eyes he's not a feast,
but you and i will never know
why Nature chose to make him so.
farewell, farewell, you old rhinoceros,
i'll stare at something less prepoceros.

OGDEN NASH, "The Rhinoceros"

Outlines

Capitalize the first word of each line of an outline.

Capitalization and Punctuation

I. Use of capital letters

   A. Proper nouns and adjectives
   B. First words

      1. Sentences
      2. Poetry
      3. Outlines
      4. Titles

II. Use of periods

Titles

Capitalize the first word, last word, and any other important words in a title.

Do not capitalize a little word such as *the, in, for, from, a,* or *an,* unless it comes first or last.

Steven Spielberg, *Close Encounters of the Third Kind* (book)

Anne Morrow Lindbergh, *Gift from the Sea* (book)

Lewis Carroll, "The Walrus and the Carpenter" (poem)

Underline the title of a book, magazine, or motion picture.

<u>Mary Poppins</u> (book title in handwriting)

When these titles are printed, they are in *italics.*

Mary Poppins, by P. L. Travers (book title in print)
Ebony Junior (magazine)
Star Wars (motion picture)

Underline the title of a painting or the name of a ship.

Washington Crossing the Delaware (painting)
Queen Elizabeth II (ship)

Put quotation marks around the titles of stories, television programs, poems, reports, articles, and chapters of a book.

"The Little Match Girl" (story)
"The Complete Hen" (poem)
"How Plastic Is Made" (student's report)
"Cubs Take Double-Header" (newspaper article)

Exercise Using Capital Letters Correctly

Copy the following titles and outline. Capitalize them correctly.

1. "highwire trapeze artist breaks record" (newspaper article)
2. *the peaceable kingdom* (painting)
3. "the brain is wider than the sky" (poem)
4. "how the mob is grabbing the mines" (magazine article)
5. *pets of the world* (magazine)
6. *the return of the king* (book)
7. "what makes the aurora" (student's report)
8. "the world's deepest caves" (article)
9. "the kiteflying tournament" (pupil's report)
10. (outline) indians of the northeast

    I. groups
        A. lake indians
        B. woodland indians
    II. important foods
        A. lake indians
            1. wild rice
            2. fish
        B. woodland indians
            1. corn
            2. deer and other game

Additional Exercises

Assign pages 358 and 359 for chapter test or review if they have not been previously assigned.

Additional Exercises

Capitalization

A. Capitalizing Proper Nouns and Adjectives Correctly
(Use after page 352.)

Number your paper from 1 to 10. Copy the following sentences. Change small letters to capital letters wherever necessary.

1. At the bus stop pam met josé and ursula.
2. The hostess, ms. barrett, introduced me to dr. and mrs. taylor.
3. Tomorrow i will go shopping.
4. Will october 31 fall on a friday this year?
5. The school year usually ends around memorial day.
6. The grand canyon is in the state of arizona.
7. The sears tower is the tallest building in chicago, illinois.
8. This restaurant serves delicious hungarian goulash.
9. The slavic languages use an alphabet different from ours.
10. Gladys's uncle is a member of the chamber of commerce.

B. Using Capital Letters Correctly (Use after page 357.)

Number your paper from 1 to 10. In each of the following sentences, poems, and outline, find the words that should be capitalized. Write the words after the proper number, using the necessary capital letters.

1. *optricks, a book of optical illusions* is a book by wentzell and holland.
2. this newspaper has an article called "runaway horse stops traffic."

3. I based my report on the article "deserts" in the *world book encyclopedia.*

4. rosalie subscribes to the magazine *skateboard world.*

5. the movie *the wizard of oz* is shown on television almost every year.

6. today monica presented a report entitled "visiting a live television show."

7. have you ever read the story "the little mermaid"?

8. when i was in kindergarten, i watched "sesame street" every day.

9. cats sleep fat and walk thin.
cats, when they sleep, slump;
when they wake, pull in —
and where the plump's been
there's skin.
cats walk thin.

ROSALIE MOORE, "Catalog"

10. (outline) some famous paintings

I. american
  a. early
    1. *death of wolfe*
    2. west's portrait of george washington
  b. modern
    1. *american gothic*
    2. *christina's world*
II. european

Chapter 23

Punctuation

When you talk with someone, you put words together in a certain way to express your thoughts. Sometimes you drop your voice. That tells your listener you have finished a thought. Sometimes you raise your voice. That tells your listener you are asking him or her a question. If you are excited, perhaps you shout. Sometimes you pause.

What happens when you write? There is no change in voice to guide the reader. Instead, there are capital letters and punctuation marks to guide him or her. They help in the same way that pauses and changes in voice help your listener.

Part 1 End Marks

The signal that shows where a sentence begins is a capital letter. The punctuation marks that show where a sentence ends are called **end marks.**

There are three important end marks: (1) the **period;** (2) the **question mark;** (3) the **exclamation point** (or **exclamation mark**).

Chapter Objectives

1. To use end mark punctuation correctly
2. To use the comma correctly
3. To use the apostrophe to form possessives and contractions
4. To use the hyphen for word division and compound numbers
5. To use quotation marks correctly

Preparing the Students

Read and discuss the introduction on page 361. Call attention to the way the students' own voices rise, fall, and pause as they discuss the material.

Additional Resources

Diagnostic Test—page 433 in this T. E. Recommended for use before teaching the chapter.

Mastery Test—pages 481 and 482 in this T. E. Recommended for use after teaching the chapter.

Additional Mastery Test—Recommended for use after any necessary reteaching. (In separate booklet, *Diagnostic and Mastery Tests, Gold Level,* pages 57 and 58.)

Skills Practice Book—pages 133–142

Duplicating Masters—pages 133–142

Part 1

Objective

To use end mark punctuation correctly

Presenting the Lesson

1. Read and discuss Part 1 on pages 361 to 363. Ask students to suggest additional examples of abbreviations they know. Have them write their own names with initials. Point out that some abbreviations do not require periods.

2. Assign and discuss Exercises A, B, C, and D on pages 363 and 364.

3. Read and discuss page 365. Have students write examples of sentences using each kind of end mark.

4. Assign and discuss Exercises A and B on pages 365 and 366.

5. See Exercise A on page 379 for additional practice.

Optional Practice

Ask students to write out their complete names and addresses, using no abbreviations. Then ask them to rewrite them, using as many abbreviations as possible.

Example:

John Allen Whitney
602 West Arbor Drive
Mission Heights, Illinois

J. A. Whitney
602 W. Arbor Dr.
Mission Hts., IL

Extending the Lesson

Students should learn the two-letter postal abbreviations for all fifty states. Have them create a map bulletin board display that presents them all.

The Period

Use a period at the end of a declarative sentence.

A **declarative sentence** tells something.

This is my poster for the exhibit.

Use a period at the end of most imperative sentences.

An **imperative sentence** requests, instructs, or orders.

Put your poster on the bulletin board.

Use a period after an abbreviation or after an initial.

We often write words in a shortened form to save time and space. These shortened forms of words are called **abbreviations.** On calendars the names of the days are often abbreviated. For example, *Mon.* stands for *Monday*. Except for such abbreviations as *Mr., Mrs., Ms., A.M.,* and *P.M.,* avoid using abbreviations when you write sentences.

We use the abbreviation *A.M.* to stand for the two Latin words, *ante meridiem*, which mean "before noon." The abbreviation *P.M.* stands for *post meridiem*, "after noon."

Here are examples of other common abbreviations. Notice how some abbreviations have two or three parts, with each part standing for one or more words. A period is then used after each part of the abbreviation.

1. St. Street or Saint
2. Mt. Mount or Mountain
3. R.R. Railroad
4. P.O. Post Office
5. U.S.A. United States of America
6. D.C. District of Columbia
7. in. inch
8. doz. dozen
9. Dr. Doctor
10. Mr. Mister

Periods are not used after some abbreviations:

CB (citizens' band) PBS (Public Broadcasting System)
FM (frequency modulation) USAF (United States Air Force)

The two-letter state abbreviations, such as *IL, OH,* and *CA,* are written with capitals and no periods.

If you are not sure whether an abbreviation should be written with or without periods, look up the abbreviation in a dictionary.

We often shorten a name to its first letter, which is called an **initial.** Always use a period after an initial.

P. L. Travers (Pamela Lyndon Travers)

J. C. Penney (James Cash Penney)

Use a period after each number or letter that shows a division of an outline or that precedes an item in a list.

Punctuation (an outline)

I. End marks
  A. The period
    1. Sentences
    2. Abbreviations and initials
    3. Outlines and lists
  B. The question mark
  C. The exclamation point
II. Commas

Talent Show Acts (a list)

1. tumblers
2. tap dancer
3. singer
4. band

Exercises Using Periods Correctly

A. Number your paper from 1 to 10. Copy the following phrases, putting periods where necessary.

1. 4 ft. 10 in.
2. Washington, D.C.
3. P. O. Box 12
4. Bedford Ave.

5. Aug. 30
6. Butterford Chocolate Co., Inc.
7. Dr. H. M. Ritchie
8. 500 mi.
9. (list) First five presidents
   1. George Washington
   2. John Adams
   3. Thomas Jefferson
   4. James Madison
   5. James Monroe
10. (outline) Super-8 Movie-Making
    I. Major equipment needed
       A. Camera
          1. For silent movies
          2. For sound movies
       B. Projector
    II. Other materials needed
       A. Film
       B. Splicer

B. Rewrite each of the following phrases, using abbreviations where possible.

E. 126 St.	1. East 126 Street	6. Raleigh, North Carolina	N.C.
N.Y.	2. New York	7. December 9	Dec.
Rev.	3. Reverend Marsh	8. Benander Game Company	Co.
gal.	4. 4 gallons	9. 10 square feet	sq. ft.
R.	5. Platte River	10. Durapools, Incorporated	Inc.

C. List the abbreviated forms you find on maps in a geography book. Beside each abbreviation, write the word it stands for.
Answers will vary.

D. List the abbreviations used in measurement problems in your arithmetic book. Beside each abbreviation, write the word it stands for. Answers will vary.

The Question Mark

Use a question mark at the end of an interrogative sentence.

An **interrogative sentence** is a sentence that asks a question.

Where are we?

The Exclamation Point (or Exclamation Mark)

Use an exclamation point at the end of an exclamatory sentence and some imperative sentences.

An **exclamatory sentence** is a sentence that expresses strong feelings.

Jackie struck out!

An exclamation point is used at the end of an imperative sentence that expresses excitement or emotion.

Be careful!

Use an exclamation point after an interjection.

An **interjection** is a word or group of words used to express strong feeling. It is one of the eight parts of speech. Words often used as other parts of speech may become interjections when they express strong feeling.

Oh! How beautiful!   Wow! What an ending!

Exercises Using End Marks Correctly

A. Copy the following sentences. Supply the missing punctuation.

1. Mr. and Mrs. Gregory go to St. Augustine every winter.
2. Ouch! This pan is hot!
3. Dr. Evans will be in his office until 4:30.

4. What circus did P. T. Barnum manage?

5. Ms. Carol F. Lunt will speak at the N.H.S. commencement exercises.

6. My new address is 600 W. 24 St.

7. Don't touch that broken glass!

8. We stopped at an L.C. Carran gas station.

9. How many Coke bottles are you returning?

10. Good grief! My kite got stuck on that tree again!

B. Follow the directions for Exercise A.

1. Terrific! We got the last four tickets!

2. How much does that album cost?

3. W.E.B. DuBois, Ph.D., was a writer and a professor of sociology.

4. Jump out of the way of that car!

5. Mail the letter to Miss Deborah K. Sobol.

6. Did Vanessa try out for the team last night?

7. The poet Hilda Doolittle signed her poems H.D.

8. Oh, no! You didn't forget the picnic lunch, did you?

Part 2

Objective

To use the comma correctly

Presenting the Lesson

1. Read pages 366 and 367. Stress that a series consists of three or more words.

2. It is suggested that Exercise A on pages 367 and 368 be done orally. Assign and discuss Exercise B.

3. Read and discuss pages 368 and 369.

Part 2 The Comma

Commas in Sentences

Commas tell the reader to pause. The pause keeps the reader from running together words that should be kept apart. Commas are a great help in reading.

When you write a series of words, use commas to separate them.

Two words are not a series. There are always three or more words in a series.

The children entered dogs, cats, and hamsters in the show.

In a series, commas are placed *after* each word except the last.

You can see how important it is to separate the parts of a series by looking at these sentences.

Bob stuffed himself with cheese, pizza, ice cream, sandwiches, chocolate, milk, and peanuts.

Bob stuffed himself with cheese pizza, ice-cream sandwiches, chocolate milk, and peanuts.

Note that both sentences contain the same words, in the same order. It is the punctuation that differs. Both sentences might be right. It depends upon what Bob ate. The writer has to use commas correctly to tell the reader what Bob ate.

Place a comma after *yes, no,* or *well* when these words start a sentence.

Yes, I'm going. Well, I'll see you there.

When you use *and, but,* or *or* to combine two sentences, put a comma before these words.

We ran fast. We nearly missed the bus.

We ran fast, but we nearly missed the bus.

Exercises Using Commas Correctly

A. Copy these sentences. Place commas where they are needed.

1. Yes, we went to the zoo last summer.
2. You can take a bus to the zoo, but we drove out.
3. We took our lunches, and we spent the whole day.
4. We saw a hippopotamus, a gorilla, and an anteater.
5. No, you can't feed the elephants.

4. Assign and discuss Exercises A and B on pages 369 and 370.

5. Read pages 370 and 371. Carefully discuss each use of the comma. Make sure that the students understand when the comma should be placed within quotation marks, and when it comes before.

6. Assign Exercises A and B on pages 371 and 372. Ask students to exchange papers for proofreading. Correct errors. Please note that in the Teacher's Answer Key, there is not always adequate space to show the correct order of punctuation marks. If a comma or end mark should be placed after a word and before quotation marks, but there is no room for it, that comma or end mark has been placed *under* the word.

7. See Exercise B on pages 379 and 380 for additional practice.

Optional Practice

Have students place commas in these sentences as needed.

1. Yes I'd love to come to your birthday party.
2. The explosion occurred on Friday June 23 1969.
3. We moved from Grand Rapids Michigan to Cranford New Jersey.
4. He asked "Where's the nearest gas station?"
5. After you move the TV set the rocker there.

Extending the Lesson

Have students write letters to the editor of your local or school newspaper expressing opinions on a current issue. Remind them to pay particular attention to the use of end marks and commas.

6. Well, we liked the monkey house best.

7. There were monkeys of every size, color, and shape.

8. Two monkeys started a fight, and another watched.

9. We took pictures, had a boat ride, and saw a movie.

10. The movie was good, but it wasn't as much fun as the animals at the zoo.

B. Follow the directions for Exercise A.

1. No, it's not raining.

2. Karen aimed, fired, and just missed the bull's eye.

3. Motels are all right, but I like campgrounds better.

4. Dawn, Ramon, and Anna dug a harbor in the sand, and Doug and Nancy built a sandcastle.

5. Yes, your answer is right.

6. Denmark, Sweden, and Norway are called Scandinavian countries.

7. Will you drive us, or should we take the bus?

8. The spaghetti, tomato sauce, and spices are in that cupboard.

9. Well, what do you think?

10. Donald Duck's nephews are Huey, Dewey, and Louie.

Use commas to set off the name of a person spoken to. If the name comes at the beginning or end of the sentence, one comma is enough. If the name comes in the middle of the sentence, place one comma before the name and another comma after it.

Please answer the phone, Jim.

Ginny, may I use your pen?

I believe, Mark, that you are right.

Set off an appositive by commas. An **appositive** is a word or group of words that means the same as the noun just before it. The appositive gives more information about the noun.

The words in italics in the following sentences are appositives. Notice that they tell more about *Mr. Lopez* and *our neighbor*. Notice also that they are set off by commas.

Mr. Lopez, *the scoutmaster*, moved away.

Our neighbor, *Ms. Carl*, drives an ambulance.

Separate the parts of a date by commas. If the date appears in the middle of a sentence, place a comma after the last part.

On November 7, 1962, Eleanor Roosevelt died.

We'll expect you on Tuesday, April 4.

Note: Do not place a comma between the month and the number of the day: April 4.

Separate the name of a city from the name of a state or country by a comma. If the two names come in the middle of a sentence, place a comma after the second name, too.

My grandmother was born in Dublin, Ireland.

We left Concord, New Hampshire, at noon.

Exercises Using Commas Correctly

A. Copy these sentences. Place commas where they are needed.

1. Last summer we went to Phoenix, Arizona.
2. Friday, May 5, was our opening night.
3. We all met the new principal, Mrs. Gomez.
4. At Kitty Hawk, North Carolina, the Wright brothers successfully flew three gliders.
5. Dad, this is Al Cresco, a friend of mine.
6. It was hot in Corpus Christi, Texas.
7. Hold the line, Gerry, and I'll ask her.
8. On Saturday, January 25, the excavation was begun.

B. Follow the directions for Exercise A.

1. Rhonda, were you born in September, 1970?
2. Albany, New York, is on the Hudson.
3. No, Mrs. Lucas, I have never lived in Dayton, Ohio.
4. Mr. Gray, let's have the exhibit on Friday, February 19.
5. The candidate, Ms. Wingreen, made a speech.
6. On October 7, 1943, my father was born.
7. You know, Adele, I'll be away tomorrow.
8. In Duluth, Minnesota, there is a statue of Jay Cooke, the financier.

Commas with Quotations

Use a comma to set off the explanatory words of a direct quotation.

When you use a quotation you are giving the words of a speaker or writer. You are said to be *quoting* the words of the speaker or writer. If you give the *exact* words, you are giving a **direct quotation.** Usually you include explanatory words of your own, like *Mary Kay said, JoAnne answered,* or *Phil asked.*

> Courtney announced, "The movie will begin in ten minutes."

In the above sentence, the explanatory words come *before* the quotation. A comma is then placed after the last explanatory word.

Now look at this quotation:

> "I want to go home," moaned Lisa.

In the above sentence, the explanatory words come *after* the quotation. A comma is then placed inside the quotation marks after the last word of the quotation.

Sometimes the quotation is separated into two parts.

> "One of the people in this room," the detective said, "is the murderer."

The preceding sentence is an example of a **divided quotation.** It is called "divided" because it is made up of two parts that are separated by the explanatory words. A comma is used after the last word of the first part. Another comma is used after the last explanatory word.

The quotations you have just looked at are all direct quotations. A quotation can be either *direct* or *indirect*. In an **indirect quotation** you change the words of a speaker or writer to your own words. No commas are used.

Clark Kent said that he had to make a phone call.

Commas in Letter Parts

Use a comma after the greeting of a friendly letter and after the closing of any letter.

Dear Agnes,   Sincerely yours,

The Comma To Avoid Confusion

Some sentences can be very confusing if commas are not used in them. Here are two examples of such sentences:

Going up the elevator lost power.
In the grocery bags were in demand.

Now notice how much clearer a sentence is when a comma is used:

Going up, the elevator lost power.

In the grocery, bags were in demand.

Use a comma whenever the reader might otherwise be confused.

Exercises Using Commas Correctly

A. Copy these sentences. Add commas where they are needed.

1. Benjamin said, "I'd like to visit Boston some day."

2. "This cake is delicious," said my father.

3. When Sheila typed, the table shook.

4. "It seems to me," Carol said, "that this puzzle is missing some pieces."

5. In the story, books were forbidden.

6. After we ate, the neighbors came to visit.

7. "Who," the caterpillar asked Alice in Wonderland, "are you?"

8. According to the paper, cups of coffee will cost a dollar each.

9. In the garden, flowers were blooming from May through September.

10. "Come here, Midnight," Ned called.

B. Follow the directions for Exercise A.

1. While Vickie painted, Eric sanded the table.

2. "Tomorrow's weather," the forecaster said, "will be sunny and warm."

3. For dinner, Tony had macaroni, salad, and dessert. (three items)

4. Ms. Gajda announced, "The concert begins at seven o'clock."

5. "The radio is too loud," my mother complained.

6. When our team lost, the players felt depressed.

7. Coming down, the tree snapped telephone lines.

8. Yvette asked, "What's on TV tonight?"

9. After Mr. Knowles left, his puppy whined.

10. "Three weeks ago today," Meg said, "I got my new bike."

Part 3

Objective

To use the apostrophe to form possessives and contractions

Part 3 The Apostrophe

Use an apostrophe to show possession.

To form the possessive of a singular noun, add an apostrophe and *s* after the apostrophe.

dog + 's = dog's   lady + 's = lady's   James + 's = James's

To form the possessive of a plural noun that does not end in *s*, add an apostrophe and an *s* after the apostrophe.

gentlemen + 's = gentlemen's   geese + 's = geese's

To form the possessive of a plural noun that ends in *s*, add only an apostrophe.

dogs + ' = dogs'   ladies + ' = ladies'

Exercises Using Apostrophes in Possessives

A. Make these words show possession. Write the possessive form.

1. island's	4. babies'	7. goalies'	10. children's
2. mechanics'	5. Chris's	8. guides'	11. golfers'
3. chickadee's	6. announcer's	9. cow's	12. frogmen's

B. Make these words show possession. Write the possessive form.

1. hunters'	4. women's	7. painter's	10. cyclist's
2. Ms. Smith's	5. Louisa's	8. cats'	11. Dr. Bliss's
3. policemen's	6. poets'	9. horse's	12. partner's

Use an apostrophe in a contraction.

A **contraction** is a word made by combining two words and omitting one or more letters. The apostrophe shows where a letter or letters have been omitted.

can not = can't	we are = we're
will not = won't	does not = doesn't
you will = you'll	he had = he'd
must not = mustn't	she would = she'd
they are = they're	are not = aren't

Presenting the Lesson

1. Read and discuss pages 372 and 373. Review the use of possessive nouns on pages 119 to 121 if necessary.

2. Assign Exercises A and B on page 373. When discussing the answers, ask students to tell whether the original word was singular or plural.

3. Read and discuss the bottom section of page 373. It is suggested that the Exercise on page 374 be done as a class activity.

4. See Exercise C on page 380 for additional practice.

Optional Practice

1. Have the students tell whether each word below is singular or plural. Ask them to write the possessive form of each word.

warden   Jess   deer
France   mice   friends

2. Have the students write the correct contraction for each of these pairs of words.

he will   do not   you are
they would   he is

Part 4

Objective

To use the hyphen for word division and compound numbers

Presenting the Lesson

1. Read and discuss Part 4 on page 374. It may be helpful to note these guidelines, also:

If a word has a double consonant, you usually divide the word between the consonants.

Proper nouns should never be divided at the end of a line.

2. Assign and discuss Exercises A and B on pages 374 and 375.

3. See Exercise D on pages 380 to 381 for additional practice.

Optional Practice

Ask students to decide whether the following words are correctly divided. Have them rewrite those that are incorrectly divided. Students should use a dictionary to check their answers.

let-ter	wr-ite	syll-able
ofte-n	di-vide	

Exercise Using Apostrophes in Contractions

Write the contractions of these words.

1. I am (I'm)	5. has not (hasn't)	9. we will (we'll)
2. are not (aren't)	6. I will (I'll)	10. is not (isn't)
3. it is (it's)	7. she is (she's)	11. that is (that's)
4. will not (won't)	8. we would (we'd)	12. had not (hadn't)

Part 4 The Hyphen

In writing, you often run out of space at the end of a line and can fit in only part of a word.

Use a hyphen after the first part of a word at the end of a line.

The second part of the word is placed at the beginning of the next line, without punctuation.

> Before you choose a career, inves-
> tigate many fields.

Only words of two or more syllables can be divided at the end of a line. Never divide words of one syllable, such as *slight* or *bounce*. If you are in doubt about dividing a word, look it up in a dictionary.

A single letter must not be left at the end of a line. For example, this division would be wrong: *a- mong*. A single letter must not appear at the beginning of a line either. It would be wrong to divide *inventory* like this: *inventor- y*.

Use a hyphen in compound numbers from twenty-one through ninety-nine.

> seventy-six trombones   Twenty-third Psalm

Exercises Using Hyphens Correctly

A. Copy the following phrases. Decide whether you can divide the word in italics into two parts, each part having more than one letter.

If you can, divide the word as you would at the end of a line. Add the necessary hyphens.

Example: the thirty eight *cannons*
the thirty-eight can-
nons

1. forty five *minutes*
2. the fifty ninth *correction*
3. twenty second Amendment
4. thirty four *years*
5. eighty one *trailers*
6. seventy nine years *ago*
7. ninety three *skateboards*
8. twenty nine *cents*
9. my sixty fourth *experiment*
10. forty *clarinets*

B. Follow the directions for Exercise A.

1. the eighty fifth *problem*
2. the forty eighth *state*
3. the seventy first *variation*
4. twenty two *classrooms*
5. ninety seven *cups*
6. the fifty fourth *contestant*
7. my seventy nine *marbles*
8. the thirty sixth *card*
9. his ninety third *birthday*
10. the sixty ninth *story*

Part 5 Quotation Marks

Direct Quotations

When you write what someone has said or written, you are using a **quotation.** If you write the person's exact words, you write a **direct quotation.** If you do not write his exact words, you have an **indirect quotation.** Study these sentences.

Direct quotation: Steven said, "I will come."
Indirect quotation: Steven said that he would come.

The quotation marks in the sample direct quotation mark off Steven's exact words. They were "I will come."

Part 5

Objective

To use quotation marks correctly

Presenting the Lesson

1. Read and discuss each item concerning direct quotations on pages 375 and 376. Emphasize these points:

a. Only the words actually spoken should be enclosed in quotation marks; words identifying the speaker or describing the situation are not enclosed in quotation marks.

b. Indirect quotations are never punctuated with quotation marks.

Stress also the correct placement of commas and end marks.

2. If necessary, review the use of commas with quotations on pages 370 and 371.

3. Assign the Exercise on page 377. Allow students to make corrections during discussion. Please note that, as in Part 2 Exercises, there is not always adequate space in the Teacher's Answer Key to show the correct order of punctuation marks. If a comma or end mark should be placed after a word and before quotation marks, but there is no room for it, that comma or end mark has been placed *under* the word.

4. Read Divided Quotations on pages 377 and 378. Some students may have difficulty with this lesson, but they should be introduced to the process.

5. Assign Exercises A and B on page 378. Allow corrections during discussion of the answers.

6. See Exercise E on page 381 for additional practice.

Optional Practice

Allow students experiencing difficulties to work in pairs for the Exercises on page 378.

Put quotation marks before and after the words of a direct quotation.

Quotation marks [“ ”] consist of two pairs of small marks that resemble apostrophes. They tell a reader that the exact words of another speaker or writer are being given.

Quotation marks are *not* used with indirect quotations.

Separate the words of a direct quotation from the rest of the sentence with a comma or end mark, in addition to quotation marks.

Jane said, “The dog is hungry.”

“The dog is hungry,” Jane said.

Notice that, in the first sentence above, the comma comes *before* the quotation marks. But the second sentence starts with the quoted words, and the comma falls *inside* the quotation marks.

Now look at these sentences carefully:

Mom asked, “Are you hungry?”

Bill replied, “We're starving!”

“We're starving!” Bill replied.

You can see that in these sentences the question marks and exclamation points fall *inside* the quotation marks.

Place question marks and exclamation points inside quotation marks if they belong to the quotation itself.

Place question marks and exclamation points outside quotation marks if they do not belong to the quotation.

Did Dad say, “Come home at seven o'clock”?
I was shocked to hear her say, “I'll go”!

Remember to capitalize the first word of a direct quotation.

Exercise Punctuating Direct Quotations

Copy these sentences. Add all the necessary punctuation marks.

1. “Drop anchor,” bellowed the captain.
2. “Don't forget your key, Jeff,” said Nina.
3. The cashier asked, “Will there be anything else?”
4. “Call me when you finish,” said Ms. Walters.
5. Kevin replied, “I am finished now.”
6. His parents have already said that Pablo can't go.
7. “Do you really believe in ESP?” asked Tammy.
8. Did Lillian say, “I'll be at the pool soon?”
9. Ron asked, “Where are you going?”
10. “Two eggs, with bacon,” shouted the waitress.
11. “What was that noise?” asked my sister.
12. “Last call for dinner,” announced the Amtrak waiter.

Divided Quotations

Sometimes a quotation is divided. Explanatory words, like *she said* or *he asked*, occur in the middle of the quotation.

“My favorite movie,” Lewis said, “is the original *King Kong*.”

Divided quotations follow the capitalization and punctuation guidelines presented already. In addition, these rules apply:

1. Two sets of quotation marks are used.

2. The explanatory words are followed by a comma or a period. Use a comma if the second part of the quotation does not begin a new sentence. Use a period if the second part of the quotation is a new sentence.

“I believe,” said Mona, “that you are wrong.”

“I can't go,” Frank said. “My homework is not done.”

Extending the Lesson

Collect a class set of single-frame newspaper cartoons that have one character speaking, such as “Dennis the Menace,” “Marmaduke,” “Family Circus.” Distribute them to the students. Ask them to rewrite the line of dialogue, using the proper forms of punctuation as the line would appear in a composition. Appropriate explanatory words can be chosen to match the content of the cartoon.

3. The second part of the quotation begins with a capital if it is the start of a new sentence, as in the second example above. Otherwise, the second part begins with a small letter.

Exercises Punctuating Divided Quotations

A. Copy these sentences, using correct punctuation and capitals.

1. Are you ready said Bryan I'll time you.
2. The crawl kick isn't hard Judy assured us just keep your knees straight.
3. Take the game home Sally said generously you can keep it.
4. What would you do Mr. Rocher asked if the rope broke?
5. How much does this spray cost Bonita inquired is it guaranteed to repel mosquitoes?
6. Captain Mr. Spock reported the ship was seriously damaged during the attack.
7. Where did you go Julia asked I couldn't find you.
8. Look at my watch exclaimed Zane it doesn't even have water in it.
9. You can pat Prince said Linda he won't bite.
10. The other way Hector insisted is much shorter.

B. Follow the directions for Exercise A.

1. Be careful shouted John the canoe will hit bottom.
2. Ask Mrs. Mitchell suggested Maureen maybe we can broadcast the announcement.
3. No answered Seth my jacket is blue.
4. If you need more spigots said the farmer they're in this sap bucket.
5. Fortunately piped up Andrea I've got fifty cents.
6. Turn the box over my brother suggested maybe the price is on the back.
7. Saturday Dora said I'll come about 8:30.
8. I'm getting cold complained Robin let's go in.

Additional Exercises

Punctuation

A. Using End Marks Correctly (Use after page 365.)

Copy the following sentences. Supply the missing periods, question marks, and exclamation points.

1. The soccer game was still going on at 8:30 P.M.
2. Does George know what a hobbit is?
3. Miguel trained his dog to catch a Frisbee in its mouth.
4. Get help fast!
5. When is Tara coming?
6. Cheryl has an appointment with Dr. H. P. Lewis tomorrow.
7. Move to a seat with a better view.
8. Wow! I never saw such a huge cave before!
9. Elena entered her giant sunflower in a contest.
10. May I borrow your ruler?

B. Using Commas Correctly (Use after page 371.)

Copy these sentences. Place commas where they are needed.

1. A catamaran has two hulls, but it has only one sail.
2. Mayor Wilmont, a friend of Senator Stevens, rode with him in the parade.
3. Charles M. Schulz is famous for drawing Charlie Brown, Lucy, and Snoopy.
4. Florence, are you going to the movie with us?
5. "Satellites," Ms. Lee said, "are used for communications, weather reporting, and navigation."
6. Do you mean Paris, France, or Paris, Ontario, Canada?
7. Well, Tracy has enough money, and she wants to buy the hat.

Additional Exercises

Assign pages 379 to 381 for chapter review if they were not previously used with individual lessons.

8. On July 20, 1969, the United States landed two astronauts on the moon.

9. "You should take an umbrella," Ned reminded his mother.

10. When Gayle moved, the street became much quieter.

C. Using Apostrophes Correctly (Use after page 373.)

Rewrite the following sentences. In each sentence make a contraction of the words in italics. Change any underlined word to show possession.

Example: *Let us* go to Valerie house.

Let's go to Valerie's house.

1. *He will* mail Mother letter. He'll, Mother's
2. *They have* always bought cider here. They've
3. Bret dog *did not* wake up. Bret's, didn't
4. I *do not* know how to ice skate. don't
5. Eddie book *was not* overdue. Eddie's, wasn't
6. *She had* already left her grandmother house. she'd, grandmother's
7. You *should not* phone again tonight. shouldn't
8. Isabelle *will not* copy anyone work. won't, anyone's
9. *You are* ready early. You're
10. The smaller children *could not* see the acrobats stunts at all. couldn't, acrobats'

D. Using Hyphens Correctly (Use after page 374.)

Copy the following phrases. Decide whether you can divide the word in italics into two parts, each part having more than one letter. If you can, divide the word as you would at the end of a line. Add the necessary hyphens.

Example: fifty two *papers*
fifty-two pa-
pers

1. the thirty-first *section*
2. my eighty-fourth *mistake*
3. sixty-five *days*
4. their forty-six *members*
5. more than seventy-two *dollars*
6. over ninety *degrees*
7. the twenty-eighth *caller*
8. only sixty-three *cents*
9. the eighty-seven *students*
10. his fifty-ninth *order*

E. Punctuating Quotations Correctly (Use after page 378.)

Copy these sentences. Add all the punctuation marks and capital letters that are needed.

1. The pharmacist said, "I'll show you how to open this bottle."
2. "Good morning, Mr. Moser," Richard called.
3. Janice said quickly, "It must be Marny's parka."
4. "Which do you like?" asked Henry. "Is this photo better?"
5. "Paul, have you ever read about old castles?" asked Veronica.
6. "Well," muttered Kim, "who asked you?"
7. "I have some money, but I'm saving it," I told Alonzo.
8. "Beat the egg whites well," Julia said, "and then blend in the sugar."
9. Heather asked, "Where is my basketball, Terence?"
10. "Take all the pie you want," Conrad's mother urged.

Chapter 24

Spelling

You won't wake up one day and find that suddenly you are a good speller. However, you can learn to spell well. It takes practice. It also takes a knowledge of some spelling rules. If you are a poor speller, you don't have to remain one.

There are many ways to approach spelling problems. These ways will be explained in this chapter.

Good spelling skills are valuable. They are important for writing reports in school. They are needed for writing different kinds of letters. They are vital for filling out forms and applications. As you grow older and write more, they will become even more necessary. To show people that you are careful and informed, you will need to be able to spell correctly.

Chapter Objectives

1. To develop habits for good spelling

2. To understand and apply common spelling rules

3. To become familiar with the use and spelling of words often confused

Preparing the Students

Students who use a structured, sequential spelling program need not study this chapter in its entirety. The chapter does, however, offer good information for review or reference.

Suggest that students develop the habit of listing new words they learn while doing reading or writing assignments. Every student, even the best speller, has personal spelling demons that he or she needs to conquer.

Read aloud the chapter introduction on page 383. Stress the need for accurate spelling in all written work. Ask if any students have developed individual schemes or reminders for dealing with certain types of spelling problems.

Additional Resources

Diagnostic Test—page 434

Mastery Test—pages 483 and 484

Additional Mastery Test—In separate booklet, *Diagnostic and Mastery Tests, Gold Level,* pp. 59, 60.

Skills Practice Book—pp. 143–152

Duplicating Masters—pp. 143–152

Part 1

Objective

To develop habits for good spelling

Presenting the Lesson

1. Read Part 1 on pages 384 and 385. Discuss each item thoroughly.

2. Careful pronunciation is helpful to correct spelling. Some words in the English language, however, show no logical link between pronunciation and spelling. Discuss these language oddities.

to, get, her—together
off, ice—office
here—there
Kansas—Arkansas
fork—work

3. Encourage proofreading of all written work. Students sometimes have difficulty spotting their own errors, but they can do a good job of editing someone else's work. Try exchanges of rough drafts for your next written assignment.

4. At least one dictionary is now available to help students who voice the age-old complaint, "How can I look up how to spell a word when I don't know how to spell it in the first place?" *The Misspeller's Dictionary* (Quadrangle/The New York Times Book Co., 1974) contains phonetic spellings and common misspellings, alphabetized with the correct spellings next to them. If possible, have a copy of this type of reference book on hand for the class to examine.

Extending the Lesson

1. Use the following word challenges to point out the importance of careful letter arrangement in words. Ask students to try to define

Part 1 How To Become a Better Speller

1. Find out your own spelling enemies and attack them. Look over your past papers and make a list of the misspelled words. Study these words until you can spell them correctly.

2. When you speak, pronounce words carefully. Sometimes people misspell words because they say them wrong. Be sure that you are not blending syllables together. For example, you may write *probly* for *probably* if you are mispronouncing it.

3. Make a habit of looking at words carefully. Practice seeing every letter. Store the letters in your memory. Many people see a word again and again but don't really look at it. Then they make mistakes like writing *safty* for *safety* or *sayed* for *said*. When you see a new word or a tricky word, like *necessary*, look at all the letters. To help yourself remember the spelling, write the word several times. You may want to keep a list of the new words for later practice.

4. Find memory devices to help with problem spellings. Memory devices link words with their correct spellings. Below are some devices. They may give you ideas for other words.

sep**arate** (*arat*). Only *a rat* makes us sep**arate**.
princi**pal** (*pal*) The princi**pal** is my *pal*.
tr**age**dy (*age*) Every *age* has its tr**age**dy.
spons**or** (*or*) *Oh, are* you the spons**or**?
pursue (*pur*) **Pur**sue *Sue's purse* snatcher!
gui**dance** (*dance*) I *dance* with gui**dance.**
emba**rrass** (*rr, ss*) I turned **r**eally **r**ed and felt **s**o **s**illy.

5. Proofread what you write. To make sure that you have spelled all words correctly, reread your work. Examine it carefully, word for word. Don't let your eyes race over the page and miss misspellings.

6. Learn the few important spelling rules given in this chapter.

How To Master the Spelling of Particular Words

1. Look at a new or difficult word and say it to yourself. Pronounce it carefully. If it has two or more syllables, say it again, one syllable at a time. Look at each syllable as you say it.

2. Look at the letters and say each one. If the word has two or more syllables, pause between syllables as you say the letters.

3. Without looking at the word, write it.

4. Now look at your book or list and see if you have spelled the word correctly. If you have, write it once more. Compare it with the correct spelling again. For best results, repeat the process once more.

5. If you have misspelled the word, notice where the error was. Then repeat steps 3 and 4 until you have spelled the word correctly three times in a row.

Part 2 Rules for Spelling

The Final Silent *e*

When a suffix beginning with a vowel is added to a word ending with a silent *e*, the *e* is usually dropped.

make + ing = making	advise + or = advisor
confuse + ion = confusion	believe + able = believable
expense + ive = expensive	fame + ous = famous

When a suffix beginning with a consonant is added to a word ending with a silent *e*, the *e* is usually kept.

hate + ful = hateful	hope + less = hopeless
bore + dom = boredom	sure + ly = surely
safe + ty = safety	move + ment = movement

each group of words with two words that are identical except for two letters that are reversed within each word. See how many your class can figure out.

Example:
a shiny metal (silver)
a small weed splinter (sliver)

a. to desire (crave)
to slice (carve)

b. peaceful (calm)
a hard-shelled sea creature (clam)

c. growing things (farming)
putting something around a picture (framing)

d. person who writes his or her own name (signer)
person who makes music with his or her voice (singer)

e. to shape (form)
a common preposition (from)

2. Try another word challenge. The word that fits the first definition of each group of words below can be changed into the word that fits the second definition by adding only one letter. See how many the students can get right.

Example:
to participate (join)
place where two bones meet (joint)

a. a fiery planet (sun)
submerged (sunk)

b. a number (ten)
a canvas house (tent)

c. feminine pronoun (her)
a brave person (hero)

d. distant (far)
place to raise livestock (farm)

e. conflict (war)
part of a hospital (ward)

Part 2

Objective

To understand and apply common spelling rules

Presenting the Lesson

1. The rules of Part 2 should be introduced over several days (or weeks). Each of the five sections should be used as an independent lesson.

2. Read The Final Silent *e* on pages 385 and 386. Discuss the two rules and the word listed as exceptions. Be sure that students know the meaning of the words used as examples. Some students may need to review the definitions of *vowel* and *consonant.*

3. Assign and discuss the Exercise on page 386.

4. See Exercise A on page 394 for additional practice with suffixes and silent *e.*

5. Read and discuss Words Ending in *y* on page 386. Can students use the example words in sentences?

6. It is suggested that you use the Exercise on page 387 as an oral exercise.

7. See Exercise B on page 394 for additional practice with suffixes and final *y.*

8. Read and discuss the prefix and suffix lesson on page 387. Discuss the meanings of the example words.

9. Assign and discuss the Exercise on page 387 and 388.

10. See Exercise C on pages 394 and 395 for additional practice with prefixes and suffixes.

11. Read and discuss page 388. Can students think of additional examples for each part of the lesson?

12. Assign and discuss the Exercise on page 389.

13. See Exercise D on page 395 for additional practice with "seed" words and *ie/ei* words.

The following words are exceptions:

truly argument ninth wholly judgment

Exercise Suffixes and Silent e

Find the misspelled words. Spell them correctly.

1. Some famous people are lonly. famous, lonely
2. Why are we haveing this silly arguement? having, argument
3. I am hopeing that this game won't remain scoreless. hoping
4. A jack is usful for changeing tires. useful, changing
5. Ms. Moore's statment was truly moveing. statement, moving
6. Terence is blameing me for the damage to his bike. blaming
7. We ordered a flower arrangment of ninty roses. arrangement ninety
8. The blazeing fire severly damaged the house. blazing, severely
9. The performance of the dareing acrobats was surly exciteing. daring, surely, exciting
10. Good writeing skills are a desirable achievment. writing achievement

Words Ending in *y*

When a suffix is added to a word that ends with *y* following a consonant, the *y* is usually changed to *i*.

noisy + ly = noisily carry + age = carriage
happy + est = happiest fifty + eth = fiftieth
try + ed = tried heavy + ness = heaviness

Note this exception: When *-ing* is added, the *y* remains.

bury + ing = burying cry + ing = crying
deny + ing = denying apply + ing = applying

When a suffix is added to a word that ends with *y* following a vowel, the *y* usually is not changed.

joy + ful = joyful pay + ment = payment
stay + ing = staying annoy + ed = annoyed

Exercise Suffixes and the Final *y*

Add the suffixes as shown and write the new word.

1. employ + er (employer)	8. sixty + eth (sixtieth)	15. boy + ish (boyish)
2. enjoy + able (enjoyable)	9. say + ing (saying)	16. lovely + er (lovelier)
3. marry + age (marriage)	10. reply + es (replies)	17. ugly + est (ugliest)
4. play + ed (played)	11. hurry + ed (hurried)	18. relay + ed (relayed)
5. carry + ing (carrying)	12. holy + ness (holiness)	19. happy + ly (happily)
6. sneaky + est (sneakiest)	13. easy + ly (easily)	20. rely + able (reliable)
7. destroy + er (destroyer)	14. ready + ness (readiness)	

The Addition of Prefixes

When a prefix is added to a word, the spelling of the word stays the same.

un + named = unnamed	re + enter = reenter
dis + appear = disappear	un + known = unknown
in + formal = informal	il + legible = illegible
im + mature = immature	in + appropriate = inappropriate

The Suffixes *-ly* and *-ness*

When the suffix *-ly* is added to a word ending with *l*, both *l*'s are kept. When *-ness* is added to a word ending in *n*, both *n*'s are kept.

mean + ness = meanness	practical + ly = practically
open + ness = openness	careful + ly = carefully

Exercise Words with Prefixes and Suffixes

Find the misspelled words. Spell them correctly.

1. Luis was imobile in a plaster cast. immobile
2. Carolyn likes this meat for its leaness. leanness

14. Read and discuss page 389. It is suggested that the Exercise on page 389 be done orally. What errors do the students need to discuss?

15. See Exercise E on page 395 for additional practice on doubling the final consonant.

Optional Practice

1. Have students add the suffix to each of these words and spell the new word correctly.

1. shape ing	5. re appear
2. make er	6. peaceful ly
3. entire ly	7. copy ing
4. bury ed	8. tap ing

2. Students should fill in the blanks with *ei* or *ie:*

1. ch_____ f	5. pr_____ st
2. fr_____ ght	6. y _____ ld
3. n_____ ce	7. dec _____ t
4. _____ ght	

Extending the Lesson

Have students proofread the following paragraph for spelling errors. It contains ten in all. (The errors have been underlined for the convenience of the teacher.)

It is great to have hobbys. Some people enjoy fling model airplanes. Others recieve pleasure from hikeing in the feilds. My sister is a trainner of dogs, but I am happyest when diging in my garden. Whatever your hobby is, I hope you sucede in haveing lots of fun.

3. Sometimes reporters are missinformed. misinformed
4. Many students become awfuly unneasy at test time. awfully uneasy
5. Mistreating animals should be ilegal. illegal
6. People who write carefuly don't often mispell words. carefully misspell
7. The unevenness of Ken's handwriting makes it ilegible. illegible
8. Idealy, citizens should not dissobey the law. Ideally, disobey
9. My mother dissapproves of my stubborness. disapproves stubbornness
10. I realy distrust people who are iresponsible. really, irresponsible

Words with the "Seed" Sound

Only one English word ends in *sede: supersede.*
Three words end in *ceed: exceed, proceed, succeed.*
All other words ending in the sound of "seed" are spelled *cede:*

concede precede recede secede

Words with *ie* or *ei*

When the sound is long *e* (ē), the word is spelled *ie* except after *c*.

I Before *E*

belief	relieve	yield	fierce	achieve
niece	brief	field	chief	shield

Except After *C*

receive	ceiling	perceive	deceit
conceive	conceited	receipt	

These words are exceptions:

either	weird	species
neither	seize	leisure

Exercise "Seed" and *ie/ei* Words

Find the misspelled words. Spell them correctly.

1. Anna recieved an award for her painting. received
2. Did the trucker excede the speed limit? exceed
3. Alvarez preceeds Sanders in the batting order. precedes
4. The mayor conceeded that she had been wrong. conceded
5. We saw a breif film about making leisure time work. brief
6. The criminal yeilded after a feirce fight. yielded, fierce
7. The outfielder prosed to snatch the line drive. proceeded
8. Weird shadows danced on the cieling. ceiling
9. Many people succede because they beleive in themselves. succeed believe
10. The police cheif siezed the thief. chief, seized

Doubling the Final Consonant

Words of one syllable, ending with one consonant following one vowel, double the final consonant before adding *-ing, -ed,* or *-er.*

sit + ing = sitting	sad + er = sadder
hop + ed = hopped	stop + ing = stopping
shop + er = shopper	let + ing = letting

The final consonant is not doubled when it is preceded by *two* vowels.

meet + ing = meeting	loan + ed = loaned
break + ing = breaking	train + er = trainer

Exercise Doubling the Final Consonant

Add the suffixes as shown and write the new word.

1. leap + ed (leaped)	6. hem + ed (hemmed)	11. near + ing (nearing)
2. fat + er (fatter)	7. scream + ing (screaming)	12. trip + ed (tripped)
3. beat + ing (beating)	8. flap + ed (flapped)	13. swim + er (swimmer)
4. cool + er (cooler)	9. hot + er (hotter)	14. leap + ing (leaping)
5. chop + er (chopper)	10. hug + ing (hugging)	15. peek + ed (peeked)

Part 3

Objective

To become familiar with the use and spelling of words often confused

Presenting the Lesson

1. Read the opening paragraphs of Part 3 on page 390. Discuss the meaning of the word *homonym.* Encourage students to learn the spelling and pronunciation of *homonym,* as well as its meaning.
2. Read through the sets of homonyms and other words on pages 390 to 392. Take time to discuss the meaning and use of each word.
3. Have students write original sentences for the sets of homonyms. Discuss the sentences in class.
4. Assign and discuss Exercises A and B on page 393. Avoid confusion in checking by spelling each correct choice from the parentheses.

Optional Practice

Try this variation on the old-fashioned spelling bee. Divide the class into two teams. One team is asked to spell a word, with each team member in order supplying a single letter. If the team spells the word incorrectly, the other team gets a turn with the same word. The first team to spell it correctly gets a point. Playing the game this way encourages good concentration and listening skills, as well as spelling skill.

Part 3 Words Often Confused

Sometimes you make a mistake in spelling simply because of your own carelessness or forgetfulness. Other times, however, your problems are caused by the language itself. In English there are many words that are easily confused. These words sound the same, or nearly the same, but are spelled differently and have different meanings. Words of this type are called **homonyms.** Here are some examples of homonyms:

horse—hoarse pare—pear—pair tail—tale do—dew—due

When you have problems with homonyms, general spelling rules won't help you. The only solution is to memorize which spelling goes with which meaning.

Here is a list of homonyms and other words frequently used and frequently confused in writing. Study the sets of words, and try to connect each word with its correct meaning. Refer to the list if you have further difficulties with these words.

accept means to agree to something or to receive something willingly.

except means to keep out or leave out. As a preposition, *except* means "but" or "leaving out."

My brother will *accept* the job the grocer offered him.
Michelle likes every flavor of ice cream *except* pistachio.

capital means chief, important, or excellent. It also means the city or town that is the official seat of government of a state or nation.

capitol is the building where a state legislature meets.

the Capitol is the building in Washington, D.C. in which the United States Congress meets.

The *capital* of Illinois is the city of Springfield.
The *capitol* of Illinois is a stately building in Springfield.
The senators arrived at the *Capitol* in time to vote.

hear means to listen to.

here means in this place.

Every time I *hear* this song, I feel happy.
Reference books stay *here* in the library.

it's is the contraction for *it is* or *it has*.

its shows ownership or possession.

It's nearly midnight.
The boat lost *its* sail during the storm.

lead (lĕd) is a heavy, gray metal.

lead (lēd) means to go first, to guide.

led (lĕd) is the past tense of *lead* (lēd).

Water pipes are often made of *lead*.
These signs will *lead* us to the hiking trail.
Bloodhounds *led* the detectives to the scene of the crime.

loose means free or not tight.

lose means to mislay or suffer the loss of something.

A rider keeps the horse's reins *loose*.
If you *lose* your book, report the loss to the library as soon as possible.

peace is calm or stillness or the absence of disagreement.

piece means a portion or part.

A sunset over the ocean is my idea of *peace*.
Who can stop after one *piece* of pie?

principal means first or most important. It also refers to the head of a school.

principle is a rule, truth, or belief.

A *principal* export of Brazil is coffee.
Our school *principal* organized a safety council.
One *principle* of science is that all matter occupies space.

Extending the Lesson

The two blanks in each sentence can be filled with a pair of homonyms.

1. ________ time for the puppy to have ________ dinner.
2. They signed a ________ of paper promising ________ in the land.
3. Our school ________ taught a lesson about the ________ of gravity.
4. ________ is the place to ________ good music.
5. I don't care ________ the ________ is rainy or sunny.

Can students think up more sentences for pairs of homonyms?

quiet means free from noise or disturbance.
quite means truly or almost completely.

The only time our classroom is *quiet* is when it's empty.
The aquarium tank is *quite* full.

their means belonging to them.
there means at that place.
they're is the contraction for *they are*.

Our neighbors sold *their* house and moved to a farm.
Please take the squirt guns over *there*.
My sisters have never skied, but *they're* willing to try.

to means in the direction of.
too means also or very.
two is the whole number between one and three.

The surgeon rushed *to* the operating room.
The lights went off, and then the heat went off, *too*.
Only *two* of the four mountaineers reached the peak.

weather is the state of the atmosphere referring to wind, moisture, temperature, etc.
whether indicates a choice or alternative.

Australia has summer *weather* when the United States has winter.
Whether we drive or take the train, we will arrive in three hours.

who's is the contraction for *who is* or *who has*.
whose is the possessive form of *who*.

Who's been chosen to be a crossing guard?
Whose skateboard was left on the sidewalk?

you're is the contraction for *you are*.
your is the possessive form of *you*.

You're going to the costume party, aren't you?
Please bring *your* sheet music to choir practice.

Exercises Words Often Confused

A. Choose the right word from the words in parentheses.

1. Janie and Alethia built (their, there, they're) own treehouse.
2. The Indian (lead, led) his tribesmen to the hunting ground.
3. (Who's, Whose) bicycle has racing stripes?
4. If I (loose, lose) this dollar bill, I won't eat lunch.
5. A shark is vicious because of (its, it's) double row of teeth.
6. Did Dwayne (accept, except) the invitation to your party?
7. I study best in a well lit, (quiet, quite) room.
8. The (capital, capitol, Capitol) in Washington, D.C., is built on a hill.
9. Are you taller than (your, you're) sister?
10. We will play the game (weather, whether) it rains or not.

B. Choose the right word from the words in parentheses.

1. We had to hunt for the gerbil that got (loose, lose).
2. The (principal, principle) character in *A Christmas Carol* is Ebenezer Scrooge.
3. Jaguars seem fierce, but (their, there, they're) afraid of dogs.
4. A fire engine will (lead, led) the parade.
5. Although bats don't see at night, they (hear, here) where they are.
6. Does your brother know that (your, you're) planning a surprise party?
7. Ceramics is creative, and it's fun, (to, too, two).
8. Eric is the only batter (who's, whose) left-handed.
9. The city of Austin is the (capital, capitol, Capitol) of Texas.
10. Everyone (accept, except) Dawn went down the giant slide.

Additional Exercises

Use the exercises on pages 394 and 395 for review if they were not previously assigned.

Additional Exercises

Spelling

A. Suffixes and Silent *e* (Use after page 386.)

Find the misspelled words. Spell them correctly.

1. May I speak to you privatly? privately
2. Lyn's lovly new jacket is reverseible. lovely, reversible
3. Cal's hobbies are bakeing and raceing stock cars. baking, racing
4. The poor stray dog was namless and homeless. nameless
5. Donna said she was sincerly sorry for leaveing. sincerely, leaving
6. The summer night was strangly peacful. strangely, peaceful
7. Raoul's behavior was completly unexpected. completely
8. Our coach was giveing us guideance in shooting baskets. giving, guidance
9. My relateives held a birthday celebrateion for my cousin. relatives, celebration
10. After escapeing from their pen, the cattle came chargeing across the field. escaping, charging

B. Suffixes and the Final *y* (Use after page 386.)

Add the suffixes as shown and write the new word.

1. fly + er (flier)	6. speedy + est (speediest)	11. deny + al (denial)
2. stay + ing (staying)	7. try + ing (trying)	12. angry + ly (angrily)
3. funny + est (funniest)	8. gray + er (grayer)	13. city + es (cities)
4. early + er (earlier)	9. copy + ing (copying)	14. portray + ed (portrayed)
5. play + ful (playful)	10. silly + er (sillier)	15. ninety + eth (ninetieth)

C. Words with Prefixes and Suffixes (Use after page 387.)

Find the misspelled words. Spell them correctly.

1. A wolf is known for its meaness. meanness

2. I missunderstood the last question. misunderstood
3. The new rules are both unnfair and ilogical. unfair, illogical
4. My notebook is dissorderly and dissorganized. disorderly disorganized
5. Kyle's parents were actually shocked by the cleaness of his room. cleanness
6. Our teacher dissapproves of imature jokes and fights. disapproves immature
7. Finaly the stagecoach reached the openess of the plains. Finally openness
8. During the winter, bears are generaly innactive. generally inactive
9. The trainer cruely whipped his horses for missbehaving. cruelly misbehaving
10. People usualy see pictures in the iregular shapes of inkblots. usually irregular

D. "Seed" and *ie/ei* Words (Use after page 388.)

Find the misspelled words. Spell them correctly.

1. The tide receeds twice a day. recedes
2. The pass receiver streaked down the feild. field
3. Mr. Johnson gave his neice a wierd mask. niece, weird
4. The Southern states seceeded from the Union. seceded
5. Some people who achieve fame become concieted. conceited
6. Marla feircely defended her beleif in ghosts. fiercely, belief
7. The parade proceded to the pier at the edge of town. proceeded
8. The fire cheif succeded in controlling the blaze. chief, succeeded
9. A detective percieved footprints on the ceiling. perceived
10. An overture preceeds either an opera or a musical. precedes

E. Doubling the Final Consonant (Use after page 389.)

Add the suffixes as shown and write the new word.

1. tour + ed (toured)	6. keep + er (keeper)	11. stir + ed (stirred)
2. moan + ing (moaning)	7. slam + ing (slamming)	12. troop + er (trooper)
3. star + ing (starring)	8. grab + ed (grabbed)	13. flat + er (flatter)
4. sip + ed (sipped)	9. leak + ing (leaking)	14. big + er (bigger)
5. seat + ed (seated)	10. mad + er (madder)	15. clap + ed (clapped)

Index

Acknowledgments

William Collins + World Publishing Company: For entries appearing on pages 173, 174, 175, 176, and 178, from *Webster's New World Dictionary of the American Language*, Students Edition; copyright © 1976 by William Collins + World Publishing Company, Inc. E. P. Dutton: For a selection from *Rascal* by Sterling North; copyright © 1963 by Sterling North. Mary Nelle Kainer: For "The Game That Almost Was," which appeared in the January, 1978, issue of *Cricket;* copyright © 1977 by Mary Nelle Kainer. The New Yorker: For "Catalog" by Rosalie Moore; copyright © 1940, 1968, The New Yorker Magazine, Inc., reprinted by permission. Harper & Row, Publishers, Inc.: For "Spaghetti," from *Where the Sidewalk Ends* by Shel Silverstein; copyright © 1974 by Shel Silverstein.

Photographs

Cover: Les Line

James L. Ballard: 64, 284, 318, 346.

The following photographs courtesy of Magnum: Paul Fusco, ii, 28, 252; Dennis Stock, xii, 302; Arthur Tress, 12; Burk Uzzle, 82, 110, 222; Costa Manos, 94, 262; René Burri, 126; Charles Harbutt, 154, 168; Burt Glinn, 180, 312, 360; David Hurn, 196; Kryn Taconis, 236; Charles Gatewood, 334, 382.

Illustrations

Donald Leake, 2, 3, 4, 5, 7, 18, 20, 22, 50, 71, 72, 80, 87, 171, 182, 193, 203, 210, 212, 216, 221, 225, 232, 244, 264, 272, 320, 323, 324, 328, 329, 331, 339, 340; Mila Lazarevich, 6, 32, 39, 67, 68, 69, 76, 84, 97, 102, 104, 105, 107, 119, 128, 136, 157, 201, 240, 269, 286, 330, 332, 335, 342, 343; Len Ebert, 116, 204; Hilary Hayton, 139, 147, 159, 228, 238, 239, 246, 259; Michael Deas, 200. Ken Izzi, mechanical artwork; Jeanne Seabright, handwritten letters.

Copy Masters

Practice Pages on Usage of Irregular Verbs

The next seventeen pages are an extension of Chapter 19, **Using Irregular Verbs,** and are recommended for use after class discussion of that chapter. The pages have been designed for the teacher's convenience in reproducing them. The publisher grants permission to the classroom teacher to reproduce any of the practice pages as needed.

A brief pretest on the usage of irregular verbs is provided on page 406. It is recommended that the teacher use the results of this pretest to group students and assign practice pages as needed. Not more than three pages should be assigned at one session.

NAME

Practice Pages on Irregular Verbs

Regular verbs have the same form for the past and past participle. Using helping verbs with the past participle is no problem.

But irregular verbs very often have different forms for the past and past participle. Since we may use helping verbs only with the past participle, we must know which form is the past participle.

The exercise below will help you find which irregular verbs give you problems. Following this exercise, there is a page of exercises for each verb tested. When you know which verbs give you difficulty, you can then turn to the exercise pages on those verbs.

Exercises Using Irregular Verbs

Underline the correct word from the two in the parentheses.

1. The game should have (began, begun) at two o'clock.
2. I have (chose, chosen) a topic for my report.
3. Last month, sixty visitors (came, come) to the school.
4. The doctors (did, done) all they could.
5. The goldfish has (ate, eaten) all the food in his bowl.
6. The TV dinner is (froze, frozen) and has to be heated.
7. All this loud music has (gave, given) me a headache.
8. My mother has (went, gone) to the store.
9. Have you (grew, grown) tomatoes at home?
10. I (knew, known) the answers to all the test questions.
11. At camp, we have (rode, ridden) horses many times.
12. By the time the rain started, the children had (ran, run) home.
13. Has everyone (saw, seen) the illustration in the book?
14. Somebody has (took, taken) my lunch.
15. Charlotte has (threw, thrown) a two-hit game!
16. Morgan has already (wrote, written) to his pen-pal three times.

1. begun
2. chosen
3. came
4. did
5. eaten
6. frozen
7. given
8. gone
9. grown
10. knew
11. ridden
12. run
13. seen
14. taken
15. thrown
16. written

NAME ____

Hear It Right   Say It Right

Begin
Began
Begun

Began and *begun* are used correctly in the following sentences. Notice that *began* is used alone, without a helping verb. *Begun* is used with a helping verb. Say each sentence to yourself.

1. The show *began* a little late.
2. The milk *has begun* to sour.
3. I just *began* my report today.
4. I should *have begun* it a month ago.
5. The recital *began* at exactly eight-thirty.
6. Our class *has begun* to study Africa.
7. We *began* reading about it yesterday.
8. Fractions *have* just *begun* to make sense to me.

> Use *began* by itself, without a helping verb.
> Use *begun* with the helping verbs *is, are, was, were, has, have,* and *had.*

Write It Right

Underline the correct verb in the parentheses. Then say the sentence to yourself, using the correct verb.

1. began
2. begun
3. began
4. began
5. begun
6. began
7. begun
8. began
9. begun
10. begun

1. The ballgame (began, begun) in spite of the rain.
2. I haven't (began, begun) my homework yet.
3. Spring vacation (began, begun) last week.
4. I never heard of a rock concert that (began, begun) on time.
5. Construction on the building was (began, begun) in May.
6. Mother (began, begun) making this quilt two years ago.
7. Our TV has (began, begun) to give us trouble.
8. A month ago, Sue (began, begun) taking guitar lessons.
9. Lately she has (began, begun) entertaining at parties.
10. Hadn't you (began, begun) to study Spanish last term?

NAME ______________________________

Hear It Right   Say It Right

Choose
Chose
Chosen

Chose and *chosen* are used correctly in the sentences below. Notice that *chose* is used alone, without a helping verb. *Chosen* is used with a helping verb. Say each sentence to yourself.

1. Have you *chosen* a book to read?
2. I *chose* this one about King Arthur.
3. Our class *has chosen* new officers.
4. We *chose* Tina again this year.
5. *Was* the All-Star team *chosen* today?
6. Paul's uncle *chose* to be a geologist.
7. He *has chosen* to live in Alaska.
8. We *were chosen* to decorate the gym for the party.

> Use *chose* alone, without a helping verb.
> Use *chosen* with the helping verbs *is, are, was, were, has, have, had.*

Write It Right

Underline the correct verb in the parentheses. Then say the sentence to yourself, using the correct verb.

1. Lucinda was (chose, chosen) to star in the play.
2. Don't you like the sweater I (chose, chosen)?
3. Frank has (chose, chosen) a good topic for his report.
4. Stand up if you have already been (chose, chosen).
5. Has a city been (chose, chosen) for the next Olympics?
6. Sarah (chose, chosen) two angelfish for her aquarium.
7. Leonard (chose, chosen) fruit instead of cake for desert.
8. Seven students were (chose, chosen) to represent our school.
9. Wanda was (chose, chosen) again, too.
10. Haven't you (chose, chosen) a record yet?

1. chosen
2. chose
3. chosen
4. chosen
5. chosen
6. chose
7. chose
8. chosen
9. chosen
10. chosen

NAME ____________________

Hear It Right   Say It Right

Came and *come* are used correctly in the sentences below. Notice that *came* is used by itself, without a helping verb. *Come* is used with a helping verb. Say each sentence to yourself.

Come

Came

Come

1. *Haven*'t the Lombardis *come* home from their trip?
2. Yes, they *came* home last night.
3. The traffic *had come* to a standstill.
4. Why *have* so many people *come* to the park?
5. They *came* to see the fireworks.
6. *Has* the mail *come* yet?
7. It *came* this morning.
8. We *had come* to the end of the road.

> Use *came* alone, with a helping verb.
> Use *come* with the helping verbs *has, have,* and *had.*

Write It Right

Underline the correct verb in the parentheses. Then say the sentence to yourself, using the correct verb.

1. You should have (came, come) to the basketball game.
2. The President had (came, come) to give a speech.
3. Who (came, come) to the door?
4. A messenger had (came, come) with a note.
5. John (came, come) to school late again.
6. Lisa has (came, come) to visit you.
7. The presents (came, come) yesterday afternoon.
8. Have you (came, come) from Denver?
9. Philip (came, come) early to help with the refreshments.
10. Has Jeannette (came, come) in on that plane?

Answers: 1. come 2. come 3. came 4. come 5. came 6. come 7. came 8. come 9. came 10. come

Building English Skills, Gold Level, Teacher's Edition.

409

NAME ____

Hear It Right   Say It Right

Do
Did
Done

Did and *done* are used correctly in the following sentences. Notice that *did* is used by itself, without a helping verb. *Done* is used with a helping verb. Say each sentence to yourself.

1. Jeff *did* the wrong math problems.
2. What *have* you *done* with my gym shoes?
3. Tell me what you *did* on your vacation.
4. Sally *has done* two extra credit projects.
5. What *was done* about the broken window?
6. Wendy *did* more than her share.
7. Robert *did* everything he could to help, too.
8. Didn't you think they *had done* an excellent job?

> Use *did* alone, without a helping verb.
> Use *done* with the helping verbs *is, are, was, were, has, have,* and *had.*

Write It Right

Underline the correct verb in the parentheses. Then say the sentence to yourself, using the correct verb.

1. Who (did, done) the dishes last night?
2. Peggy certainly (did, done) a good job on the mural.
3. Haven't you (did, done) your homework?
4. Nothing had been (did, done) about the gutted building.
5. Who (did, done) that drawing of Rod Carew?
6. Midge has never (did, done) needlepoint.
7. Our dog (did, done) every trick we taught him.
8. Has Roberto (did, done) all of the questions?
9. I could have (did, done) another lap across the pool.
10. What was (did, done) with the extra cookies?

1. did
2. did
3. done
4. done
5. did
6. done
7. did
8. done
9. done
10. done

NAME

Hear It Right Say It Right

Eat

Ate

Eaten

Ate and *eaten* are used correctly in the sentences below. Notice that *ate* is used alone, without a helping verb. *Eaten* is used with a helping verb. Say each sentence to yourself.

1. I *ate* too much cake at the party.
2. I wish I *had eaten* less.
3. *Were* all of the cupcakes *eaten*, too?
4. One *was eaten* by a dog.
5. Those peaches will spoil if they *are*n't *eaten*.
6. We *ate* earlier than usual tonight.
7. *Have*n't you *eaten* your broccoli yet?
8. Nicole *has* never *eaten* Mexican food before.

> Use *ate* alone, without a helping verb.
> Use *eaten* with the helping verbs *is, are, was, were, has, have,* and *had.*

Write It Right

Underline the correct verb in the parentheses. Then say the sentence to yourself, using the correct verb.

1. Who (ate, eaten) the watermelon?
2. Keith has (ate, eaten) most of it.
3. Snails are (ate, eaten) in France.
4. Was the knight (ate, eaten) by the dragon?
5. No, the dragon (ate, eaten) only his armor.
6. The gerbils have (ate, eaten) all of their food.
7. Rosa (ate, eaten) lunch with us today.
8. Never go swimming right after you have (ate, eaten).
9. How many of the doughnuts were (ate, eaten)?
10. My baby brother has (ate, eaten) my homework!

Answers:
1. ate
2. eaten
3. eaten
4. eaten
5. ate
6. eaten
7. ate
8. eaten
9. eaten
10. eaten

411

NAME

Hear It Right   Say It Right

Freeze
Froze
Frozen

Froze and *frozen* are used correctly in the sentences below. Notice that *froze* is used by itself, without a helping verb. *Frozen* is used with a helping verb. Say each sentence to yourself.

1. Let's skate when the pond *is frozen.*
2. Kate says it *froze* last night.
3. Many foods *are frozen* to preserve them.
4. The rabbit *froze* when it saw me.
5. My fingers *were* nearly *frozen* from the cold.
6. The soda pop *had frozen* and burst the bottle.
7. Mom *froze* the fish we caught to keep it fresh.
8. *Haven't* you ever *frozen* a snowball?

> Use *froze* by itself, without a helping verb.
> Use *frozen* with the helping verbs *is, are, was, were, has, have,* and *had.*

Write It Right

Underline the correct verb in the parentheses. Then say the sentence to yourself, using the correct verb.

1. Our car radiator (froze, frozen) last night. 1. froze
2. We walked in the cold until our toes nearly (froze, frozen). 2. froze
3. Berries are often (froze, frozen) as soon as they are picked. 3. frozen
4. The stalking lioness (froze, frozen) in the brush. 4. froze
5. After the streets had (froze, frozen), traffic moved cautiously. 5. frozen
6. See if the popsicles have (froze, frozen). 6. frozen
7. The puddles on the walk were (froze, frozen) by morning. 7. frozen
8. You shouldn't have (froze, frozen) the pie. 8. frozen
9. In the experiment, the mercury thermometer (froze, frozen). 9. froze
10. Our homemade ice cream never (froze, frozen). 10. froze

412

NAME

Hear It Right Say It Right

Give
Gave
Given

Gave and *given* are used correctly in the following sentences. Notice that *gave* is used alone, without a helping verb. *Given* is used with a helping verb. Say each sentence to yourself.

1. The doctor *gave* me a booster shot.
2. *Have* you ever *given* a dog a bath?
3. Judy *has*n't *given* her speech.
4. Raymond *gave* me a puzzle for my birthday.
5. I *have given* Mary all of her assignments.
6. Who *gave* you the chewing gum?
7. The princess *was given* a golden pear.
8. My older sister *had given* me a ride on her motorcycle.

> Use *gave* by itself, without a helping verb.
> Use *given* with the helping verbs *is, are, was, were, has, have,* and *had.*

Write It Right

Underline the correct verb in the parentheses. Then say the sentence to yourself, using the correct verb.

1. I wish I knew who had (gave, given) me the mumps.
2. The Drama Club (gave, given) the play last night.
3. All the actors have (gave, given) excellent performances.
4. Hasn't Michael (gave, given) your pen back?
5. Uncle Dave (gave, given) me two passes to the Dodgers' game.
6. This award is (gave, given) to the best students.
7. I still haven't (gave, given) my science project any thought.
8. I (gave, given) my sister the keys.
9. Mr. Fabri has (gave, given) us our band uniforms.
10. The President (gave, given) another press conference.

1. given
2. gave
3. given
4. given
5. gave
6. given
7. given
8. gave
9. given
10. gave

NAME ______

Hear It Right   Say It Right

Go
Went
Gone

Went and *gone* are used correctly in the following sentences. Notice that *went* is used alone, without a helping verb. *Gone* is used with a helping verb. Say each sentence to yourself.

1. *Have* you ever *gone* trout fishing?
2. I *went* once with my dad.
3. An hour *had gone* by.
4. My grades *went* from bad to worse.
5. The cheesecake *was gone* in no time.
6. *Has* Roxanna *gone* camping?
7. She *went* with her family this morning.
8. We should *have gone* to the water show.

> Use *went* alone, without a helping verb.
> Use *gone* with the helping verbs *is, are, was, were, has, have,* and *had.*

Write It Right

Underline the correct verb in the parentheses. Then say the sentence to yourself, using the correct verb.

1. Both of my parents (went, gone) to college. 1. went
2. Do you know anyone who has (went, gone) to England? 2. gone
3. Allen (went, gone) last summer. 3. went
4. When we looked, the candlesticks were (went, gone). 4. gone
5. After everyone had (went, gone), Victor did the dishes. 5. gone
6. When have you (went, gone) to a professional hockey game? 6. gone
7. Karen (went, gone) through her pockets for her bus fare. 7. went
8. Have you (went, gone) jogging lately? 8. gone
9. I (went, gone) just this morning. 9. went
10. We watched TV after my little sister had (went, gone) to bed. 10. gone

414

NAME

Hear It Right Say It Right

Grow
Grew
Grown

Grew and *grown* are used correctly in the following sentences. Notice that *grew* is used by itself, without a helping verb. *Grown* is used with a helping verb. Say each sentence to yourself.

1. Uncle Henry *has grown* a mustache.
2. We *grew* many of our own vegetables.
3. Where *are* pineapples *grown?*
4. The crowd *grew* quiet.
5. This lizard *has grown* a new tail.
6. Ellen *has grown* prettier in the last year.
7. My sweet-potato plant never *grew.*
8. I *had grown* two inches over the summer.

> Use *grew* alone, without a helping verb.
> Use *grown* with the helping verbs *is, are, was, were, has, have,* and *had.*

Write It Right

Underline the correct verb in the parentheses. Then say the sentence to yourself, using the correct verb.

1. The sky suddenly (grew, grown) dark.
2. What crops are (grew, grown) in California?
3. Indians were the first people who (grew, grown) corn.
4. The ficus plant has (grew, grown) taller.
5. The young child (grew, grown) restless.
6. Have you ever (grew, grown) a Japanese bonsai tree?
7. Marcia has (grew, grown) too big for that jacket.
8. The horses (grew, grown) impatient and pawed the ground.
9. Look how the tomatoes have (grew, grown).
10. Has your butterfly collection (grew, grown) much this year?

1. grew
2. grown
3. grew
4. grown
5. grew
6. grown
7. grown
8. grew
9. grown
10. grown

415

NAME

Hear It Right   Say It Right

Know

Knew

Known

Knew and *known* are used correctly in the following sentences. Notice that *knew* is used by itself, without a helping verb. *Known* is used with a helping verb. Say each sentence to yourself.

1. I *knew* Marguerite would recognize me.
2. We *had known* each other from Girl Scouts.
3. Gerard never *knew* her.
4. Wisconsin *is known* for its dairy products.
5. Who *knew* about the test?
6. I wish I *had known* it would be on multiplication.
7. How could Thelma *have known* about the surprise party?
8. None of us *knew* the story.

> Use *knew* alone, without a helping verb.
> Use *known* with the helping verbs *is, are, was, were, has, have,* and *had.*

Write It Right

Underline the correct verb in the parentheses. Then say the sentence to yourself, using the correct verb.

1. Ships have been (knew, known) to disappear suddenly.
2. We hadn't (knew, known) that we would end up in Montreal.
3. We felt lucky that we (knew, known) some French.
4. Mr. McNab asked if I (knew, known) the capital of Austria.
5. The number zero was (knew, known) to the ancient Maya.
6. Have you (knew, known) Sam for a long time?
7. I've (knew, known) him since third grade.
8. Teri already (knew, known) about the picnic.
9. Ms. Thomas never (knew, known) I came in late.
10. I (knew, known) my spelling words by heart.

1. known
2. known
3. knew
4. knew
5. known
6. known
7. known
8. knew
9. knew
10. knew

NAME

Hear It Right Say It Right

Rode and *ridden* are used correctly in the sentences below. Notice that *rode* is used by itself, without a helping verb. *Ridden* is used with a helping verb. Say each sentence to yourself.

Ride
Rode
Ridden

1. *Have* you ever *ridden* in a helicopter?
2. Dolores *rode* in one last summer.
3. Vince *had* never *ridden* on a roller coaster.
4. Where *are* llamas *ridden?*
5. We *rode* in the Jacksons' new camper.
6. Melanie *has ridden* on a elephant.
7. Peter could *have ridden* my bike.
8. A teenage jockey *rode* the winning horse.

Use *rode* alone, without a helping verb.
Use *ridden* with the helping verbs *is, are, was, were, has, have, had.*

Write It Right

Underline the correct verb in the parentheses. Then say the sentence to yourself, using the correct verb.

1. Which horse has never been (rode, ridden)?
2. We never (rode, ridden) so slowly before.
3. Sedan chairs were (rode, ridden) long ago.
4. Have you ever (rode, ridden) in an antique car?
5. Bonnie has (rode, ridden) the roller coaster nine times.
6. The team (rode, ridden) to the game in two separate vans.
7. Where are street cars still (rode, ridden)?
8. Tanya (rode, ridden) in the boat while Scott water-skied.
9. A bobsled is (rode, ridden) on an ice track.
10. Who (rode, ridden) to school on the bus today?

1. ridden
2. rode
3. ridden
4. ridden
5. ridden
6. rode
7. ridden
8. rode
9. ridden
10. rode

NAME

Hear It Right   Say It Right

Run
Ran
Run

Ran and *run* are used correctly in the sentences below. Notice that *ran* is used alone, without a helping verb. *Run* is used with a helping verb. Say each sentence to yourself.

1. Jane's dog *ran* after my cat.
2. Which way *have* the boys *run?*
3. We *ran* all the way home.
4. The Kentucky Derby *is* always *run* in May.
5. *Has* Sandy ever *run* a movie projector?
6. She *ran* it the last time we saw a movie in class.
7. The grandfather clock *had* finally *run* down.
8. The trains *ran* on time.

> Use *ran* alone, without a helping verb.
> Use *run* with the helping verbs *is, are, was, were, has, have,* and *had.*

Write It Right

Underline the correct verb in the parentheses. Then say the sentence to yourself, using the correct verb.

1. The batteries in your calculator may have (ran, run) down. 1. run
2. Frank Shorter has (ran, run) in the Boston Marathon. 2. run
3. He also (ran, run) marathons in two Olympics. 3. ran
4. Our bus had (ran, run) out of gas. 4. run
5. Have you ever (ran, run) that fast before? 5. run
6. My digital watch has always (ran, run) well. 6. run
7. I (ran, run) two miles before school this morning. 7. ran
8. Who (ran, run) against Lyndon Johnson in 1964? 8. ran
9. The Indianapolis 500 wasn't (ran, run) because of rain. 9. run
10. Raise your hand if you haven't (ran, run) the fifty-yard dash. 10. run

418

NAME

Hear It Right   Say It Right

Saw and *seen* are used correctly in the following sentences. Notice that *saw* is used alone, without a helping verb. *Seen* is used with a helping verb. Say each sentence to yourself.

See
Saw
Seen

1. *Has* Mrs. Levy's class *seen* *Where the Lilies Bloom?*
2. We *saw* a great dolphin show at Marineland.
3. A tall, bearded man *was seen* leaving the bank.
4. No one ever *saw* him again.
5. *Have* you ever *seen* a triple play?
6. No, but I once *saw* a grand slam homerun.
7. Mona *saw* *Star Wars* twice.
8. Giant Pandas *are* seldom *seen* outside of China.

> Use *saw* alone, without a helping verb.
> Use *seen* with the helping verbs *is, are, was, were, has, have,* and *had.*

Write It Right

Underline the correct verb in the parentheses. Then say the sentence to yourself, using the correct verb.

1. Terence (saw, seen) *Fantasia* last night.
2. He could have (saw, seen) it with us tonight.
3. Our class (saw, seen) the Jacques Cousteau special on whales.
4. I haven't (saw, seen) Maria all day.
5. Some sports broadcasts are not (saw, seen) locally.
6. You look as if you had (saw, seen) a ghost.
7. Has anybody (saw, seen) my sweatshirt?
8. We (saw, seen) a movie on Ferdinand and Isabella of Spain.
9. Betty (saw, seen) an accident on her way downtown.
10. Have you ever (saw, seen) a bear on this ranch?

1. saw
2. seen
3. saw
4. seen
5. seen
6. seen
7. seen
8. saw
9. saw
10. seen

NAME

Hear It Right   Say It Right

Take
Took
Taken

Took and *taken* are used correctly in the following sentences. Notice that *took* is used by itself, without a helping verb. *Taken* is used with a helping verb. Say each sentence to yourself.

1. What *took* you so long?
2. You must *have taken* a wrong turn at the stoplight.
3. My brother *has taken* my bike to Hill Park.
4. He *took* it early this morning.
5. The second graders *were taken* to the circus.
6. *Have* you ever *taken* a ferryboat ride?
7. We *took* one when we went to New York.
8. Who *took* my pencil?

> Use *took* alone, without a helping verb.
> Use *taken* with the helping verbs *is, are, was, were, has, have,* and *had.*

Write It Right

Underline the correct verb in the parentheses. Then say the sentence to yourself, using the correct verb.

1. Ted's family (took, taken) a plane to San Diego.
2. Have you (took, taken) your medicine?
3. Who (took, taken) the Ping-Pong paddles?
4. It has (took, taken) Brad an hour to get ready for school.
5. Latonya (took, taken) the science test this morning.
6. I had already (took, taken) my test.
7. It (took, taken) us two hours to get through the traffic.
8. Why have you (took, taken) my math book?
9. We should have (took, taken) the shortcut home.
10. Julie was (took, taken) to the nurse's office.

1. took
2. taken
3. took
4. taken
5. took
6. taken
7. took
8. taken
9. taken
10. taken

1. threw
2. thrown
3. threw
4. thrown
5. thrown
6. threw
7. threw
8. thrown
9. thrown
10. threw

NAME ___

Hear It Right Say It Right

Throw
Threw
Thrown

Threw and *thrown* are used correctly in the following sentences. Notice that *threw* is used alone, without a helping verb. *Thrown* is used with a helping verb. Say each sentence to yourself.

1. The rookie pitcher *threw* his first shutout.
2. *Have* you ever *thrown* a boomerang?
3. The cranky baby *threw* a tantrum.
4. Now here's a horse that *has* never *thrown* anyone.
5. The ball *was thrown* to the catcher.
6. Who *threw* that airplane?
7. Tommy *has thrown* the Frisbee on the roof.
8. Perhaps you *threw* your paper away.

> Use *threw* alone, without a helping verb.
> Use *thrown* with the helping verbs *is, are, was, were, has, have,* and *had.*

Write It Right

Underline the correct verb in the parentheses. Then say the sentence to yourself, using the correct verb.

1. The quarterback (threw, thrown) a pass to his receiver.
2. The first pass he had (threw, thrown) had been intercepted.
3. Who (threw, thrown) that gum wrapper on the floor?
4. Mom asked Bob if he had (threw, thrown) away the garbage.
5. The fighting players were (threw, thrown) out of the game.
6. Tommy (threw, thrown) a snowball at me.
7. The relief pitcher (threw, thrown) a few warm-up pitches.
8. Why have you (threw, thrown) away my button collection?
9. Pecos Bill was never (threw, thrown) by a horse.
10. All the graduates (threw, thrown) their hats into the air.

NAME ______________________________

Hear It Right   Say It Right

Write
Wrote
Written

Wrote and *written* are used correctly in the sentences below. Notice that *wrote* is used alone, without a helping verb. *Written* is used with a helping verb. Say each sentence to yourself.

1. Kevin *wrote* Mother another letter.
2. He *has written* to her every week.
3. Who *wrote Treasure Island?*
4. It *was written* by Robert Louis Stevenson.
5. Louise *wrote* a very funny story.
6. Raoul *had written* the letter in both Spanish and English.
7. Carol King *has written* many popular songs.
8. Ms. Novak *wrote* our assignments on the chalkboard.

> Use *wrote* by itself, without a helping verb.
> Use *written* with the helping verbs *is, are, was, were, has, have,* and *had.*

Write It Right

Underline the correct verb in the parentheses. Then say the sentence to yourself, using the correct verb.

1. Have you (wrote, written) your report yet?
2. I (wrote, written) half of it.
3. Had Mark Twain (wrote, written) *Tom Sawyer* by 1880?
4. Stacy has (wrote, written) a letter to the newspaper.
5. Lennon and McCartney (wrote, written) many Beatles songs.
6. The suspect (wrote, written) a full confession.
7. Was *Mary Poppins* (wrote, written) by P. L. or L. P. Travers?
8. It was P. L. Travers who (wrote, written) that novel.
9. Has anyone (wrote, written) to Darren?
10. Was the note (wrote, written) or typed?

1. written
2. wrote
3. written
4. written
5. wrote
6. wrote
7. written
8. wrote
9. written
10. written

Copy Masters

Diagnostic and Mastery Tests

The Diagnostic Tests. These tests should be given to students before their study of this text. The purpose of the tests is to diagnose which skills the students have mastered from their study of the preceding level of *Building English Skills*.

The tests diagnose the students' skills in the following areas: sentence structure and grammar, usage, capitalization, punctuation, and spelling.

For each test, the maximum score is 100 points.

The Mastery Tests. Each test may be given immediately after the students have studied the corresponding chapter in *Building English Skills, Gold Level*. The tests measure students' mastery of vocabulary, writing skills, grammar and usage, capitalization, punctuation, and spelling.

Alternatively, the tests may be given near the end of the year for the purpose of measuring achievement. No more than two tests should be administered at any given session.

For each test, the maximum score is 100 points.

Individual Student's Record

Name ______________________

May be duplicated for each student

Diagnostic Tests

			Score
1	Using Complete Sentences	p. 425	______
2	The Sentence and Its Parts	426	______
3	Using Nouns	427	______
4	Using Verbs	428	______
5	Using Pronouns	429	______
6	Using Adjectives	430	______
7	Using Adverbs	431	______
8	Capitalization	432	______
9	Punctuation	433	______
10	Spelling	434	______

Mastery Tests

Chapter 1	How Our Language Grows	pp. 435–436	______
Chapter 2	Developing a Vocabulary of Specific Words	437–438	______
Chapter 3	Learning About Sentences	439–442	______
Chapter 4	Writing Good Paragraphs	443–444	______
Chapter 5	Ways of Developing a Paragraph	445–446	______
Chapter 6	Different Kinds of Paragraphs	447–448	______
Chapter 7	Using Nouns	449–450	______
Chapter 8	Using Verbs	451–454	______
Chapter 9	Using Pronouns	455–456	______
Chapter 10	Using the Dictionary	457–458	______
Chapter 11	Using the Library	459–460	______
Chapter 12	Writing Compositions and Reports	461–462	______
Chapter 13	Different Kinds of Compositions	463–464	______
Chapter 14	Using Adjectives	465–466	______
Chapter 15	Using Adverbs	467–468	______
Chapter 16	Using Prepositions and Conjunctions	469–472	______
Chapter 17	Writing Letters	473–474	______
Chapter 18	Making Subjects and Verbs Agree	475–476	______
Chapter 19	Using Irregular Verbs	477–478	______
Chapter 22	Capitalization	479–480	______
Chapter 23	Punctuation	481–482	______
Chapter 24	Spelling	483–484	______

NAME ______________________ SCORE __________

Diagnostic Test 1

Using Complete Sentences

Part 1 Sentences and Fragments Write *sentence* in the space before each complete sentence. Write *fragment* before any group of words that is not a complete sentence. (6 points each)

Answer		
1. sentence	1. __________	Start now
2. fragment	2. __________	Bringing home a kitten
3. fragment	3. __________	The stapler on Mr. York's desk
4. sentence	4. __________	Canaries sing beautifully
5. fragment	5. __________	Nosey chipmunks and bold squirrels
6. fragment	6. __________	Harry Houdini, the famous magician
7. sentence	7. __________	Park the car in the lot
8. fragment	8. __________	That twelve-string guitar
9. sentence	9. __________	Crystal glasses break easily
10. fragment	10. __________	An advanced art class

Part 2 Kinds of Sentences In the first blank, place the end mark needed for each sentence. In the second blank, name the kind of sentence. Write **D** for declarative, **IMP** for imperative, **INT** for interrogative, or **E** for exclamatory. (4 points each blank)

Answer		
1. **! E**	1. ______ ______	What a perfect day this has been
2. **? INT**	2. ______ ______	Where is the Frisbee packed
3. **. D**	3. ______ ______	The cookies are in the basket
4. **! E**	4. ______ ______	Stop splashing me this instant
5. **. IMP**	5. ______ ______	Bring me a towel, please

NAME SCORE

Diagnostic Test 2

The Sentence and Its Parts

Part 1 Complete Subjects and Predicates Draw a line between the complete subject and the complete predicate in each of the sentences. (5 points each sentence)

1. Teresa's old jalopy broke down last week.
2. The green buds burst into flowers.
3. My friends bowl at least once a month.
4. Ice cold lemonade tastes refreshing.
5. Henry talks on the phone constantly.
6. The basketball team won the game.
7. Poisonous snakes have triangular-shaped heads.
8. The old trunk in the attic holds family treasures.

Part 2 Simple Subjects and Verbs Underline the simple subjects once. Underline the verbs twice. (6 points each)

1. Jack cooked spaghetti for dinner.
2. The fierce dog frightened the children.
3. Our new neighbor collects stamps.
4. That red T-shirt faded in the wash.
5. Surfers use special wax on their surfboards.
6. Do you want mustard on your hot dog?
7. Gary found a dollar on the beach.
8. Penelope did not take the bus to Texas.
9. These old gloves will protect your hands.
10. Mr. Allen waxed his pick-up truck.

1. jalopy | broke
2. buds | burst
3. friends | bowl
4. lemonade | tastes
5. Henry | talks
6. team | won
7. snakes | have
8. trunk in the attic | holds

	subjects	verbs
1.	Jack	cooked
2.	dog	frightened
3.	neighbor	collects
4.	T-shirt	faded
5.	Surfers	use
6.	you	Do want
7.	Gary	found
8.	Penelope	did take
9.	gloves	will protect
10.	Mr. Allen	waxed

1. jets, airport, house
2. Nancy Lopez, golfer
3. Arthur, June, Ben, contest
4. Shirley, pickles, olives
5. Linus, friend, Charlie Brown, blanket, security
6. Egypt, Israel, peace, Middle East
7. pencil, eraser, test
8. person, courage, beliefs

beets juries

elves churches

sheep children

lanes alleys

combs stereos

1. Fred's

2. Mrs. Williams's

3. men's

4. turtles'

NAME SCORE

Diagnostic Test 3 Using Nouns

Part 1 Identifying Nouns Underline all of the nouns in the following sentences. (7 points each sentence)

1. The jets from the airport fly over our house.
2. Nancy Lopez is a famous golfer.
3. Arthur, June, and Ben entered the contest.
4. Shirley likes pickles better than olives.
5. Linus, a friend of Charlie Brown, needs a blanket for security.
6. Egypt and Israel want peace in the Middle East.
7. Bring a pencil and an eraser for the test.
8. A person must have the courage to stand up for his or her beliefs.

Part 2 Plurals Write the plural form of each noun. (2 points each)

beet ________	jury ________
elf ________	church ________
sheep ________	child ________
lane ________	alley ________
comb ________	stereo ________

Part 3 Possessives Write the italicized word to show possession. (6 points each)

1. *Fred* new minibike ________
2. *Mrs. Williams* book ________
3. *men* volleyball team ________
4. the two *turtles* shells ________

NAME SCORE

Diagnostic Test 4

Using Verbs

Part 1 Finding Verbs Underline the verb in each of the following sentences. On the blank tell whether it is an action verb or a state-of-being verb. (6 points each sentence)

1. ______ Jemima is an honor student.
2. ______ The elephant crashed through the forest.
3. ______ Fred Astaire danced his way to fame.
4. ______ The oleander is a poisonous plant.
5. ______ Bjorn Borg has beaten Jimmy Connors.
6. ______ Dr. Clark prescribed penicillin for my cold.
7. ______ This chocolate cake tastes delicious.
8. ______ Our class has broken the record.
9. ______ Could Muhammad Ali win another fight?
10. ______ Nancy works at a day-care center.

1. is (state-of-being)
2. crashed (action)
3. danced (action)
4. is (state-of-being)
5. has beaten (action)
6. prescribed (action)
7. tastes (state-of-being)
8. has broken (action)
9. Could win (action)
10. works (action)

Part 2 Choosing the Correct Verb Underline the correct verb in each sentence. (5 points each)

1. (Leave, Let) the dog come in, please.
2. "(Lay, Lie) the money on the counter!" shouted the thief.
3. Each 4-H club member can (rise, raise) an animal as a project.
4. Georgia is (learning, teaching) Harry to play chess.
5. Mom was (laying, lying) in the hammock.
6. You (can, may) go to the movies tonight.
7. Don't (leave, let) your bicycle in the driveway.
8. The calico cat (set, sat) in the sun all day.

1. Let
2. Lay
3. raise
4. teaching
5. lying
6. may
7. leave
8. sat

NAME ______________________ SCORE ______

Diagnostic Test 5

Using Pronouns

Part 1 Finding Pronouns Underline the pronouns in the following paragraph. (3 points each pronoun)

My, me, it
it, it
my, she
I, my
She, my
My, her
his, him

My grandparents made a very special gift for me. It is a patchwork quilt. The reason it is so special is that it is made from scraps of material Gram saved from my clothes. For example, she used pieces of the blanket I used as a baby and the pockets from my first pair of jeans. She even used the number from my first football jersey. My grandfather helped her sew the patches to a blanket that his father had given him. The gift is really unique.

Part 2 Choosing the Correct Pronoun Underline the correct pronoun in each sentence. (5 points each)

1. me
2. he
3. them
4. she
5. me
6. me
7. It's
8. they
9. We
10. she
11. its

1. The police chief praised my dad and (me, I) for our bravery.
2. Lois and (he, him) repair bikes for a hobby.
3. Gracie sits behind (they, them) in math.
4. The new class president is (she, her).
5. Mr. Cobb helped Joan and (me, I) with our speeches.
6. The song "Getting To Know You" was sung by Ann and (me, I).
7. (Its, It's) a beautiful day for a parade.
8. It was (they, them) who called last night.
9. (We, Us) two are going to watch the eclipse of the sun.
10. Was it (she, her) wearing the sunglasses?
11. The camel kicked (its, it's) master.

NAME SCORE

Diagnostic Test 6 Using Adjectives

Part 1 Finding Adjectives On the first blank, write the adjective in each sentence. Write the word it describes on the second blank. Ignore *a, an,* and *the.* (3 points each blank)

1. ________ ________ Laura bought a new album.
2. ________ ________ The antique mirror was for sale.
3. ________ ________ Come here this minute!
4. ________ ________ Karen wrote the best story.
5. ________ ________ George did a graceful dive.
6. ________ ________ The baby seems fussy today.
7. ________ ________ Ellen is furious with you.
8. ________ ________ Several days have passed since the storm.
9. ________ ________ We had Russian tea and cookies for dessert.
10. ________ ________ The editor received fifty letters.

Part 2 Choosing the Correct Adjective Underline the correct word. (5 points each sentence)

1. That peach pie is the (baddest, worst) I've ever eaten.
2. (This, These) kinds of plants can survive in a cold climate.
3. (Them, Those) flowers are wilting.
4. Harry can get only two of (them, those) tickets.
5. That arrow is the (sharper, sharpest) of all.
6. (A, An) omelette makes a good dinner.
7. That messenger service is the (fastest, most fastest).
8. Marie is the (taller, tallest) of the two.

1. new album
2. antique mirror
3. this minute
4. best story
5. graceful dive
6. fussy baby
7. furious Ellen
8. Several days
9. Russian tea
10. fifty letters

1. worst
2. These
3. Those
4. those
5. sharpest
6. An
7. fastest
8. taller

1. loudly

2. now

3. outside

4. often

5. very

6. merrily

7. well

8. silently

9. really

10. too

1. well

2. harder

3. really

4. worse

5. more carefully

6. later

7. quickly

8. faster

NAME SCORE

Diagnostic Test 7 Using Adverbs

Part 1 Identifying Adverbs Read these sentences. Find the adverbs. Write them on the blanks. (6 points each blank)

1. ____________ The band played loudly.
2. ____________ Leave this room now.
3. ____________ Joe and Eddy played outside.
4. ____________ Grandpa often tells riddles.
5. ____________ Julie is a very helpful person.
6. ____________ The birds chirped merrily.
7. ____________ You play the piano well.
8. ____________ The sailboat slipped silently into the harbor.
9. ____________ The monster really frightened the children.
10. ____________ It is too cold for skating.

Part 2 Using Adverbs Underline the correct word for each sentence below. (5 points each)

1. Marcy swam (good, well) in the meet.
2. Rub (harder, more hard) to get a good shine on that car.
3. *The Pigman* is a (real, really) good book.
4. John dances (more badly, worse) than I do.
5. The baby walked (more careful, more carefully) after he fell.
6. The train from New York ran (later, more late) than usual.
7. Adam runs (quick, quickly) to his bus stop every morning.
8. Of the two joggers, the one on the right runs (faster, fastest).

NAME SCORE

Diagnostic Test 8 Capitalization

In the following sentences, copy the words that should be capitalized. Use capital letters. (10 points each sentence)

1. russell and i hate green beans. ______

2. the wells fargo bank is in california. ______

3. phoenix, arizona is in the southwest. ______

4. meet me at the corner of elm street and grant avenue. ______

5. call dr. devore on monday. ______

6. i love spring flowers. ______

7. support the pittsburgh steelers. ______

8. jan rode an arabian horse in the show. ______

9. that house was designed by frank lloyd wright. ______

10. i read the short story "the gift of the magi" and the book *a wrinkle in time.* ______

1. Russell, I
2. The, Wells Fargo Bank, California
3. Phoenix, Arizona, Southwest
4. Meet, Elm Street, Grant Avenue
5. Call, Dr. Devore, Monday
6. I
7. Support, Pittsburgh Steelers
8. Jan, Arabian
9. That, Frank Lloyd Wright
10. I, "The Gift of the Magi," *A Wrinkle in Time*

1. Stop! I forgot my hat, my scarf, and my gloves.
2. "Who is number twenty-nine?" asked Mr. Berman.
3. This check must reach Ames, Iowa, by May 2, 1980.
4. "No, I won't try out for the team," said Sonya.
5. Mr. Smith's cookies are good, but his cupcakes are better.
6. Does the ladies' luncheon begin at 12:30 P.M.?
7. "I can't do it!" shouted Molly's little brother.
8. Well, friend, I'll see you later.
9. Pearl Harbor, Hawaii, was attacked on December 7, 1941.
10. Mt. Vesuvius, the volcano that destroyed Pompeii, is still active.

NAME ______________________ SCORE ________

Diagnostic Test 9 Punctuation

Rewrite the following sentences. Punctuate them correctly. (10 points each sentence)

1. Stop I forgot my hat my scarf and my gloves

   ____

2. Who is number twenty nine asked Mr Berman

   ____

3. This check must reach Ames Iowa by May 2 1980

   ____

4. No I wont try out for the team said Sonya

   ____

5. Mr Smiths cookies are good but his cupcakes are better

   ____

6. Does the ladies luncheon begin at 12:30 PM

   ____

7. I cant do it shouted Mollys little brother

   ____

8. Well friend Ill see you later

   ____

9. Pearl Harbor Hawaii was attacked on December 7 1941

   ____

10. Mt Vesuvius the volcano that destroyed Pompeii is still active

   ____

NAME SCORE

Diagnostic Test 10 Spelling

Part 1 Prefixes and Suffixes Combine the following root words with the prefix or suffix provided. Drop, change, or add the necessary letters. (5 points each)

1. come + ing ______
2. employ + ment ______
3. stern + ness ______
4. fry + ing ______
5. notice + able ______
6. rain + ing ______
7. re + appear ______
8. scrub + ed ______
9. run + er ______
10. un + clear ______
11. real + ly ______
12. fussy + est ______
13. true + ly ______
14. live + ly ______
15. thin + est ______

1. coming
2. employment
3. sternness
4. frying
5. noticeable
6. raining
7. reappear
8. scrubbed
9. runner
10. unclear
11. really
12. fussiest
13. truly
14. lively
15. thinnest

Part 2 Choosing the Correct Spelling Underline the correct word for each sentence. (5 points each)

1. When (your, you're) sick, call the doctor.
2. The Russells had (their, there, they're) furniture shipped.
3. The pig wallowed in the mud in (it's, its) pen.
4. Put the groceries over (their, there, they're).
5. That color is (to, too, two) dark to match the curtains.

1. you're
2. their
3. its
4. there
5. too

1. compound
2. echoic
3. borrowed
4. clipped
5. blended
6. echoic
7. compound
8. clipped
9. borrowed
10. clipped
11. blended
12. compound
13. technical
14. echoic
15. clipped

NAME ______ SCORE ______

Mastery Test Chapter 1

How Our Language Grows

Part 1 Understanding How Words Are Added to English Decide whether the italicized words are *borrowed* words, *echoic* words, *clipped* words, *technical* words, *compound* words, or *blended* words. Write your answer in the blank. (4 points each)

1. ______ The *slumlord* neglected the building.
2. ______ Steaks *sizzled* on the grill.
3. ______ All of the items on the menu were *a la carte.*
4. ______ The movie star arrived in a pink *limo.*
5. ______ *Motocross,* cross-country biking, is a popular sport.
6. ______ The floorboards *creaked.*
7. ______ My *backpack* weighed thirty pounds.
8. ______ Agent 006 lost the secret *memo.*
9. ______ Our school had a fall *fiesta.*
10. ______ The secretary made a *typo* in the letter.
11. ______ The *smog* drifted over the valley.
12. ______ "I just had a *brainstorm,*" said Sam.
13. ______ A computer needs good *input* to do its job.
14. ______ The car *screeched* to a halt.
15. ______ Fill the tank with *gas.*

Mastery Test
Chapter 1

NAME ______________________________

Part 2 Making Acronyms What new words are formed by shortening these word groups to acronyms? (2 points each)

1. __________ Volunteers in Service to America
2. __________ self-contained underwater breathing apparatus
3. __________ Cooperative for American Relief Everywhere
4. __________ television
5. __________ People United to Save Humanity

Part 3 Words from Famous People or Places Fill in the blanks. (5 points each)

1. Louis Braille was a teacher of the blind. He created an alphabet of raised dots that is read by touch. His alphabet is called __________.
2. Marie Curie discovered radium. A unit of radioactivity is a __________.
3. In Limerick, a county in Ireland, people at social gatherings would take turns making up verses to the song "Will You Come Up to Limerick?" Now a type of humorous poem is called a __________.
4. James Bowie was an American soldier and pioneer. A knife named after him is the __________.
5. Frankfurt on the Main is a city in Germany known for its sausages. Sometimes our hot dogs are called __________.
6. Waterloo is a village in Belgium where Napoleon was soundly defeated. Today when someone has had a crushing defeat, we say that person has met his or her __________.

Part 2 answers:
1. VISTA
2. scuba
3. CARE
4. TV
5. PUSH

Part 3 answers:
1. Braille
2. curie
3. limerick
4. bowie
5. frankfurters
6. Waterloo

436

NAME SCORE

Mastery Test Chapter 2

Developing a Vocabulary of Specific Words

Part 1 Specific Words for *Go, Big,* and *Small* Read the following word list. Write the word that *best* fits each sentence. (5 points each)

bulky—having an unwieldy size
charge—to rush violently at
dash—to rush
fat—chubby, obese
glide—to move smoothly
imposing—impressive because of size or stateliness
microscopic—so small as to be invisible without a microscope
modest—not showy or extravagant
petite—small in stature or figure
plunge—to throw oneself, dive, or rush into something
puny—weak, under-sized
spacious—having a great area

1. microscopic
2. bulky
3. charge
4. plunge
5. modest
6. imposing
7. glide
8. spacious
9. puny
10. dash

1. The scratch on the contact lens was __________.
2. The bales of cotton were __________.
3. Will bulls __________ if they see the color red?
4. The diver will __________ into the icy water.
5. Our house is a __________ five-room ranch.
6. The World Trade Center towers are __________.
7. The dancers seemed to __________ across the stage.
8. The __________ dining room seated twenty people.
9. That __________ child looks underfed.
10. Les would __________ eagerly to the ball field every day after school.

Mastery Test
Chapter 2

NAME ______________________________

Part 2 Specific Words for *Make, Good,* and *Bad* Read the following word list. Write the word that *best* fits each sentence. (5 points each)

adequate—barely suitable
cause—to bring about
compose—to create
concoct—to make by combining ingredients
delicious—pleasing to taste or smell
design—to prepare preliminary plans
devastating—overwhelming
harmful—dangerous
illegal—against the law
naughty—mischievous; disobedient
prepare—to make ready
proper—suitable; appropriate to the purpose
shoddy—poorly made or done
useful—serving some purpose

1. The damage from the hurricane was ______________. 1. devastating
2. Sean bakes ______________ fudge brownies. 2. delicious
3. The Doctor Jazz Ice Cream Parlor can ______________ a fantastic sundae. 3. concoct
4. The architect will ______________ the new building. 4. design
5. Running a red light is ______________. 5. illegal
6. The size of this room is ______________ for no more than twenty students. 6. adequate
7. The ______________ toddler pulled Lisa's hair. 7. naughty
8. Dad and Mom will ______________ their income tax forms. 8. prepare
9. Smoking can ______________ lung disease. 9. cause
10. Mark will ______________ a song for June's birthday. 10. compose

438

NAME SCORE

Mastery Test Chapter 3

Learning About Sentences

Part 1 Sentences and Fragments Next to each group of words put **S** for sentence or **F** for fragment. (2 points each)

1. F
2. F
3. S
4. F
5. S
6. F
7. S
8. F
9. S
10. S

1. ______ The deep, dark dungeon of the castle
2. ______ Our new aluminum canoe
3. ______ Follow that taxi
4. ______ The Louisiana hot sauce in the chili
5. ______ We ate beans and rice for dinner
6. ______ Cows along the road in Mexico
7. ______ Halt
8. ______ San Francisco, the city with cable cars
9. ______ They won the game
10. ______ Try this one

Part 2 Kinds of Sentences To each sentence, add the correct end punctuation. Then write whether the sentence is *declarative, interrogative, imperative,* or *exclamatory.* (2 points each)

1. **.** declarative
2. **.** imperative
3. **?** interrogative
4. **!** exclamatory
5. **.** declarative

1. ____________________ Dodo birds are extinct
2. ____________________ Sign on the dotted line
3. ____________________ Did you enjoy reading *The Secret Garden*
4. ____________________ What a great song that is
5. ____________________ I'll have a peanut butter and jelly sandwich

439

NAME ____________________

Part 3 Complete Subjects and Predicates Draw a line between the complete subject and the complete predicate. (1 point each sentence)

1. Mary Ellen takes karate lessons.
2. The books on those shelves have beautiful illustrations.
3. The wind chimes tinkled in the breeze.
4. Luis smashed the cockroach with his shoe.
5. The upholstery in the car needs some patches.
6. The artist Monet painted the same scene many times.
7. The comfortable leather chair adjusts to any position.
8. We played gin rummy on the train.
9. Ms. Carter sews many of her own clothes.
10. Ralph's peanut butter toast landed on the floor.

Part 4 Main Verbs and Helping Verbs Write **H.V.** above each helping verb. Write **M.V.** above each main verb. (1 point each sentence)

1. The movie star was accompanied by her bodyguard.
2. That bill should have been paid last week.
3. The grass is usually mowed once a week.
4. That casserole should heat for thirty minutes.
5. Ms. Brachman would not accept our excuse.
6. Dad will have been napping for two hours.
7. Cranberries are usually served with turkey.
8. Flight 942 will be departing from Gate H-11.
9. Lisa must pass her science test.
10. Beatles fans would pay a fortune for tickets to one last concert.

1. Mary Ellen | takes . . .
2. The books on those shelves | have . . .
3. . . . chimes | tinkled . .
4. Luis | smashed . . .
5. The upholstery in the car | needs . . .
6. . . . Monet | painted . . .
7. . . . chair | adjusts . . .
8. We | played . . .
9. Ms. Carter | sews . . .
10. . . . toast | landed . . .

	H.V.	M.V.
1.	was	accompanie
2.	should have been	paid
3.	is	mowed
4.	should	heat
5.	would	accept
6.	will have been	napping
7.	are	served
8.	will be	departing
9.	must	pass
10.	would	pay

1. ice cream dripped
2. part was played
3. Cathy is taking
4. key is
5. tadpoles swam
6. horse is limping
7. parade was canceled
8. "Broom Hilda" is
9. (You) stop
10. saw should be used

Mastery Test
Chapter 3

NAME ______________________________

Part 5 Subjects and Verbs Write the subject and the verb of each sentence on the blanks after the sentence. (2 points each sentence)

1. Erin's ice cream dripped on her jacket.

   s: ____________ v: ____________

2. The part of Dorothy in *The Wiz* was played by Diana Ross.

   s: ____________ v: ____________

3. Cathy is taking voice lessons once a week.

   s: ____________ v: ____________

4. Where is the key for the garage door?

   s: ____________ v: ____________

5. Under the lily pads swam the tadpoles.

   s: ____________ v: ____________

6. Craig's horse is limping back to the barn.

   s: ____________ v: ____________

7. The Labor Day parade was canceled due to the rain.

   s: ____________ v: ____________

8. What a hilarious comic strip "Broom Hilda" is!

   s: ____________ v: ____________

9. Stop at the corner.

   s: ____________ v: ____________

10. A saw should be used carefully.

    s: ____________ v: ____________

Mastery Test
Chapter 3

NAME ______________________________

Part 6 Compound Subjects Underline each part of the compound subject. Write the conjunction on the line. (2 points each sentence)

1. __________ Bob and Al vacationed in Wisconsin.
2. __________ Cake, pie, and ice cream were the choices for dessert.
3. __________ Coffee and tea were the only beverages available.
4. __________ Tulips, daffodils, and crocuses are popping out now.
5. __________ Alex's dad or Tony's brother will drive us to the circus.
6. __________ The thunder and the lightning scared the dog.

Part 7 Compound Predicates Underline each part of the compound predicate. (2 points each sentence)

1. Mario played his guitar and sang a song.
2. The passengers fastened their seat belts and put their seats in an upright position.
3. Mrs. O'Leary's cow kicked over a lantern and started the Chicago Fire.
4. Every day Jim runs a mile or jumps rope for five minutes.
5. The heavy snow covered the streets and caused traffic jams.
6. Lillian weeded the garden and watered the plants.
7. The bell captain took our suitcases, led us to our room, and opened the door.
8. Carla ate her lunch and paid the bill.
9. The gymnast twisted his ankle and fell off the balance beam.

1. Bob, Al (and)
2. Cake, pie, ice cream (and)
3. Coffee, tea (and)
4. Tulips, daffodils, crocuses (and)
5. dad, brother (or)
6. thunder, lightning (and)

1. played his guitar
   sang a song
2. fastened their seat belts
   put their seats in an upright position
3. kicked over a lantern
   started the Chicago Fire
4. runs a mile
   jumps rope for five minutes
5. covered the streets
   caused traffic jams
6. weeded the garden
   watered the plants
7. took our suitcases
   led us to our room
   opened the door
8. ate her lunch
   paid the bill
9. twisted his ankle
   fell off the balance beam

NAME SCORE

Mastery Test
Chapter 4

Writing Good Paragraphs

Part 1 Sticking to the Main Idea Find the sentence that does **not** support the main idea. Circle the letter of the sentence. (8 points each)

1. b

1. a. Diamonds are not only beautiful but useful.
   b. There are diamonds found in Siberia.
   c. Eye surgeons use super-sharp diamond knives for cataract operations.
   d. NASA uses a diamond disk to measure the temperature of stars.

2. b

2. a. James Cook claimed Australia for Great Britain in 1770.
   b. The opera house in Sydney is world famous.
   c. Many of the first settlers were convicts from England.
   d. Australia has an interesting history.

3. c

3. a. A basic need is food from the protein group.
   b. Learning to eat a balanced diet is important for your health.
   c. Running can burn up calories from overeating.
   d. Green vegetables and fresh fruits provide needed vitamins.

4. d

4. a. In 1976 Ella Grasso was elected governor of Connecticut.
   b. Women are becoming more visible in politics.
   c. Jane Byrne became mayor of Chicago in 1979.
   d. Corporations are hiring more women executives.

5. a

5. a. A movie camera is harder to use than a still camera.
   b. A photographer must remember a few rules for taking good pictures.
   c. The lighting must be right.
   d. Centering the subject in the view finder is important.

443

NAME ______________________________

Part 2 The Topic Sentence Circle the numbers of the topic sentences that are interesting enough to catch the reader's attention. (8 points each)

1. Never have a three-year-old child help you bake cookies.
2. Can you imagine eating an eel?
3. This paragraph is about my dog.
4. There are many kinds of fresh-water fish.
5. Out of the darkness appeared a smiling unicorn.

Numbers to be circled: 1, 2, 5

Part 3 Supporting the Topic Sentence Read the following paragraph. Answer the questions below it. (10 points each)

If you want to have healthy house plants, you must give them tender, loving care. Water your plants once a week, and fertilize them several times a year. Cactus plants need less care than other plants. In addition, give your plants adequate light, pull off dead leaves, and watch for insects. If you follow these simple steps, you'll have a great indoor garden.

1. What is the topic sentence of this paragraph?

____

____

1. If you want to have healthy house plants, you must give them tender, loving care.

2. One sentence does not support the topic sentence. Write the unrelated sentence on the blank.

____

____

2. Cactus plants need less care than other plants.

NAME SCORE

Mastery Test Chapter 5

Ways of Developing Paragraphs

Part 1 Using Details Read the paragraph and answer the question. (8 points each item)

The grass was spongy with dew and the air was cool and sweet, filling his lungs until they pressed against his ribs and a stitch ran up and down his side. Then he was crunching over gravel. The sky was blood-red. It was going to be another warm day but not yet. He couldn't help smiling, he'd sing if he had the breath. He was all alone in the park.

—ROBERT LIPSYTE, *The Contender*

List three specific details the author uses. Tell whether each detail appeals to the sense of sight, sound, smell, taste, or touch.

spongy (touch)
cool (touch)
sweet (smell)
lungs . . . pressed (touch)
crunching (sound)
blood-red (sight)

1. ______
2. ______
3. ______

Part 2 Using One Example Read the paragraph and answer the questions. (15 points each)

Actually, Norton is a social outcast. He's been a social outcast since his freshman year in high school when he got caught stealing a bag of marshmallows from the supermarket. He never recovered from that because they put his name in the newspaper and mentioned that the entire loot was a bag of marshmallows. Ever since then everybody calls him The Marshmallow Kid.

—PAUL ZINDEL, *The Pigman*

1. first sentence

1. What is the topic sentence of the paragraph?

______

2. Norton's theft of the marshmallows

2. What one example does the author use to develop the topic?

______

______

NAME ______________________________

Part 3 Using Several Examples Read the paragraph and answer the questions. (8 points each item)

As a city addicted to sports, both collegiate and professional, Los Angeles likes winners, and winners it has. On the football field it's the Rams, and on the basketball court, the Lakers. But most of all it's the Dodgers on the baseball diamond. And now the city is preparing to host the 1984 Summer Olympic Games.

—WILLIAM S. ELLIS, *National Geographic*

List three examples the author uses to develop the topic.

1. ______________________________
2. ______________________________
3. ______________________________

1. Rams are winners.
2. Lakers are winners.
3. Dodgers are winners.

Part 4 Ways of Developing a Paragraph (11 points each question)

As he came near, what impressed me first was his clothes. He wore dark trousers of some serge material tucked into tall boots and held at the waist by a wide belt. Boots and belt were soft black leather tooled in an intricate design. A coat of the same dark material as the trousers was neatly folded and strapped to his saddle-roll. His shirt was finespun linen, rich brown in color. The handkerchief knotted loosely around his throat was black silk. His hat was not the familiar Stetson, not the familiar gray or muddy tan. It was a plain black, soft in texture, unlike any hat I had ever seen, with a creased crown and a wide curling brim swept down in front to shield the face.

—JACK SCHAEFER, *Shane*

1. What is the topic sentence?

____

____

1. first sentence

2. How did the author develop this paragraph?

____

2. using details

NAME SCORE

Mastery Test Chapter 6

Different Kinds of Paragraphs

Part 1 Identifying Kinds of Paragraphs Would the paragraph following each of these topic sentences most likely be *narrative, descriptive,* or *explanatory?* Answer in the blanks. (5 points each)

1. explanatory
2. descriptive
3. explanatory
4. descriptive
5. narrative

1. ______ Making marshmallow fudge is easy if you have a good recipe.
2. ______ The Picasso sculpture in the Daley Center is an unusual piece of art.
3. ______ The graduated length method of learning to ski, or GLM, has several steps.
4. ______ Our neighborhood is made up of many beautiful old buildings.
5. ______ Early yesterday morning, I decided to wallpaper my room.

Part 2 Developing Paragraphs What is the *best* way to organize a paragraph on each of the following topics?

A. By following time sequence
B. By using details
C. By giving reasons

Put the letter of the answer next to the topic. (6 points each)

1. A
2. B
3. B
4. A
5. C

______ 1. How to make an apple pie

______ 2. The first robin of spring

______ 3. A rock singer's costume

______ 4. The life of Margaret Mead

______ 5. Smoking can be hazardous to your health

Building English Skills, Gold Level, Teacher's Edition.

Mastery Test
Chapter 6

NAME ______________________________

Part 3 Kinds of Paragraphs Read the following paragraphs. Answer the questions about them. (5 points each question)

Crabbing is a pastime that requires patience. First you tie the bait to the crab trap. Then you lower the trap into the water so that it rests on the sand. Next you wait. And then you wait some more. Occasionally you pull the trap up to see if the bait is still there. With a little luck you will be looking eye-to-eye with a crab.

1. What kind of paragraph is this? ______________________
2. How is the paragraph organized? ______________________
3. List two details used by the author to develop the topic.

____

Nervous is too mild to describe how I felt on my first day at the new school. I was in a panic! To start the day off right, I spilled orange juice down my blouse. Then I missed the bus; therefore I was late for my first class. During the day I forgot my locker combination, tripped down the stairs, and went to the wrong math class. The only bright spot in my day was the 3:30 bell.

1. What kind of paragraph is this? ______________________
2. How is the paragraph organized? ______________________
3. List three details used to develop the topic.

____

Resting on black velvet, the necklace in the jewelry store window is breathtaking. The chain is made of the finest yellow gold. The pendant suspended from the chain is a brilliant emerald. Fiery diamonds and blood-red rubies create a halo around the green gem. It surely must have been designed for a queen.

1. What kind of paragraph is this? ______________________
2. The writer of this paragraph uses many details that appeal to the sense of __________.
3. Name two specific details. ______________________

1. explanatory—"how"
2. time sequence (step-by-step)
3. Any two:
   tie bait to trap, lower trap, wait, check the trap occasionally

1. narrative
2. time sequence
3. Any three:
   spilled juice, missed bus, late for class, forgot combination, tripped, went to wrong class

1. descriptive
2. sight
3. Any two:
   on black velvet, finest yellow gold, brilliant emerald, fiery diamonds, blood-red rubies, halo

448

NAME SCORE

Mastery Test Chapter 7

Using Nouns

Part 1 Recognizing Nouns Underline all of the nouns in the following sentences. (3 points each)

1. Spinach and broccoli are full of vitamins and minerals.
2. Carlos, Carmen, and Linda speak Spanish.
3. Patience and kindness are good qualities.
4. The shark slowly circled the boat.
5. The frightened dog backed into the cactus.
6. Tina hit the ball into the outfield.
7. Passengers need exact change to ride the bus.
8. My dream is to be a veterinarian.
9. Chris and Jim played Monopoly for hours.
10. The baby smiled with glee and clapped her hands.

Answers:
1. Spinach, broccoli, vitamins, minerals
2. Carlos, Carmen, Linda, Spanish
3. Patience, kindness, qualities
4. shark, boat
5. dog, cactus
6. Tina, ball, outfield
7. Passengers, change, bus
8. dream, veterinarian
9. Chris, Jim, Monopoly, hours
10. baby, glee, hands

Part 2 Proper Nouns Write the proper nouns from each sentence on the blanks. Capitalize correctly. (4 points each)

1. jackie is teaching joe to speak french.

____

2. Meet me at the corner of park avenue and linden street.

____

3. The golden gate bridge in san francisco is beautiful.

____

4. pope john paul II was born in poland.

____

5. Do you have a silver dollar with a likeness of susan b. anthony on it?

____

Answers:
1. Jackie, Joe, French
2. Park Avenue, Linden Street
3. Golden Gate Bridge, San Francisco
4. Pope John Paul II, Poland
5. Susan B. Anthony

Mastery Test
Chapter 7

NAME ______________________________

Part 3 Plurals Write the plural form of the following words. (2 points each)

calf ________	pizza ________	calves	pizzas
mess ________	fox ________	messes	foxes
goose ________	apartment ________	geese	apartments
potato ________	kettle ________	potatoes	kettles
screen ________	peony ________	screens	peonies

Part 4 Possessives Write the italicized words to show possession. (3 points each)

1. ________ *Susan* dog had puppies. — 1. Susan's
2. ________ The *President* plane has landed. — 2. President's
3. ________ The *children* room is full of toys. — 3. children's
4. ________ The *prince* castle was surrounded by a moat. — 4. prince's
5. ________ The two *students* project won first prize at the science fair. — 5. students'
6. ________ Nurse Jones took *Toby* temperature. — 6. Toby's
7. ________ The *waitress* pencil broke. — 7. waitress's
8. ________ Those *campers* tents look alike. — 8. campers'
9. ________ *Ms. Middleton* car has a flat tire. — 9. Ms. Middleton's
10. ________ The *triplets* outfits are identical. — 10. triplets'

NAME SCORE

Mastery Test Chapter 8

Using Verbs

Part 1 Finding Action Verbs and State-of-Being Verbs Underline the verb in each sentence. Write *action* or *state-of-being* in the blank. (2 points each sentence)

1. ______________ The skateboard rolled down the hill without the rider.
2. ______________ The kangaroo punched the zookeeper in the nose.
3. ______________ The valentine pleased my mother.
4. ______________ Flag football is a popular sport.
5. ______________ The popcorn popped out of the pan and onto the floor.
6. ______________ Monster movies give me the creeps.
7. ______________ Mary, Sue, and Fred have chicken pox.
8. ______________ Chocolate chip cookies are delicious.
9. ______________ The baby smeared spaghetti in her hair.
10. ______________ Claire is a fine musician.
11. ______________ The cheerleaders formed a pyramid at halftime.
12. ______________ Kate dreamed about a trip to Disney World.
13. ______________ Dill pickles are sour.
14. ______________ King Midas turned his daughter into gold.
15. ______________ Sam's boat was full of fish.

1. rolled (action)
2. punched (action)
3. pleased (action)
4. is (state-of-being)
5. popped (action)
6. give (action)
7. have (action)
8. are (state-of-being)
9. smeared (action)
10. is (state-of-being)
11. formed (action)
12. dreamed (action)
13. are (state-of-being)
14. turned (action)
15. was (state-of-being)

451

Mastery Test
Chapter 8

NAME ______________________________

Part 2 Helping Verbs On the first line after each sentence write the helping verb or verbs, **H.V.** On the second line write the main verb, **M.V.** (2 points each sentence)

1. Lisa would like the tangerine sherbet.

H.V. ____________ **M.V.** ____________

2. George will not sing in front of an audience.

H.V. ____________ **M.V.** ____________

3. Max will have eaten eleven donuts!

H.V. ____________ **M.V.** ____________

4. Our car can be started in any weather.

H.V. ____________ **M.V.** ____________

5. You must return your library books today.

H.V. ____________ **M.V.** ____________

Part 3 Finding Direct Objects Read the sentences below. Underline the verb. Circle the direct object. (2 points each sentence)

1. Ted will knit a scarf.
2. The softball broke the window.
3. Ancient Egyptians built the pyramids.
4. Geraldine answered the question correctly.
5. Lou's dog bit the stranger.
6. Traffic officers sometimes ride motorcycles.
7. Barbara roasted some marshmallows.
8. Joel forgot his keys again.

	H.V.	M.V.
1.	would	like
2.	will	sing
3.	will have	eaten
4.	can be	started
5.	must	return

	V.	D.O.
1.	will knit	scarf
2.	broke	window
3.	built	pyramids
4.	answered	question
5.	bit	stranger
6.	ride	motorcycles
7.	roasted	marshmallow
8.	forgot	keys

Mastery Test
Chapter 8

NAME ____________________

Part 4 Linking Verbs Write the subject of the sentence on the first line. Then write the linking verb. On the third line write the word that is linked to the subject. (3 points each sentence)

1. room is mess

1. That room is a mess.

______ ______ ______

2. sherbet tastes tart

2. Lemon sherbet tastes tart.

______ ______ ______

3. album was gift

3. This album was a gift from my aunt.

______ ______ ______

4. Dick is leader

4. Dick is the leader of the band.

______ ______ ______

5. Alice is angry

5. Is Alice angry?

______ ______ ______

6. Frank seems upset

6. Frank seems upset about football tryouts.

______ ______ ______

Part 5 Tense Write the correct tense of each verb on the blank. (2 points each)

1. laughed

1. (*laugh*-past) The audience ______ at the clown.

2. will run

2. (*run*-future) Marietta ______ in the marathon.

3. teases

3. (*tease*-present) The dog ______ the cat.

4. thought

4. (*think*-past) John ______ about his plans for summer.

Building English Skills, Gold Level, Teacher's Edition.

NAME ______________________________

Part 6 Using the Right Word Underline the correct word in each sentence. (1 point each)

1. Mike usually will (lay, lie) down on the sofa after dinner.
2. The price of movie tickets is (raising, rising) faster than my allowance.
3. Gertrude will (learn, teach) me to yodel.
4. (May, Can) I go to the roller rink tonight?
5. (Raise, Rise) the shade to let in more light.
6. (Leave, Let) your books in the room during the assembly.
7. (Sit, Set) the flowerpot on the windowsill.
8. The baby (may, can) walk by himself now.
9. There isn't (no, any) dessert left.
10. Easter eggs were (laying, lying) all over the lawn.
11. Mom will not (leave, let) my brother babysit on weekdays.
12. Don't you want (any, no) cookies?
13. The farmer (raises, rises) hogs and chickens.
14. I found Jeff (sitting, setting) by the pool.
15. Andy is (learning, teaching) Ken to play the guitar.
16. (Lie, Lay) your cards on the table.
17. Mary Lynne was (lying, laying) in the hammock.
18. Herb hasn't done (nothing, anything) to help.

1. lie
2. rising
3. teach
4. May
5. Raise
6. Leave
7. Set
8. can
9. any
10. lying
11. let
12. any
13. raises
14. sitting
15. teaching
16. Lay
17. lying
18. anything

They (Bob and Charlotte)

they (Bob and Charlotte)

it (race)

He (Bob)

his (Bob)

she (Charlotte)

her (Charlotte)

They (Bob and Charlotte)

them (Bob and Charlotte)

their (the winners)

1. his

2. her

3. their

NAME ____________________ SCORE ________

Mastery Test Chapter 9

Using Pronouns

Part 1 Finding Pronouns Read the paragraph. Write the pronouns in the column on the left. Next to each pronoun, write the word the pronoun stands for. (2 points each blank)

Bob and Charlotte entered the sack race at the annual Fourth of July picnic. They thought they could win it easily. He was the track champ at his school, and she was the fastest runner at her school. They didn't win, though. The winners told them their secret—practicing together.

________________ ________________

________________ ________________

________________ ________________

________________ ________________

________________ ________________

________________ ________________

________________ ________________

________________ ________________

________________ ________________

________________ ________________

Part 2 Possessive Pronouns Write the possessive pronoun that can take the place of the noun in italics. (5 points each)

1. ________________ *John's* bike

2. ________________ *Dorothy's* dog

3. ________________ *children's* games

NAME ______________________________

Part 3 Choosing the Correct Pronoun Write the correct pronoun for each sentence on the blank. (3 points each blank)

1. __________ (He, Him) and the paramedic will accompany the victim in the ambulance. — 1. He
2. __________ John clocked (he, him) running the mile at 4 minutes 52 seconds. — 2. him
3. __________ Gram kissed Mom, Dad, and (me, I). — 3. me
4. __________ Our class lost (it's, its) best speller when Carl moved away. — 4. its
5. __________ Marge and (me, I) will meet at the bus stop. — 5. I
6. __________ The best actors in the play were you and (them, they). — 6. they
7. __________ It is (they, them) who are painting our house. — 7. they
8. __________ Was it (her, she) who answered the question? — 8. she
9. __________ (We, Us) five formed a basketball team. — 9. We
10. __________ In the choir I sit beside (she, her). — 10. her
11. __________ The magician amazed Jill and (me, I) with her tricks. — 11. me
12. __________ Dan, George, and (me, I) are going to race slot cars. — 12. I
13. __________ The cat scratched Laurel and (me, I) before we got it to the vet. — 13. me
14. __________ The Snoopy poster is a gift from (me, I). — 14. me
15. __________ My favorite restaurant keeps (it's, its) best recipes secret. — 15. its

456

1. Chattanooga
2. Chicago
3. Greenwich
4. Minneapolis
5. Montreal
6. Provo
7. Salem
8. Seattle
9. Williamsburg

1. architect
2. carpenter
3. electrician
4. engineer
5. landscaper
6. mason
7. painter
8. plumber
9. surveyor

1. 459 6. 460

2. 461 7. 461

3. 460 8. 459

4. 460 9. 461

5. 459 10. 459

NAME SCORE

Mastery Test Chapter 10

Using the Dictionary

Part 1 Using Alphabetical Order Rewrite these two sets of words in alphabetical order. (2 points each)

1. ________	Seattle	1. ________	carpenter
2. ________	Minneapolis	2. ________	plumber
3. ________	Williamsburg	3. ________	engineer
4. ________	Chicago	4. ________	architect
5. ________	Montreal	5. ________	mason
6. ________	Greenwich	6. ________	painter
7. ________	Chattanooga	7. ________	surveyor
8. ________	Salem	8. ________	electrician
9. ________	Provo	9. ________	landscaper

Part 2 Using Guide Words By using the sample guide words given below, write the page on which each of the given words would be found. (2 points each)

459	460	461
evoke—examine	**example—exchequer**	**excide—exculpatory**

1. ________	exalted	6. ________	exchange
2. ________	excite	7. ________	exclude
3. ________	except	8. ________	evolve
4. ________	excess	9. ________	exclaim
5. ________	exam	10. ________	ewe

NAME ______________________________

Part 3 Using a Dictionary Entry Answer the questions about the following dictionary entry from *Webster's New World Dictionary of the American Language,* Student's Edition. (4 points each)

si·lent (sī′lənt) ***adj.*** [< L. < prp. of *silere,* to be silent] **1.** making no vocal sound; mute **2.** seldom speaking; not talkative **3.** free from sound or noise; quiet; still [a *silent* place to study] **4.** not spoken, expressed, etc. [*silent* grief, the *silent* "b" in "debt"] **5.** making no mention, explanation, etc. [the newspaper is *silent* on that matter] **6.** not active [factories now *silent*] **7.** designating or of films without synchronized sound —**si′·lent·ly** ***adv.***
SYN.—**silent** is the simple, direct word for one who is temporarily not speaking or who seldom speaks; **taciturn** applies to a somewhat gloomy and unsociable person who has a habit of not talking or expressing his feelings; **reserved** implies that one has a habit of being withdrawn in speech and self-controlled or cool in manner; **reticent** implies a lack of desire, sometimes temporary as from shyness or embarrassment, to express one's feelings or to speak freely about certain matters; **secretive** suggests the sneaky or overly cautious reticence of one who hides things even when there is no need to do so—***ANT.*** **talkative, voluble**

1. Copy the pronunciation of *silent.* ______________________ 1. sī′ lənt

2. What part of speech is *silent?* ______________________ 2. adjective

3. Underline the word history for *silent.* 3. from Latin, *silere,* to be silent

Name three synonyms for *silent.*

4. ____________ 5. ____________ 6. ____________ 4.,5.,6. (any three): taciturn, reserved, reticent, secretive

How is *silent* used in the following sentences? Put the number of the definition next to each sentence.

7. ________ Only at night were the machines silent. 7. 6

8. ________ Did you see the silent films on TV last Saturday? 8. 7

9. ________ The Governor remained silent on the tax issue. 9. 5

10. ________ The word *gnat* has a silent *g.* 10. 4

11. ________ Ernest is rarely silent at home, but he is less talkative at school. 11. 2

NAME ____________________ SCORE ________

Mastery Test Chapter 11

Using the Library

Part 1 Arranging Fiction Books Put the books in each list in the order that you would find them on a library shelf. Number each from one to ten, one being the first book you would find on the shelf. (2 points each)

1. 6 — 1. ______ O'Dell, Scott. *The Black Pearl*

2. 8 — 2. ______ Rockwell, Thomas. *Hiding Out*

3. 4 — 3. ______ First, Julia. *Flat on My Face*

4. 7 — 4. ______ O'Dell, Scott. *Island of the Blue Dolphins*

5. 1 — 5. ______ Chittum, Ida. *The Hermit Boy*

6. 5 — 6. ______ Gold, Sharla. *Amelia Quackenbush*

7. 3 — 7. ______ Corbett, Scott. *The Home Run Trick*

8. 9 — 8. ______ Rodgers, Mary. *A Billion for Boris*

9. 2 — 9. ______ Cooper, Elizabeth. *The Wild Cats of Rome*

10. 10 — 10. ______ Steptoe, John. *Train Ride*

Part 2 Call Numbers Put the following call numbers in the order that you would find them on the library shelf. Number each from one to ten, one being the first you would find. (2 points each)

Answers					
3 9 1 4 10	____591.042 C172s	____592 W82t	____529.09 S711u	____591.09 H271s	____593.7 S892j
5 6 7 8 2	____591.16 C651a	____591.188 S181v	____591.188 T462b	____591.4 L781d	____587.2 Z222a

459

Part 3 Using the Card Catalog If you were using the card catalog to locate each of the following items, would you be looking for an **author** card, **title** card, or a **subject** card? (5 points each number)

1. *A Calf Is Born* _____

1. title

2. books by Beverly Cleary _____

2. author

3. *Away Went the Balloons* _____

3. title

4. a book by Roald Dahl _____

4. author

5. a book about dinosaurs _____

5. subject

6. *Across Five Aprils* _____

6. title

7. a book about cats _____

7. subject

8. *Fireweed* _____

8. title

Part 4 Using Encyclopedias If you were looking for answers to the following questions, what *key word* in each question would you look for in the encyclopedia index? (4 points each)

1. What did Clara Barton do? _____

1. Barton

2. When was the cotton gin invented? _____

2. cotton gin

3. What is Brazil's chief export? _____

3. Brazil

4. How does the Wankel engine work? _____

4. Wankel engine

5. Explain the process of photosynthesis. _____

5. photosynthesis

NAME _______________ SCORE _______________

Mastery Test Chapter 12

Writing Compositions and Reports

Part 1 Narrowing the Subject Each of the following subjects is too broad to be handled in a composition. Narrow each subject. Write the new subject on the blank. (4 points each)

Answers will vary.

1. American Indians ______________________
2. Magic ______________________
3. Our government ______________________
4. Trees found in the Midwest ______________________
5. Conservation ______________________
6. Animals ______________________
7. Summer camps ______________________
8. Comic book characters ______________________

Part 2 The Introductory Paragraph A good introductory paragraph should catch the reader's interest and introduce the subject of the composition. Using the list of facts given below, write an introductory paragraph. (18 points)

My sister is two years old.
We took her to a nice restaurant.
She said, "Hi, doll," to everybody as we entered.
I was embarrassed.

Answers will vary.

____

____

____

____

____

____

NAME ______________________________

Part 3 Organizing Ideas Organize the following ideas into the outline below. (5 points each)

Smaller, lighter cars steer easily.
They emit fewer pollutants.
They conserve gas.
They save on gas and oil bills.
Parking is easy.
License plates and stickers are cheaper.
Most small cars are less expensive than larger cars.

ADVANTAGES OF A SMALL CAR

I. Introduction
II. Small cars save money.
    A. ______________________________
    B. ______________________________
    C. ______________________________
III. Small cars are good for the environment.
    A. ______________________________
    B. ______________________________
IV. Small cars are easy to handle.
    A. ______________________________
    B. ______________________________
V. Conclusion

(Order of ideas may vary.)
II. Small cars save money.
    A. They save on gas and oil bills.
    B. License plates and stickers are cheaper.
    C. Most small cars are less expensive than larger cars.
III. Small cars are good for the environment.
    A. They emit fewer pollutants.
    B. They conserve gas.
IV. Small cars are easy to handle.
    A. Smaller, lighter cars steer easily.
    B. Parking is easy.

Part 4 Writing Endings The following sentences were written to conclude the composition about small cars that you outlined in Part 3. If the sentence is a *good* ending sentence, put a **G** in the blank. If it is *poor*, put a **P** in the blank. (5 points each)

1. ______ Of course, small cars also have disadvantages.
2. ______ Well, that ends my composition on small cars.
3. ______ Small cars can save you money and energy while getting you where you want to go easily.

1. **P**
2. **P**
3. **G**

NAME SCORE

Mastery Test
Chapter 13

Different Kinds of Compositions

Part 1 Kinds of Compositions Read the following introductory paragraphs. Does each introduce a *descriptive,* a *narrative,* or an *explanatory* composition? Write your answer in the blank. (15 points each)

It all started one day while I was hoeing corn down in our field close to the river. Across the river, a party of fishermen had been camped for several days. I heard the old Maxwell car as it snorted and chugged its way out of the bottoms. I knew they were leaving. Throwing down my hoe, I ran down to the river and waded across at a place called the Shannon Ford. I hurried to the camp ground.

—Wilson Rawls

1. narrative

1. ____________________

To the swelling thunder of hooves, the hunt chief climbed to a perch atop the medicine post. Clad in a buffalo-skin robe and headdress, he held a staff adorned with feathers. Near him was the ritual post that had been planted beside a streambed deep with snow. —Dennis Stanford

2. descriptive

2. ____________________

You had better be both young and patient to try growing house plants from seeds. It can take anywhere from six months to seven years before you reach the size plant you want.

—Maggie Baylis

3. explanatory

3. ____________________

The day my son Laurie started kindergarten, he renounced corduroy overalls with bibs and began wearing blue jeans with a belt. I watched him go off the first morning with the older girl next door, seeing clearly that an era of my life was ended, my sweet-voiced, nursery-school tot replaced by a long-trousered, swaggering character who forgot to stop at the corner and wave good-bye to me. —Shirley Jackson

4. narrative

4. ____________________

NAME ______________________________

Part 2 Using Time Sequence Arrange the following topic sentences in proper time sequence. Place a *1* next to the first event, and so on. (5 points each)

_____ Decorating the house is done the week before Christmas. 5

_____ Another project we start weeks early is baking Christmas cookies for all of our friends. 4

_____ Preparing for the Christmas holidays, for instance, is as much fun as Christmas itself. 2

_____ Right after Thanksgiving my family begins making Christmas cards. 3

_____ Our family traditions make an already joyous holiday even better. 1

_____ Trimming the tree on Christmas Eve is the last preparation before the festive occasion. 6

Part 3 Using Logical Order Arrange the following topic sentences in logical order for a "why" explanatory composition. (2 points each) (Answers may vary.)

_____ An unexpected benefit of the lower maximum speed limit is that there are fewer highway deaths. 3

_____ If every driver does his or her part, the highway will be safer, and there will be gas to spare. 5

_____ Drivers should obey the 55 mile per hour speed limit. 1

_____ A practical reason to obey the speed limit is to avoid a speeding ticket. 2

_____ The main reason the maximum speed limit is set at 55 miles per hour is to conserve gas. 4

1. sweet, warm

2. Fifty, eager

3. stiff, silk

4. Dark, gloomy

5. spicy, tangy, raw, fresh

6. new, low, sleek

7. Fierce, several, small

1. Oriental

2. Swiss

3. Idaho

4. French

5. Chinese

NAME ______________________________ SCORE __________

Mastery Test Chapter 14

Using Adjectives

Part 1 Finding Adjectives Write the adjectives in these sentences on the blanks. Ignore *a, an,* and *the.* (5 points each sentence)

1. The sweet coating on the candy melted in the warm sun.

   ____

2. Fifty eager fans rode the bus to the game.

   ____

3. George hated wearing the stiff shirt and the silk tie.

   ____

4. Dark, gloomy clouds threatened to ruin the carnival.

   ____

5. I love hamburgers with spicy mustard, tangy catsup, raw onions, and fresh tomatoes.

   ____

6. The new car has low, sleek lines.

   ____

7. Fierce winds blew several small trees down.

   ____

Part 2 Proper Adjectives Write the proper adjectives on the blanks. Capitalize correctly. (3 points each)

1. ____________ Those oriental rugs are valuable.
2. ____________ Jed's favorite flavor is swiss mocha.
3. ____________ I love sour cream on baked idaho potatoes.
4. ____________ Julia Child teaches french cooking.
5. ____________ Have you ever tasted chinese green tea?

NAME ______________________________

Part 3 Predicate Adjectives Write the subject of each sentence on the first blank. Write the predicate adjective in each sentence on the second blank. (6 points each sentence)

1. This cheese smells awful.

_______________ _______________

2. Casey is wild about country music.

_______________ _______________

3. The noise of the jackhammer is terrible.

_______________ _______________

4. Gayle seems angry about something.

_______________ _______________

5. The new motorcycle poster looks fantastic in your room.

_______________ _______________

Part 4 Choosing the Correct Adjective Underline the correct word. (2 points each)

1. I had toast, bacon, and (a, an) egg for breakfast.
2. (This, These) kind of shoe is comfortable.
3. Which person in the story was (braver, bravest), Lee or Chuck?
4. The third model's outfit is the (more stylish, most stylish).
5. Penny's cold was (worse, worser) in the morning.
6. Mr. Hirsch opened one of (them, those) windows.
7. Sue's goal is to be (a, an) honor student.
8. That monster is (scariest, most scariest) of all.
9. Craig's art teacher is the (bestest, best) artist I know.
10. (That, Those) kind of watch is very expensive.

Part 3 answers:
1. cheese awful
2. Casey wild
3. noise terrible
4. Gayle angry
5. poster fantastic

Part 4 answers:
1. an
2. This
3. braver
4. most stylish
5. worse
6 those
7. an
8. scariest
9. best
10. That

466

NAME SCORE

Mastery Test Chapter 15

Using Adverbs

Part 1 Finding Adverbs Write the adverbs on the lines following each sentence. Then write whether the adverb tells *how, where, when,* or *to what extent.* (5 points each sentence)

1. My dad often pops popcorn in the fireplace.
2. Jerry slammed the door angrily.
3. Our next door neighbors hang their wash outside.
4. Climbing mountains is too dangerous for me.
5. Alice stamped her foot stubbornly.
6. We will go in soon.
7. Carl stared dreamily into the air.
8. That comedian is really hilarious!
9. My older sister Loretta pitches well.
10. The stranger lurked suspiciously around the parking lot.

1. often (when)
2. angrily (how)
3. outside (where)
4. too (to what extent)
5. stubbornly (how)
6. soon (when)
7. dreamily (how)
8. really (to what extent)
9. well (how)
10. suspiciously (how)

Building English Skills, Gold Level, Teacher's Edition.

467

NAME ______________________________

Part 2 Comparatives and Superlatives Write the correct form of the word on the blank . (5 points each)

1. ______________ That test was the (superlative of *hard*) we've ever had.
2. ______________ Cynthia draws (comparative of *good*) than I.
3. ______________ Adam builds models (superlative of *skillfully*).
4. ______________ Bob sings even (comparative of *badly*)!
5. ______________ The hungry elf ate (superlative of *greedily*).
6. ______________ Simon plays checkers (comparative of *well*) than Jeff.

Part 3 Adjective or Adverb Underline the correct word in each sentence. (2 points each sentence)

1. Sam plays air hockey (good, well).
2. *National Geographic* is a (real, really) interesting magazine.
3. The toreador approached the bull (careful, carefully).
4. The skydivers fell (dangerous, dangerously) close to the ground before opening their parachutes.
5. The strawberry pie smells (good, well).
6. The ants marched (slow, slowly) through the kitchen.
7. Mama Cat put her kittens (gentle, gently) into their basket.
8. The typist worked (noisy, noisily).
9. Mrs. Bell attached the antenna (permanent, permanently) to the roof.
10. Heidi's grandfather spoke (gruff, gruffly) to her at first.

Part 2 answers:

1. hardest
2. better
3. most skillfully
4. worse
5. most greedily
6. better

Part 3 answers:

1. well
2. really
3. carefully
4. dangerously
5. good
6. slowly
7. gently
8. noisily
9. permanently
10. gruffly

NAME SCORE

Mastery Test Chapter 16

Prepositions and Conjunctions

Part 1 Prepositional Phrases Find the prepositional phrases. Underline them. (2 points each sentence)

1. on the telephone
2. beyond that field
3. under my chair
4. through the Rocky Mountains
5. During the storm
6. in our garden
7. by a sixth-grade student
8. around the lake

1. Katie talked on the telephone.
2. The barn is beyond that field.
3. The puppy scooted under my chair.
4. Driving through the Rocky Mountains is breathtaking.
5. During the storm we had a power failure.
6. George and I planted squash in our garden.
7. That oil painting was done by a sixth-grade student.
8. We drove around the lake.

Part 2 Pronouns as Objects of Prepositions Underline the correct pronoun. (1 point each item)

1. her
2. me
3. him
4. me
5. us
6. me
7. them

8.,9. them, us

1. Is there any mail for (she, her)?
2. Everyone but Jesse and (I, me) has the flu.
3. The card I sent to David and (he, him) never arrived.
4. The prize money will be divided among Jack, Doug, and (I, me).
5. Everyone but that boy and (we, us) got a seat.
6. Joy's Toy Store refunded the money to the twins and (I, me).
7. The teacher divided her time between our project group and (they, them).

8.,9. The race for all-city band champion is between (they, them) and (we, us).

NAME ______________________________

Part 3 Preposition or Adverb For each sentence write whether the italicized word is used as an **adverb** or as a **preposition.** (1 point each sentence)

1. ______________ Look *out!*
2. ______________ The gum wrapper flew *out* the window.
3. ______________ Crowds of people walked *up* the aisle.
4. ______________ The gas tank had been filled *up.*
5. ______________ I feel as though I've been here *before.*
6. ______________ Be home *before* noon.
7. ______________ Turn the light *off.*

1. adverb
2. preposition
3. preposition
4. adverb
5. adverb
6. preposition
7. adverb

Part 4 Compound Sentence Parts Identify the italicized compound sentence parts. In the blank write **CS** for compound subject, **CP** for compound predicate, or **CO** for compound object. Underline the conjunction. (2 points each sentence)

1. ______ Janice *curled her hair* and *polished her nails.*
2. ______ *Rita Coolidge* and *Kris Kristofferson* are married.
3. ______ Mom got *travel posters* and *brochures* about Germany.
4. ______ Allen *went to the show* but *left the movie early.*
5. ______ Juan planted *corn, tomatoes,* and *zucchini* in his garden.
6. ______ *Matthew* or *Lucas* will represent the class.
7. ______ Lucy *watered the lawn* but *forgot the vegetable garden.*
8. ______ Dad bought *three bags of groceries* and *two cases of pop.*
9. ______ Is a *flare* or a *flashlight* in the car?

1. **CP** (and)
2. **CS** (and)
3. **CO** (and)
4. **CP** (but)
5. **CO** (and)
6. **CS** (or)
7. **CP** (but)
8. **CO** (and)
9. **CS** (or)

470

Mastery Test
Chapter 3

NAME ____________________

Part 5 Compound Sentences Rewrite the following sentences, combining each pair with *and, but,* or *or.* Use commas where needed. (3 points each)

1. . . . diseased, and it . . .

2. . . . movie, but her . . .

3. . . . pizza, or do you . . .

4. . . . trash, and John . . .

5. . . . Saturday, and the . . .

1. The elm tree was diseased. It had to be cut down.

____

2. Jonelle wanted to see the movie. Her friends didn't.

____

____

3. Do you want to order a pizza? Do you want to make tacos?

____

____

4. Cassie took out the trash. John did the dishes.

____

5. The rock concert is on Saturday. The symphony performs on Sunday.

____

____

Part 6 Combining Sentences In each sentence below, a conjunction is used to combine sentences, or it is used to join parts of sentences. Write **CS** if the conjunction joins two sentences. Write **CP** if it joins parts of sentences. (2 points each)

1. **CS**
2. **CP**
3. **CP**
4. **CS**
5. **CP**

1. ______ Maria fed the dog, and Susan fed the cats.
2. ______ Tulips, daffodils, and crocuses are spring flowers.
3. ______ The used car lot sells Chevrolets, Fords, and Dodges.
4. ______ Was that Shaun Cassidy, or was it a look-alike?
5. ______ The Great Pumpkin and the Easter Beagle can be found in the Peanuts comics.

NAME ____________________

Part 7 Avoiding Run-on Sentences Read each word group. If it is a *run-on*, write **RO** in the blank. If it is a *sentence*, write **S.** (2 points each sentence)

1. ______ Carl is a freshman his sister is in sixth grade.
2. ______ After the car wash, the band had enough money to buy new uniforms.
3. ______ Baked potatoes aren't as fattening as butter and sour cream.
4. ______ The jade plant is a succulent it doesn't need much water.
5. ______ My shoelace broke I fell down the stairs at school.
6. ______ Terrifying the crowd, the lion frantically paced in his cage.
7. ______ Kathy and Sue each ordered a sundae.
8. ______ This day has been miserable everything went wrong.

Part 8 Identifying Parts of Speech Tell how the italicized word is used in each sentence. It may be a **noun, verb, adjective, adverb,** or **preposition.** (1 point each sentence)

1. ____________ *Meet* me at the soda shop after school.
2. ____________ The cross-country *meet* begins at 3:00.
3. ____________ Myra sat *down* in the middle of the gym.
4. ____________ Grandma's *hurricane* lamp is an antique.
5. ____________ City dwellers *lock* their doors at night.
6. ____________ Eric bought buttered popcorn *before* the show.
7. ____________ Paste *wax* protects furniture and makes it shine.
8. ____________ Close your *test* booklet when you finish.
9. ____________ You have to take a driving *test* before you can get a driver's license.

1. **RO**
2. **S**
3. **S**
4. **RO**
5. **RO**
6. **S**
7. **S**
8. **RO**

1. verb
2. noun
3. adverb
4. adjective
5. verb
6. preposition
7. noun
8. adjective
9. noun

NAME SCORE

Mastery Test Chapter 17

Writing Letters

Part 1 Kinds of Letters and Their Parts Match the terms on the left with the proper definitions. (2 points each)

1. ______ salutation
2. ______ inside address
3. ______ closing
4. ______ R.S.V.P.
5. ______ heading
6. ______ bread-and-butter note
7. ______ note of acceptance or regret
8. ______ body
9. ______ invitation
10. ______ signature

a. where and when the letter was written
b. the farewell
c. an abbreviation for a French phrase meaning "please respond"
d. the name of the writer
e. a thank-you for hospitality
f. a reply to an invitation
g. where a business letter is going
h. the greeting
i. the information in a letter
k. a request for the reader to attend a social event

1. h
2. g
3. b
4. c
5. a
6. e
7. f
8. i
9. k
10. d

Part 2 Using Correct Capitalization and Punctuation Read these letter parts. Circle *letters* that should be capitalized. Add any needed *punctuation marks* and circle them, too. (5 points each number)

1. 951 kinkade court
2. olson tennessee 37115
3. january 5 1980
4. dear michael
5. dear sir or madam
6. yours truly
7. sincerely

1. Kincade Court
2. Olson, Tennes-see
3. January 5, 1980
4. Dear Michael,
5. Dear Sir or Madam:
6. Yours truly,
7. Sincerely,

NAME ______________________________

Part 3 Business Letters Using your home address, today's date, and the information below, compose a business letter. Follow all capitalization and punctuation rules.

Write a letter to Mr. Paul E. Russell at the Florida Tourist Bureau in Orlando, Florida. Request information on tourist attractions in the Orlando area. Explain that you plan to vacation in Florida. The Tourist Bureau office is located at 65 Ovieda Boulevard, and the ZIP code is 32807.

____

Heading ______________________________

____

(10 points)

Inside Address

____

____

____

______________________________ (15 points)

Salutation

______________________________ (5 points)

Body

____

____

____

____

(10 points)

____

Closing ______________________________

(5 points)

Signature ______________________________

Answers will vary.

474

1. (things) happen
2. (Houseplants) need
3. (members) practice
4. (sandwiches) stick
5. (stores) open
6. (players) use
7. (Two) clash
8. (player) drops

1. doesn't
2. have
3. are
4. were
5. Are
6. are

NAME SCORE

Mastery Test Chapter 18

Making Subjects and Verbs Agree

Part 1 Making the Subject and Verb Agree Underline the subject of each sentence. Then circle the correct verb. (4 points each sentence)

1. Strange things (happen, happens) in the old haunted house.
2. Houseplants (needs, need) tender loving care.
3. The members of the team (practices, practice) every night.
4. Peanut butter sandwiches (stick, sticks) to the roof of your mouth.
5. The stores in the mall (open, opens) at noon.
6. Soccer players really (uses, use) their heads.
7. Two of these paint colors (clash, clashes) with the carpeting.
8. A player on our team (drops, drop) the bowling ball on someone's foot every week.

Part 2 Special Verb Forms Write the correct verb form for each sentence on the blank. (3 points each sentence)

1. ______ Mr. Hale (don't, doesn't) take cream in his coffee.
2. ______ Cheryl's feet (has, have) blisters from her new shoes.
3. ______ The lenses for this camera (is, are) very expensive.
4. ______ The gorillas in the zoo (was, were) making faces at the visitors.
5. ______ (Is, Are) the Girl Scouts in the parade this year?
6. ______ Some friends of my brother (is, are) coming for dinner.

Mastery Test
Chapter 18

NAME ______________________________

Part 3 Tricky Subjects Underline the subject in each sentence. Write the correct verb on the blank. (4 points each sentence)

1. ____________ One of the triplets (have, has) brown hair. 1. (One) has
2. ____________ Neither of the students (want, wants) to miss the spelling bee. 2. (Neither) wants
3. ____________ Each of the shirts (have, has) a monogram on the pocket. 3. (Each) has
4. ____________ Here (is, are) the strawberries. 4. (strawberries) are
5. ____________ Everybody in these apartments (attend, attends) the block party. 5. (Everybody) attends
6. ____________ Anyone with perfect attendance (get, gets) a free ticket to a Sox game. 6. (Anyone) gets
7. ____________ Where (is, are) the new magazines? 7. (magazines) are
8. ____________ There (was, were) thirteen doughnuts in the bag. 8. (doughnuts) were

Part 4 Verbs with Compound Subjects For each sentence, write the correct verb form on the blank. (3 points each sentence)

1. ____________ Shields and Yarnell (is, are) mimes. 1. are
2. ____________ Either the principal or our teacher (present, presents) the awards. 2. presents
3. ____________ Neither Cecil nor his brothers (is, are) going to summer school. 3. are
4. ____________ Joliet and Marquette (was, were) early explorers. 4. were
5. ____________ Either the Smiths or Mr. Brown (is, are) meeting us at the airport. 5. is
6. ____________ Marge or Sharon (is, are) the hall monitor this week. 6. is

476

NAME ______________________________ SCORE ________

Mastery Test Chapter 19

Using Irregular Verbs

Part 1 Principal Parts of Verbs Fill in the principal parts for each of the following verbs. (1 point each blank)

	Present	Past	Past Participle
1.	wash	______	______
2.	______	broke	______
3.	swim	______	______
4.	need	______	______
5.	carry	______	______
6.	sit	______	______
7.	come	______	______
8.	throw	______	______
9.	______	wrote	______
10.	go	______	______
11.	walk	______	______
12.	______	took	______
13.	teach	______	______
14.	help	______	______
15.	______	rode	______
16.	know	______	______
17.	sing	______	______
18.	______	______	run
19.	lie	______	______
20.	begin	______	______

1. washed, washed
2. break, broken
3. swam, swum
4. needed, needed
5. carried, carried
6. sat, sat
7. came, come
8. threw, thrown
9. write, written
10. went, gone
11. walked, walked
12. take, taken
13. taught, taught
14. helped, helped
15. ride, ridden
16. knew, known
17. sang, sung
18. run, ran
19. lay, lain
20. began, begun

Mastery Test
Chapter 19

NAME ______________________________

Part 2 Using Principal Parts of Verbs Write the indicated verb form in the blank. Remember to use a helping verb when needed. (4 points each)

1. ______________ That table leg (present of *wobble*).
2. ______________ Ron (past of *feel*) dizzy after riding the roller coaster.
3. ______________ Dad (future of *grow*) tomatoes in the garden.
4. ______________ The ranch hands (past participle of *ride*) all day.
5. ______________ The Avon lady (past of *ring*) the bell.
6. ______________ It is so cold that the pond (past participle of *freeze*).
7. ______________ The Declaration of Independence (past participle of *write*) in 1776.
8. ______________ Roz (past of *begin*) her judo lessons yesterday.
9. ______________ The sun (past participle of *rise*).
10. ______________ The voters (past of *choose*) Jimmy Carter in 1976.
11. ______________ The swallows (past participle of *fly*) back to Capistrano.
12. ______________ The swim team (past participle of *swim*) in several meets so far.
13. ______________ Jerry (future of *lay*) the tile.
14. ______________ Carolyn (past of *know*) the solution to the riddle.
15. ______________ Chris (past participle of *throw*) the ball through the picture window.

(Helping verbs may vary.)
1. wobbles
2. felt
3. will grow
4. had ridden
5. rang
6. has frozen
7. was written
8. began
9. has risen
10. chose
11. have flown
12. has swum
13. will lay
14. knew
15. had thrown

**Mastery Test
Chapter 22** **Capitalization**

Part 1 Proper Nouns and Adjectives Find the words that should be
capitalized. Write them correctly on the blanks. (5 points each sentence)

1. Glenbrook
 South High
 School Band,
 Rose Bowl
 Parade

 1. The glenbrook south high school band marched in the 1979 rose bowl
 parade.

2. Mr. Paulus,
 South

 2. When mr. paulus moved to the south, he gave us his toboggan.

3. Bible

 3. Our church will have a bible study class next fall.

4. Monday, Me-
 morial Day

 4. Next monday is memorial day.

5. Collins Avenue
 Miami
 Beach,
 Florida

 5. We drove down collins avenue in miami beach, florida.

6. Parthenon
 Restaurant,
 Greek

 6. The parthenon restaurant is famous for its greek food.

7. New England,
 I, Bradford

 7. On my trip to new england i will visit the bradford family.

8. Chinese

 8. The high school now offers a course in chinese.

9. Joe, Harry, I

 9. In the spring joe, harry, and i are going canoeing.

10. Italian

 10. Huge slabs of italian marble fell off the side of the building.

Building English Skills, Gold Level, Teacher's Edition.
Copyright © 1980 by McDougal, Littell & Company, Evanston, Illinois

NAME ______________________________________

Part 2 First Words and Titles Circle all letters that should be capitalized. (10 points each number)

1. the song of canaries
   never varies
   and when they're moulting
   they're pretty revolting.
   —Ogden Nash
2. your homework for tomorrow is to read the story "the emperor's new clothes."
3. for my birthday I received a book entitled *a day no pigs would die* and the sound track album from *star wars.*
4. john used an article from the *chicago tribune,* "conservation groups meet in washington," as a source for his current events report.
5. (outline) houseplants that require little care
   I. succulents
      A. burro tail
      B. jade plant
   II. cactuses
      A. prickly pear
      B. christmas cactus
   III. leafy plants
      A. umbrella tree
      B. piggy-back plant

1. The song . . .
   Never . . . .
   And when . . .
   They're . . .
2. Your, "The Emperor's New Clothes"
3. For, *A Day No Pigs Would Die,* *Star Wars*
4. John, *Chicago Tribune,* "Conservation Groups Meet in Washington"
5. Houseplants That Require Little Care
   I. Succulents
      A. Burro tail
      B. Jade plant
   II. Cactuses
      A. Prickly pear
      B. Christmas cactus
   III. Leafy plants
      A. Umbrella tree
      B. Piggy-back plant

1. What an interesting speaker Dr. Freeman is!

2. What time is it in England when it is 9:00 A.M. here?

3. Is Mr. C. W. Johnson in the audience?

4. Ouch! Watch out for broken glass!

5. Will Mr. Thorpe, Ms. Smith, or Dr. Martin be our substitute teacher?

1. Noreen, paper, pen,

2. Yes, Street, Chicago,

3. I, skaters,

4. ate,

5. 20, 1969,

NAME SCORE

Mastery Test Chapter 23

Punctuation

Part 1 End Marks Rewrite the following sentences adding the correct punctuation. (6 points each sentence)

1. What an interesting speaker Dr Freeman is

2. What time is it in England when it is 9:00 AM here

3. Is Mr C W Johnson in the audience

4. Ouch Watch out for broken glass

5. Will Mr Thorpe, Ms Smith, or Dr Martin be our substitute teacher

Part 2 Commas In each of the following sentences, insert commas where they belong. (6 points each sentence)

1. Noreen please bring me some paper a pen and the tape.
2. Yes our new address is 12 E. Oak Street Chicago Illinois.
3. Richard and I the expert skaters are going to the roller rink.
4. As we ate the campfire crackled.
5. On July 20 1969 the first human walked on the moon.

NAME ______________________________

Part 3 Apostrophes and Hyphens Rewrite the following words or phrases inserting the correct punctuation. (2 points each)

1. ladies hats ____________
2. babys toy ____________
3. Id ____________
4. ninety nine ____________
5. couldnt ____________
6. havent ____________
7. Marys wallet ____________
8. twenty first ____________
9. mens store ____________
10. Draculas face ____________

1. ladies' hats
2. baby's toy
3. I'd
4. ninety-nine
5. couldn't
6. haven't
7. Mary's wallet
8. twenty-first
9. men's store
10. Dracula's face

Part 4 Quotations Rewrite the following sentences inserting the correct punctuation. (4 points each sentence)

1. Debby asked Will we see the Grand Ole Opry

____

2. Riding a bike said Dad is as easy as falling off a log

____

3. Did she say Meet me at the gym at noon

____

4. About face shouted the drill sergeant

____

5. I'm tired said Roland let's go home

____

1. Debby asked, "Will we see the Grand Ole Opry?"
2. "Riding a bike," said Dad, "is as easy as falling off a log."
3. Did she say, "Meet me at the gym at noon"?
4. "About face!" shouted the drill sergeant.
5. "I'm tired," said Roland. "Let's go home."

482

NAME SCORE

Mastery Test Chapter 24

Spelling

Part 1 Recognizing Spelling Errors Correct the spelling errors in the following sentences. Write the misspelled words correctly on the blank line. (4 points each sentence)

1. Artificially, carried

1. Artificialy sweetened soft drinks are carryed by our grocer.

2. thief, busily

2. The theif was busyly emptying the jewels into his bag.

3. babysitter, reliable

3. That babysiter is the most relyable teen-ager I know.

4. really, receive

4. Tom realy wants to recieve the perfect attendance award.

5. regretfully, conceded

5. Mayor Brown regretfuly conceeded defeat to the challenger.

6. baking, chop-ping, beating

6. Sean helped with the bakeing by choping the nuts and beatting the eggs.

7. hotter, swim-ming

7. The hoter it got, the more the boys wanted to go swiming.

8. truly, outfielder

8. Jenny is truely a good outfeilder.

9. chief

9. The retired police cheif lives in San Diego.

10. leisure, riding

10. He spends his liesure time rideing his moped on the beach.

NAME ______________________________

Part 2 Prefixes and Suffixes Combine these root words with the prefixes or suffixes given. Drop, add, or change letters as needed. (2 points each)

1. achieve + ment ______________ 1. achievement
2. gleeful + ly ______________ 2. gleefully
3. bid + ing ______________ 3. bidding
4. sixty + eth ______________ 4. sixtieth
5. pry + ing ______________ 5. prying
6. un + named ______________ 6. unnamed
7. fury + ous ______________ 7. furious
8. re + evaluate ______________ 8. reevaluate
9. meet + ing ______________ 9. meeting
10. stubborn + ness ______________ 10. stubbornness

Part 3 Words Often Confused Underline the correct word for each sentence. (5 points each sentence)

1. Paul and Bonny let (their, there, they're) pet snake Nadine loose in the house. 1. their
2. Beth wants (to, too, two) go (to, too, two) Disney World (to, too, two). 2. to, to, too
3. (Who's, Whose) Frisbee is that? 3. Whose
4. Mark's (principle, principal) objection to skydiving is that it is dangerous. 4. principal
5. We often (hear, here) sirens at night. 5. hear
6. Our tour of Washington, D.C., included the (capital, capitol, Capitol). 6. Capitol
7. Jerry can babysit every night (accept, except) Thursday. 7. except
8. (Your, You're) flight for Puerto Rico leaves in ten minutes. 8. Your

484